ISBN 978-1-397-32457-3
PIBN 11374551

1896   1897

ANNOUNCEMENT

OF THE

COLLEGE OF

Physicians and Surgeons

OF ONTARIO,

And Report of Proceedings of Ontario Medical Council,
: : : : June, 1896 : : : :

FOR THE ACADEMIC YEAR, 1896-97.

By Authority.

REGISTRY OFFICE, COLLEGE OF PHYSICIANS AND SURGEONS OF ONTARIO,

SOUTH-EAST CORNER BAY AND RICHMOND STREETS, TORONTO.

JUNE, 1896.

ANNOUNCEMENT

OF THE

College of Physicians and Surgeons

OF ONTARIO

FOR THE ACADEMIC YEAR, 1896-97.

BY AUTHORITY.

REGISTRY OFFICE:

COLLEGE OF PHYSICIANS AND SURGEONS OF ONTARIO,

SOUTH-EAST CORNER BAY AND RICHMOND STREETS,

TORONTO.

JUNE, 1896.

01

Contents and Index to Proceedings.

THE COUNCIL

OF THE

College of Physicians and Surgeons of Ontario

TERRITORIAL REPRESENTATIVES.

J. L. Bray, M.D., Chatham, Ont....................................	No. 1 Division.	
J. A. Williams, M.D., Ingersoll, Ont.............................	ıı 2	ıı
W. F. Roome, M.D., London, Ont	ıı 3	ıı
W. Graham, M.D., Brussels, Ont	ıı 4	ıı
L. Brock, M.D., Guelph, Ont	ıı 5	ıı
J. Henry, M.D., Orangeville, Ont.................................	ıı 6	ıı
G. Shaw, M.D., Hamilton, Ont.............................	ıı 7	ıı
J. P. Armour, M.D., St. Catharines, Ont...........................	ıı 8	ıı
I. Hanly, M.D., Midland, Ont....................................	ıı 9	ıı
E. J. Barrick, M.D., Toronto, Ont	ıı 10	ıı
H. T. Machell, M.D., Toronto, Ont.................................	ıı 11	ıı
J. H. Sangster, M.D., Port Perry, Ont.............................	ıı 12	ıı
J. W. McLaughlin, M.D., Bowmanville, Ont....................	ıı 13	ıı
T. H. Thornton, M.D., Consecon, Ont	ıı 14	ıı
W. W. Dickson, M.D., Pembroke, Ont	ıı 15	ıı
R. Reddick, M.D., Winchester, Ont	ıı 16	ıı
A. F. Rogers, M.D., Ottawa, Ont	ıı 17	ıı

COLLEGIATE REPRESENTATIVES.

W. Britton, M.D., Toronto, Ont......................	University of Toronto.
J. W. Rosebrugh, M.D., Hamilton, Ont	ıı Victoria College.
V. H. Moore, M.D., Brockville, Ont	ıı Queen's College.
W. T. Harris, M.D., Brantford, Ont.................	ıı Trinity College.
J. H. Thorburn, M.D., Toronto, Ont	Toronto School of Medicine.
F. Fowler, M.D., Kingston, Ont	{ Royal College of Physicians and Surgeons, Kingston.
W. B. Geikie, M.D., Toronto, Ont...................	Trinity Medical College.
W. H. Moorhouse, M.D., London, Ont	Western University, London.

HOMŒOPATHIC REPRESENTATIVES.

George Logan, M.D., Ottawa, Ont.
G. Henderson, M.D., Strathroy, Ont.
C. T. Campbell, M.D., London, Ont.
L. Luton, M.D., St. Thomas, Ont.
W. J. H. Emory, M.D., Toronto, Ont.

Medical Registration Office of the College of Physicians and Surgeons of Ontario, south-east corner Bay and Richmond Streets, Toronto.

Office Hours: 2 to 4 p.m.

ROBERT A. PYNE, M.D., M.C.P.S.O., Toronto, Ont., *Registrar.*

OFFICERS

OF THE

College of Physicians and Surgeons of Ontario

FOR 1896-97.

President.....................A. F. ROGERS, M.D., Ottawa, Ont.

Vice-President.................J. THORBURN, M.D., Toronto, Ont.

Treasurer.....................W. T. AIKINS, M.D., Toronto, Ont.

Registrar.....................R. A. PYNE, M.D., Toronto, Ont.

BOARD OF EXAMINERS, 1896-97.

DR. F. LeM. GRASETT, Toronto, Ont...	*Anatomy, Descriptive.*
DR. D. E. MUNDELL, KINGSTON, Ont. ..	*Theory and Practice of Medicine.*
DR. H. HOWITT, Guelph, Ont..........	*{ Midwifery, Operative and other than Operative, and Puerperal and Infantile Diseases, etc.*
DR. A. S. FRASER, Sarnia, Ont.	*Physiology and Histology.*
DR. A. B. Welford, Woodstock, Ont..,.	*Surgery, Operative and other than Operative.*
DR. H. WILLIAMS, London, Ont........	*Medical and Surgical Anatomy.*
DR. G. ACHESON, Galt, Ont............	*Chemistry, Theoretical, Practical and Toxicology.*
DR. H. B. SMALL, Ottawa, Ont.	*Materia Medica and Pharmacy.*
DR. C. V. EMORY, Hamilton, Ont.	*Medical Jurisprudence and Sanitary Science.*
DR. C. O'REILLY, Toronto, Ont........	*Assistant Examiner to the Examiner on Surgery.*
DR. J. THIRD, Kingston, Ont.	*1st Assistant Examiner to Examiner on Medicine.*
DR. W. P. CAVEN, Toronto, Ont........	*{ 2nd Assistant to the Examiner on Medicine, Pathology and Therapeutics.*
DR. D. J. SINCLAIR, Woodstock, Ont....	*Homœopathic Examiner.*

STANDING COMMITTEES OF COUNCIL

OF THE

College of Physicians and Surgeons of Ontario

FOR 1896-97.

REGISTRATION COMMITTEE.

Dr. Rosebrugh (*Chairman*).	Dr. Barrick.	Dr. Roome.
Dr. Campbell.	Dr. Hanly.	Dr. Shaw.
Dr. Dickson.		

RULES AND REGULATIONS COMMITTEE.

Dr. Reddick (*Chairman*).	Dr. Hanly.	Dr. Machell.
Dr. Emory.	Dr. Luton.	

FINANCE COMMITTEE.

Dr. Henderson (*Chairman*).	Dr. Bray.	Dr. Dickson.
Dr. Armour.	Dr. Brock.	

PRINTING COMMITTEE.

Dr. Barrick (*Chairman*).	Dr. Henry.	Dr. McLaughlin.
Dr. Emory.	Dr. Luton.	

EDUCATION COMMITTEE.

Dr. Britton (*Chairman*).	Dr. Harris.	Dr. Moorhouse.
Dr. Fowler.	Dr. Logan.	Dr. Sangster.
Dr. Graham.	Dr. Moore.	Dr. Williams.

PROPERTY COMMITTEE.

Dr. Machell (*Chairman*).	Dr. Emory.	Dr. Thornton.
Dr. Barrick.	Dr. McLaughlin.	

COMPLAINTS COMMITTEE.

Dr. Henry (*Chairman*).	Dr. Geikie.	Dr. Shaw.
Dr. Armour.	Dr. Reddick.	

EXECUTIVE COMMITTEE.

Dr. Rogers (*Chairman*).	Dr. Thorburn.	Dr. Campbell.

DISCIPLINE COMMITTEE.

Dr. Bray (*Chairman*),	Dr. Moore,	Dr. Logan,
Chatham, Ont.	Brockville, Ont.	Ottawa, Ont.

The President and Vice-President are *ex officio* members of all Committees, excepting the Discipline Committee, and the Chairman of any Committee is *ex officio* a member of any Sub-Committee thereof.

OFFICERS

OF THE

College of Physicians and Surgeons of Ontario

FROM 1866 TO 1896-97.

PRESIDENTS.*

1.	JOHN R. DICKSON	...From 1866 to 1867	17.	D. BERGIN	.........From 1881 to 1882
2.	JOHN TURQUAND	..... " 1867 " 1868	18.	J. L. BRAY	.... " 1882 " 1883
3.	JAMES A. GRANT	..... " 1868 " 1869	19.	G. LOGAN	.... " 1883 " 1884
4.	WILLIAM CLARK	..... " 1869 " 1870	20.	H. W. DAY	.... " 1884 " 1885
5.	WILLIAM H. BROUSE.	" 1870 " 1871	21.	D. BERGIN	.... " 1885 " 1886
6.	CHAS. W. COVERNTON.	June to Dec., 1871	22.	H. H. WRIGHT	...... " 1886 " 1887
7.	WILLIAM CLARK	....Dec.,† 1871 to 1872	23.	G. HENDERSON	...... " 1887 " 1888
8.	J. F. DEWAR	.......From 1872 to 1873	24.	J. H. BURNS	.... " 1888 " 1889
9.	WILLIAM CLARK	..... " 1873 " 1874	25.	J. G. CRANSTON	...... " 1889 " 1890
10.	M. LAVELL	.... " 1874 " 1875	26.	V. H. MOORE	.... " 1890 " 1891
11.	E. G. EDWARDS	...... " 1875 " 1876	27.	J. A. WILLIAMS	..... " 1891 " 1892
12.	DANIEL CLARK	...... " 1876 " 1877	28.	F. FOWLER	.... " 1892 " 1893
13.	DANIEL CLARK	...... " 1877 " 1878	29.	C. T. CAMPBELL	...... " 1893 " 1894
14.	D. CAMPBELL	.... " 1878 " 1879	30.	D. L. PHILIP	.... " 1894 " 1895
15.	J. D. MACDONALD	.... " 1879 " 1880	31.	W. T. HARRIS	.... " 1895 " 1896
16.	W. ALLISON	.... " 1880 " 1881	32.	A. F. ROGERS	.... " 1896 " 1897

VICE-PRESIDENTS

1.	WM. H. BROUSE	.....From 1866 to 1870	15.	H. W. DAY	.........From 1883 to 1884
2.	CHAS. W. COVERNTON.	" 1870 " 1871	16.	E. W. SPRAGGE	...... " 1884 " 1885
3.	JAMES HAMILTON	.... " 1871 " 1872	17.	R. DOUGLAS	.... " 1885 " 1886
4.	D. CAMPBELL	.... " 1872 " 1873	18.	G. HENDERSON	...... " 1886 " 1887
5.	JOHN MUIR	.... " 1873 " 1874	19.	J. H. BURNS	.... " 1887 " 1888
6.	E. G. EDWARDS	...... " 1874 " 1875	20.	J. G. CRANSTON	..... " 1888 " 1889
7.	E. M. HODDER	...... " 1875 " 1876	21.	V. H. MOORE	.... " 1889 " 1890
8.	D. CAMPBELL	.... " 1876 " 1877	22.	J. A. WILLIAMS	...... " 1890 " 1891
9.	D. CAMPBELL	.... " 1877 " 1878	23.	F. FOWLER	.... " 1891 " 1892
10.	W. ALLISON	.... " 1878 " 1879	24.	C. T. CAMPBELL	...... " 1892 " 1893
11.	G. LOGAN	.... " 1879 " 1880	25.	D. L. PHILIP	.... " 1893 " 1894
12.	D. BERGIN	.... " 1880 " 1881	26.	W. T. HARRIS	.... " 1894 " 1895
13.	J. L. BRAY	.... " 1881 " 1882	27.	A. F. ROGERS	.... " 1895 " 1896
14.	W. B. GEIKIE	.... " 1882 " 1883	28.	J. THORBURN	.... " 1896 " 1897

TREASURER.

W. T. AIKINS ....From 1866

REGISTRARS AND SECRETARIES.

HENRY STRANGE........From May 3rd, 1866, to September 2nd, 1872.

THOMAS PYNE.......... " September 2nd, 1872, to July 15th, 1880.

ROBERT A. PYNE........ " July 15th, 1880.

---

* The President, Vice-President, Treasurer and Registrar of the College are elected at the Annual Meeting of the Council, and hold office until their successors are elected.

† Dr. William Clark was elected December 12th, 1871, at a special meeting of the Council, in consequence of the resignation of Dr. C. W. Covernton.

College of Physicians and Surgeons

OF ONTARIO.

ANNOUNCEMENT FOR THE ACADEMIC YEAR 1896-97.

"THE COLLEGE OF PHYSICIANS AND SURGEONS OF ONTARIO" is the name adopted by the Medical Profession of the Province of Ontario in its corporate capacity. As every legally qualified medical practitioner in the Province is a member of this College, it is not an institution for the teaching of medicine.

The Medical Profession of Ontario was first incorporated under this name by an Act of the Parliament of Canada, passed in 1866. This Act was subsequently repealed by the Legislature of Ontario in 1869, and now the affairs of the Profession in this Province are regulated by an Act passed in 1874 (37 Vic., Cap. 30), commonly known as the "Ontario Medical Act," and further amended in 1887, 1891, 1893 and 1895.

By this Act, the "COUNCIL OF THE COLLEGE OF PHYSICIANS AND SURGEONS OF ONTARIO" is empowered and directed to enact by-laws for the regulation of all matters connected with medical education ; for the admission and enrolment of students of medicine ; for

determining from time to time the curriculum of the studies to be pursued by them, and to appoint a Board of Examiners before whom all must pass a satisfactory examination before they can be enrolled as members of the College, and thus be legally qualified to practise their profession in the Province of Ontario.

The Council, moreover, has power and authority conferred upon it by this Act to fix the terms upon which practitioners of medicine, duly qualified in other countries, may be admitted as members of the College of Physicians and Surgeons of Ontario, this being the only mode in which they can become legally entitled to practise their profession in this Province.

For the information and guidance of students of medicine, the Profession, and the public generally, the Council, in conformity with the Ontario Medical Act, hereby promulgates for the year 1896–97 the REGULATIONS which herein follow, repealing all others heretofore in force.

REGULATIONS FOR 1896-97.

SECTION I.—MATRICULATION.

Everyone desirous of being registered as a matriculated medical student in the Register of this College, except as hereinafter provided, shall be required to pay a fee of twenty dollars and to conform to the following regulations :

1. Any person who presents to the Registrar of the Medical Council a certificate that he has passed the examination conducted by the Education Department on the course prescribed for matriculation in arts, including chemistry and physics, and approved by the Lieutenant-Governor in Council, shall be entitled, on payment of the lawful fees in that behalf, to registration as a medical student within the meaning of Section 11 of the Ontario Medical Act.

2. Any person who before the 15th day of June, 1896, had not passed the examination in all the subjects prescribed for matriculation as aforesaid, shall be entitled to registration as a medical student on submitting to the Registrar a certificate that he has completed such examination by passing in the remaining subjects of such matriculation, including chemistry and physics.

3. Any student in medicine who submits to the Registrar certified tickets that he has attended not less than two courses of lectures at any chartered medical school or college in Canada, shall be entitled, on payment of the lawful fees in that behalf, to take the Primary examination, provided that the standing obtained at such examination may not be allowed until such student presents to the Registrar the matriculation certificate.

4. A certificate from the Registrar of any chartered university conducting a full arts course in Canada, that the holder thereof matriculated prior to his enrolment in such university, and passed the examination in arts prescribed for students at the end of the first year, shall entitle such student to registration.

5. Any person who on or before the 1st day of November, 1895, had passed the examination of any university in Canada for matriculation in arts, or the matriculation examination conducted by the Education Department entitling to registration in arts with any university in Canada—or an examination entitling to registration with the Medical Council subsequent to July 1st, 1888—shall be entitled to registration on submitting to the Registrar a certificate to that effect, signed by the proper officer in that behalf.

6. Gratuates in arts, in any university in Her Majesty's dominions, are not required to pass this examination, but may register their names with the Registrar of the College upon giving satisfactory evidence of their identity and certificate of qualifications and upon paying the fee of twenty dollars.

SECTION II.—MEDICAL CURRICULUM.

1. On and after the 1st day of July, 1892, every student must spend a period of five years in actual professional studies, except as hereinafter provided ; and the prescribed period of studies shall include four winter sessions of not less than six months each, and one summer session of ten weeks ; or four winter sessions of eight months each and be exempt from summer session. The fifth year shall be devoted to clinical work, six months of which may be spent with a registered practitioner in Ontario, and six months at one or more public hospitals, dispensaries or laboratories devoted to physiological or pathological research, Canadian, British or foreign, attended after having been registered as a medical student in the Register of the College of Physicians and Surgeons of Ontario—" But any change in the curriculum of studies fixed by the Council shall not come into effect until one year after such change is made."

Homœopathic students who attend four sessions at any medical college where nine-month sessions are taught, to be held equal to four winter sessions and one summer session of this College. This shall not in any way interfere with the practical and clinical work as prescribed by the Medical Council of Ontario for the fifth year.

2. Graduates in arts or science of any college or university recognized by the Council who shall have spent a year in the study of physics, chemistry and biology, and have passed an examinations in the subjects for degrees in arts or science, shall be held to have completed the first year of the five years of medical study, and will only be required to pass three years after graduating in at-

tendance upon medical studies, and having spent one year thereafter in practical clinical work before being admitted to their final examination.

No tickets for lectures will henceforward be accepted by the Council unless it is endorsed thereon that the pupil has attended at least 75 per cent. of each course of said lectures, as shown by teacher's own roll.

3. Application for every professional examination must be made to the Registrar of the College of Physicians and Surgeons of Ontario two weeks prior to examinations. No application will be received unless accompanied by the necessary tickets and certificates, and by the Treasurer's receipt showing the fees have been paid.

4. Each " six months' course " shall consist of not less than fifty lectures, and each "three months' course " of not less than twenty-five lectures.

5. Every student must attend the undermentioned courses of lectures in a university, college or school of medicine approved of by the Council, viz. :

Two courses of not less than six months each (in the different years) upon—
Anatomy.
Practical Anatomy.
Physiology (including Histology).
Theoretical Chemistry.
Materia Medica and Therapeutics.
Principles and Practice of Medicine.
 "   "   " Surgery.
Midwifery and Diseases of Women.
Clinical Medicine.
 " Surgery.

One course of not less than six months upon—
Medical Jurisprudence.
Medical, Surgical and Topographical Anatomy.

Two courses of not less than three months each (in different years) upon—
Diseases of Children.
Practical Chemistry (including Toxicology).

One course of not less than three months upon—
Sanitary Science.
Practical Pharmacy.
To be taken prior to candidate presenting himself for examination on Materia Medica and Pharmacy.

One course of ten lectures upon—
Mental Diseases.

One course of fifty demonstrations upon—
Physiological Histology.

6. Every candidate will be required to prove that he has carefully dissected the adult human body.

7. The following are the text books recommended by the Council in the various branches :

GENERAL TEXT BOOKS.

Anatomy—Gray, Qnain, Cunningham's Practical Anatomy.
Physiology—Foster, Kirke, Yeo.
Chemistry—Roscoe, Attfield, Remsen and Jones, Richter, Simons.
Materia Medica—Ringer, Mitchell Bruce, Hare's Therapeutics, British Pharmacopœia.
Surgery—Erichsen, Treves, Mansell Moulin, Walsham.
Medicine — Hilton Fagge, Strumpell, Osler.
Clinical Medicine—Gibson and Russel, Vierordt.
Midwifery and Gynæcology—Lusk, Thomas Mundé, Playfair, Hart and Barber, American Text Book of Obstetrics.
Medical Jurisprudence and Toxicology—Taylor, Reese.
Pathology — Ziegler, Green, Woodhead, Coates.
Sanitary Science—Wilson, Louis C. Parke.
Diseases of Children — Eustace Smith, Ashby and Wright, Goodhart.

HOMŒOPATHIC TEXT BOOKS.

Materia Medica—Hahnemann, Hering.
Medicine and Therapeutics — Goodno, Arndt, Raue's Pathology and Diagnostics, Lilienthal.
Surgery—Fisher, Helmuth.
Midwifery—Guernsey, Ludlam.

8. Also must have attended the practice of a general hospital for twenty-four months during the first four years of study.

9. Also must have attended six cases of midwifery.

10. Also must, before being registered as a member of the College of Physicians and Surgeons of Ontario, have passed all the examinations herein prescribed, and attained the full age of twenty-one years.

11. Graduates in medicine from recognized colleges outside the Dominion of Canada, who desire to qualify themselves for registration, must pass the matriculation required by the Council ; and must attend one or more full winter courses of lectures in one of the Ontario medical schools, and must complete fully the practical and clinical curriculum required by the Council after the fourth year, and shall pass before the examiners appointed by the Council all the examinations hereinafter prescribed, so as to complete fully the curriculum.

12. That British registered medical practitioners, on paying all fees and passing the Intermediate and Final examinations, be reg-

istered, provided they have been domiciled in Britain for five years after becoming so registered.

SECTION III.—EXAMINATIONS.

1. The professional examinations are divided into three parts : A "Primary," "Intermediate" and "Final."

2. The Primary examination shall be undergone after the second winter session, and the Intermediate after the third or fourth winter session, the Final after the fifth year.

3. The following branches shall be embraced in the Primary examination :

a. Anatomy.
b. Physiology and Histology.
c. Chemistry (Theoretical and Practical).
d. Materia Medica and Pharmacy.

4. Every candidate for the Primary examination will be required to present, with his lecture tickets, a certificate of having undergone and passed an examination at the school he has attended at the close of his first winter session on Primary branches. Also a certificate of ability to make and mount microscopic specimens.

5. Each candidate for final examination must present a certificate of attendance at six post mortem examinations, and a certificate of ability to draw up a report of a post mortem examination ; and a certificate of having reported satisfactorily six cases of clinical medicine, and six cases of clinical surgery, and of having attended twenty-five pathological demonstrations, and of having passed his Intermediate examination. The certificates to be signed by the teachers referred to upon these subjects, or the practitioner holding post mortem. At the Spring examination, to be held in 1896 and thereafter, all candidates shall (except arts graduates) present a certificate of having passed at the close of their third session in the college or school they may have attended, an examination in such parts of medicine, surgery and midwifery as may be thought advisable by the faculties of the respective colleges or schools. This examination is not in any way to interfere with any of the examinations of the Council.
The following branches shall be embraced in the intermediate examination :

a. Medical, Surgical and Topographical Anatomy.
b. Principles and Practice of Medicine.
c. General Pathology and Bacteriology.
d. Surgery, other than Operative.
e. Surgery, Operative.
f. Midwifery, other than Operative.
g. Midwifery, Operative.
h. Medical Jurisprudence, including Toxicology and Mental Diseases.
i. Sanitary Science.
j. Diseases of Children.

k. Diseases of Women.
l. Therapeutics.

7. The Primary and Intermediate examinations shall be " written " and " oral." The Final " oral " and " clinical."

8. The following branches will be embraced in the Final examination :

a. Clinical Medicine.
b. Clinical Surgery (including Vaccination).
c. Diseases of Women.
d. Diseases of Children, Medical and Surgical.

9. Any candidate who makes 60 per cent. in three or more branches, but fails in the others, shall receive credit for the subjects so passed, and be compelled to pass in the other branches only at a subsequent examination.

10. Candidates who intend to be examined by the homœopathic Examiner in special subjects, shall signify their intention to the Registrar at least two weeks previous to the commencement of the examination, in order that he may provide means of preventing their identification by the other students, or by the Examiners.

11. In the event of any candidate signifying his intention to the Registrar to be examined and registered as a homœopathic practitioner, due notice of such must be submitted to the Registrar, so that the examinations may be conducted by the parties appointed for that purpose ; prior to the acceptance of such notice from the candidate, the usual fees must be paid. In the event of any candidate presenting himself for such examination, due notice must be given by the Registrar to the special Examiner.

12. A professional examination will be held in Toronto on the third Tuesday in September, 1896. Candidates who have failed in a former examination to pay a fee of twenty dollars for this examination. The next professional examinations will be held at Toronto and Kingston on the third Tuesday in May, 1897.

SECTION IV.—FEES.

1. The following scale of fees has been established by the Council of the College of Physicians and Surgeons of Ontario :

a. Registration of matriculation...$20 00
b. Primary examination.......... 20 00
c. Final examination, including registration 30 00
These fees are to be paid to the Treasurer of the College before each examination.
d. Registration of persons duly qualified before 23rd day of July, 1870.................. 10 00
e. Registration of persons duly qualified after 23rd day of July 1870 .... 25 00

f. Registration of additional degrees or titles 2 00
This fee is only payable when the additional titles are registered at different times, but any number of such titles as are allowed to be registered, may be put on record at the first registration, for the registration fee.

g. Diploma of membership of the College..................... 5 00
This diploma is granted free of charge to all those members of the College who attain their membership by passing the examinations of the College. All other members may obtain it on application to the Registrar, and paying the above named fee.

h. Annual assessment due by members of the College for the year
1892, payable to the Registrar. 2 00
1893   ,,   ,,   ,,   2 00
1894   ,,   ,,   ,,   2 00
1895   ,,   ,,   ,,   2 00
1896   ,,   ,,   ,,   2 00
This fee is payable by every member of the College.

Fees after 1st July, 1889 :
a. Registration of matriculation... 20 00
b. Primary examination.......... 30 00
c. Intermediate and Final examination, including registration ... 50 00
   This is not to affect any student who is registered as a matriculate prior to 1st July, 1889.

2. All fees must be paid in lawful money of Canada to the Treasurer of the College.

3. No candidate will be admitted to any examination until the fee for such examination is paid in full.

4. Candidates who have failed in any professional examination shall pay a fee of twenty dollars for each subsequent examination.

SECTION V.—EXAMINATIONS.

RULES FOR THE GUIDANCE OF THE BOARD OF EXAMINERS.

1. The Registrar or Deputy Registrar must be present at every examination.

2. At the end of each written examination upon any subject, the answers to the questions are to be handed to the Registrar, who will open the envelopes, in which they are hereinafter directed to be enclosed, and to each set of papers affix a number by which the author will be known to the Examiners during the examination. The Registrar will then deliver the papers to the member of the Board of Examiners appointed by the Council to examine upon the subject.

3. The papers, when delivered to the member of the Board of Examiners appointed by the Council to examine upon the subject, are to be by him examined, and the relative value of answers marked by means of numbers in a schedule which will be furnished to him by the Registrar, ranging for the Primary subjects as follows :

4. That the percentage in the Primary branches be as follows, ranging from 0 to 100 on all subjects :

	Honors.	Pass.
Anatomy	75	50
Physiology and Histology	75	50
Chemistry — Theoretical and Practical	75	50
Materia Medica and Pharmacy	75	50

INTERMEDIATE.

Medical, Surgical and Topographical Anatomy	0 to 100
Principles and Practice of Medicine......................	0 to 100
General Pathology and Bacteriology	0 to 100
Surgery, other than Operative...	0 to 100
Surgery, Operative............	0 to 100
Midwifery, other than Operative.	0 to 100
Midwifery, Operative	0 to 100
Medical Jurisprudence, Toxicology and Mental Diseases....	0 to 100
Sanitary Science...............	0 to 100
Diseases of Children, Medical and Surgical	0 to 100
Diseases of Women	0 to 100
Therapeutics	0 to 100

Marks required for honors and pass :

Medical. Surgical and Topographical Anatomy	75	50
Principles and Practice of Medicine......................	75	50
General Pathology and Bacteriology......................	75	50
Surgery, other than Operative.	75	50
Surgery, Operative	75	50
Midwifery, other than Operative	75	50
Midwifery, Operative	75	50
Medical Jurisprudence, Toxicology and Mental Diseases...	75	50
Sanitary Science..............	75	50
Diseases of Children, Medical and Surgical	75	50
Diseases of Women..........	75	50
Therapeutics.................	75	50

That the percentage in the Final branches be as follows : 0 to 100 on all subjects. Honors 75, pass 50.

5. The values awarded by the individual Examiners to the answers of candidates are not to be subject to revision, except by an appeal by the candidate to the Council, when special cases of hardship may seem to have occurred.

6. The Examiners shall return the schedules to the Registrar, with values inserted, within seven days of notice to be sent by the Registrar. From these values a general schedule is to be prepared by the Registrar, and no change of value can be made after such schedules have been returned by the Examiners to the Registrar. The general schedule so prepared is to be examined as to its correctness by the President, and the results announced by the President.

7. Papers on the homœopathic subjects are to be finally submitted to the Examiner approved of for that purpose by the representatives of that system in the Council.

8. All oral examinations are henceforth to be as clinical, demonstrative and practical as possible, and the candidate shall be known to the Examiners by number only.

9. That it be an instruction to the Examiners, in the questions in their respective subjects, to confine themselves to the text books in ordinary use (see page x. of this Announcement), also that in referring to diseases or operations of any kind, the names of such diseases or operations most commonly in use should be employed.

The Examiners are instructed to attach to each question a printed number as the value of a full and correct answer thereof—the whole of such numbers to amount to 100— also that in reading the paper they mark in colored chalk what they regard as the numerical value of the answer given.

10. That it be an instruction to the President that he shall in no case report a candidate as having passed an examination when on any subject he makes less than the minimum of marks set by the Council for a pass on that subject. But in any case where he thinks there are special reasons for granting a license to such candidate, he shall report the same to the Council for its action.

RULES FOR CANDIDATES WHEN IN THE EXAMINATION HALL.

11. Each candidate shall receive from the Registrar a programme containing a list of subjects upon which the candidate is to be examined, and it will admit him to the examination hall during the progress of the examinations upon such subject, but at no other time.

12. Candidates must write the answers to the questions given by the Examiners legibly and neatly upon one side only of each page of a book, which will be furnished to each candidate, and the number given with each question is to be put at the head of the answer to it, in such a manner as to have the first page facing outward to the view ; they are then to be folded once and enclosed in an envelope, on the outside of which each candidate is to write his name. The packet is then to be handed to the Registrar, or some one deputed by him. Neither signature, number or sign, by which the writer could be recognized by the Examiner, is to be written or marked upon any portion of the book to be enclosed in the envelope.

13. The questions of the Examiners in the homœopathic subjects will be handed in writing, at the beginning of the general examination on the same subject, by the Registrar, to such candidates as have given him notice in accordance with Section III., Sub-secs. 10, 11. They shall write the answers to these questions in the same hall with the other candidates, and hand their papers, when finished, to the Registrar in the same manner as provided for other candidates, to be by him given for examination to the homœopathic member of the Board of Examiners appointed to examine on that subject.

14. If any abbreviations are used in answering the questions, candidates must be careful that they are such as are generally understood, or which cannot be mistaken.

15. No candidate will be allowed to leave the hall after the questions are given out, until his answers have been handed in.

16. No candidate will be allowed in the hall during the hours of examination, except those who are actually undergoing examination.

17. Any candidate who may have brought any book or reference paper to the hall, must deposit it with the Registrar before the examination begins.

18. Candidates must not communicate with each other while examinations are going on, either by writing, signs, words, or in any manner whatever.

19. Candidates must at all times bear themselves toward the Registrar and Examiners with the utmost deference and respect ; and they will not be permitted in any manner to manifest approbation or disapprobation of any member of the Board of Examiners during the progress of the examination.

20. Candidates must not only conduct themselves with decorum while any examination is going on, but they will be held strictly responsible for any impropriety of conduct during the whole progress, both of the written and the oral examinations.

21. Any infraction of the above rules will lead to the exclusion of the candidate who is guilty of it from the remainder of the examination ; and he will not receive credit for any examination papers which he may have handed to the Registrar previous to his being detected in such misconduct.

22. And be debarred from further privileges, at the discretion of the Council.

LIST OF STUDENTS OF MEDICINE

WHO HAVE PASSED THE

Matriculation ·Examination

BEFORE THE EXAMINERS APPOINTED BY THE COUNCIL,
AND REGISTERED AS MATRICULATES
WITH THE

College of Physicians and Surgeons of Ontario.

Abbott, Clarence...........Toronto 1883
Adamson, H. A.............Ottawa 1889
Airth, H. W...............Renfrew 1886
Aitchison, William.......'..St. George 1870
Alexander, L. H........Owen Sound 1892
Alexander, W. E...Hemmingford, Q. 1892
Alexander, W. J........ Thornbury 1887
Alexander, W. W...Hemmingford, Q. 1892
Allen, William G..............Perth 1875
Allen, Thomas......·......Toronto 1888
Allingham, A. W.........Warkworth 1884
Alway, F. J................'.Vittoria 1891
Alway, J. H.............Grimsby 1890
Anderson, J. J............Kingston 1883
Anderson, A. F...........Peterboro' 1894
Anderson, R..............Hornby 1886
Ardiel, L. M.............Thorndale 1887
Armstrong, Moore..........Kingston 1873
Arnold, H. T.............Watford 1885
Arnold, John R...........Harriston 1880
Arnott, D. H.............London 1895
Atkinson, V. T.............Nelson 1875
Austin, G. H.............Lansdowne 1891
Auld, E...................Toronto 1896
Aylen, Walter W............Quebec 1885
Aylen, E. D.............Montreal 1889
Aylesworth, A. C......Mount Forest 1884

Babbitt, W..........Parrsboro', N.S. 1888
Baily, Eli H...........Mount Forest 1881
Baker, E................Springfield 1892
Baker, J. A..............Hamilton 1894
Bain, W. L..............Parkdale 1884
Baldwin, H. F............Toronto 1877
Banting, W. T............London 1888
Barber, Robert A..........Berlin 1880
Barclay, Thomas ....Hamilton 1871
Barlee, H. J. W..........Montreal 1888
Baston, John.............Kingston 1870
Bayne, C. W..............Ottawa 1887
Barnett, T. J.............Almonte 1896
Bauer, J. A..............Hamilton 1894
Bayne, John G...........Newbury 1891
Beamish, George.........Port Hope 1876
Beattie, D. A..................Galt 1888
Beatty, E. D.........South March 1891

Beandry, J. S.............Montreal 1883
Beemer, W. C.............Simcoe 1888
Belanger, R. U.............Ottawa 1892
Belch, J. A...............Kingston 1887
Bellamy, A. W........North Augusta 1888
Bell, A. W................Toronto 1887
Bell, Basil H........New Edinburgh 1886
Bell, J. C...............Strathroy 1877
Bell, John C................Nairn 1881
Bell, A..................Agincourt 1892
Belton, W. J.............Kingston 1885
Bennett, J. E.................Reach 1895
Bennett, W. H............Toronto 1895
Bennie, Robert............Sudbury 1892
Bentley, F. M..........Newmarket 1887
Bensley, B. A.............Toronto 1894
Berwick, G. A.............Farnham 1888
Berwick, R. H.........Cowansville 1887
Bickstead, Morris.........Morrisburg 1874
Birge, A. H................Toronto 1891
Birks, William R...........Prescott 1891
Birmingham, F. H........Kingston 1888
Blewett, W. J.......Little Britain 1886
Blewett, W. G.............Lindsay 1892
Block, B. F......... :......Kingston 1891
Blunt, H. W.........Knowlton, Que. 1888
Boddy, James...............Toronto 1889
Boynton. W. J.........Prince Albert 1895
Bolton, T. B...............Toronto 1881
Booth, John A............Brantford 1890
Bonter, G. S..............Trenton 1869
Bosanko, Arthur.......Gravenhurst 1875
Bowan, Hector A............Albion 1873
Bouillon, A..............Montreal 1890
Bowles, G. H..............Sandhill 1888
Bradley, T..............Georgetown 1893
Brethour, H. F.........Sunderland 1895
Brewster, William..........Toronto 1873
Bridgman, O. M............London 1882
Britton, Fred.............Brantford 1892
Broad, R................Coboconk 1892
Brown, Campbell... .....Acton Vale 1870
Brown, W...............Heathcote 1894
Brown, Charles.......Carleton Place 1892
Brown, Kent A......St. Catharines 1881
Brown, E. L...'.........Chesterville 1886

Brown, James E............Tyrone 1881
Brown, F. W............Brockville 1888
Bryce, W...................Keene 1892
Bucke, E. P...............London 1896
Buck, Katie L...... .....Peterboro' 1892
Buck, R. A..... ......Avonbank 1888
Burnham, J. H..........Peterboro' 1887
Burns, T. B...............Toronto 1875
Butler, Charlton..........Strathroy 1876
Burd, W. S.............Parry Sound 1892
Burrows, Frederick N..........Bath 1880
Burk, John A.........Amherstburg 1892

Casselman, P. C.........Morrisburg 1894
Caldwell, H. J.............Toronto 1881
Cameron, Alex. D......River Raisin 1878
Cameron, Duncan............Perth 1873
Cameron, Duncan,
    85 Hayter St., Toronto 1870
Cameron, John D.........L'Orignal 1892
Cameron, Duncan.........Strathroy 1880
Cameron, J. B. Montague,
    Prince Edward Island 1872
Campbell, A. L...........Kingston 1883
Campbell, David................. 1879
Campbell, G. G.........Truro, N.S. 1888
Campbell, James ....London 1873
Campbell, George J..........Blyth 1893
Carbert, Joseph A.......Orangeville 1870
Carry, Chester............Florence 1870
Case, J. H................Colborne 1872
Carter, L. H...............Picton 1884
Carroll, R. W............Stratford 1889
Cawthorpe, F. J........Thamesford 1894
Chappell, W..... ......St. Mary's 1896
Chambers, W. J.............Paisley 1881
Christie, Andrew..........Bradford 1880
Christin, J. A............Montreal 1892
Chance, J. Broomley......Brantford 1876
Chestnut, George.................. 1866
Chisholm, J. S ....Wingham 1894
Church, F. W. H..........Hull, Que. 1888
Church, A. H............Montreal 1892
Clarke, Geo. L.............London 1895
Clarke, E. A...............Aylmer 1887
Clark, F. G. R..........Collingwood 1871
Clark, J. A. M..........Ridgetown 1891
Clark, J. L.............Waterloo 1883
Clarkson, Frederick A......Seaforth 1891
Clayes, George..........Brockville 1892
Cleaver, John C..........Kingston 1875
Cleaver, Wm. F..........Kingston 1875
Close, James A.................. 1869
Clindinin, S. L...........Brighton 1892
Cloutier, F..............Kingston 1884
Coad, George...... ...Smith's Falls 1892
Code, W. E. R............Toronto 1894
Coffee, R. H.............Toronto 1883
Cole, J. A..............Freelton 1880
Coleman, Il. Kay........Gananoque 1876
Coleman, Mary E.........West Hill 1880
Coleman, T..............Seaforth 1886
Collfas, W. F...........Morriston 1892
Collins, H. L..........Kincardine 1894
Collins, E. P.............Princeton 1892
Collison, G. W......Dixon's Corners 1892

Collville, J................Leskard 1894
Conerby, M................Trenton 1886
Connor, F. E............Gananoque 1896
Cooke, C. F................Gesto 1886
Cook, E. L. B............Toronto 1876
Cook, J. D................Paris 1875
Cooke, Sheldon R.........Aultsville 1878
Cooper, E. G............Kingston 1894
Cooper, J. J............Chatham 1887
Cooper, M. A.........Howick, Que 1888
Coote, Frank............Montreal 1885
Corson, Douglas.......Woodstock 1881
Cosford, John B............Toronto 1876
Cowan, J. J............Goderich 1880
Cowley, Daniel K...........Ottawa 1876
Craig, J. E................Toronto 1893
Creighton, E...........Thamesford 1894
Crosby, Arthur...........Uxbridge 1880
Crosby, F. H............Uxbridge 1884
Cron, William.............Batteau 1890
Crowe, W. B...............Trenton 1894
Cumberland, Thomas....Mono Centre 1880
Curzon, Edith M............Toronto 1890
Cuzner, Mark R........Aylmer, Que. 1878
Cunningham, J. D..........Osborne 1892
Cuzner, G...............Montreal 1895

Dady, Ralph.. ....Toronto 1877
Darling, Elsie L...........Rosedale 1892
Dargavel, J...............Durham 1887
Dancey, J. H.............Aylmer 1892
Davis, H. C.................Dundas 1892
Davis, Murdock L..........Norham 1872
Davis, T. B.........Wakefield, Que. 1880
Davis, W...................... 1872
Davis, John ....Kingston 1893
Davidson, A. E..........Woodstock 1894
Deane, M. B..............Brighton 1894
Dean, W. E..............Toronto 1892
Deeks, W. E............Montreal 1889
Delaney, W. F........:...Peterboro' 1885
Dettrick, H..........St. Catharines 1896
Denis, A...........Vaudreuil, Que. 1889
Dewar, Alexander.........Montreal 1887
Dilane, K............Tottenham 1894
Dillabough, H. W..........Hamilton 1891
Dickson, G. J.............Paisley 1887
Dingham, H................Picton 1871
Disney, H. C......... .....London 1880
Dobbie, W. J............Guelph 1893
Doherty, Charles E........Eglinton 1891
Doherty, George..........Markham 1875
Donovan, Patrick......Campbellford 1881
Donovan, E. J............Kingston 1881
Donald, William............Goderich 1881
Dougherty, J. W..............Eden 1881
Dorais, U. A............Montreal 1884
Dougan, R. P............Thorold 1886
Douglas, A. E............Warwick 1889
Douglas, James H..........Norham 1876
Dow, J. D..............Pembroke 1881
Dowsley, G. W. O..........Burford 1895
Doyle, C. S..............Toronto 1885
Doyle, J. M............Caledonia 1884
Drain, J. F..........Campbellford 1891
Drummond, P............Almonte 1884

B

Wilson, Henry H	Kingston	1872
Wyatt, W. C	Custom's Corners	1874
Wood, James S	Kingston	1878
Whiting, John	Brantford	1878
Williams, Joseph	London	1878
Wilson, Charles James		1879
Warren, Edward		1879
Whetham, James	Toronto	1880
Wright, Henry	Toronto	1883
Wait, G. N	Harriston	1881
Watson, E. C	Kingston	1894
Watson, John C	Belleville	1885
Watson, W. R	Waterdown	1883
Weir, E S. G	Toronto	1894
Wells, W	Flesherton	1895
Wickens, A. E	Brantford	1894
Williams, E. P	Ottawa	1883
Williamson, W. P	Buckhorn	1884
Willmott, W. E	Toronto	1885
Winch, H. C	Hastings	1895
Wonder, W. M	St. Catharines	1883
Woodruff, T. A	St. Catharines	1883
Woolway, E. W	St. Mary's	1884
Wright, H. A	Guelph	1882
Wright, W	Kingston	1882
Welsh, H. A	Quebec	1886
Williamson, H. M	Guelph	1886
Watson, G. C	Hawkesbury	1885
Wagner, C. J	Toronto	1895
Walker, C. W	Petrolea	1894
Whyte, J. J	Lancaster	1885
Ward, W. L	Acton	1884
Wideman. H. B	Ringwood	1887
Whitely, R	Goderich	1887
Wilson, A	Kingston	1887
Woods, C. R	Brockville	1887
Woods, A. C	Barrie	1894
Willoughby, G. A. F., Saskatoon, N. W.T.		1886

Wickman, L. G	Toronto	1885
White, James G	Thessalon	1884
Watson, N. M	Williamstown	1887
Walker, W. G	Stratford	1888
Wheeler, J. W	Kingston	1888
Watson, R	Newmarket	1888
Williamson, T	Picton	1888
Watson, N. M	Williamstown	1888
Wilson, J. T	London	1889
Wilson, Thomas	Toronto	1890
Ward, Marjory	Kingston	1890
Wilson, George B	Toronto	1890
Williams, J. A	Carleton Place	1891
Wood, D. M	Kenmore	1892
Weisbrod, S. L	Aylmer	1892
Webster, J. D	Toronto	1894
Welch, G	Toronto	1893
Whiteley, A. G	Goderich	1892
White, R. W. K	Hamilton	1892
Whilton, D. A	Ottawa	1894
Williams, E. J	Montreal	1894
Williamson, A. R	Kingston	1895
Walker, H	Belleville	1892
Weaver, W. J	Toronto	1892
White, R. B	Pembroke	1892
White, W. R	Toronto	1894
York, F. E	Aurora	1883
Yeomans, P. H	Mount Forest	1888
Yates, H. B	Brantford	1888
Yourex, Ed. L	Belleville	1888
Young, F. A	Toronto	1894
Young, T. A	Brougham	1891
York, H. E	Montreal	1892
Yeo, W. T	Little Britain	1892
Young, W. Y	Toronto	1892
Zimmerman, Solomon	Toronto	1876
Zangg, A. A. C	Montreal	1883

FIRST YEAR'S EXAMINATION.

Bosanko, S. A.	1877	McConnell, B. J		1878
Neilson, A	1877	McCauley, John		1878
Shaw, Frank	1877	McDonald, Walter		1878
Shepherd, O. B	1877	Poole, W. H		1878
Steffins, John	1877	Reid, W. D		1878
Atkinson, H. H	1878	Serviss, T. W		1878
Baker, George W	1878	Sullivan, Thomas		1878
Campbell, James	1878	Watson, M. J		1879
Cotton, Robert	1878	Burton, R. J. F		1879
Cooper, R. E	1878	Carson, S. H		1879
Dupuis, James	1877	Fairbairn, F. W		1879
Haken, George W	1878	Harvie, John C		1879
Holcomb, S. D	1878	Higginson, Henry		1879
Houston, D. W	1878	Kerr, Henry		1879
Island, Robert	1878	Mordy, A. A		1879
Keam, A. P	1878	McLachlan, D. D		1879
Lang, W. A.	1878	O'Keefe, Henry		1879
Mewburn, F. H	1878	Shaw, Alexander		1879
Milne, G. L	1878	Smith, Edwin A		1879
Munro, Lawrence	1878	Wilson, Herbert C.		1879
Mickle, Herbert	1878			

SECOND YEAR'S EXAMINATION.

Aikins, William Heber	1878	Empey, C. T.	1879
Black, James	1878	Ferguson, J.	1879
Christie, J	1878	Hatton, E. T	1879
Donovan, J. C.	1878	Meikle, Hamilton	1879
Eccles, R. M.	1878	McCracken, C. L.	1879
Hunter, J. B.	1878	Ross, J. W.	1879
Lindsay, Ninian	1878	Smith, H. W.	1879
Marsh, Edward	1878	Thompson, G. B.	1879
Montgomery, W. A. D	1878	Wilson, Robert	1879
Sutherland, W. R.	1878	Witherspoon, W.	187
Van Norman, H. C.	1878	Harris, A. B.	1881
Beatty, William	1879		

THIRD YEAR'S EXAMINATION.

Cross, W. J.	1879	Montgomery, D. W.	1881
Howitt, F. W	1880	Nicholson, M. A.	1879

PRIMARY EXAMINATION.

Bell, James	1876	Murray, T. W.	1883
Betts, Alfred H.	1876	Phillips, J. R.	1883
Burton, W. H.	1874	Wattam, G. S.	1883
Cameron, D. H.	1876	Wilson, A. B.	1883
Cameron, L. D.	1877	Charlesworth, W. H	1884
Cannon, Gilbert	1876	Simenton, G.	1884
Cluxton, Frederick C.	1870	Smith, C. J.	1884
Cormon, John W.	1874	Wilson, W. A.	1884
Dunsmore, John	1876	Green, W. D.	1885
Glasgow, James H.	1876	Gardiner, A. W.	1885
Gray, J. W.	1872	Hotson, A.	1885
Greer, Thomas E.	1875	Thompson, A. B.	1885
Henderson, Kenneth	1876	Woodhull, F.	1885
Howey, William	1877	Dowson, W. H.	1886
Lewis, Ford	1877	James, Charles	1886
McArthur, J.	1877	Berry, R. P.	1887
McCrimmon, John	1877	Brown, J. F.	1887
Mellmoyl, Henry Allen	1875	Cross, J. A.	1887
McKinley, J. H.	1877	Cooke, W. H.	1887
Rae, George W.	1874	Edgar, A. E.	1887
Stevenson, Charles S.	1875	Ferguson, F. F.	1887
Stevenson, Sabin	1875	Hotson, J. M.	1887
Ferguson, A. H.	1880	Johnston, T. H	1887
Ferrier, James	1880	Kennedy, J. D.	1887
Herrington, A. W	1880	Mason, H.	1887
McCarthy, W. T.	1880	Mitchell, D.	1887
Ogden, H. V.	1880	Millman, M. G.	1887
Panton, A. C.	1880	McKellar, A.	1887
Denike, G. H.	1881	McBride, J.	1887
Johnston, Joseph	1881	Ogden, J. P.	1887
Snider, S. H.	1881	Potts, J. M.	1887
Graham, George	1882	Patterson, A. G.	1887
Menzies, John	1882	Patrick, T. A.	1887
Thompson, A. S.	1882	Quarry, H. D.	1887
Walmsley, P. C.	1882	Rice, P. J.	1887
Brown, W. M.	1883	Salter, F. G.	1887
Logan, J. R.	1883	Tyrell, J	1887

Westlake, H. W	1887	Rutledge, C. N	1892
Wilson, M.	1887	Roles, J. A	1893
Watson, L.	1887	Shaw, C	1893
Walker, S. R.	1887	Thom, W	1893
Allingham, L. W.	1888	Alway, W. R	1895
Cram, G. D.	1888	Addy, A. H	1895
Dougan, R. P.	1888	Boyd, H. O.	1895
Ferguson, M.	1888	Brown, A. I	1895
Ironsides, A. S.	1888	Bell, J. H.	1895
Jones, W. A	1888	Cockburn, Hattie	1895
Owen, C. B	1888	Campbell, P. M.	1895
Paterson, J. A.	1888	Churchill, B. P	1894
Preiss, F	1888	Copp, C. J	1895
Reid, A. L	1888	Campbell, A. M	1895
Starr, F. H.	1888	Campbell, Geo. I	1895
Turnbull, W. J.	1888	Cummings, I. A	1895
Cook, W. A.	1889	Cairnes, Geo	1895
Irwin, W. T.	1889	Campbell, C. A	1895
Lockridge, J.	1889	Crosskerry, E. A	1895
Porter, H. W	1889	Dales, F. A.	1895
Philp, W. S	1889	Dyde, C. B	1895
Stewart, A	1889	Downing, J. J	1895
Schlenker, T. W	1889	Davis, James	1895
Todd, S. G.	1889	Cook. G. E.	1894
Wilson, A. C	1889	McLean, J. D.	1894
Williams, A. A.	1889	MacCallum, Maggie	1894
Wall, J. R	1889	Millichamp, G. E	1894
Campbell, J. S.	1889	McInnes, N. W	1894
Dean, L. W	1889	McCarter, J. M	1894
Shirton, G. K	1889	Elliott, J. H.	1895
Brown, A. M	1890	Forster, F. J. F	1895
Brown, W. E.	1890	Gillies, J. M. H	1895
Brown, W. F	1890	Graham, W. L	1895
Chambers, W	1890	Jamieson, D	1894
Hersbey, J. A	1890	Ludwig, A	1895
Herald, D.	1890	Laidlaw, W. C	1895
Kennedy, J. T.	1890	Moore, S	1895
Lloyd, H. M.	1890	Maybury, W. F	1895
Mathew, W. E.	1890	Morgan, J. A	1895
MacLennan, D. N	1890	Pickard, H. G.	1894
Meecham, G. P.	1890	Parlow, A. B	1894
McConnell, H. B.	1890	Pritchard, J	1894
McLean, E. H. S.	1890	Routledge, J. W	1894
Northrup, W.	1890	Reeves, J	1894
Shaw, R. W	1890	Skinner, Emma	1894
Armstrong, F. K.	1890	Sneath, C. R.	1894
Morrow. W. S.	1890	Smith, F. W	1894
MacPherson, W. A.	1891	Tyndall, J. E	1894
McGill, H. G	1891	Teetzell, W. M.	1894
Paterson, Eliza	1891	Turner, Adelaide	1894
Tuttle, H. E.	1891	Weekes, E. C	1894
Whitelock, F. C	1891	Muelin, J. H	1895
Black, B. F	1892	Macdonald, J. M.	1895
Connell, W. T.	1892	Morton, J. P	1895
Grant, H. A.	1892	Mills, G. B	1895
Richardson, A	1892	Mylks, G. W	1895
Shirra, Jennie S	1892	McEachern, J. S	1895
Elliott, George A	1893	McNulty, F. P.	1895
Ford, J. N.	1893	McGillivray, D.	1895
Fleming, Maggie A.	1893	McCallum, E. C. D	1895
Hunter, H A	1893	McKenzie, D. C	1895
Hurdon, Elizabeth	1893	McNamara, A T	1895
Leith, J. D.	1893	McGregor, M	1895
McLachlan, A. R.	1893	Nicholl, R.	1895
Orr, C. A.	1893	Pallister, W. T.	1895
Parker, W. M.	1893	Perry, R. M	1895

Quesnel, E. G	1895	Fadden, W. S	1896
Reynar, A. F	1895	Garner, E. L	1896
Radcliffe, S. W	1895	Grange, T. A	1896
Royce, G	1895	Gould, Maggie	1896
Sills, C. H	1895	Grant, J	1896
Shultis, J	1895	Henderson, W	1896
Steele, F. C	1895	Howey, R	1896
Scott, F. A	1895	Hossack, J. G	1896
Taylor, W. H	1894	Hume, J. J. C	1896
Thompson, J. B	1895	Hogg, J. S	1896
Wesley, W. J	1895	Hassard, G. A	1896
Wilson, F. W. E	1895	Jackson, G. H	1896
Willson, Jennie M	1895	Lang, C. A	1896
Wade, G. H	1895	Lovett, A. S	1896
Yeomans, L. W	1895	Large, R. W	1896
Bradshaw, Kate	1895	Lundy, J. E	1896
Beatty, H. A	1895	Lawrence, T. H	1896
Clarke, J. T	1885	Moffatt, W	1896
Klotz, J. E	1895	Mitchell, J. P	1896
McCormick, T. A	1895	Moore, F	1896
McGuire, J. C	1895	McMurrich, J. B	1896
Ashton, E. C	1896	McEwen, D	1896
Anderson, D. M	1896	McCrae, J	1896
Alexander, N. B	1896	McDermid, A	1896
Bennett, W. H	1896	McKay, A. R	1896
Baker, M. D	1896	McDougall, T. A	1896
Bell, B. C	1896	McDonald, A. J	1896
Bethune, F. H	1896	Nixon, J. R	1896
Birnie, Jessie	1896	O'Connor, C. E	1896
Butler, J. A	1896	Paulin, S	1896
Crawford, M	1896	Redmond, R. C	1896
Cahoon, F	1896	Roberts, J. A	1896
Crane, J. W	1896	Sutherland, G. A	1896
Charlesworth, J. E	1896	Smith, R. H	1896
Campbell, J. B	1896	Spence, H. W	1896
Cunningham, W. F	1896	Shepard, A. A	1896
Clark, W. J	1896	Stewart, A. D	1896
Clemes, S. R	1896	Stewart, C. M	1896
Cruickshank, Jean	1896	Scott, W. A	1896
Callendar, C. N	1896	Stephens, W	1896
Delmage, F. W	1896	Tillman, W. J	1896
Dunsmore, J. M	1896	White, W. C	1896
Easton, J. L	1896	Willson, Geo. S	1896
Fallis, M. P	1896		

MEMBERS

College of Physicians and Surgeons of Ontario

WHO HAVE ATTAINED THEIR MEMBERSHIP
BY PASSING THE

FINAL EXAMINATION

Before the Board of Examiners appointed by the Council of the College.

Adams, S. A. J.	Kinmount	1887
Adams, W. A.	Lakefield	1876
Alexander, R. A.	Stony Creek	1871
Alguire, D. O.	Lunenburg	1873
Alt, A.	Toronto	1877
Anderson, J. B.	Watford	1875
Armstrong, F. R.	Stouffville	1874
Arnott, H.	Brampton	1870
Armour, J.	Hastings	1877
Atkinson, J. S.	Hamilton	1875
Adair, J.	Oshawa	1878
Algie, J.	Ayr	1879
Ashby, T. H.	Woodbridge	1878
Abbott, R. H	Stony Point	1879
Anderson, J. D.	Port Perry	1879
Armstrong, G. S.	McKellar	1879
Ames, F. H. S.	Martintown	1880
Anderson, J.	Hamilton	1880
Allen, W. L.	Ridgeway	1880
Aikens, H. W.	Toronto	1881
Alexander, F. R	Ottawa	1881
Anglin, W. G.	Kingston	1883
Addison, J. L.	St. George	1884
Anderson. J. E. W	Boston	1884
Acheson, G.	Toronto	1887
Aikins, N.	Caistorville	1887
Applebe, J.	Belle Ewart	1887
Armstrong, W.	Zephyr	1887
Avison, O. R.	Toronto	1887
Allen. A. G.	Deseronto	1887
Anglin, J. V.	Kingston	1887
Amos, T. A.	West McGillivray	1887
Arthur, E. C.	Brighton	1888
Ardagh, A. E.	Barrie	1888
Anderson, C. N.	Comber	1888
Auld, L.	Toronto	1888
Almas, W. E.	Hagersville	1889
Anderson, R. K.	Hornby	1889
Armstrong, W. J.	Bayfield	1889
Armstrong, H. W.	Bailieboro'	1889
Adams, E. H.	Toronto	1890
Agar, J. S.	Chatham	1890
Agar, Mary L.	Chatham	1890

Aldrich, A. G.	Port Hope	1890
Archer, D.	Burketon	1890
Ardagh, A. P.	Barrie	1890
Arnall, H. T.	Barrie	1890
Auld, J. C.	Forest	1890
Abraham, C. F. P.	Hamilton	1891
Almas, J. S.	Hagersville	1891
Amyot, J. A.	St. Thomas	1891
Arthur, J. L.	Shanty Bay	1891
Ashbaugh, J. A.	Aylmer	1891
Anderson, H. B.	Apsley	1891
Awde, A. E.	Toronto	1892
Armstrong, M. A. V.	Bayfield	1892
Archer, Robt.	Milton, Dakota	1892
Austin, J. H.	Brampton	1893
Alway, R. D.	Grimsby	1893
Anderson, N.	Toronto	1893
Armstrong, J. M.	Walton	1893
Arnott, W. J.	Toronto	1893
Armstrong, J. J. P.	Moore	1893
Alger, H. H.	Port Colborne	1893
Agnew, T.	Belgrave	1894
Alexander, W. H.	Bolton	1894
Allen, J. R.	Napanee	1894
Anderson, W. J.	Shanly	1894
Armour, D. J.	Cobourg	1894
Armstrong, H. E.	Orono	1894
Arrell, Wm.	Caledonia	1894
Addison, W. L. T.	Toronto	1895
Aiken, A. W.	Orangeville	1895
Allen, Mary E	Fordwich	1895
Amyot, N. J.	St. Thomas	1895
Arkell, H. E.	St. Thomas	1896
Argue, J. F	Carp	1896
Allin, J. H.	Orono	1896
Backhouse, John B.	Simcoe	1870
Bain, Hugh Urquhart	Angus	1875
Baird, J. G.	Montreal	1872
Ball, Jerrold	Meaford	1874
Balmer, J. S.	Oakville	1874
Barkwell, R. H.	Port Hope	1874
Bates, S. L.	Bowmanville	1871

Beeman, Milton J.	Selby	1873
Beemer, N. H.	Brantford	1874
Bell, Forest F.	Amherstburg	1870
Bell, Robert	Carleton Place	1870
Bell, Samuel	Alliston	1874
Bennett, J. H.	Toronto	1875
Bently, R. J.	Kettleby	1877
Birdsall, S. E.	Canboro'	1876
Bonner, H. A.	Albion	1877
Black, Wm. S.	Barrie	1871
Bowen, G. H.	Kingston	1877
Bowerman, A. C.	Toronto	1876
Boyle, W. S.	Bowmanville	1872
Brattan, J. R.	London	1875
Bray, Alfred	Angus	1874
Brent, H.	Port Hope	1874
Brereton, W. J.	Bradford	1871
Brete, R. G.	Arkona	1874
Brewster, N.	Ridgeway	1873
Bridgland, S.	Bracebridge	1870
Brien, James	Essex Centre	1870
Britton, Wm.	Brantford	1875
Brock, Wm.	Jarvis	1875
Brown, Miles	Winchester	1871
Buchanan, Geo.	Rodgerville	1871
Burgess, T. J.	Toronto	1870
Burnham, G. H.	Peterboro'	1875
Burns, W. J.	Streetsville	1876
Buchart, J. L.	Ingersoll	1877
Burt, W.	St. George	1870
Byam, J. W.	Campbellford	1875
Baines, A. M.	Toronto	1878
Bennett, Henry	Peterboro'	1878
Bentley, W. H.	Newmarket	1878
Bonnar, J. D.	Kingston	1878
Burt, Franklin	Paris	1878
Black, Fergus	Uxbridge	1879
Beeman, Thomas	Centreville	1879
Bremner, W. W.	Minesing	1879
Baldwin, J. B.	Toronto	1879
Butler, Billa F.	Stirling	1879
Brown, J. L.	Chesterville	1879
Bowlby, D. A.	Simcoe	1879
Brooke, D. E.	Chatham	1879
Boileau, Jules M.	Crysler	1880
Bowman, Geo.	Penetanguishene	1880
Boyce, W. W.	Warkworth	1880
Brownlee, Milne	Millbrook	1880
Buchner, D. C.	Delhi	1880
Berry, F. R. R.	Simcoe	1881
Bingham, Geo. S.	Waterloo	1881
Baugh, Jas.	Hamilton	1881
Beck, G. S.	Orillia	1882
Bedard, E.	Pembroke	1882
Bell, J. F.	Toronto	1882
Bentley, F.	Toronto	1882
Bentley, L.	Toronto	1882
Book, E. H.	Drummondville	1882
Bonnar, Wm.	Albion	1882
Brereton, T. G.	Bethany	1882
Brett, W. M.	Arkona	1882
Burt, J. C.	Bolton	1882
Bray, J.	Enfield	1883
Bates, F. D.	Hamilton	1883
Belt, R. W.	Brussels	1883
Bell, W. D. M.	Bear Brook	1883

Bingham, G. A.	Manilla	1884
Beatty, Elizabeth R.	Lansdowne	1884
Burgess, J. A.	Toronto	1885
Baumann, A. F.	Waterloo	1885
Britton, C. H.	Brantford	1885
Barber, J.	Nassagaweya	1885
Beemer, F.	New Durham	1886
Brock, L.	Guelph	1886
Brodie, G. M.	Markdale	1886
Bateman, R. M.	Port Perry	1886
Brennan, F. H.	Peterboro'	1886
Bromley, E.	Pembroke	1886
Birkitt, H. S.	Hamilton	1886
Beaman, W. C.	Ventnor	1886
Burdett, H. E.	St. Paul, Minn.	1887
Brown, J. J.	Owen Sound	1887
Barnett, A. D.	Fergus	1887
Barton, S. G. T.	Toronto	1887
Bradford, A.	Vachell	1887
Begg, J. W.	Kingston	1887
Bell, J.	Caledon	1887
Balfour, J. D.	Russelldale	1887
Bolby, G. H.	Berlin	1888
Bell, G.	Owen Sound	1888
Bishop, E. R.	Brantford	1888
Bechard, D.	Stony Point	1888
Bradley, W. J.	Ottawa	1888
Bibby, F. T.	Brighton	1888
Barber, W. C.	Toronto	1888
Bell, S. T.	Alliston	1888
Bapti-, G.	Ottawa	1888
Burns, R. A. E.	Toronto	1888
Bradd, F. J.	Campbellford	1889
Brown, J.	Campbellford	1889
Bateman, W. E.	Cresswell	1889
Birdsall, W. W.	Delhi	1889
Bolton, A. E.	Portland	1889
Broad, J. J.	Cobocook	1889
Bowman, J. E.	Dundas	1889
Becker, H.	Crieff	1889
Beeman, T. A.	Bancroft	1889
Bull, R.	Weston	1889
Bowman, G. M.	Hamilton	1889
Brown, P.	Oshawa	1889
Berden, O L.	Strathroy	1889
Bateman, F. J.	Christina	1890
Baldwin, W. W.	Toronto	1860
Bayly, B.	London	1890
Bowes, E. J.	Ottawa	1890
Brown, Minnie	Strathroy	1890
Berry, J. D.	Warkworth	1890
Bigelow, G. T.	Port Perry	1890
Bray, R. V.	Chatham	1890
Boyes, E. T.	Binbrook	1890
Bryans, W. F.	Toronto	1890
Boyle, Susanna P.	Toronto	1890
Bond, W. L.	Newmarket	1890
Baker, W. A.	Stouffville	1890
Black, M. C.	Glammis	1890
Burger, J. H.	Toronto	1890
Barker, L. F	Ingersoll	1890
Boyes, E. J.	Toronto	1890
Bell, J. H.	Colborne	1890
Baker, T. C.	Chatham	1890
Beatty, A. C.	Elizabethville	1890
Bedard, J. A.	St. Eugene	1890

Bell, J. C................ Strathroy 1890
Bowie, E. F............... Toronto 1890
Bueglass, A. S.............. Bright 1890
Barnhart, W. N......Mitchell Square 1891
Beath, T.................Columbus 1891
Bennett, T. E.............. Toronto 1889
Bolster, L. E.............. Orillia 1891
Bowie, R. A.............Brockville 1891
Boyd, G.................Toronto 1891
Brown, W. A........... Chesterville 1891
Burritt, C. H............ Lyndhurst 1891
Boultbee, A................. Toronto 1892
Bowles, G. H.............. Sandhill 1892
Bissonette, J. D...........Napanee 1892
Boyce, B. F................ Norham 1892
Bruce, H. A............. Port Perry 1892
Beattie, D. A................. Galt 1892
Blain, E. B...............Hamilton 1892
Bensley, R. R............. Hamilton 1892
Barber, H D.............. Cobourg 1892
Brown, J. N. E.............Medina 1892
Bownes, T. C.............. Addison 1892
Balfe, T. H............Smith's Falls 1892
Burkholder, J. F...........London 1892
Bourns, W. H...........Frankville 1892
Burrows, J. G.............Napanee 1892
Brown, P. M............. Camlachie 1892
Bentley, D. B...............Forest 1892
Ball, F. J................... Rugby 1893
Brown, W. F.............. Medina 1893
Burrows, F. J.............Lambeth 1893
Bowie, I...................Embro 1893
Brodie, R.............. Claremont 1893
Bird, C. H.................Barrie 1893
Brander, Minnie M........ Priceville 1893
Blanchard, F.............. Sutton 1893
Bruce, R. F.....New Lathrop, Mich. 1893
Barker, A. N........... Seeley's Bay 1893
Brown, W. E..........Rush, N.Y. 1893
Baker, M.................Springfield 1894
Boyd, W. B.............. Uxbridge 1894
Bradley, J. L................. Airlie 1894
Bull, J. H...............Weston 1894
Ball, W. A................. Toronto 1894
Burt, Ellen A. A............Toronto 1894
Badgerow, G. W............Eglinton 1895
Bean, S. B................. Bright 1895
Becket. Jas............ Thamesville 1895
Brien, J. W..........Essex Centre 1895
Brown, Geo. W..............Aylmer 1895
Boucher, R. B............Peterboro' 1895
Bouck, C. W..............Inkerman 1895
Boileau, F. X........Sturgeon Falls 1896
Basken. J. T.............. Dunrobin 1896
Blow, T. H........ South Mountain 1896
Berry, G. H.............. Gananoque 1896
Burt, G. S................ Hillsburg 1896
Bier, T. H...............Brantford 1896
Bedell, T. C................ Picton 1896
Buchanan, D................. Galt 1896
Beasley, W. J.............. Weston 1896
Boyle, J. F................ Toronto 1896
Beatty, A. A............... Toronto 1896
Bell, T. H.............Peterboro' 1896
Byers, W. G. N.......... Gananoque 1896
Beatty, W. J.............Glencairn 1896

Barber, G. W.............Hartford 1896
Brereton, C. H.......... Schomberg 1896

Caldwell, William......... Brantford 1875
Cameron, I. H............. Toronto 1874
Campbell, A. L............ Brooklin 1874
Carmichael, Duncan.......... Ottawa 1877
Carscallen, A. B............Petworth 1875
Carthew, C. E.. .... Guelph 1877
Case, G. X.................London 1875
Case, A. H............... Hamilton 1870
Cash, Edward............ Markham 1871
Cassels, J. McN,............ Quebec 1875
Clarke, R. A............. Oakville 1872
Clarke, John............. Peterboro' 1872
Claxton, William........... Verona 1876
Clement, John.......... Streetsville 1871
Cole, H. J.................Brantford 1871
Cook, A. B............... Welland 1875
Copeland, W. L....... St. Catharines 1875
Cornell, C. M. B............ Toledo 1872
Cotton, J. H..............Garafraxa 1875
Coverton, T. S..............Toronto 1875
Cowan, G. H............Princetown 1871
Crawford, Allen............Yorkville 1870
Crozier, J. B.......... London, Eng. 1872
Cameron, J. D............Glengarry 1878
Campbell, A. D............ Toronto 1878
Clarke, C. K..............Toronto 1878
Clinton, George...... Prince Edward 1878
Cornell, S. A.................London 1878
Cornell, Wagner............ Arkona 1878
Craig, H. A.............North Gower 1878
Comfort, William..........Ridgeville 1878
Chisholm, Thomas.......... Fergus 1879
Clapp, R. E................. Lochiel 1879
Caughlin, J. W..........St. Thomas 1879
Chappell, W. F............. Thorold 1879
Cattanach, A. J.............Fergus 1879
Chisholm, Alexander....... Lochiel 1879
Campbell, A. W........... Toronto 1880
Chown, H. H.... Emerson, Manitoba 1880
Clark, W. S................ Toronto 1880
Clemens, G. H............... Blair 1880
Clements, L. B.............Breslau 1880
Colquhoun, George......... Iroquois 1880
Cotton, Jas. M....... Burnhamthorpe 1880
Cameron, Paul............ Lancaster 1881
Clarke, J. G...............Meaford 1881
Cameron, Alexander.........Vachel 1882
Charlton, W. J............. Weston 1882
Cleland, G. S.............. Niagara 1882
Clendenan, G. W............. Jordan 1882
Cornell, A. P............. Kingston 1882
Coulter, R. M........ Richmond Hill 1882
Clarke, H. S...............Toronto 1883
Cuthbertson, William........Toronto 1883
Collver, M. K........... Wellandport 1883
Casgrain, H. R............ Windsor 1883
Chaffee, C. W.............. Toronto 1883
Carleton, W. H............Hamilton 1883
Case, T. E................ Exeter 1883
Cryan, John..... North Williamsburg 1883
Canfield, F. D..............Ingersoll 1884
Carveth, G. H................Orono 1884
Clerk, J. W................Kinsale 1884

Campbell, D	Ontario, N. Y.	1884
Cochrane, J. M	Toronto	1884
Cook, E. M	Belleville	1884
Coughlan, Richard	Hastings	1884
Courtney, J. D	Hamilton	1885
Cowan, T. C	Iona	1884
Corlis, M. A	St. Thomas	1885
Cane, F. W	Newmarket	1885
Cunningham, H. C	Kingston	1885
Couch, J. A	Queensboro'	1885
Campbell, Frank	Wiarton	1885
Conerty, J. M	North Augusta	1886
Caven, W. P	Toronto	1886
Cruickshank, G. R	Weston	1886
Clemison, J. McD	Wellington	1886
Casselman, J. P	N. Williamsburg	1886
Collins, Cornelius	Peterboro'	1886
Carruthers, J. B	Barrie	1886
Cullen, L. F	Woodstock	1886
Cassidy, J. I	Goldstone	1886
Cassidy, G. A	Moorefield	1886
Campbell, T. F	Newbury	1886
Cale, W. F	Mitchell	1886
Cutbertson, C. R	Toronto	1886
Campbell, J. F	Toronto	1886
Creggan, J. G	Kingston	1886
Cornell, S. S	Farmersville	1886
Charteris, C. R	Chatham	1887
Collins, A. E	St. Catharines	1887
Cameron, Daniel	Perth	1887
Cameron, J. M	Galt	1887
Campbell, Edwin	Port Perry	1887
Caron, G. G	Aylmer	1887
Clouse, Elias	Simcoe	1887
Clarke, W. H	Meaford	1887
Campbell, A. W	Montreal	1887
Cline, L. F	Springfield	1888
Campbell, D. M	St. Thomas	1888
Carson, Miss Susie	Strathroy	1888
Chamberlain, W. P	Morrisburg	1888
Cummings, S	Hamilton	1888
Connell, J. C	Kingston	1888
Cowan, F. P	Toronto	1888
Craine, Miss Agnes	Smith's Falls	1888
Conroy, C. P	Martintown	1888
Campeau, W. J	Amherstburg	1888
Campbell, D. W	Petrolea	1888
Clutton, W. H	Dunlop	1888
Castleman, A. L	Williamsburg	1888
Crosthwaite, G. K	Bartonville	1889
Campbell, J	Mapleton	1889
Collins, J. H	Whitby	1889
Campbell, J. T	Whitby	1889
Carruthers, John	Cayuga	1889
Chambers, G	Woodstock	1889
Clark, C. P	St. Mary's	1889
Chapple, H	Newcastle	1889
Crawford J	Glencoe	1889
Clapp, W. H	Toronto	1889
Carson, Jennie S	Strathroy	1889
Creasor, J. A	Owen Sound	1889
Channonhouse, R. C	Eganville	1889
Cooper, R M	London	1889
Cline, C. A	Belmont	1889
Carbert, G. B	Orangeville	1889
Coutlee, H. N	Sharbot Lake	1889
Cornu, F	Montreal	1889
Clerihew, E. M	Kingston	1889
Chisholm, W. P	Hamilton	1889
Comfort, F. S	Campden	1890
Coleman, A. H	Belleville	1890
Cullen T. S	Sarnia	1890
Chrystal, R. J	Avonton	1890
Clarke, F. R	Colborne	1890
Coughlin, C. B	Hastings	1890
Carveth, C. B	Port Hope	1890
Copeland, E. M	Ealing	1890
Cunningham, D	Kingston	1890
Clendenan, C. W	Toronto	1890
Coon, D. A	Elgin	1890
Cunningham, F. W	Hespeler	1890
Cameron, W. A	Smith's Falls	1891
Campbell, J. W	Kingston	1891
Carmichael, A	Spencerville	1891
Chown, A. P	Kingston	1891
Clemesha, J. C	Port Hope	1891
Clendenan, A. E	Cambray	1891
Clune, P. J	Wooler	1891
Crawford, R. J	Owen Sound	1891
Campbell, W. A	Whitby	1892
Chabot, J. L	Ottawa	1892
Crawford, W	Galt	1892
Clark, A. M	Wellandport	1892
Chambers, Annie	Port Elgin	1892
Chalmers, A. P	Poole	1892
Crichton, A	Toronto	1892
Closson, J. H	Toronto	1892
Clark, D. A	Agincourt	1892
Chevrier, G. R	Ottawa	1892
Cooke, G. H	Chesley	1892
Clingan, G	Toronto	1892
Chambers, W	Toronto	1893
Campbell, L. H	Bradford	1893
Campbell, N	Cookstown	1893
Carlaw, T. W	Warkworth	1893
Calder, R. M	Grimsby	1893
Countryman, J. E	Tweed	1893
Creighton, J. K	Millstown	1893
Carter, C	Toronto	1893
Carveth, Annie E	Toronto	1893
Corbett, R. T	Toronto	1893
Campbell, B	Parkhill	1894
Coleman, F	Hamilton	1894
Crain, W E	Brockville	1894
Crawford, J	Toronto	1894
Curtis, J. D	St. Thomas	1894
Cuthbertson, H. A	Chicago, U.S.A.	1894
Coulthard, W. L	Toronto	1894
Caven, James G	Toronto	1895
Chapin, C. D	Brantford	1895
Chapman, W. J	Toronto	1895
Cormack, J. H	Kingston	1895
Cowper, J. A	Welland	1895
Craft, R. A	Chisholm	1895
Currie, M	Picton	1895
Cameron, D. A	Wallacetown	1896
Cranston, J. G	Arnprior	1896
Carron, F. B	Brockville	1896
Connolly, B. G	Trenton	1896
Crawford, D. T	Thedford	1896
Clare, H	Chapman	1896
Campbell, P. M	Admaston	1896

David, A	Port Lambton	1874
Davidson, Alex	Berlin	1877
Day, Jonathan	Port Hope	1877
Day, W. D. P. W	Harrowsmith	1874
DeCow, A	Thamesville	1870
Dee, J. M	Stamford	1872
De La Mater, R. H	Fonthill	1871
Deynard, A. B	Picton	1875
Dingham, W. E	Milford	1875
Dingwall, A. M	Mount Hope	1875
Donaldson, John	Singhampton	1872
Dorland, James	Adolphustown	1872
Douglas, Alex	Avon	1876
Douglas, W. J	Norman	1876
Dowsley, D. H	Owen Sound	1870
Dumble, T. H	Gananoque	1877
Dumble, W. C	Owen Sound	1870
Dunsmore, J. McA	Mitchell	1870
Dafoe, Wm	Toronto	1878
De Lom, H. A	London	1878
Duggan, F. J	Lloydtown	1878
Dunfield, J	Peterboro'	1878
Davies, R. A	Easton's Corners	1879
Dryden, J. R	Eramosa	1879
Dowling, J. F	Eganville	1879
Duck, W. B	Morpeth	1879
Des Rosiers, dit Lafreniets, Alex. N		
	Clarence Creek	1880
Dickson, J. F	Goderich	1880
Duncan, J. H	Bayfield	1881
Davidson, J. G	Lynden	1882
Dickson, C. R	Wolfe Island	1882
Dowsley, G. C	Wingham	1882
Duncan, J. T	Toronto	1882
Drake, F. P	Kingsmill	1883
Dickson, W. F	Ingersoll	1883
Derby, W. J	Rockland	1883
Davis, W. N	Aylmer	1884
Duff, H. R	Kingston	1884
Doolittle, P. E	Toronto	1885
Dales, J. R	Dunbarton	1885
Dewar, P. A	Essex Centre	1885
Dwyer, A. W	Elgin	1885
Drummond, H. E	Pontypool	1886
Dunton, Daniel	Britannia	1886
Dickison, G. J	Mildmay	1886
Dow, W. G	Fergus	1886
Dow, Wm	Barnett	1886
Dixon, M. L	Frankville	1886
Dame, A. A	Jordan	1886
Dobie, D. A	Strathburne	1887
Dryden, G. F	Rockwood	1887
Durand, C. F	Toronto	1887
Dickson, Miss Annie	Brockville	1887
Downing, W. H	Kingston	1888
Dawson, F. J	Toronto	1888
Dewar, C. P	Ottawa	1888
Dewar, M. C	Weston	1889
David, W. C	Kingston	1889
Dixon, W. A	Toronto	1889
Dickinson, G. A	Zion	1889
Duff, John	Inverary	188?
Davis, Lelia A	King	1889
De'a, H. J	Moorefield	1888
Douglas, S	Marshville	1890
Drake, F. A	South Cayuga	1890

Dinwoody, J. A	Clover Hill	1890
Dolan, J. F	Belleville	1890
Danby, J. J	Ottawa	1890
Day, S. D	St. Thomas	1891
Dow, J	Fergus	1891
Dunning, M	Orangeville	1891
Day, A. R. A	Guelph	1892
Davis, S. N	York	1892
Dwyer, R. J	Toronto	1892
Dymond, Bertha	Toronto	1892
Duncan, J. H	Emery	1893
Darling, R. E	Goodwood	1893
Douglas, W	Harrison	1893
Doan, W	New Sarum	1893
Dunn, D. J	Rosemont	1893
Danard, A. L	Allenford	1894
Devitt, T. G	Bobcaygeon	1894
Drysdale, W. F	Perth	1894
Delahaye, F. C	Pembroke	1895
Douglas, W	Chatham	1895
Dow, Jeamie I	Fergus	1895
Downey, R. A	Toronto	1895
Drummond, C. A	Meaford	1895
Downing, A	Toronto	1895
Davidson, A	Burns	1895
Deacon, J. D	Pembroke	1896
Drennan, Jennie G	Kingston	1896
Deacon, G. R	Stratford	1896
Eakins, J. E	Newbury	1875
East, C	Moray	1873
Edwards, O. C	Clarence	1873
Ellison, S. B	St. Thomas	1873
Esmond, J. J	Belleville	1877
Evans, H. E	Pembroke	1878
Emerick, F	Simcoe	1878
Edwards, J. S	London	1879
Ellis, Judson	St. George	1880
Emory, C. Van N	Galt	1881
Eastwood, W, F	Whitby	1882
Emory, W. J. H	Burlington	1883
Elliott, J. E	Toronto	1884
Ewing, William	Hawkesbury	1885
Ellis, D.D	Tilbury Centre	1885
Elberts, D. W	Chatham	1885
Eadie, A. B., jun	Toronto	1886
Eadie, A. B., sen	Toronto	1886
Edmison, A. H	Roseneath	1886
English, W. M	London	1886
Earl, E. H	Port Hope	1886
Ego, Angus	Sutton West	1886
Eastwood, J. H	Whitby	1887
Erritt, A. I	Merrickville	1887
Easton, C. L	Smith's Falls	1887
Evans, E	Seaforth	1887
Eaton, J. M	Lakeview	1888
Embury, Miss E	Napanee	1888
Earley, W. J	Owen Sound	1889
Emery, G. F	Gananoque	1889
Elliott, A. R	Belleville	1889
Egbert, W	Dunville	1889
Emmerson, A. T	Peterboro'	1889
Elliott, H. C. S	Toronto	1889
Ellis, T. H	Pembroke	1890
Ellis, A. D	Norwich	1890
Echlin, E. B	Copetown	1891

Edgar, J. W	Hamilton	1891
Empey, W. A	Winchester	1891
Ewing, F. J	Seaforth	1891
Evans, J. A. C	Bradford	1892
Earl, W. M	Bishop's Mills	1892
Elliott, W	Mitchell	1893
Elliott, George	Toronto	1895
Elliott, A. S	Scotch Block	1895
Ellis, George	Dundela	1896
Elliott, F. B	Mayfair	1896
Elliott, Geo. A	Oury	1896
Embury, A. T	Belleville	1896
Elliott, J. J	Brantford	1896
Farewell, Adolphus	Oshawa	1874
Farewell, G. W	Stouffville	1874
Farley, John J	Belleville	1877
Faulkner, George W	Belleville	1871
Fenwick, Kenneth N	Kingston	1874
Field, Byron	Toronto	1877
Fisher, David M	Toronto	1877
Forest, William	Mount Albert	1871
Francks, William	Port Elgin	1877
Fraser, Alex. C	Wallaceburg	1877
Fraser, Donald B	Shakespeare	1874
Fraser, Duncan	Shakespeare	1874
Fraser, John	Strabane	1871
Freel, Eugene I	Markham	1875
Freeman, Wm. Clarkson	Scotland	1877
Fulton, James	Fingal	1876
Faulkner, D. W	Holloway	1878
Forbes, John M	Caledonia	1878
Fraser, John R	Hawkesbury	1878
Fraser, Henry Donald	Pembroke	1881
Fisher, Richard M	Toronto	1882
Freel, Ira Albert	Markham	1882
Fairchild, Rich. Melvin	Brantford	1883
Frost, Robt. Samuel	Kinmount	1883
Freeman, Wm. Francis	Milton	1883
Fierheller, G	Parry Sound	1886
Foster, Chas. Manley	Toronto	1884
Fraser, Robert Nelson	Westmeath	1884
Ferguson, James	Cumberland	1884
Fielde, Ed. Cazalet	Prescott	1884
Ferguson, John	Berlin	1885
Ford, Henry Bernice	Bouck's Hill	1885
Fox, Wm. Henry	Mono Road	1886
Fraser, John Wilson	London	1886
Foley, Declan Ed	Westport	1886
Forster, James Moffatt	Oakville	1886
Forin, Alexander	Belleville	1886
Freeman, Albert Ed	Invermay	1887
Free, Ed. John	Campbellford	1887
Funnell, Ada Alferetta	Trenton	1887
Fraser, Jas. Mitchell	Hawkesbury	1887
Fish, William A	Newton Brook	1887
Foster, Alonzo Barton	Waterford	1887
Féré, G. A	Toronto	1888
Fisher, J. H. C. F	Bailieboro'	1888
Fisher, A. J	Wiarton	1888
Francy, C. H	Gormley	1888
Ferguson, J. G	Cookstown	1888
Ferguson, T. A	Toronto	1888
Fraser, J. B	Brockville	1888
Fitzgerald, T. A	Millbrook	1889
Fraser, S. M	London	1889

Ferguson, W. S	Avonbank	1890
Ferguson, R	London	1890
Forfar, J. E	Toronto	1890
Fletcher, W. J	Toronto	1890
Flatt, C. E	Millgrove	1890
Fairfield, C. A. D	St. Catharines	1890
Freeland, A	Ottawa	1890
Funnell. Roselle V	Kingston	1890
Ferguson, W. D. T	Rocklands	1890
Fairchild, C. C	Brantford	1891
Farmer, G. D	Ancaster	1891
Field, A. B	Blackstock	1891
Fotheringham, J. T	Toronto	1891
Forrest, J	Mount Albert	1892
Forrest, R. F	Mount Albert	1892
Fowler, R. V	Colborne	1892
Fenton, F	Toronto	1892
Ferguson, M	Harriston	1892
Foster, Mattie I	Welland	1892
Fraleigh, A. E	Arva	1892
Foley, J. G	Westport	1892
Futcher, T. B	St. Thomas	1893
Ferguson, J. B	Toronto	1893
Farley, F. J	Smithfield	1894
Farncomb, T. S	Newcastle	1894
Ferguson, A. K	Kirkton	1894
Field, C. C	Cobourg	1894
Field, G. H	Cobourg	1894
Fletcher, A. G. A	Toronto	1894
Ford, J. W	Woodham	1894
Frank, H. R	Brantford	1894
Ferris, G. M	Campbellford	1894
Farrell, T. H	Kingston	1895
Feader, W. A	Iroquois	1895
Featherstone, H. M	Nelson	1895
Ferguson, J. H	Toronto	1895
Flaherty, T. F	Thorndale	1895
Fleming, S. E	Millbank	1895
Gaboury, Ulric	Belle River	1875
Gahan, Beresford T	Toronto	1870
Gaviller, Edwin A	Bond Head	1873
Geikie, Walter W	Toronto	1875
Gibson, A. M	Newburgh	1874
Gilbert, Thomas M	Bowmanville	1875
Gillies, Neil	Chesley	1874
Golden, John	Blenheim	1873
Gordon, George	Bluevale	1877
Gracey, Wm. John	Blyth	1877
Graham, Peter L	Lobo	1877
Graham, Wm. Henry	Gilford	1871
Grasett, F. LeM	Toronto	1877
Grant, Andrew	Woodville	1877
Gray, John S	Bailieboro'	1886
Gray, Wesley	Cartwright	1874
Griffin, Herbert Spohn	Hamilton	1877
Griffin, Walter Scott	Peterboro'	1870
Griffiths, John Auckland	Guelph	1874
Groves, A	Fergus	1871
Gunn, John	Beaverton	1874
Glasgow, Sinclair H	Drummondville	1878
Grant, Wm. F. H	Tullamore	1878
Gilmour, John F	Port Hope	1878
Gardner, John H	Farquhar	1878
Groves, James W	Pakenham	1878
Gravely, Edward J	Cornwall	1878

Greenwood, F. J.	St. Catharines	1878
Graham, Kenneth	Ottawa	1878
Gould, David	Stroud	1878
Groves, George Hodgins	Carp	1879
Geikie, Arch. James	Toronto	1879
Galbraith, John E.	Bowmanvinle	1880
Glendinning, J. I.	Streetsville	1880
Gordon. John	Luther	1880
Greer, T. N.	Millbrook	1880
Gray, William L.	Pembroke	1881
Gibson, William J.	Kingston	1882
Garrett, R. W.	Kingston	1882
Gaviller, A. C.	Beeton	1882
Gilpin, William	Brechin	1882
Gullen, J. B.	Toronto	1883
Gordon, C. M.	Ottawa	1883
Graham, Angus	Glencoe	1885
Gunn, W. J.	Portage la Prairie	1885
Gordon, D. McD.	St. Helen's	1886
Galligan, T. D.	Arnprior	1886
Grant, J. H. Y.	Ottawa	1886
Gibson, Robert	Watford	1886
Giles, William	Haliburton	1886
Graham, A. D	Lobo	1887
Galloway, James	Beaverton	1887
Guinane, Joachin	Toronto	1887
Galloway, H. P. H	Toronto	1887
Gillespie, W. R.	Cannington	1887
Glassford, W. J.	Toronto	1887
Glass, M. J	Poplar Hill	1887
Graham, W. F	Ottawa	1887
Gallaghar, Morton	Portland	1887
Grasett, J. C. C	Simcoe	1888
Gunne, N. D.	Seaforth	1888
Garratt, A. H	Toronto	1888
Groves, O.	Fergus	1888
Grant, John	Beaverton	1888
Gamble, J. B.	Jarvis	1889
Godfrey, F. E.	Belgrave	1889
Gilchrist, W. C.	Barrie	1889
Greenlaw, J. A.	Palmerston	1889
Gillrie, M. E.	St. Mary's	1889
Grundy, H	Toronto	1889
Garrow, A. E.	Ottawa	1889
Gordon, G.	Toronto	1889
Gandier, A.	Kingston	1889
Gemmill, E. W.	Almonte	1889
Groves, W. H.	Burnhamthorpe	1889
Gorrell, A. S.	Brockville	1890
Ghent, J. A.	Toronto	1890
Gimby, J. H.	Owen Sound	1890
Goold, A. J.	Mount Pleasant	1890
Gibson, J. A.	London	1890
Gordon, A. R.	Toronto	1890
Greene, E H.	Toronto	1890
Gray, W. A.	Perth	1890
Gee, J. J.	Toronto	1890
Gimby, W. E.	Goodwood	1890
Gordon, E. P.	Rosedale	1890
Guest, Frederick	London	1890
Gardiner, R. J.	Seeley's Bay	1891
Gibeault, A. A.	Alfred	1891
Gibson, R. J.	Clinton	1891
Gifford, Mary A.	Meaford	1891
Gillespie, P. A.	Cannington	1891
Graham, Lucinda	Toronto	1891

Griffith, R. C	Picton	1891
Gould, G. W	Colborne	1892
Gowland, R. H	Hamilton	1892
Grant, H. A	Pembroke	1892
Gray, Eliza R.	Toronto	1892
Gray, Jennie	Toronto	1892
Greene, S. D.	Arnprior	1892
Green, F. T	Stony Creek	1892
Green, R. H	Sheffield	1892
Groves, W	Quyon, Que.	1892
Graham, W. C. R	Prescott	1892
Gowan, T. J.	Creemore	1892
Gear, H	Marshville	1892
Gibson, J. C.	Milverton	1892
Gordon, J. K. M.	St. Helen's	1893
Glaister, W.	Cross Hill	1893
Gibson, J. L.	Cherry Valley	1893
Glasco, G. S.	Hamilton	1893
Goode, E. W	Toronto	1893
Grant, F. E.	Richmond Hill	1893
Galloway, A.	Beaverton	1894
Graham, E. D.	Sutton West	1894
Gray, G. B.	Elora	1894
Gibson, A.	Orton	1895
Gibson, J. F.	Kingston	1895
Gorrell. C. W. F	Brockville	1895
Greenwood, A. B.	Keswick	1895
Gun, A.	Durham	1895
Grant, J. A. C	Gravenhurst	1895
Grant, A. J.	Pembroke	1896
Gardner, A. E.	Belleville	1896
Goldie, W.	Ayr	1896
Graef, Chas.	Clifford	1896
Gibbs, Joseph	Meaford	1896
Goldsmith, P. G.	Peterboro'	1896
Gibson, J. C.	Kingston	1896
Gwyn, N. B	Dundas	1896
Hagel, S. D.	Toronto	1873
Hamilton, Alexander.	Onondaga	1871
Hamilton, J. R.	Stratford	1872
Hamilton, Robert	Athlone	1874
Hanover, Wm	Almonte	1876
Harris, W. T	Onondaga	1874
Hart, J. M.	Wilford	1871
Harvey, W. A.	Harriston	1875
Heally, L. D.	Springfield	1874
Henderson, A. A.	Ot'awa	1871
Henning, N. P	Tyrrell	1871
Hickey, S. A.	Aultsville	1876
Higgins, E. M.	Ottawa	1877
Higginbotham, Wm	Bridgewater	1871
Hill, Alfred H	Woodstock	1877
Hobley, Thomas	Toronto	1875
Hockridge, T. G.	Newmarket	1874
Hodge, George	Orono	1870
Holmes, F. L	Farmersville	1877
Holmes, T. G.	Holmesville	1875
Honeywell, Wm	Toronto	1877
Hopkins, E. L	Stony Creek	1877
Hourigan, A. B	Peterboro'	1877
Howitt, Henry	Guelph	1874
Hudson. Samuel	Roslin	1871
Hunter, John	St. George	1875
Hartman, Jacob	Hamilton	1878
Howe, F. M.	Cartwright	1878

Hutchinson, T. S	Exeter	1878
Hamilton, C. J	Goderich	1879
Horton, R. N	New Dublin	1879
Hossie, T. R	Cataraqui	1879
Hanna, Frank	Lansdowne	1876
Hunt, Henry	Williamstown	1879
Hyde, J. G.	Stratford	1879
Hamil, W. E	Aurora	1880
Hoig, D. S.	Oshawa	1880
Howie, W. H	Courtland	1880
Hart, G. C	Osnabruck Centre	1880
Heyd, H. E	Brantford	1881
Hall, J. B.	Toronto	1881
Hanbridge, Wm	Dunblane	1882
Henwood, A. J	Brantford	1882
Hansler, J. E	Fonthill	1883
Hislop, Robert	Detroit	1883
Hearn, Richard	Toronto	1883
Hickey, D. C	Kingston	1883
Hall, W. R	Chatham	1884
Hixon, E. F	Priceville	1884
Hamilton, W. H	Stratford	1884
Hunt, C. W.	Listowel	1884
Herald, John	Kingston	1884
Hall, E. A	Hornby	1884
Harrison, W. S	Milton	1885
Hamilton, H. J	Brampton	1885
Harvie, A. R	Orillia	1885
Howell, J. H	Fonthill	1885
Hawley, H. H	Trenton	1885
Hanks, A. R	Florence	1885
Harkin, F, McD	Vankleek Hill	1885
Hunter, J. W	Buffalo	1886
Hillier, Reil	Cottam	1886
Heggie, W. C	Brampton	1886
Hunt, George	Rosemont	1886
Hart, J. W	Fleetwood	1886
Hay, W. W	Watford	1886
Hopkins, W. B	Marshville	1886
Hamilton, J. H	Hillsburg	1886
Harvie, J. A	Coldwater	1886
Hamilton, J. A	Woodhill	1886
Heath, F. C	Brantford	1886
Hanna, J. E	North Gower	1886
Hughes, P. H	Leamington	1886
Hoover, J. H	Aylmer	1887
Hopkins, R. R	Harrison	1887
Halstead, T. H	Mount Forest	1887
Hawke, Benjamin	Hawkesville	1887
Hart, M. W	Prescott	1887
Hay, H. R	Listowel	1887
Hall, Wm	Lloydtown	1887
Hunter, A. J	Rochester, Mich.	1888
Hotson, A. N	Innerkip	1888
Hart, J. F	Prescott	1888
Harris, W. H	Canton	1888
Hæntschell, C. W	Pembroke	1888
Horsey, E. H	Ruthven	1888
Hanvey, C. B. H	St. Thomas	1888
Hyttenranch, L. J	London	1888
Hutton, John	Priceville	1888
Hotson, Alex	London	1888
Hoare, C. W	Walkerville	1888
Howitt, J. A	Gourock	1888
Henderson, D	Bradford	1889
Halliday, A. H	Bellwood	1889

Hart, J. S	Toronto	1889
Harding, W. E	Brockville	1889
Hickson, L. J	Lasalle, N.Y., U.S.	1889
Honner, R. H	London	1889
Holdcroft, J	Tweed	1889
Harkness, F. B	Kingston	1889
Hamilton, C. H	Oakville	1889
Henwood, J. M	Toronto	1889
Hamilton, W	Beaverton	1889
Herriman, W. C	Lindsay	1890
Hutchison, D. H	Ingersoll	1890
Hayes, A. N	Parkhill	1890
Hobbs, A. T	London	1890
Hilliary, R. M	Aurora	1890
Harrison, G	Toronto	1890
Hutton, Mary	Forest	1890
Hodgetts, C. A	Toronto	1890
Hill, R	Aylmer	1890
Howell, R. G	Jarvis	1890
Holdcroft, W. T	Tweed	1890
Hanley, J. F	Waubaushene	1890
Harrington, A. J	Toronto	1890
Harrison, E. D	Picton	1891
Hay, R. F	Watford	1891
Heaslip, A. W	Niagara Falls	1891
Henry, T. H	Orangeville	1891
Herriman, W. D. D	Lindsay	1891
Hett, J. E	Berlin	1891
Hilliard, W. L	Waterloo	1891
Hunter, A. C	Newcastle	1891
Hunter, W. R	Clarksburg	1891
Hutt, W. G	Aurora	1891
Hagerman, F. H	Parkhill	1892
Haig, A	Menie	1892
Halliday, V. S	Peterboro'	1892
Heggie, D. L	Brampton	1892
Henderson, E. M	Brockville	1892
Henderson, J	Warkworth	1892
Henry, E. A	Mono Centre	1892
Hough, A. H	St. Catharines	1892
Hughes, T. A. M	Ilderton	1892
Heming, F. H	Toronto	1892
Harper, J. J	Rosemont	1892
Holmes, W. L	Walkerton	1892
Hershey, J. A	Garrison Road	1892
Harvey, E. E	Newry	1893
Hopkins, J. R	Stony Creek	1893
Harvie, J. N	Orillia	1893
Hyndman, H. K	Exeter	1893
Henderson, J. A	Orangeville	1893
Haight, M	New Durham	1893
Hubbard, J. P	Thamesford	1893
Hackett, W. A	Belfast	1894
Harris, N. M	Toronto	1894
Hastings, R. J	Guelph	1894
Hodgson, T. C	Beaverton	1894
Hogg, D. H	London	1894
Hughes, F. W	Thorndale	1894
Hulet, Gertrude	Norwich	1894
Hagar, F. C	Kingston	1895
Hall, G. W	Little Britain	1895
Harris, F. C	Tuscarora	1895
Hewson, T. B	Port Hope	1895
Hill, Jennie	Bond Head	1895
Hird, W	Uxbridge	1895
Hunter, A. J	Toronto	1895

c

Hutchinson, J. C .... Fordwich 1895
Hutchinson, — ...... Richmond Hill 1895
Hogg, L. .... London 1895
Hooper, E. M .... Toronto 1896
Henderson, W. J ..... Little Britain 1896
Hodgins, F. W .... Lucan 1896
Hodgins, A. G. .... Lucan 1896
Hicks, E. S. .... Pt. Dover 1896
Harcourt, G. V .... Port Hope 1896

Irving, W .... Toronto 1874
Inksetter, D. G. .... Copetown 1880
Ivey, J. A. .... Jarvis 1889
Irwin, T. W. .... Pembroke 1889
Inksetter, W. E. .... Copetown 1890
Irwin, H. .... Pembroke 1890
Irwin, A. F. .... Chatham 1890
Irvine, Emily J. .... Brampton 1890
Irwin, E. E. .... Newmarket 1890
Irwin, T. C. .... Cloverhill 1890

Jackes, G. W .... Unionville 1875
Jackson, F. W. .... Brockville 1873
Jackson, N. M. .... Port Lambton 1876
Jakeway, C. E. ..... Holland Landing 1871
James, W. .... Mount Albert 1872
Jeffs, T. W. .... Union, B.C. 1895
Jessop, E. .... Port Perry 1876
Johnson, A. J .... Yorkville 1873
Johnson W. H. .... Fergus 1875
Johnston, J. S. ...... Mount Charles 1873
Johnston, T. G. .... Sarnia 1878
Jones, J. R. .... Toronto 1878
Jamieson, D. .... Mount Forest 1878
Judson, G. W. .... Westport 1880
Jamieson, J. .... Kars 1881
Jones, A. C. .... Cummingsville 1881
Josephs, G. E. .... Pembroke 1881
Jarvis, C. E. .... London 1882
Johnston, W. H. .... Toronto 1882
Johnston, D. A. .... Bridgewater 1882
Johnston, J. M. .... Kincardine 1882
Jacques, W. .... Jarvis 1883
Jackson, J. M. .... Arva 1882
Johnston, G. L. .... Winthrop 1883
Johnston, F. H. .... Brantford 1884
Jones, J. A. .... Kemptville 1884
Jones, D. O. R. .... Toronto 1885
Johnston, D. R. .... Ancaster 1886
Johnson, D. .... Buck's Hill 1887
James, M. .... Centreville 1887
Jones, S. J. .... Stony Creek 1887
Jones, G. F. .... Lucan 1887
Johnson, J. W. .... Farmersville 1887
Jeffs, W. H. .... Hoard's 1888
Jamieson, D. .... Kars 1888
Jamieson, T. J. .... Kars 1888
Jento, C. B. .... Brockville 1890
Johnson, D. .... Underwood 1891
Johnston, W. J. ...... Carleton Place 1891
Jamieson, Alison .... Wicklow 1892
Johnston, Albert .... Ottawa 1892
Jones, W. A. .... Clandeboye 1892
James, H. J. .... Clayton 1893
Johnston, H. A. .... Toronto 1894
Jardine, J. .... Sunderland 1894

Jary, J. M. .... Norwood 1894
James, J. F. .... Strathroy 1895
Johnston, C. G. .... Athens 1895
Jones, W. W. .... Mount Forest 1896

Kains, Robert. .... St. Thomas 1871
Kennedy, Alexander. .... Bath 1876
Kennedy, J. B. .... Welland 1872
Kennedy, William .... Sandhill 1875
Kidd, Edward. .... Manotick 1872
King J. S. .... Toronto 1876
Kitchen, Edward. .... St. George 1877
Kittson, Ed. G. .... Hamilton 1883
Kennedy, G. A. .... Dundas 1878
Kennedy, W. B. .... Pembroke 1878
Kidd, P. E. .... Kingston 1877
Kirk, G. W. .... Pembroke 1878
Kilborn, R. K. .... Frankville 1879
Kidd, T. A. .... Carp 1886
Kippax, J. R. .... Toronto 1880
Kidd, J. F. .... Kingston 1883
Kent, F. D. .... Bracebridge 1884
Knight, J. H. .... Wallaceburg 1885
Kinsley, A. B. .... Port Colborne 1885
Krick, C. A. .... Elcho 1885
Kyle, W. A. ..... North Winchester 1885
Kester, D. W. .... Princeton 1886
Keane, M. J. .... Toronto 1887
Kennedy, R. A. .... Rockland 1887
Kelly, J. A. A. .... Woodbridge 1887
Karn, C. J. W. .... Woodstock 1888
Kidd, D. A. .... French River 1888
Kennedy, J. H. .... Lindsay 1888
Kerr, W. .... Toronto 1889
Kilborn, O. L. .... Kingston 1889
Kalbfleisch, F. H .... Paisley 1899
Kaiser, T. E. .... Edgeley 1890
Kennedy, J. P. .... London 1891
Kidd, W. E. .... Kingston 1891
Knechtel, R. .... Brussels 1891
Kilbourne, B .... Parkhill 1892
Kirk, F. J. .... Kingston 1892
Koyle, F. H. .... Brockville 1893
King, James. .... St. Thomas 1893
King, J. E. .... Elder's Mills 1893
King, R. .... Elder's Mills 1893
Kingston, C. M. .... Stirling 1894
Kerr, Thomas. .... Toronto 1894
Keith, W. D. .... Toronto 1895
Kellam, E. T. .... Seaforth 1895
Kelly, C. J. .... West Flamboro' 1895
Klotz, M. O. .... Ottawa 1895
Kelly, J. K. .... Almonte 1896

Lafferty, James .... Perth 1875
Lane, Joseph .... North Williamsburg 1871
Lang, Hugh .... Granton 1873
Lang, William. .... Keene 1871
Langstaff, G. A. .... Thornhill 1878
Lawrence, Robert. .... Honeywood 1871
Lean, Thomas .... Cobourg 1872
Leitch, Archibald. ..... St. Catharines 1875
Leitch, D. .... St. Thomas 1870
Leslie, R. B. .... Toronto 1874
Lett, Stephen .... Toronto 1870
Lindsay, N. J. .... Alvinston 1874

Locke, C. F. A.	Barrie	1871
Lovekin, J. P.	Newcastle	1871
Lovett, William	Ayr	1870
Lowey, W. H.	Guelph	1874
Lumley, W. G.	Delaware	1870
Lynd, Adam	Bond Head	1875
Lackner, H. G.	Hawkesville	1876
Lowe, J. H.	Haliburton	1878
Langstaff, J. E.	Richmond Hill	1878
Langlois, Onesine	Windsor	1878
Lewis, F. W.	Toronto	1878
Lehman, William	Ringwood	1878
Lynch, D. P.	Kingston	1878
Lowry, David	Cavanville	1878
Lloyd, David	Strathroy	1879
Lefevre, J. M.	Brockville	1879
Leonard, R. A.	West Brook	1879
Lundy, F. B.	Galt	1880
Lavell, W. A.	Newburg	1881
Lennox, L. J.	Thornton	1881
Lesslie, J. W.	Toronto	1881
Lafferty, James	Hamilton	1882
Lepper, W. J.	Toronto	1883
Langstaff, L. G.	Thornhill	1884
Lake, A. D.	Drumbo	1884
Lockhart, R. J.	Hespeler	1886
Lynch, W. V.	Lindsay	1885
Little, A. T.	Allandale	1885
Lucy, Robert	Glen Allan	1885
Leitch, H. D.	Flesherton	1885
Lundy, F. G.	Sheffield	1885
Lapp, T. C.	Grafton	1886
Logie, W. J.	London	1886
Logie, William	Sarnia	1886
Lawson, Alexander	Greensville	1887
Lackner, A. E.	Hawkesville	1887
Loucks, W. F.	Stirling	1887
Lawrence, F.	St. Thomas	1887
Livingstone, Miss M.	Kingston	1887
Langford, C. B.	Kent Bridge	1888
Lammiman, B.	Solina	1888
Little, T. H.	Owen Sound	1888
Lawyer, Miss Annie	Ottawa	1888
Lane, I. J.	North Williamsburg	1888
Lang, C. M.	Owen Sound	1888
Lanfear, H. O.	Lakefield	1889
Little, W. C.	Barrie	1889
Lynd, Ida E.	Bond Head	1890
Lockhart, G. D.	Mount Brydges	1890
Liddell, G. L.	Cornwall	1890
Lambert, E. M.	Ottawa	1891
Langrill, W. F.	Ohsweken	1891
Langstaff, R. L.	Richmond Hill	1891
Lundy, P.	Toronto	1891
Leininger, J. W.	Gladwin, Mich.	1892
Lucas, M. F.	Grimsby	1892
Lambert, W. H.	Arnprior	1893
Lehman, J. E.	Orillia	1893
Laird, C. J.	Guelph	1893
Locke, J. A.	Brinston's Corners	1893
Lockhart, A	Sydenham	1893
Lapp, L.	Toronto	1893
Large, S. H.	King City	1893
Lawson, J. A.	Brampton	1894
Leith, J. D.	Dromore	1894
Lipsey, R. M.	St. Thomas	1894
Livingstone, H. D.	Georgetown	1894
Laidlaw, W. C.	Toronto	1895
Lambert, A. C.	Toronto	1895
Lamont, J. G.	Ripley	1895
Lancaster, J. B.	Culloden	1895
Langrill, A. S.	Ohsweken	1895
Laurie, C. N.	Coboconk	1895
Lawrason, L.	Dundas	1895
Lennox, Eleanore G.	Toronto	1895
Lynch, D. P.	Chapeau, Que.	1896
Lee, J. P.	Toronto	1896
MacColl, D. S.	Eagle	1891
Macdonald, A. A.	Guelph	1872
Machell, H. T.	King, Co. York	1873
Mackie, J. McD.	Clifford	1876
Macklim, M.	Markham	1877
Marlatt, C. W.	Yarmouth Centre	1871
Marlatt, G. A.	Yarmouth	1877
Mathieson, J. H.	Embro	1871
Mattice, R. I.	Moulinette	1875
Meldrum, N. W.	Harrington	1873
Metcalf, W. G.	Uxbridge	1872
Millar, A. H.	St. Thomas	1877
Miller, L. F.	Kingston	1877
Miller, T. M.	Keene	1877
Minaker, Wm.	Milford	1875
Minshall, H.	Thamesville	1875
Mitchell, Fred.	London	1874
Mitchell, J. C.	Clarke	1878
Moore, C. S.	London	1874
Moore, C. G.	Brampton	1871
Moore, J. T.	Woodstock	1874
Moore, V. H.	Merrickville	1870
Moore, L. M.	Duntroon	1872
Moorehouse, H.	Toronto	1871
Moorhouse, W. H.	London	1875
Moran, J. B.	Frankfort	1872
Munro, J. T.	Notfield	1876
Munro, W. A.	Chesterfield	1877
Murphy, J. B.	Norwood	1876
Murray, C. S.	Toronto	1876
Murray, Robt.	Innerkip	1877
Murray, S. S.	Thorndale	1875
Mylius, G. R.	Berlin	1878
MacArthur, Jas.	Ailsa Craig	1878
Meek, Harry	Port Stanley	1878
Merrison, J. E.	Sarnia	1878
Millman, T.	Toronto	1878
Milis, T. W.	Hamilton	1878
Mills, R. P.	Iona	1879
Macklin, W. E.	Poplar Hill	1880
Mackid, H. G.	Goderich	1880
Machell, A. G.	Aurora	1881
Mearns, W. A.	Tara	1881
Mennie, J. G.	Fergus	1882
Milroy, T. M.	Galt	1882
Meldrum, J. A.	Morrison	1883
Meikle, T. D.	Argenteuil, Que.	1883
Martin, H. S.	Craigholme	1884
Mott, T. H.	Mount Vernon	1884
Minchin, D. J.	Shakespeare	1885
Mothersill, L. J.	Tuscarora	1885
Marty, J.	Mitchell	1885
Mitchell, W. J.	London	1885
Mather, W. M.	Plainfield	1886

Moffatt, J. C............Smith's Falls	1886
Mundell, D. E..............Kingston	1886
Mellow, S. J.................Bath	1886
Mitchell, Daniel.........Coldstream	1887
Mullock, M. J............Bearbrook	1887
MacMahon, J. A............Toronto	1887
Moore, C. F.................Toronto	1887
Maybee, M.................Odessa	1887
Maybee, J. E...............Odessa	1887
Moore, T. A...............Kingston	1887
Mundell, J.................Kingston	1887
Myers, A....................Barrie	1888
Merritt, W. H.........St. Catharines	1888
Meyers, D. C................Toronto	1888
Mallory, C. N...............Escott	1888
Marling, J. H. O...........Toronto	1888
MacNaughton, P............Norwood	1888
MacCallum, A. B...........Toronto	1888
Moffatt, R. D.............Toronto	1888
Morrow, C..................Vernon	1888
MacDonnell, A. J........Morrisburg	1888
MacDougall, D. S...........Russell	1888
MacDonald, O. F...........Toronto	1888
Manes, J. T...............Sheffield	1888
Minchin, H. A............Brantford	1888
Montgomery, R. G........Wroxeter	1888
Meiklejohn, H. J............Stirling	1889
Milne, W. J..................Blyth	1888
MacAulay, A. J..........Frankford	1889
Maxwell, W. J........Bishop's Mills	1889
Meek, E.....................Alton	1889
Moher, T. J...........South Douro	1889
Muirhead, D. A.......Carleton Place	1889
Mulcahy, M. V..............Orillia	1889
Mulligan, W. H..............Toronto	1889
Milner, B. Z................Toronto	1889
MacArthur, R. A............Toronto	1889
Murray, M. W..........Beechwood	1890
Macdonald, J. A............Toronto	1890
Mitchell, A. V.............Toronto	1890
MacFarlane, M. T........Ridgetown	1890
Morrison, W. C............Elmwood	1890
Morton, E. R................Barrie	1890
Macdonald, J. R..........Wingham	1890
Murray, W. C. B.....Harrington, W.	1890
Macklin, E.................London	1890
Mavety, A. C...............Odessa	1890
Mason, R. H................Barrie	1890
MacCartney, G. P..........Thorold	1891
MacKay, C................Seaforth	1891
Mark, G. K.................Keene	1891
Martyn, J. B.............Alvinston	1891
Mead, Letitia ....Nassagaweya	1891
Montgomery, W..........Perrytown	1891
Moore, J. J................Shirley	1891
Mowat, M. M..........Williamstown	1891
MacGregor, J. A...........London	1891
Maybury, A. W............Toronto	1892
Middlebro', T. H.......Owen Sound	1892
Millard, H. P...........Newmarket	1892
Mitchell, R. M...........Shrigley	1892
Morgan, E. M...............Perth	1892
Murray, A. J...............Embro	1892
Murphy, A. L............Rosemont	1892
Mair, A. W....Portage du Fort, Que.	1892
Moss, F. H................Toronto	1892

Martin, F....................Erin	1893
MacDonald, R. E.........Stratford	1893
Mulligan F. A............Millbrook	1893
Macmillan, J. A..........Strathroy	1893
Maloney P. J............Ennismore	1893
MacDonald, W. S..........London	1893
Machendrick, H. F...........Galt	1893
Minnes, R. S..............Kingston	1893
Murphy, J. E............Newboro'	1893
Mackenzie, J. R............Toronto	1893
Meikle, W. F......Cowansville, Que.	1893
Marr, D.................Ridgetown	1893
Moore, John....Bath, Mich., U.S.A.	1893
Mackay, R. B..............Toronto	1893
Mitchell, J. A..........Caistorville	1893
MacCarthy, G. S............Ottawa	1884
Mencke, J. R..............Toronto	1894
Millen, W. H..............Cottam	1894
Morden, F. W..............Picton	1894
Murphy, S. H.............Renfrew	1894
Mackechnie, W. G..........Brighton	1895
Macklin, Daisy............Stratford	1895
Mackay, A...............Creemore	1895
Marseles, E. H.........Bouck's Hill	1895
Merritt, A. K.............Scotland	1895
Milligan, A. A..............Toronto	1895
Monteith, J. D.............Stratford	1895
Miller, H. W................Orillia	1895
Metcalfe, A. A.............Almonte	1896
Musson, George............ Toronto	1896
Morris, J. S................Oshawa	1896
Marquis, J. A............Brantford	1896
Malloy, J. A.............. Preston	1896
Moore, R................. Maple	1896
MacLaren, P. S..........Tiverton	1896
Malloch, W. J. O..........Meaford	1896
More, George...............Kirkton	1896
Macklin, Alt............ Stratford	1896
Murray, H. G.............Kingston	1896
McAlpine, John............. Appin	1875
McArton, Stewart......Carleton Place	1876
McBain, John........ Martintown	1876
McCallum, J. S............ Dunville	1872
McConkey, T. C............Barrie	1874
McCurdy, Archibald........Otterville	1876
McDermid, William............Athol	1877
McDermitt, James.......Bond Head	1870
McDiarmid, Duncan........ Malvern	1875
McDiarmid, J. C............Prospect	1877
McDonald, D. F........... Ardock	1877
McDonald, Peter...... Brucefield	1872
McDonnell, Alex......... Alexandria	1875
McEwan, Findlay............Toronto	1871
McFayden, Duncan........ Nobleton	1877
McGregor, J. O............Lowville	1875
McKay, Andrew.........Woodstock	1871
McKay, Angus............Ingersoll	1871
McKeough, G. T............Chatham	1877
McKinnon, A. H............Norval	1877
McKinnon, A.......... Ospringe	1871
McLaren, Alexander........Delaware	1874
McLaren, A. L............ Sarnia	1874
McLarty, Colin.......... St. Thomas	1875
McLay, P. W. McM........ Toronto	1870
McLean, John...............Barrie	1876

McLean, J. C.	Centre Augusta	1874
McLean, Peter	Morrison	1874
McLellan, Charles	Walton	1872
McClure, William	Thorold	1875
McNicholl, Eugene	Norwood	1877
McPhedran, Alexander	Toronto	1875
McRae, George	Toronto	1876
McWilliam, James	Galt	1876
McCort, T. J.	Tormore	1878
McCrimmon, Wilton	Ancaster	1878
McDonagh, G. R.	Carlow	1878
McGrath, John	Lucan	1878
McKay, William	St. Thomas	1878
McKelvey, Alexander	Seaforth	1878
McLennan, J. H.	London	1878
McNamara, G. W.	Gorrie	1878
McDiarmid, Andrew	Fingal	1878
McCullough, George	St. Mary's	1878
McArthur, J. A.	North Bruce	1879
McIlhargy, J. J.	Lucan	1879
McFadden, J. J.	Stratford	1879
McLean, Peter	Jarratt's Corners	1879
McCammon, James	North Augusta	1879
McCarroll, John	Barrie	1880
McGuigan, William	Point Edward	1880
McKenzie, B. E.	Aurora	1880
McKinnon, R. J.	York	1880
McWilliam, Robert	Hespeler	1880
McLain, George	Nanticoke	1881
McGannon, E. A.	Prescott	1881
McCausland, H. P.	Aylmer	1882
McGill, H. R.	Janetville	1882
McMahon, T. F.	Fergus	1882
McPhaden, Murdock	Brussels	1882
McConochie, S. W.	Bowmanville	1883
McMurchy, Archibald	Strange	1883
McGillivray, Mrs. Alice	Kingston	1884
McLaren, D. C.	Galt	1885
McGannon, M. C.	Prescott	1885
McCormack, Norman	Pembroke	1885
McKenzie, A. F.	Belgrave	1886
McAllister, J. C.	Wendigo	1886
McEwan, Thomas	Hagersville	1886
McCallum, H. A.	London	1886
McEdwards, Duncan	Thedford	1886
McLaughlin, Edward	Harrowsmith	1886
McCabe, J. C.	Phelpton	1886
McKenzie, John	Poplar Hill	1886
McKague, W. H.	Cobourg	1886
McVety, A. F.	Kingston	1886
McGannon, T. G.	Prescott	1886
McPhail, D. P.	Iona Station	1887
McCasey, J. H.	Wingham	1887
McKenzie, Thomas	Toronto	1887
McDonald, C. D.	Rodney	1887
McLurg, James	Woodstock	1887
McLean, C. H.	Barrie	1887
McKenzie, Dugald	Dromore	1887
McFaul, A. McN.	Caledon	1887
McCullough, H. R.	Georgetown	1887
McEwan, Ewan	Franktown	1887
McDonald, A. L.	Glen Donald	1887
McCordick, A. W.	North Gower	1888
McClinton, J. B. H.	Black Bank	1888
McLaughlin, P.	Dundela	1888
McKay, Miss M. B.	Stellarton, N.B.	1888
McGrath, E.	Campbellford	1888
McLaughlin, Miss A.	Toronto	1888
McFarlane, M. A.	Arnprior	1888
McDonald, J. A.	Kintall	1888
McKibbon, L. G.	Teeswater	1888
McGillawee, J.	Shakespeare	1888
McLennan, D.	Renfrew	1888
McMartin, D. R.	Toronto	1888
McCarthy, J. G.	Sorel, Que.	1888
McDonald, D. D.	North Lancaster	1888
McFaul, J. H., sen.	Toronto	1888
McCullough, T. P.	Alliston	1888
McNally, T. J.	Walkerton	1889
McKay, D.	Bradford	1889
McCabe, J. R.	Adelaide	1888
McLachlin, J. Y.	London	1889
McFarlane, J. M.	Toronto	1889
McLachlan, C.	Toronto	1889
McIntosh, D. H.	Carleton Place	1889
McEwan, Hugh	Carleton Place	1889
McDonald, George	Renfrew	1889
McRitchie, T. L.	Harwich	1889
McKeown, P. W. H.	Toronto	1889
McKercher, H.	Camlachie	1889
McKillop, J. T.	Beachburg	1889
McConville, Isabel	Kingston	1889
McNamara, C. J.	Walkerton	1889
McGillivray, C. J.	Hamilton	1889
McEwen, J. A.	London	1890
McColl, H. A.	Georgetown	1890
McGillivray, W.	Whitby	1890
McNaughton, J. D. Worth	Keppel	1890
McFaul, J. H.	Seaforth	1890
McCarty, O. C.	Belleville	1890
McGillivray, C. F.	Whitby	1890
McLeod, D.	Cannington	1890
McQueen, D. K.	Ripley	1890
McGregor, J. A.	Longwood	1890
McCullough, J. W. S.	Dundalk	1890
McPherson, W. A. A.	Prescott	1890
McDonald, A.	Vankleek Hill	1890
McKellar, Maggie	Ingersoll	1890
McKenty, James	Kingston	1890
McGee, Robert	Collingwood	1890
McClelland, M.	Bensfort	1891
McColl, A. E.	Campbellford	1891
McCrimmon, F.	London	1891
McCuen, J. A.	Guelph	1891
McCulloch, J. S.	Toronto	1891
McCulloch, O.	Everton	1891
McGorman, G.	St. Mary's	1891
McKenzie, G.	Wingham	1891
McLaughlin, T. P.	Fish Creek	1891
McLean, D.	Elmgrove	1891
McNeill, D. G.	London	1891
McQueen, J.	Sheffield	1891
McAsh, J.	Varna	1892
McCammon, F. J.	Kingston	1892
McCormick, H.	Walkerton	1892
McCoy, S. H.	Brantford	1892
McCullough, H. A.	Georgetown	1892
McDonald, H. F.	Rodney	1892
McDonald, P. A.	Alexandria	1892
McDonald, P. J.	Barrie	1892
McEachern, D.	Harriston	1892
McEwen, W. H.	Paris	1892

McCullough, E. F	Everton	1892
McPherson, D. A	Toronto	1892
McConaghy, F	Richmond Hill	1892
McGinnis, John	Arva	1892
McKenzie, W. J	Warwick	1893
McGarry, J. H	Niagara Falls	1893
McGrath, G	Campbellford	1893
McLennan, K	Dunvegan	1893
McNaughton, J. A	Cornwall	1893
McClenahan, D. A	Tansley	1894
McCollum, W. J	Toronto	1894
McCrimmon, A. A	St. Thomas	1894
McKee, J. F	Aurora	1894
McIntosh, J. W	Gore Bay	1894
McIntosh, L. Y	Strathmore	1894
McMaster, J	Toronto	1894
McIlwraith, K. C	Hamilton	1894
McArthur, W. T	Moorefield	1895
McBroom, J. A	Washburn	1895
McCallum, Annie B	Gananoque	1895
McCrae, T	Guelph	1895
McDonald, H. S	Kingston	1895
McDonald, A	Guelph	1895
McKay, T. W. G	Toronto	1895
McKechnie, W. B	Aberdour	1895
McLennan, F	Lochalsh	1895
McNiven, J. A	Dorchester	1895
McPhail, M	Sonya	1895
McPherson, D. W	Toronto	1895
McKee, C. S	Peterboro'	1896
McCaig, A. S	Collingwood	1896
McIntosh, W. A	Simcoe	1896
McRae, J. R	Lochalsh	1896
McCammon, S. H	Kingston	1896
McConnell, J. F	Toronto	1896
McPherson, Chas	Prescott	1896
Newell, J	Springfield	1877
Nichol, A	Stratford	1873
Nichol, Wm	Brantford	1876
Norton, T	Horning's Mills	1875
Nunan, D	Guelph	1875
Nevitt, R. B	Toronto	1878
Neilson, W. J	Perth	1878
Newlands, George		1879
Nelles, D. A	Waterford	1879
Noecker, C. F	Waterford	1886
Nicholls, W. R	Plattsville	1886
Newell, W	Strathroy	1887
Niemeier, O. G	Ayton	1887
Nairn, J. M	Port Dover	1887
Nimmo, J. H	Kingston	1887
Norman, T. J	Schomberg	1887
Neff, J. A	Springfield	1888
Nesbitt, W. B	Toronto	1888
Nasmyth, W. W	Toronto	1889
Northmore, H. S	Cataraqui	1889
Niddrie, R. J	Hampton	1890
Noble, John	Arthur	1890
Noble, C. T	Sutton West	1890
Nixon, A. W	Esquesing	1891
Nichol, A. H	Listowel	1893
New, C. F	London	1894
Northwood, A. E	Chatham	1895
Noble, R. T	Norval	1895
Nichol, W. H	Brantford	1896

Oakley, W. D	Plattsville	1887
Ogilvie, R. C	Toronto	1878
O'Neil, E	Belleville	1875
Orr, R. B	Toronto	1877
Ogg, A. S	Dundas	1878
O'Gorman, C	Hastings	1879
O'Reilly, G	Hamilton	1879
O'Brien, D	Renfrew	1879
Odlum, J	Lucknow	1879
O'Shea, J. F	Norwood	1881
O'Keefe, J. F	Henderson	1882
O'Reilly, E. B	Hamilton	1883
Orr, J. O	Toronto	1884
Ovens, Thomas	Ailsa Craig	1884
Olmstead, Ingersol	Ancaster	1886
Osborne, A. B	Hamilton	1886
Orton, T. H	Hamilton	1886
Ochs, A	Hespeler	1887
O'Neill, T	Belleville	1888
Oliver, C. B	Motherwell	1890
Old, F. J. T	Caledonia	1891
Oldright, H. H	Toronto	1891
Orton, R. H	Guelph	1891
Oldham, J. H	Marlbank	1892
Olmstead, W. E	Ancaster	1893
O'Connor, E. J	Ottawa	1895
Oliver, J. H	Sunderland	1896
Park, Hugh	Caistorville	1875
Parke, W. T	Seneca	1877
Parker, James	Frankville	1871
Parker, William	Ashton	1871
Parsons, J. H	Yorkville	1871
Paterson, C. A	Streetsville	1873
Paterson, H	Berlin	1872
Pettigrew, G. A	Norwood	1876
Phelan, D	Ottawa	1877
Phelan, J. B	Toronto	1877
Phillip, T. W	Port Perry	1870
Philip, William	Port Perry	1874
Pringle, A. R	Unionville	1876
Potter, S	Manotick	1875
Potter, D	Hazeldean	1875
Powell, N. A	Cobourg	1875
Powell, R. H	Ottawa	1876
Preston, R	Newburg	1878
Pringle, H. H	Port Perry	1877
Prosser, Wm. O	Newington	1877
Pomeroy, J. R	Newburg	1878
Pyne, R. A	Toronto	1878
Prouse, E	Little Britain	1879
Park, T. J	Amherstburg	1879
Patterson, R	Ilderton	1880
Piper, J. M	London	1880
Peters, W. F	Michipicoten Island	1882
Prevost, L. C	Ottawa	1882
Park, John	Saintfield	1883
Patterson, J. W	Harrowsmith	1884
Pringle, A. F	Mount Albert	1884
Peters, G. A	Toronto	1885
Paul, J. J	Sebringville	1885
Parry, W. T	Dunville	1885
Pickard, J. E	Thamesville	1885
Palmer, G. F	London	1885
Peaker, J. W	Burnhamthorpe	1885
Pattee, R. P	Plantagenet	1886

Philp, T. S.	Colborne	1887
Palmer, J. A.	Richmond Hill	1887
Pirie, A. F.	Dundas	1887
Pyne, A. R.	Toronto	1887
Piper, D. H.	London	1887
Phillips, J. A.	Guelph	1887
Perfect, A. 11	Orangeville	1887
Pare, L. T.	Sandwich	1887
Palling, J. F.	Allandale	1888
Patton, J. C.	Toronto	1888
Pickering, Mrs. Annie L.	Toronto	1888
Proudfoot, J. A.	London	1888
Park, P. C.	Durham	1888
Paterson, J. A.	Port Elgin	1889
Palmer, R. H.	Danforth	1889
Patterson, T. C.	Grafton	1889
Philip, W. S.	Brampton	1889
Pomeroy, L. E. M.	Tweed	1889
Pratt, W. F.	Ottawa	1889
Phair, W. R. G.	Uxbridge	1889
Phelan, D.	North Gower	1890
Parker, S. G.	Toronto	1890
Pugh, W. M.	Milverton	1890
Philp, W. H.	Waldemar	1890
Patterson, C. J.	Ottawa	1890
Pape, T.	Concord	1891
Penhall, F. W.	Port Perry	1891
Potts, R. B.	Toronto	1891
Parkyn, H. A.	Toronto	1892
Parson, H. C.	Toronto	1892
Peters, J. B.	Toronto	1893
Pease, H. D.	Toronto	1893
Pirritte, F. W.	Toronto	1893
Park, W. F.	Chatham	1893
Pearson, F. G. E.	Weston	1893
Parfitt, C. D.	London	1894
Park, J.	Bruce Mines	1894
Parlow, A. B.	Iroquois	1894
Porter, G. D.	Brantford	1894
Pritchard, J.	North Wakefield	1894
Procter, E. C.	Toronto	1894
Parker, F.	Stratford	1895
Paterson, H. M.	Rodney	1895
Pickard, H. G.	Glammis	1895
Pratt, J. I.	Heathcote	1895
Pringle, Rose	Fergus	1895
Pearson, H. C.	Demorest	1895
Phillip, J. R.	Northfield, Dak.	1896
Purvis, J. W. F.	Lyn	1896
Partridge, A. W.	Crown Hill	1896
Quance, S. H.	Elfrid	1887
Quackenbush, Allen	Morpeth	1889
Quackenbush, A	Mountain View	1892
Rattray, C. J.	Cornwall	1871
Read, William	London	1874
Reeve, J. E.	Toronto	1878
Renwick, J. W.	Scotland	1871
Reynolds, T. N.	Meaford	1870
Richards, N. D.	Castleton	1877
Richardson, G. T.	Wyoming	1880
Richardson, Jos.	Toronto	1875
Richardson, Samuel	Toronto	1871
Robertson, Hugh	St. Catharines	1871
Robertson, J. A.	Shakespeare	1871

Robinson, R. H.	Toronto	1874
Robinson, Wesley	Markham	1874
Rodgers, Amos	Ottawa	1876
Rolston, H. J.	Toronto	1874
Ross, Hugh	Brucefield	1872
Ross, W. D.	Ottawa	1875
Ross, R. A.	Barrie	1877
Routledge, G. A.	Lambeth	1877
Rowan, P. J.	Toronto	1870
Rutherford, James	Orono	1870
Rutherford, S. G.	Shakespeare	1871
Ryerson, G. A. S.	Toronto	1878
Rankin, J. P.	Tavistock	1878
Riddell, George	Cold Springs	1888
Ross, J. F. W.	Toronto	1887
Robson, W. T.	Toronto	1878
Robinson, Alexander	Beaverton	1878
Reddick, Robt.	West Winchester	1878
Rowe, G. G.	Georgetown	1879
Radford, J. H.	Perth	1880
Robinson, Jonathan	Uxbridge	1881
Reynolds, T. W.	Brockville	1881
Rogers, D. H.	Gananoque	1881
Reeve, H. H.	Minesing	1882
Riordan, B. L.	Toronto	1882
Rose, David	Simcoe	1882
Rutherford, D. B.	Belleville	1882
Robinson, T. H.	Nobleton	1883
Robinson, W. J.	Fergus	1883
Ross, W. A	Barrie	1882
Rattray, J. C.	Cobden	1883
Ray, J. W	Little Britain	1883
Routhier, L. G	Curran	1884
Robertson, W. N.	Stratford	1884
Rice, A. T.	Woodstock	1884
Ruttan, R. F.	Montreal	1884
Roberts, H. G.	Elora	1885
Rutherford, J. A	Millbank	1885
Reynolds, Helen E.	Mount Forest	1885
Russell, D. G.	Mankato, Minn.	1885
Reeve, J. L.	Clinton	1886
Riddell, A. B.	King	1886
Richardson, W. A.	Toronto	1886
Robinson, T. M.	St. Jacob's	1886
Reaume, J. O	Windsor	1886
Reid, J. A.	Sault Ste. Marie	1887
Rea, J	Pickering	1887
Richardson, G. C.	Arnprior	1887
Ross, J. W.	Brockville	1887
Ross, R. R.	Bervie	1887
Ross, L. F	Point Edward	1887
Ross, D. L.	Winthrop	1887
Reid, J. B.	Orangeville	1887
Robinson, E. H.	Hamilton	1888
Reavley, E.	Port Robinson	1888
Rivet, A. N.	Emburn	1888
Robinson, R. P.	Williamsville	1888
Roger, J. P.	Fergus	1889
Rennie, G. S	Hamilton	1888
Reynolds, A. J	Mount Forest	1889
Rutherford, S. T.	Millbank	1889
Rose, D. A.	Toronto	1889
Ross, J. A.	Barrie	1889
Rankin, W. H	Collin's Bay	1889
Reid, J. H.	Dundalk	1889
Rowan, J. W.	Toronto	1889

Rogers, J. T	Gananoque	1889
Ryan, E	Kingston	1889
Robertson, W	Chesterfield	1890
Russell, T	Alton	1890
Rice, L. E	Embro	1890
Richardson, T. B	Goderich	1890
Robinson, J. A. R	New York, U.S.	1890
Rooney, R. W	Shelburne	1890
Reid, H. A. L	Bowmanville	1891
Robertson, T. F.	Brockville	1891
Rogers, J. F. B	Toronto	1891
Rowan, R	Stouffville	1891
Richardson, C. C	Vandorf	1892
Robertson, P	Botany	1892
Ross, J. F	Argyle	1892
Rosebrugh, F. A	Hamilton	1892
Rogers, J. M	Toronto	1893
Robinson, J. T	Collingwood	1893
Rykert, A. F	St. Catharines	1893
Rorke, R. F	St. Thomas	1893
Rutton, F. S	Sydenham	1893
Ryan, Eva J	Trafalgar	1893
Reeves, J	Eganville	1894
Russell, J. P	Toronto	1894
Rutledge, H. N	Streetsville	1894
Ratz, J. H	Elmira	1895
Richardson, E. K	Flesherton	1895
Rounthwaite, F. S	Collingwood	1895
Rannie, J. A	Chatham	1896
Rivers, J. H	Sarnia	1896
Robinson, E. L	Toronto	1896
Roberts, E. L	Lyndoch	1896
Ross, H. H	Clinton	1896
Ruppert, A	New Hamburg	1896
Sanderson, A	Mono Road	1875
Schmidt, G	Berlin	1874
Scott, A	Midland City, Mich.	1872
Scott, J. G	Seaforth	1870
Scovill, S. S	Portland	1877
Secord, L	Toronto	1877
Shaver, A. W	Ancaster	1877
Shaw, G	Woodburn	1874
Sinclair, A. J	St. Thomas	1875
Sinclair, C	St. Thomas	1876
Sinclair, J. A	Colborne	1877
Sievewright, J. A., jr	Chatham	1870
Sievewright, J. P	Chatham	1876
Smellie, T. S. T	Fergus	1877
Smith, C. M	Owen Sound	1870
Smith, J. B	Glanford	1877
Smith, J. W	Dundas	1876
Snider, F. S	Simcoe	1877
Sovereen, A. W	Delhi	1870
Stalker, J	Harwich	1876
Standish, J	Hillsburg	1870
Stark, W. G	Hamilton	1877
Steacy, G	Brockville	1872
Stevens, R. J	Collingwood	1877
Stevenson, J. A	Cayuga	1873
Stevenson, R. A	Strathroy	1871
Stewart, Alex	Hamstead	1872
St. John, L	St. Catharines	1872
Stone, D. F	Milton	1871
Stewart, D	Crieff	1876
Stewart, D	Ailsa Craig	1877

Strangways, W. F	Pennville	1876
Stuart, W. T	Toronto	1877
Sutton, M	McGillivray	1877
Sylvester, G. P.	Galt	1875
Shupe, C.	Toronto	1878
Sheard, C	Toronto	1878
Stalker, M	Orono	1878
Stanley, U. M	Lucan	1878
Smith, D. F	Listowel	1878
Smith, R. W. B.	Cataraqui	1879
Stevenson, F. C	Ancaster	1879
Spencer, B	Guelph	1879
Scott, J. G	Bearbrook	1880
Shepherd, L. E	Uttoxeter	1880
Small, H. B	Ottawa	1880
Smith, G. A	Ottawa	1880
Soper, A.	Preston	1886
Spence, T. C	Walkerton	1880
Simpson, J	Bowmanville	1881
Snow, W. H	Hamilton	1881
Sweetnam, L. M	Toronto	1891
Shaw, W. F	Bracebridge	1882
Shore, J. E	White Oak	1882
Smith, A. D	Watford	1882
Stark, A	Berwick	1882
Stark, T. H	Toronto	1882
Stewart, J. M	Portsmouth	1882
Symington, T. J	Camlachie	1883
Sawers, F. H	Peterboro'	1883
Stowe, Miss Augusta	Toronto	1883
Spilsbury, E. A	Toronto	1883
Scott, W. O	Mono Road	1884
Shoutts, G	Park Hill	1884
Sangster, A	Stouffville	1884
Shaw, J. M	Keene	1884
Smyth, R. A	North Williamsburg	1884
Sprague, W. E		1884
Stewart, S	Wallaceburg	1884
Spence, J	Fergus	1884
Staebler, D. M	Port Elgin	1884
Stewart, R. L., Jamestown, N.Y., U.S.		1884
Stirling, J. E	Kingston	1884
Smith, Elizabeth	Hamilton	1884
Snelgrove, C. F	Griersville	1885
Simmons, J. U	Trenton	1885
Shaver, A. M	Innerkip	1885
Scott, S	Toronto	1885
Sutherland, J. G	Cookstown	1885
Stacey, C. E	Fleetwood	1885
Stirling, J. A	Kingston	1885
Smith, E. A. C	Toronto	1885
Spankie, W	Kingston	1885
Sanford, C. M	Brighton	1885
Sanson, G	Petrolea	1885
Soden, J. J	Bailieboro'	1886
Shaw, J. P	Orono	1886
Smith, L. G	Glanford	1886
Storms, D. G	Hamilton	1886
Shaw, J. M	Mallorytown	1886
Scadding, H. C	Orillia	1886
Staples, C. R	Princeton	1887
Shillington, J. W	Ottawa	1887
Stewart, W. O	Guelph	1887
Shaw, W. R	Brantford	1887
Smith, J. C	Dayton, Dakota	1887
Sinclair, Duncan	Tonawanda, U.S.	1887

Shannon, W. A	Marmora	1887
Shannon, J. R	Goderich	1887
Stevenson, A. J	Brantford	1887
Smith, R. S	London	1887
Scales, Thos	Kingston	1887
Stevenson, W. J	Aurora	1887
Stewart, Geo	Cedar Mills	1887
• Shepherd, H. E	Stouffville	1887
Scott, W. D	Peterboro'	1887
Smith, G. O	L'Orignal	1887
Steele, M	Avon Bank	1888
Smith, W. H	Toronto	1888
Sisley, E	Toronto	1888
Scott, J. A	McIntyre	1888
Stinson, A. W	Coderington	1888
Sinclair, D. J	Ann Arbor, Mich.	1888
Struthers, R. B	Montreal	1888
Scott, P. J	Saugeen	1888
Smith, W. A	Welland	1888
Smellie, D. M	Chesley	1888
Smith, A. A	Ridgetown	1889
Sangster, W. A	Stouffville	1889
Silverthorne, G	Toronto	1889
Scott, A. Y	Toronto	1889
Snider, E. T	Toronto	1889
Stewart, H. A	Toronto	1889
Stevens, R. H	Detroit	1889
Starr, F	Brooklin	1889
Starr, F. N. G	Toronto	1889
Stone, J. R	McKellar	1889
Sands, E	Sandbury	1889
Sisley, O	Toronto	1889
Sheppard, C	Toronto	1890
Springer, W. D	Nelson	1890
Sifton, J. M	Thamesford	1890
Smith, D	Belmont	1890
Starr, C. L	Brooklin	1890
Shiel, R	Plattsville	1890
Stenton, D. K	Port Lambton	1890
Stringer, T. L	Chatham	1890
Shannon, J. R	Kingston	1890
Sherk, F. H	Berlin	1890
Smith, J. L	Monck	1890
Speers, A. H	Burlington	1890
Spence, A. M	Fordwich	1890
Sargent, W. A	Centreton	1891
Scott, W. J	Renfrew	1891
Shannon, G. A	Orangeville	1891
Sharp, M	Delaware	1891
Shaw, J. W	Brussels	1891
Smith, C. F	Winchester	1891
Smith, J. C	Mitchell	1891
Spier, J. R	Lindsay	1891
Sutherland, A. A	Fingal	1891
Sutherland, J	Strathroy	1891
Sinclair, L. C	Tilsonburg	1892
Smith, J. R	Glanford	1890
Spankie, J. E	Kingston	1892
Sparling, A. J	Pembroke	1892
Sullivan, D. V	Kingston	1892
Saulter, W. W	Toronto	1892
Skippen, A	Hillsburg	1892
Switzer, F. L	Carleton Place	1892
Shaw, R. W	Hudson, Mich.	1892
Smuck, J. W	Renforth	1893
South, T. E	St. George	1893

Sanderson, H. H	Sparta	1893
Stafford, E. H	Chicago	1893
Stinson, J. C	Brantford	1893
Story, S. G	Cedar Springs	1893
Shouldice, J. H	Hamilton	1893
Smith, R. G	Perth	1893
Singleton, A. B	Newboro'	1893
Seager, J	Ottawa	1894
Shuttleworth, C. B	Toronto	1894
Sinclair, J. P	Toronto	1894
Smith, F. A	Sheffield	1894
Smyth, C. E	Toronto	1894
Stephen, W	Wallaceburg	1894
Scott, W. H	Toronto	1894
Sinclair, H. H	Walkerton	1894
Shillington, A. T	Kemptville	1894
Shurie, J. S	Trenton	1894
Somerville, J. T	Clifford, Mich.	1894
Stenhouse, J	Toronto	1894
Stockton, F. W	Richwood	1894
Seabarn, E	London	1895
Sheahan, J	Newark	1895
Shier, D. W	Cannington	1895
Simpson, D. K	Hamilton	1895
Sloan, J. G. M	Annan	1895
Small, A. A	Toronto	1895
Sneath, T. H	Midhurst	1895
Stevenson, H. A	London	1895
Symington, Maggie	Brighton	1895
Sharpe, W. D	London	1895
Sager, D. S	Brantford	1895
Shaw, R. W	Lotus	1895
Smith, M. B	Glanford	1895
Stammers, C. L	Toronto	1895
Sinclair, Christine	Ottawa	1896
Sutherland, J. A	Toronto	1896
Smith, I. G	Ridgetown	1896
Steele, F. C	Orillia	1896
Stevenson, W. J	London	1896
Snider, R. O	Toronto	1896
Silcox, W. L	Delhi	1896
Smith, C. H	Bradford	1896
Tamblyn, T. J	Newcastle	1872
Taylor, Alexander	Whitby	1871
Taylor, A. B	Belmont	1876
Taylor, C. E. S	Dundas	1875
Telgman, J. F	Kingston	1877
Teskey, Luke	Toronto	1877
Thompson, J. N	Orono	1874
Thornton, T. H	Consecon	1870
Tisdale, Walter	Simcoe	1877
Trimble, R. J	Brampton	1875
Trout, Mrs. J. K	Toronto	1875
Tucker, M. M	Brighton	1870
Tuttle, Leslie	Centreville	1875
Tyrell, R. S	Weston	1876
Thurreson, Eyre	Ancaster	1879
Todd, J. A	Churchill	1879
Tracey, T. H	Aurora	1880
Tracey, W. J	Aurora	1880
Thompson, L. W	Hawkesville	1885
Totten, Osborne	Toronto	1885
Trow, Charles	Toronto	1885
Trudel, Aime	Ottawa	1885
Tracey, A. F	Holyoke, Mass.	1886

Tuck, J. A	Mount Forest	1886
Toole, C. A	Newmarket	1886
Tovel, Matthew	Everton	1887
Thompson, J. M	Strathroy	1887
Thorburn, J. D	Toronto	1887
Thomson, Adam	Bracebridge	1887
Tyrrell, J. D	Toronto	1887
Thorne, S. H	Brighton	1887
Taylor, O	Princeton	1888
Thompson, P. W	Toronto	1888
Thompson, F. G	Queensboro'	1888
Tufford, A. F	Aylmer	1888
Thomson, H. C	Barrie	1888
Towle, R. E	Kintore	1888
Turner, H. A	Millbrook	1889
Turnbull, J. L	Newton	1889
Topp, R. U	Bracebridge	1889
Thompson, W. W	Toronto	1889
Thistle, W. B	Toronto	1890
Temple, C. A	Toronto	1891
Third, James	Campbellford	1891
Thompson, B. E	Waterdown	1891
Thomson, W. A	Galt	1891
Taylor, T. T	Chatham	1892
Teeter, O	Grimsby	1892
Tilley, A. S	Bowmanville	1892
Thompson, J. J	Avonton	1892
Troy, Wm	Lawrence, Mass.	1892
Tye, W. H	Chatham	1892
Thomas, Julia	Toronto	1892
Tyerman, R. D	Toronto	1893
Taylor, C. J	Toronto	1893
Tomlinson, E	Brantford	1893
Thompson, C. W	St. Mary's	1893
Tufford, W. H	Toronto	1893
Tegart, A. H. F	Schomberg	1893
Thomson, W. P	Toronto	1893
Thomson, D	Woodbridge	1894
Tremayne, H. E	Mimico	1895
Tait, N. J	St. Thomas	1896
Thomas, C. H	Toronto	1896
Thorne, J. S	Belleville	1896

Uren, J. F	Medina	1890

Van Allan, J. R	Chatham	1874
Vrooman, Adam	Vroomanton	1871
Vanderburg, J. F	Merritton	1878
Vandervoort, E. D	Queensboro'	1882
Vrooman, J. P	Yarker	1888
Valleau, A. J	Napanee	1891
Vaux, F. L	Brockville	1895
Verth, Annie	York	1896

Wagner, Adam Dixon,	Dickinson's Landing	1872
Wagner, W. J	Toronto	1870
Warren, Frank	Brooklin	1874
Washington, Nelson	Solina	1871
Waugh, Wm	London	1872
Wells, S. M	Laskay	1871
White, James	Hamilton	1875
White, J. E	Toronto	1870
Whiteman, Robert	Shakespeare	1874
Wigle, Hiram	Wiarton	1877
Wilkinson, Arthur	Alliston	1872

Wilkinson, F. B	London	1877
Wilkinson, Jonathan	Longwood	1870
Williams, Alfred	Toronto	1870
Williams, G. A	Chatham	1877
Wilson, J. D	London	1875
Wilson, T. H	Unionville	1877
Wilson, W. J	Toronto	1877
Winskil, W. E	Kelvin	1877
Wishart, John	Fergus	1875
Wood, C. A	Ottawa	1877
Worsfold, Wm	Eramosa	1872
Wright, A. H	Trenton	1875
Wright, H. P	Ottawa	1871
Wilson, Archibald	Lifford	1878
Wilson, D. H	Carp	1878
Ward, G. C. T	Napanee	1879
Wallace, Mat	Lockton	1880
Watt, Hugh	Meaford	1880
White, J. V	Meaford	1880
Wilson, Thos	Glencoe	1880
Wagner, George Corodon,	Dickinson's Landing	1881
Walker, John	Glencoe	1881
Wallace, David	North Gower	1881
Wilson, E. S	Bobcaygeon	1881
Woolverton, F. E	Hamilton	1882
Wallace, R. R	Hamilton	1882
Weagant, C. A	Yarker	1882
Welford, A. B	Woodstock	1882
Whitely, J. B	Goderich	1883
Woods, E. R	Galt	1883
Wilson, J. D	London	1883
Webster, H. E	Whitby	1884
Watson, J. A	Toronto	1885
Wright, W. H	Glen Allan	1885
Woodward, A. F	Hawkesville	1885
Wishart, D. J. G	Madoc	1885
Wood, E. G	Londesboro'	1885
West, Stephen	Ivy	1886
Wilson, R. J	Toronto	1886
Watts, E. J	Easton's Corners	1886
West, Robert	Woodstock	1886
Winnett, Frederick	Toronto	1886
Wilson, G. H	London	1886
Weeks, W. J	Thorndale	1888
Wright, E. W	Bath	1886
Waddell, W. H	Perth	1886
Walters, W. R	Coleman	1887
Walsh, W. J	Guelph	1887
Warner, A. F	Napanee	1887
Wardlaw, J. S	Galt	1888
Weir, T. P	Toronto	1888
Watson, G. R	Wellington	1888
Walker, R. E	Orillia	1888
Whitney, A. W	Morrisburg	1888
Walker, A. D	Shannonville	1888
Weagant, A. A	Dickinson's Landing	1888
Willmott, J. W	Unionville	1888
Wallwin, H	Toronto	1888
Wilkins, H. P	Toronto	1889
Wiley, J. I	Wisbeach	1889
Willson, A. J	Berlin	1889
Wade, R. J	Brighton	1889
Wade, W. R	Dunchurch	1889
Wills, A. E	Belleville	1889
Wilson, H. W	Toronto	1889

Wright, W. M............ Flesherton	1889	
Webster, J.................. Toronto	1889	
William, H. T. H............London	1889	
Westley, R. A........ Williamstown	1889	
Whiteman, G. A........ Shakespeare	1889	
Webster, T. E................Fergus	1889	
Walsh, F...................Guelph	1890	
Wright, G.................Wheatley	1890	
Walker, Hattie A........ Pitt's Ferry	1890	
Webster, E. H.............. Preston	1890	
Welch, H. W....Cook's Mills, Algoma	1890	
Walker, A. E.................Arva	1891	
Watson, J.................Sherwood	1891	
Webster, D. F..............Glencoe	1891	
Webster, R. E............ Brockville	1891	
Wells, F. H................. Aurora	1891	
Wesley, J. H............ Newmarket	1891	
White, R. H.............Bailieboro'	1891	
Wilson, C. W........Buckingham, Q.	1891	
Walker, N.................Toronto	1892	
Wasson, H. J.............Peterboro'	1892	
Way, H. J.................Toronto	1892	
Wheeler, J. W.........Wolfe Island	1892	
White, J. W.............Branchton	1892	
Wigle, F. A.............Kingsville	1892	
Wilson, J. A............... Lakelet	1892	
Wilson, W. T.............Dundas	1892	
Wood, Isaac...............Kingston	1892	
Walker, W. G......... .Stratford	1892	
Wardell, H. A............. Dundas	1893	
Williams, J. J...........Tottenham	1893	
Wilson, J. A. G.........Warkworth	1893	
Wakefield, W. F. B.........Thorold	1893	
Wickson, D. D.............Toronto	1893	
Wood, P. B................ London	1893	

Wallace, N. C................ Alma	1894	
Wells, R. B............... Toronto	1894	
White, J. A............... Oakwood	1894	
Whitelaw, T. H............. Guelph	1894	
White, P. D................ Glencoe	1894	
Wickett, T............. Belleville	1894	
Windell, J. D............. Pontypool	1894	
Wilson, Thomas...............Elm	1894	
White, F. A............... Aylmer	1894	
Walker, R. J.............Strathroy	1895	
Wallace, H. E............ Port Elgin	1895	
Wallbridge, F. G......... Belleville	1895	
Whitteker, W. C..North Williamsburg	1895	
Wiley, W. D...............Dresden	1895	
White, E. A............... Toronto	1895	
Wade, A. S........St. Lambert, Que.	1895	
Webb, A.................Newmarket	1896	
Westman, S. H.............Toronto	1896	
White, E. B..............Chatham	1896	
Webster, B. E.............Kingston	1896	
Weir, W. H............ .. Brantford	1896	
Youker, W................Holloway	1870	
Young, R. C............. Hamilton	1873	
Young, O................... Whitby	1877	
Yourex, J. McG...........Belleville	1877	
Young, W. J.............Wingham	1884	
Yelland, A. E............ Peterboro'	1887	
Young, S. N.............Ridgetown	1889	
Yeomans, H. A............ Belleville	1889	
Youell, J. H. G.............Aylmer	1892	
Young, G. S............. Stouffville	1895	
Zwick, F.................Belleville	1890	
Zumstein, J. M...............Elcho	1895	

EXAMINATION QUESTIONS.

September, 1895, and April, 1896.

Primary.

ANATOMY.

Value 0 to 100.   Time 2½ hours.

Values.
25   1. Describe the shaft of the femur.
25   2. Give the dissection necessary to expose the prostate gland.
25   3. Describe the diaphragm under (a) origin and insertion, (b) structure, (c) foramina, (d) nerve supply, (e) action.
25   4. Describe the ophthalmic division of the fifth nerve. Name and describe briefly its branches.

F. LE M. GRASETT, F.R.C.S.E.,
Examiner.

PHYSIOLOGY AND HISTOLOGY.

Value 0 to 100.   Time 2½ hours.

Values.
20   1. Give the location and histological characters of the following : Locus niger, locus cæruleus, locus ruber, and the ependyma.
15   2. Explain the relation of blood to the tissues as a factor in the maintenance of the circulation.
25   3. Give the average daily quantity of the chief urinary constituents. Mention some of the causes of the variations to which they are liable. Prove that glomerular secretion is not entirely dependent upon blood pressure.
20   4. Describe the peculiarities of the respiratory centre. Give an account of the nervous and muscular mechanisms concerned in (a) ordinary respiration, (b) labored breathing.
20   5. Describe the course taken by each of the different products of digestion from the interior of the small intestine to the blood. Why may we not consider absorption an ordinary process of diffusion ?

A. S. FRASER, M.D., Examiner.

CHEMISTRY.

Value 0 to 100.   Time 2½ hours.

Values.
10   1. "If a chemical change occurs when two given substances are brought in contact, the nature of it will depend principally upon the electrical relations of the elements concerned." Explain and illustrate this statement, and mention any influences that may modify this mode of chemical action.
10   2. Explain the principles involved in the Bunsen burner and the Davy safety lamp ; and define accurately the meaning of the term "explosion."
20   3. Write out a list of the more important elements, classifying them in groups according to their chemical relationships, and giving a brief synopsis of the characters of each group.
10   4. A sheet of white paper is moistened with a solution of lead acetate and exposed for a few minutes to the fumes of ammonium sulphide. It is then dried and brushed over with a solution of peroxide of hydrogen. Explain the chemical changes which have taken place, giving equations, and describe the mode of preparing hydrogen peroxide.
10   5. Give the names and constitutional formulæ of all the oxides of nitrogen ; and explain the presence of nitrites and nitrates in sewage-contaminated water.
10   6. Give the preparation and properties of acetylene ; and write structural formulæ for all the hydrocarbons of the composition $C_4 H_6$.
10   7. Explain how it is that there are three series of di-substitution products of benzene known as the ortho-, meta- and para-series. Give reasons for regarding salicylic acid (hydroxy-benzoic acid) as belonging to the ortho- series.
10   8. Write out a scheme for the qualitative analysis of a mixture of soluble salts of lead, copper, mercury, bismuth and cadmium.
10   9. Describe the method of making a chemical examination of the contents of the stomach for clinical purposes, having reference specially to the determination of total acidity, free hydrochloric, and lactic acids.

GEO. ACHESON, M.A., M.B. (Tor.),
Examiner.

TOXICOLOGY.

Value 0 to 100.   Time 1 hour.

Values.
25   1. Give the symptoms, post mortem appearances, and treatment of poisoning by oxalic acid.
25   2. Describe the symptoms, mode of death, and post mortem appearances of chronic phosphorus poisoning.
25   3. An adult takes two drachms of liquor strychninæ in mistake for quinine mixture. Describe the course of events apart from treatment.

25 4. What is the poisonous ingredient with its appropriate antidote in each of the following: Rough on rats,* Dover's powder, aqua lauro-cerasi, Goulard's lotion, oil of tar?

GEO. ACHESON, M.A., M.B. (Tor.), Examiner..

MATERIA MEDICA AND PHARMACY.

Value 0 to 100. Time 2½ hours.

Values.

20 1. Describe the following drugs:
Ipecacuanha.
Camphora.
Calx chlorinata.
Ammonii carbonas.

20 2. Describe the active principles of jaborandi, belladonna, podophyllum.

20 3. Name the official preparations of metallic mercury, and give strength of each.

20 4. Acidum hydrochloricum.
(a) Name the official preparations, and give the strength of each.
(b) Give its physiological action.

20 5. Aconitum napellus.
(a) Describe the parts employed.
(b) Give its physiological action.

H. BEAUMONT SMALL, M.D., Examiner.

Intermediate and Final.

THEORY AND PRACTICE OF MEDICINE.

Value 0 to 100. Time 2½ hours.

Values.

15 1. Name the causes which lead to ascites. Describe in a well-marked case, the symptoms obtained by inspection, palpation and percussion.

20 2. Name in order of frequency the varieties of cancer found in the stomach. Give the prominent symptoms of the most frequent variety and diagnose it from chronic gastritis.

10 3. In what diseases, other than surgical, may blood be found in the urine?

20 4. In making a differential diagnosis between the various forms of valvular disease of the heart, point out the advantages to be derived from observing the time and points of maximum intensity at which the murmurs are heard.

20 5. Give the causes and varieties of torticollis. What is aphasia? Clinically, what distinction is to be drawn between sensory and motor aphasia?

15 6. Define acne vulgaris. Describe the characteristic appearance and treatment of acne pustulosa.

R. W. GARRETT, M.A., M.D., Examiner.

Intermediate and Final.

PATHOLOGY.

Value 0 to 100.—All questions equal.
Time 3 hours.

1. Give a classification of the sarcomata indicating the main histological features of each class, and the relative standing of each as regards malignancy.

2. Describe and give the life history of trichina spiralis.

3. (a) Describe the pathological changes which take place in the kidney during an attack of acute Bright's disease. (b) What morbid ingredients would be found in the urine on a chemical and microscopical examination in such a case?

4. Describe in detail the method of isolating and determining the character of the various bacteria which may be found in a drop of pus.

THERAPEUTICS.

1. Discuss the principle involved in the use of serum-antitoxine in the treatment of diphtheria. Describe the method of producing the serum.

2. How do the following therapeutic agents act as antipyretics:—Quinine, phenacetin, alcohol, cold sponging?

BACTERIOLOGY.

1. Explain in detail the method of staining sputum, so as to detect the presence of tubercle bacilli.

2. Give some account of the life-history, mode of growth, and pathological effects of pneumococcus.

GEO. A. PETERS, M.B., F.R.C.S., Eng., Examiner.

N.B.—Candidates for Final write on Pathology and Therapeutics only. Candidates for Intermediate write on Pathology and Bacteriology only.

Intermediate and Final.

MIDWIFERY, OTHER THAN OPERATIVE,

PUERPERAL AND INFANTILE DISEASES.

Value 0 to 100. Time 2½ hours.

Values.

20 1. State important points to be remembered when attending labor cases with the following complications. Limit answers as indicated in each case.
(a) In puerperal eclampsia in reference to the safety of the mother.
(b) In breech presentations in regard to the life of the child.
(c) In face presentations in the interest of the medical attendant.

16 2. State the causes of flooding before, during and after labor, and give treatment of post partum hæmorrhage.

12 3. Describe the umbilical cord ; mention its anomalies and state the complications that may arise from it before and during labor.

10 4. Mention the signs and symptoms of pregnancy in the order in which they usually occur.

10 5. Give ætiology and treatment of hydramnios.

18 6. Classify puerperal insanity ; state causes, symptoms and treatment of the most common variety and mention a serious complication.

14 7. Give diagnosis and treatment of gonorrhœal ophthalmia in the new-born.

H. Howitt, M.D., Examiner.

————

Intermediate and Final.

MIDWIFERY, OPERATIVE.

Value 0 to 100. Time 2½ hours.

Values.

20 1. State the complications of labor in which you would resort to craniotomy.

20 2. Are there any circumstances in which it is justifiable to turn when the life of mother is neither in danger nor threatened ? If so, give an illustration, and your method of operating.

20 3. Give the indications for cæsarean section ; briefly describe the operation and state what part of the child it is preferable first through wound.

20 4. State how you would induce labor at the seventh month when time is an important factor.

20 5. Supposing that you have a labor case which results in complete laceration of the perineum, and that you have only ligatures, antiseptics and an anæsthetic in your bag, but neither surgical instruments nor skilled assistance within reach, state what steps you would take to repair the injury and give your subsequent treatment.

H. Howitt, M.D., Examiner.

————

Intermediate and Final.

SURGERY, OTHER THAN OPERATIVE.

Value 0 to 100. Time 2½ hours.

Values.

20 1. Describe the position of the foot and the parts injured in Pott's fracture. Dislocation at the ankle. Give treatment.

15 2. Give the symptoms and clinical features of renal calculi.

25 3. What injury at the elbow joint may be mistaken for a fracture just above the articular surfaces of the lower end of the humerus, and what are the points of difference ?

25 4. Give the treatment of chronic cystitis, the result of enlarged prostate.

15 5. What are the clinical and pathological differences between false and true keloid. Give the treatment of true keloid.

A. Beverly Welford, M.B., Examiner.

————

Intermediate and Final.

SURGERY, OPERATIVE.

Value 0 to 100. Time 2½ hours.

Values.

25 1. What are the relative values of cholecystotomy and cholecyst-enterostomy? Describe the performance of the latter.

25 2. Give the symptoms and radical cure for internal hæmorrhoids. Which method would you prefer, and why ?

20 3. What are the causes which necessitate excision of the elbow joint ? Describe in detail the operation and dressing.

15 4. Give pathology, causes and treatment of chronic genu-synovitis.

15. 5. Describe the operation for hypospadias ?

A. Beverly Welford, M.B., Examiner.

————

Intermediate and Final.

MEDICAL AND SURGICAL ANATOMY.

Value 0 to 100. Time 2½ hours.

Values.

25 1. (a) Locate the nerves and arteries in relation to the ankle. (b) What would be the results if in an incised wound one of these nerves were severed ?

25 2. Describe external auditory canal and tympanic membrane.

25 3. (a) Give attachments of the capsule of hip and of shoulder joints. (b) How much of the upper extremity of the humerus and of the femur form the epiphysis ?

25 4. (a) During tenotomy of the outer hamstring, what important nerve is in danger ? (b) In division of this nerve, at this point, what position would the foot assume ?

Hadley Williams, M.D., Examiner.

————

Intermediate and Final.

MEDICAL JURISPRUDENCE.

Value 0 to 100.—All questions equal. Time 2½ hours.

1. Distinguish between insensibility as a result of alcoholism, opium, compression and concussion.

2. A person alleges he was assaulted. You examine the wounds, and from their nature decide they were self-inflicted. Give your reasons.

3. (a) What is rigor mortis? (b) What conditions may accelerate its appearance (c) Distinguish between muscular spasm occurring at moment of death and rigor mortis. (d) Distinguish between ecchymosis and hypostasis.

4. Define the four great classes of wounds. Distinguish between those inflicted before and after death.

5. You hold a post mortem and determine starvation as cause of death. Give your reasons.

TOXICOLOGY AND MENTAL DISEASES.

1. Describe carefully the symptoms of poisoning by antimony (tartar emetic), and the post mortem appearances.

2. Give symptoms and treatment of poisoning by opium.

3. Define the following: Lunacy, somnambulism, kleptomania. Give measure of legal responsibility in each case.

4. Distinguish between lunacy and idiocy, and between illusions and delusions.

C. VAN NORMAN EMORY, M.D.,
Examiner.

N.B.—Candidates for Final write on Jurisprudence only. Candidates for Intermediate write on Jurisprudence, Toxicology and Mental Diseases.

Intermediate and Final.

SANITARY SCIENCE.

Value 0 to 100. Time 1½ hours

Values.

20 1. (a) Describe changes produced in the atmosphere of a room by respiration. (b) Distinguish between air rendered impure by combustion as from gas jets, etc., and that vitiated by respiration.

25 2. What diseases may be caused by impure drinking water, giving nature of impurity in each case?

15 3. Give general causes of zymotic diseases and measures to prevent their spread.

20 4. What points are necessary to be considered in providing for proper ventilation of a room?

20 5. Give some diseases caused by parasites in meat with main symptoms of the diseases.

C. VAN NORMAN EMORY, M.D.,
Examiner.

Intermediate.

THERAPEUTICS.

Value 0 to 100.—All questions equal.
Time 2½ hours.

1. Enumerate the various anodynes. Give indications and contra-indications for the use of each. What ill effects may follow the use of opium, belladonna, gelsemium?

2. Write a prescription for a single dose of a (1) Diuretic mixture. (2) A soporific draught. (3) A purgative pill.

3. Discuss the principle involved in the serum-antitoxine treatment of diphtheria. Describe the method of producing the serum.

4. Give the therapeutic actions of the following drugs: Strychnia, digitalis, chloral hydrate, phenacetin.

GEO. A. PETERS, M.B., F.R.S.C., Eng.,
Examiner.

Intermediate.

DISEASES OF CHILDREN.

Value 0 to 100. Time 2½ hours.

Values.

20 1. Give the differential diagnosis between scarlet fever and measles, and mention the complications and sequelæ of each separately.

20 2. Give the symptoms and morbid anatomy of infantile syphilis.

20 3. State symptoms and points in clinical history which in convulsions indicate intracranial lesion.

20 4. Give briefly diagnosis and prognosis of broncho-pneumonia in a patient under three years of age; also your treatment.

20 5. Write a prescription for incontinence of urine in a child five years old.

H. HOWITT, M.D., Examiner.

Intermediate.

DISEASES OF WOMEN.

Value 0 to 100. Time 2½ hours.

Values.

20 1. Mention and classify the more important general causes of disease peculiar to women.

16 2. Mention the displacements of the non-pregnant uterus, and differentiate between antiflexion and retroversion.

24 3. Name the abnormal conditions of the fallopian tubes, and give briefly the clinical history, diagnosis and treatment of pyosalpinx.

26 4. Give the predisposing and exciting causes, physical signs and treatment of chronic cervical endometritis.

14. 5. Write a prescription for a severe dysmenorrhagia in a young lady to relieve pain during attack.

H. HOWITT, M.D., Examiner.

BY-LAWS OF THE MEDICAL COUNCIL

OF THE

College of Physicians and Surgeons of Ontario

BY-LAW No. 39.

Rules and Regulations for conducting the proceedings of the Medical Council of the College of Physicians and Surgeons of Ontario.

MEETINGS.

1. The annual session of the Council shall take place on the first Tuesday of July in each year, at Toronto ; but special sessions may be called by the President whenever he may consider it advisable. And it shall be the duty of the President to call special sessions on a requisition signed by two-thirds of the members. No business shall be taken up at a special session except that for which the session has been called, and of which every member has been notified.

2. At the annual session of the Council the President (or, in his absence, the Vice-President) shall take the chair and declare the Council organized, when the Council shall proceed to elect officers. In the absence of the President and Vice-President the Council shall appoint a Chairman, *provided* that at the first meeting of a new Council the Registrar shall call the Council to order, read over the names of the members, and shall call on the Council to elect a President.

3. The President and Vice-President shall be elected from among the members of the Council, after nomination, by ballot, and a majority of the votes of the members present shall be necessary to an election ; *provided* that in case of a tie, the election shall be decided by the member representing the greatest number of registered practitioners.

4. The first business after the organization of the Council and the election of officers, shall be the appointment of a Committee to Nominate the Standing Committees.

OFFICERS.

1. The officers of the Council shall be a President, Vice-President, Registrar, Treasurer and Solicitor, and such others as the Council may deem necessary.

2. The salaried officers shall be elected after nomination, and shall hold office during the pleasure of the Council.

RULES OF ORDER.

1. The President shall preside at all meetings, call the Council to order at the hour appointed, and cause the minutes of the preceding meeting to be read, confirmed and signed.

2. In the absence of the President, the Vice-President shall call the meeting to order, or a Chairman *pro tem.* may, in the absence of the latter, be chosen by the Council.

3. When the President or other presiding officer is called on to decide a point of order or practice, he shall state the rule applicable to the case without argument or comment, subject to an appeal to the Council.

4. The President shall declare all votes ; but if any member demands it, the President, in case of open vote, without further debate on the question, shall require the members voting in the affirmative and negative respectively to stand until they are counted, and he shall then declare the result. At the request of any member the yeas and nays shall be taken and recorded.

5. The President or other presiding officer may express his opinion on any subject under debate ; but in such case he shall leave the chair until the question is decided, appointing some other member to take it. But he shall decide points of order or practice without leaving his place.

6. When any member is about to speak in debate he shall rise in his place and address the presiding officer, confining himself to the question under debate and avoiding personality.

7. When two or more members rise at the same time, the President or presiding officer shall name the member who is first to speak.

8. No member while speaking shall be interrupted by another, except upon a point of order, or for the purpose of explanation. The member so rising shall confine himself strictly to the point of order, or the explanation.

9. If any member, in speaking or otherwise, transgresses the rules, the President shall, or any member may, call him to order ; in which case the member so called shall immediately sit down, unless permitted to

xplain; and the Council, if appealed to, shall decide on the case, but without debate.

10. No member shall speak more than once upon any resolution or motion, except the proposer, who shall be permitted to reply; nor shall any member speak longer than a quarter of an hour on the same question without the leave of the Council, except in explanation, and then he must not introduce new matter.

11. Any member of the Council may require the question under discussion to be read at any time of the debate, but not so as to interrupt a speaker.

12. No member shall speak to any question after the same has been put by the President.

13. Notice shall be given of all motions for introducing new matter, other than matters of privilege and petitions, at a meeting previous to that at which it comes up for discussion, unless dispensed with by a three-fourths vote of the members present. Any matter when once decided by the Council shall not be re-introduced during the continuance of that session, unless by a two-thirds vote of the Council then present.

14. A motion must be put in writing and seconded before it is stated by the President, and then shall be disposed of only by a vote of the Council, unless the mover, by permission of the Council, withdraws it. Every member present shall vote unless excused by the Council.

15. At the close of the annual session the minutes of the last meeting shall be read over, adopted and signed by the President or other presiding officer.

16. The Registrar shall make a list of all resolutions and reports on the table, which shall be considered "The General Orders of the Day," the order of the same to be as follows :

(1) Calling names of members and marking them as present or absent.

(2) Reading of the minutes.

(3) Notices of motion.

(4) Reading of communications, petitions, etc., to the Council.

(5) Motions of which notice has been given at a previous meeting.

(6) Inquiries.

(7) Reports of standing and special committees.

(8) Consideration of reports.

(9) Unfinished business from previous meetings.

(10) Miscellaneous business.

No variation in the foregoing order of business shall be permitted, except by the consent of the Council.

17. When a question is under debate, no motion shall be received unless—

(1) To adjourn.

D

(2) The previous question.

(3) To postpone.

(4) To lay on the table.

(5) To refer.

(6) To amend.

The Chairman shall put the previous question in this form : "Shall the main question be now put?" and its adoption shall end all debate and bring the Council to vote upon the main question.

18. The Chairman shall consider a motion to adjourn as always in order, and that motion and the motion to lay on the table shall be decided without debate.

19. Any member who has made a motion may withdraw the same by leave of the Council, or it may be allowed to stand, such leave being granted without a negative voice.

COMMITTEES.

1. The Standing Committees shall be the following :

(a) Registration, consisting of seven members.

(b) Education, consisting of nine members.

(c) Finance, consisting of five members.

(d) Rules and Regulations, consisting of five members.

(e) Printing, consisting of five members.

(f) On Complaints, consisting of five members.

(g) Executive, consisting of three members.

(h) On Property, consisting of five members.

(i) On Discipline, consisting of three or five members.

2. A majority of a committee shall constitute a quorum.

3. When a committee presents its reports, such report shall be received without motion or debate. On reading the Order of Business for the "Consideration of Reports," the reports previously received shall be taken up in the order of their reception, and may be acted on directly by the Council or referred to Committee of the Whole.

4. When the Council shall determine to go into Committee of the Whole, the Chairman shall name the member who will take the chair.

5. The rules of the Council shall be observed in Committee of the Whole, except the rules respecting the yeas and nays and limiting the number of times of speaking ; and no motion for the previous question or for an adjournment can be received, but a member may at any time move that the chairman leave the chair or report progress, or ask leave to sit again ; and all original motions shall be put in the order in which they are proposed, and shall not require to be seconded.

6. On motion in committee to rise and report, the question shall be decided without debate.

7. Every member who shall introduce a petition or motion upon any subject which may be referred to a select committee appointed to consider such motion or petition, shall, during the sittings of the Council, be one of the committee without being named by the Council. Any member of the Council may be placed upon a committee, notwithstanding the absence of such member at the time of his being named to such committee.

8. Committees appointed to report on any subject referred to them by the Council shall report a statement of facts and also their opinion thereon in writing, and it shall be the duty of the chairman, or acting chairman, to sign and present the report.

9. All petitions or communications on any subject within the cognizance of a standing committee shall, on presentation, be referred by the Chairman or presiding officer to the proper committee, without any motion ; but it shall be competent for the Council, by a three-fourths vote, to enter on immediate consideration thereof.

10. The President and Vice-President shall be *ex-officio* members of all committees of the Council, standing and special, excepting " Committee on Discipline."

DUTIES OF THE COMMITTEES—COMMITTEE ON FINANCE.

1. The Committee on Finance shall have the supervision of the fiscal concerns of the Council, and report the condition of the various funds.

2. They shall prepare a detailed statement of the necessary estimates of money required by the Council for the year, and report the same for the consideration and action of the Council.

3. They shall consider and report on all matters referred to them by the Council.

EXECUTIVE COMMITTEE.

The Executive Committee shall take cognizance of and action upon all such matters as may be delegated to it by the Council, or such as may require immediate interference or attention between the adjournment of the Council and its next meeting.

DUTIES OF THE REGISTRAR.

1. The Registrar shall attend all meetings of the Council, and record minutes of the proceedings of such meetings.

2. He shall give notice to each member of all meetings of the Council or its committees twenty days before each meeting.

3. He shall conduct all correspondence.

4. He shall receive and submit all documents for the Council or standing committees, take charge of all reports, correspondence, accounts, and other documents, and fyle the same.

5. He shall make returns of all salaries, make out all orders for payment, and keep full accounts of all expenditure.

6. He shall examine the credentials of candidates for examination and make the necessary preparation for examinations, and every candidate shall fyle with his application a statutory declaration that the schedule he has signed and presented is correct.

7. He shall number all by-laws, and affix the seal of the College thereto.

8. He shall, on the 31st day of October in each and every year, send to each member of the College of Physicians and Surgeons of Ontario who has up to that date failed to pay his dues and take out his annual certificate, a registered letter addressed to the registered address of such member, informing him that unless the said dues are paid by the 31st December of that year his name shall be erased from the Register of the College of Physicians and Surgeons of Ontario, and the Registrar shall erase the names from the Register of all persons who have not paid their dues for one year, counting such year from the 31st December in one year to the same date in the next.

DUTIES OF THE TREASURER.

1. The Treasurer shall keep a detailed statement of receipts and expenditure and submit annually a balance sheet, setting those forth fully, as well as a statement of sundries, and the particular accounts to which these belong, and pay out moneys in settlement of all accounts that have been certified correct and signed by the President, Chairman of the Executive Committee, and Registrar.

SOLICITOR.

1. The Solicitor shall give to the Council or its President his advice or opinion upon any question of the law (properly) submitted to him for that purpose.

2. He shall also give, on requisition signed by the President, his opinion in the same way to any officer now appointed, or who may be hereafter appointed by the Council.

3. It shall be the duty of all officers of the Council to furnish the Solicitor, upon request, with any documents, books or papers in the custody or possession of such officers, and to give to the said Solicitor such other aid and assistance as he may require in the performance of the duties of said office.

AUDITOR.

The Auditor shall audit all the accounts of the Council and present his annual report on the same on or before the first day of June in each year.

BY-LAWS.

1. After notice of motion given at a previous meeting, a proposed by-law may be introduced, read a first time, and referred to Committee of the Whole.

2. The second reading shall take place in Committee of the Whole, and shall be clause by clause.

3. When the Committee of the Whole report the proposed by-law, it shall be read a third time in Council, and if adopted on such third reading, the President shall declare the by-law passed, and shall sign the same.

AMENDMENTS.

No amendment or addition to any of the foregoing rules and regulations shall be made unless the notice, setting forth the proposed amendment or addition, shall have been given at a meeting previous to that at which the same comes up for discussion, and all resolutions of the Council inconsistent with the above rules and regulations are hereby repealed.

All of which is respectfully submitted.

(Signed) HENRY W. DAY, Chairman.

Adopted as amended. J. L. BRAY,
Chairman Com. of Whole.

By-law read a third time and declared passed. J. G. CRANSTON,
President.

Wednesday, June 12, 1889,

TORONTO, ONT. [SEAL.]

BY-LAW No. 47.

For fixing the salary of the Registrar.

Whereas power hath been granted to the Council of the College of Physicians and Surgeons to make by-laws, be it therefore and it is hereby enacted : That the salary of the Registrar be fixed at $1,800.00 per annum, to be paid monthly or quarterly.

Adopted in Committee of the Whole.

R. B. ORR, Chairman.

Adopted and read a third time in Council.

V. H. MOORE, President.

BY-LAW No. 52.

Whereas power has been given to the College of Physicians and Surgeons of Ontario to make by-laws, be it therefore and it is hereby enacted : That the Treasurer and Registrar of the Medical Council of the College of Physicians and Surgeons of Ontario are hereby authorized to jointly borrow in their official capacity, as officers of the College, upon the security of the College, such sum and sums of money as may be required for the use of the College, not, however, to exceed in the aggregate at any one time $12,000.00, from the Imperial Bank of Canada, or other chartered banks in good standing, and that for such sums they are authorized to use promissory notes, each of such notes to be signed by the Treasurer and Registrar of the Council of the College of Physicians and Surgeons of Ontario. Such sums are to be placed to the credit of the College, subject, like other College funds, to the order or cheque of the Treasurer of the Medical Council of the College of Physicians and Surgeons of Ontario.

Read first, second and third time, and adopted.

G. HENDERSON,
Chairman Committee of Whole.

J. ARTHUR WILLIAMS,
President.

BY-LAW No. 53.

A By-law to amend By-law No. 39.

Whereas power has been given to the College of Physicians and Surgeons of Ontario to make by-laws, be it therefore enacted : That the Registrar shall, on the 31st day of October in each and every year, send to each member of the College of Physicians and Surgeons of Ontario who has up to that date failed to pay his dues and to take out his annual certificate, a registered letter addressed to the registered address of such member, informing him that unless the said dues are paid by the 31st December of that year his name shall be erased from the Register of the College of Physicians and Surgeons of Ontario, and the Registrar shall erase the names from the Register of all persons who have not paid their dues for one year, counting such year from the 31st December in one year to the same date in the next.

Adopted. J. L. BRAY,
Chairman Committee of Whole.

Adopted in Council.

J. ARTHUR WILLIAMS,
President.

By-Law No. 58.

To amend By-law No. 39 as amended by By-law No. 50.

1. Clause (meetings) is amended by erasing the word "seven" (7) in the seventh line thereof, and substituting therefor the words "two-thirds of the."

2. Clause (committees) is amended by erasing the word "three" in line "h," and substituting therefor the word "five."

Adopted.   D. L. Philip, President.

By-Law No. 59.

By-law to provide for the election of the territorial members of the Medical Council of the College of Physicians and Surgeons of Ontario.

Whereas power hath been granted to the Medical Council of the College of Physicians and Surgeons of Ontario to make by-laws to regulate the time and manner of holding the elections under the provisions of the Ontario Medical Act, R.'S. O. 1887, C. 142, 56, 50 V., C. 24, S. I., and amendments thereto, be it therefore enacted as follows :

1. That this by-law shall only apply to the election of territorial representatives of the divisions named in Schedule "A" and appended to the amended Medical Act of 1893, and for appointing returning officers for the ensuing elections of territorial representatives to serve in the Medical Council for the time allotted to them, in accordance with the amendments to the Medical Act as made in 1893 ; that is to say :

No. 1. For the counties of Essex, Kent and Lambton, Dr. J. P. Rutherford, Chatham, Ont.

No. 2. The counties of Elgin, Norfolk and Oxford, Dr. C. E. Duncombe, St. Thomas, Ont.

No. 3. County of Middlesex, Dr. B. Bayly, London, Ont.

No. 4. Counties of Huron and Perth, Dr. A. Taylor, Goderich, Ont.

No. 5. Counties of Waterloo and Wellington, Dr. A. MacKinnon, Guelph, Ont.

No. 6. Counties of Bruce, Grey and Dufferin, Dr. C. Barnhart, Owen Sound, Ont.

No. 7. Counties of Wentworth, Halton and Peel, Dr. F. E. Woolverton, Hamilton, Ont.

No. 8. Lincoln, Welland, Haldimand and Brant, Dr. U. M. Stanley, Brantford, Ont.

No. 9. Simcoe, districts of Muskoka, Parry Sound, Nipissing, Algoma, including Manitoulin, Thunder Bay and Rainy River, Dr. J. L. G. McCarthy, Barrie, Ont.

No. 10. The city of Toronto lying east of Yonge street, Dr. George Bingham, Toronto, Ont.

No. 11. The city of Toronto lying west of Yonge street, Dr. R. B. Orr, Toronto, Ont.

No. 12. Counties of Ontario, Victoria and York, exclusive of Toronto, Dr. J. F. Gilmour, Toronto Junction, Ont.

No. 13. Northumberland, Peterboro', Durham and Haliburton, Dr. R. P. Boucher, Peterboro', Ont.

No. 14. Counties of Prince Edward, Hastings and Lennox, Dr. H. W. Day, Belleville, Ont.

No. 15. Counties of Frontenac, Addington, Renfrew and Lanark, Dr. A. S. Oliver, Kingston, Ont.

No. 16. Counties of Leeds, Grenville and Dundas, Dr. W. P. Buckley, Prescott, Ont.

No. 17. Counties of Carleton, Russell, Prescott, Glengarry and Stormont, Dr. E. C. Malloch, Ottawa, Ont.

2. That any member of the College presenting himself for election as the representative to the Medical Council of the College of Physicians and Surgeons of Ontario for a territorial division, must receive a nomination of at least 20 (twenty) registered practitioners resident in such division, and that such nomination paper must be in the hands of the returning officer of the division not later than the hour of 2 o'clock p.m. on the 9th of October, the second Tuesday in October, 1894.

In the event of only one candidate receiving such nomination, it shall then be the duty of the returning officer to declare such candidate duly elected, and to notify the Registrar of the College by sending him such declaration in writing.

3. That the Registrar of the College shall send to every registered member of the College of Physicians and Surgeons of Ontario (excepting only those who are registered as the homœopathic members thereof), a voting paper (in accordance with the residence given on the Register) in form of Schedule "A" attached to this by-law, and a circular directing the voter to write his or her name as the voter, and his or her place of residence, and the county in which his or her place of residence is situated, and to fill up said voting paper on form of Schedule "A" attached to this by-law, as directed in circular to be enclosed.

The Registrar shall, fifty (50) days before the time for receiving nominations for the elections, which time is second Tuesday (9th) of October, 1894, send a post-card to every registered medical practitioner, excepting the homœopathic members, in the Province, in accordance with address in hands of Registrar, giving the dates up to which nominations for representatives to the Medical Council of the College of Physicians and Surgeons will be received.

.The Registrar shall advertise in the medical journals published in Toronto, during August and September, 1894, the fact that elections for the Medical Council are to be held, stating the time that nominations will be received up till, and the time of holding the election.

Also a voting paper shall be sent to every registered practitioner entitled to receive the same, by the third Tuesday (16th) of October, 1894, and that every member of the College not having received a voting paper, when a candidate has been properly nominated for their division, shall send by post to the Registrar their name and address, and the Registrar will forward paper to member so applying.

The voter is to be directed in the circular, which is to accompany the voting paper, to send by post or mail the voting paper properly filled up, giving the name and residence of the person for whom he or she votes, enclosed in an envelope, which shall be forwarded along with the circular and voting paper. The envelope in which the voter is to place his or her voting paper shall have the name and the address of the returning officer appointed to act in the territorial division in which the voter resides.

4. That the Registrar of the College shall mail the voting paper to the members of the College of Physicians and Surgeons of Ontario who are legally entitled to vote, according to their addresses in the possession of the Registrar on the third Tuesday (16th) of October, 1894, the postage, etc., all of which is to be paid by the College, and that the Registrar shall forward to any member making application a voting paper for his division after the 16th of October, upon application.

That the Registrar shall place a stamp upon each of the enclosed envelopes, which are to be used by the members of the College in sending their voting paper to the returning officer for the division. That the returning officer shall receive the votes sent to him up to the hour of 2 o'clock p.m. on the 30th of October, 1894.

5. That the returning officer in each division at the hour of two o'clock p.m. on the 30th of October, 1894, shall open the

envelopes and carefully count and examine the voting papers, and make a record of the entire number of votes cast, together with the declaration of the name of the person and address who has received the greatest number of votes, who shall be declared elected as the representative of the division, and in case two or more candidates receive an equal number of votes, the returning officer shall give the casting vote for one of such candidates, which shall decide the election ; and then at the hour of 2 o'clock p.m. on the 30th of October, 1894, when the returning officer opens the envelopes he has received and counts the votes, all or any of the candidates in the division, or their agents, may be present if duly appointed and authorized to act in writing on behalf of any candidate, and see the envelopes opened and the votes counted, and they shall be permitted to examine all voting papers to satisfy themselves as to the voting papers being properly filled up, and that the persons signing the voting papers were duly registered members of the College of Physicians and Surgeons of Ontario, and entitled to vote at the election of territorial representatives in the Medical Council of the College of Physicians and Surgeons of Ontario.

6. The returning officer in each division shall not open any envelopes he may receive as returning officer until the hour of 2 o'clock p.m. arrives on the 30th of October, 1894, and that the returning officers, respectively, shall seal up and return all the voting papers connected with the election to the Registrar of the College within six (6) days from the time appointed for holding the election, which time is 2 o'clock p.m. on the 30th of October, 1894.

That the returning officer shall reject all voting papers that are not properly filled up in accordance with instructions contained in circular which is to be sent with each voting paper.

The returning officer shall return all envelopes received after 2 o'clock p.m on the afternoon of the 30th of October, 1894, stamped as returning officer of the division, to the Registrar of the College, unopened and marked "too late."

7. That the Registrar, on receiving declaration from the returning officer, declaring a candidate has received the largest number of votes in the division, shall forthwith inform the candidate declared elected that he has been chosen to represent said division in the Medical Council of the College of Physicians and Surgeons of Ontario, and the Registrar shall inform each member so elected of the time and place of the first meeting of the Council after the said election shall have taken place.

It shall be the duty of the Registrar to attend the said meeting of the Council, and to have with him there and then all the papers and documents sent to him by the returning officers, in order that they may be submitted to the Council, and the representatives so named by the returning officers as duly elected shall form the territorial representatives to the Medical Council of the College of Physicians and Surgeons of Ontario.

8. It is hereby enacted that the returning officer of each division is to be named by the Council or Executive Committee and appointed by the Council, and in case any returning officer appointed either refuses to act or is incapacitated, that the Registrar shall fill such vacancy by appointing some member of the College residing in the territorial division on recommendation of the Executive Committee of the Council.

That the fee for acting as returning officer shall be ten dollars ($10.00) for each division.

9. The form of voting paper to be sent to each member of the College, and the form of circular to be used at the election of territorial representatives to the Medical Council is to be the same as that on Schedules " A " and " B," appended to this by-law.

D. BERGIN,
Chairman Committee of the Whole.

June 14th, 1894.

SCHEDULE " A."

The name of the candidate for whom your vote is cast .... Residence of Candidate......	MEDICAL REGISTRATION OFFICE S. E. Cor. Bay and Richmond Sts., TORONTO.

SCHEDULE " B."

COLLEGE OF PHYSICIANS AND SURGEONS OF ONTARIO.

Election for territorial representatives to the Medical Council of Ontario, 1894.

The voting paper herewith enclosed is to be filled up carefully and put into the enclosed envelope, which is directed to the returning officer, and mailed in time to reach him not later than 2 o'clock p.m. on Tuesday, October 30th, 1894.

Sign your name to voting paper.

R. A. PYNE, Registrar,
Coll. Phys. and Surgs. Ont.,
Toronto, Ont.

Adopted.   D. BERGIN.

———

BY-LAW No. 60.

To provide for the election of the homœopathic members of the Medical Council of the College of Physicians and Surgeons of Ontario :

Whereas power hath been given to the College of Physicians and Surgeons of Ontario to regulate the time and manner of holding the election under the provisions of the Ontario Medical Act, R.S.O. 1877, C. 142, 56, 50 V., C. 24, S.I., and amendments thereto, be it therefore enacted as follows :

1. This by-law shall only apply to the election of the homœopathic members to the Medical Council of Ontario.

2. That the Registrar shall send to every registered homœopathic member of the College of Physicians and Surgeons of Ontario a voting paper and circular, directing each to write his name, his residence, etc.

3. That on or before a certain time, to be named in the circular sent to each voter, the voter shall send by post or mail to the Registrar of the College, so that the Registrar shall receive the same on or before the 30th day of October, 1894, the said voting paper, enclosed in an envelope, which is to be sent to the voter, with the voting paper filled up properly with his name and residence, and the person or persons for whom he voted.

4. That R. A. Pyne, M.D., Registrar of the College of Physicians and Surgeons of Ontario, is hereby appointed returning officer for the said homœopathic elections to take place on the 30th day of October, 1894, at the hour of 2 o'clock p.m., and in case a tie occurs, the returning officer is to give the casting vote, which will decide the election.

5. The said returning officer shall carefully preserve the voting papers sent to him, and shall upon the day appointed, at the hour of 2 o'clock p.m. on the said day, open and examine the voting papers sent to him, and carefully count the votes, and make a record thereof of the votes cast, and shall inform by letter the five homoeopathic candidates having the greatest number of votes that they are elected as the homoeopathic representatives in the Medical Council of the College of Physicians and Surgeons of Ontario.

And the said returning officer shall, after counting carefully the votes contained in the envelopes, preserve the voting papers and all other documents, envelopes, etc., sent to him connected with the election of the homoeopathic members of the College of Physicians and Surgeons of Ontario, and present the same to the Medical Council.

6. The returning officer shall not open any paper or document he may have received as returning officer for the homoeopathic elections after 2 o'clock p.m. on the 30th day of October, 1894.

7. The returning officer shall not count any voting paper that is not properly filled out, in accordance with instructions contained in the circular which has accompanied the voting paper when sent to the voter.

8. The returning officer shall permit any candidate, and the agent of any candidate duly appointed and authorized in writing to act on behalf of any candidate, to be present at the counting of the votes, and who shall be permitted to satisfy himself as to the voting paper being properly filled up, and that the person signing the voting paper was a duly registered member of the College of Physicians and Surgeons of Ontario, and entitled to vote at the election of the homoeopathic representatives in the Medical Council of the College of Physicians and Surgeons of Ontario, and who may examine any or all of the voting papers.

9. The form of voting paper and circular for the homoeopathic elections is to be the same as that on Schedules "A" and "B," to this by-law appended.

10. It shall be the duty of the Registrar of the College of Physicians and Surgeons of Ontario to inform the said elected members of the time and place of the first meeting of the Medical Council of the College of Physicians and Surgeons of Ontario.

J. L. BRAY,
Chairman Committee of the Whole.

Adopted in Council.

D. L. PHILIP, President.

HOMŒOPATHIC ELECTIONS, 1894.

SCHEDULE "A."

COLL. PHYS. & SURG. OF ONT. OFFICE OF MEDICAL REGISTRATION.

S. E. cor. Bay & Richmond Sts., Toronto.

SCHEDULE "B."

COLLEGE OF PHYSICIANS AND SURGEONS OF ONTARIO.

Election for homœopathic representatives to the Medical Council of Ontario, 1894.

The voting paper herewith enclosed is to be filled up carefully and put into the enclosed envelope, which is directed to the returning officer, and mailed in time to reach him not later than 2 o'clock p.m. on Tuesday, October 30th, 1894.

Sign your name to voting paper.

R. A. PYNE, Registrar,
Coll. Phys. and Surgs. Ont.,
Toronto, Ont.

BY-LAW No. 68,

Council of the College of Physicians and Surgeons of Ontario, to amend By-law No. 39 as amended by By-law No. 50.

Whereas power hath been granted to the Medical Council of the College of Physicians and Surgeons of Ontario to make by-laws under the Ontario Medical Act, be it enacted as follows :

1. That Article 3 of the duties of the Finance Committee, page lvii, be amended by striking out the whole clause and substituting therefor these words, "They shall consider and report on all matters referred to them by the Council."

Also,

2. That Clause 1 on duties of the Treasurer, page lvii, be amended by striking out all the words alter "moneys" in the fourth line and inserting in lieu thereof the following words: "In settlement of all accounts that have been certified correct and signed by the President, Chairman of the Executive Committee and Registrar.".

3. The Auditor shall audit all the accounts of the Council and present his annual report on the same on or before the first day of June in each year.

JAMES HENRY, Chairman of Com.

June 26th, 1895.

WILLIAM T. HARRIS, President.

BY-LAW No. 69.

Whereas by Section 6 of the Ontario Medical Amendment Act, 1893, 56 Vic., Chap. 27, Sec. 27 of the "Ontario Medical Act" (R. S. O. 1887, C. 148) and Sec. 41a amending the same, enacted by the Act passed in the 54th year of Her Majesty's reign, Chap. 26, and entitled, "An Act to amend the Ontario Medical Act," were suspended, and it was by the said Act declared that the said section should continue suspended unless and until after the elections of 1894 a by-law should be passed by the Council of the College adopting the same in whole or in part.

And whereas this College has a floating debt which must be provided for and outstanding assessments which if made available would cover the same, it is therefore necessary and expedient that the same shall be adopted and put in force.

And whereas it is necessary and expedient that the same should be adopted.

Now therefore the Council of the College of Physicians and Surgeons of Ontario enacts as follows:

1. Section 27 of the Ontario Medical Act (R. S. O. 1887, C. 148) and Section 41a amending the same, enacted by the Act passed in the 54th year of Her Majesty's reign, Chapter 26, and entitled "An Act to amend the Ontario Medical Act," are hereby adopted.

2. Each member of the College shall pay to the Registrar towards the general expenses of the College an annual fee amounting to two dollars ($2.00) pursuant to the provisions of Section 27 of the Ontario Medical Act aforesaid for year 1895.

3. It is further hereby declared and enacted that the said suspended sections are adopted by the Council of the said College and the suspension thereof abrogated from the

day of the date when the same were by the Ontario Medical Amendment Act, 1893, suspended, and that each member of the College shall pay to the Registrar pursuant to the provisions of Section 27 aforesaid the annual fee of two dollars ($2.00) for each year during the time when the said sections were so suspended, viz.: for years 1893 and 1894.

4. The Registrar is hereby directed to collect the annual fee hereinbefore fixed and determined, together with all other fees and dues in arrear and owing by any member of the said College, and to enforce all provisions of the Ontario Medical Act as amended. Upon default, subject to the provisions of this by-law.

5. And be it further enacted, that part of Clause 1 known as 41a be suspended until the first of June, 1896, then to come into force in case a sufficient amount of dues is not paid over to the bank liability.

6. And be it further enacted, that the Registrar be required to send to each practitioner a registered letter, enclosing a copy of the by-law, together with a circular letter, and account of dues, explaining the necessity of imposing the fee, and calling special attention to the suspension of 41a until June 1st, 1896.

Adopted in Committee of the Whole as amended.

V. H. MOORE,
Chairman Committee of Whole.

Adopted in Council, June 28th, 1895.

WILLIAM T. HARRIS, President.

BY-LAW No. 70.

That this By-law shall apply to the payment of members of Council, members of committees, members of Board of Examiners;

Whereas power hath been granted to the Medical Council of the College of Physicians and Surgeons of Ontario to fix the amount to be paid its members and officers, under Sections 12 and 13 of the Ontario Medical Act, be it therefore and it is hereby enacted:

1. That each member of Council shall receive $12.50 per diem for days necessarily absent from home, with an allowance of four cents per mile for each mile travelled.

2. That each member of the Discipline Committee shall be paid the same and mileage per diem as is paid members of this Council at its meetings.

3. That members of committees other than Discipline Committee when meeting during the recess of the Council shall be paid a per

diem allowance of $8.00 and four cents per mile for each mile travelled.

4. That each Examiner shall receive the sum of $20.00, and in addition thereto he shall receive thirty-five cents for each paper he may have to read over the number of fifty. Each Examiner shall also receive $12.50 per diem for each day's attendance at oral examinations and meetings, with the same allowance of four cents per mile for the distance travelled to and from the examinations to place of residence.

That the oral examinations shall continue for five hours each day until they are completed.

5. That an allowance of $50.00 be paid to the Examiner on Descriptive Anatomy for providing wet preparations and dissections upon Descriptive Anatomy.

6. That By-law No. 22, and reports dealing .with payment of members of Council, committee members, and members of the Board of Examiners are hereby repealed.

H. T. MACHELL,
Chairman Committee of Whole.

Passed in Council, June 27th, 1895.

WILLIAM T. HARRIS, President.

———

BY-LAW No. 71.

Whereas power hath been granted to the Medical Council of the College of Physicians and Surgeons of Ontario under Section 13 of the Ontario Medical Act, R.S.O. 1877, C. 142, be it therefore enacted as follows :

1. This Council hereby appoints Dr. James Carlyle as Auditor for the purpose of auditing the accounts of the Council.

2. The remuneration to be paid by the Council to tne Auditor for his services shall be forty dollars ($40.00).

Adopted as amended.

W. H. MOORHOUSE,
Chairman Committee of Whole.

Adopted in Council.

A. F. ROGERS.

———

BY-LAW No. 72.

Under and by virtue of the powers and directions given by Sub-section 2 of Section 36 of the Ontario Medical Act, Revised Statutes of Ontario, 1887, Chapter 148, the Council of the College of Physicians and Surgeons of Ontario enacts as follows :

1. By-law No. 65, appointing a Discipline

E

Committee and passed upon the 13th day of June, A.D. 1895, is hereby repealed.

2. The committee appointed under the provisions and for the purposes of the said sub-section shall consist of three members, three of whom shall form a quorum for the transaction of business.

3. The said committee shall hold office for one year, and until their successors are appointed, *provided* that any member of such committee appointed in any year shall continue to be a member of such committee notwithstanding anything to the contrary herein, until all business brought before them during the year of office has been reported upon to the Council.

4. The committee under said section shall be known as the Committee on Discipline.

5. Dr. J. L. Bray, of Chatham, Ont.; Dr. Geo. Logan, of Ottawa, Ont.; Dr. V. H. Moore, of Brockville, Ont., are hereby appointed the committee for the purpose of said section for the ensuing year.

Adopted.

J. W. McLAUGHLIN,
Chairman Committee of Whole.

Read a third time and passed.

A. F. ROGERS, President.

———

BY-LAW No. 73.

Whereas by By-law No. 69, passed under the authority of Section 6 of Chapter 27 of the Ontario Medical Amendment Act, 1893, the Council of the College of Physicians and Surgeons of Ontario adopted Section 27 of the Ontario Medical Act, R.S.O. 1887, Cap. 148 and Section 41a amending the same of an Act passed in the 54th year of Her Majesty's reign, Chapter 26, entitled "An Act to amend the Ontario Medical Act;"

And whereas by the said Section 6 of the Ontario Medical Amendment Act, 1893, the Council have power from time to time to vary such by-law ;

And whereas it is expedient that any member of the College of Physicians and Surgeons of Ontario who may not practice in any year should be relieved of payment of the annual fee for such year ;

Now therefore the Council of the College of Physicians and Surgeons of Ontario enacts as follows :

1. By-law No. 69 above referred to is hereby varied as follows : The annual fee determined by by-law of the Council under the authority of Section 27 of the Ontario Medical Act shall not be due and payable by any member of the College who, by reason of absence from the Province, or for any other reason, shall in no way practise medi-

cine, surgery and midwifery in Ontario during the year for which such annual fee may be imposed.

Any registered. medical practitioner who shall apply to the Registrar for a certificate in accordance with Section 41a of the Ontario Medical Act, claiming to have been relieved by this by-law of payment of the annual fee for any year, shall prove to the satisfaction of the Registrar that he has not practised his profession during the year for which such fee has been imposed, and shall, if the Registrar so requires it, make a statutory declaration to that effect, and furnish such other evidence as may be required.

The decision of the Registrar upon such application as to the liability of the applicant for the fee in question shall be final and conclusive.

Adopted in Committee of the Whole.

R. REDDICK, Chairman.

Read a third time and adopted in Council.

A. F. ROGERS, President.

———

BY-LAW No. 74.

To amend By-law No. 70.

That Paragraph 2 of Section 4 is amended by erasing the word "seven" and substituting therefor the word "five."

J. H. SANGSTER,
Chairman Committee of Whole.

Adopted in Council.

A. F. ROGERS, President.

———

BY-LAW No. 75.

Whereas it is necessary and expedient that an annual fee be paid by each member of the College of Physicians and Surgeons of Ontario towards the general expenses of the College;

And whereas by By-law No. 69 of the Council of the said College it was enacted

that Section 41a of the Ontario Medical Act be suspended until the 1st day of June, 1896, then to come into force in case a sufficient amount of dues is not paid to cover the bank liability;

And whereas a sufficient amount of dues has not been paid and it is expedient to remove all doubts as to the coming into force of the said section;

Now. therefore the College of Physicians and Surgeons of Ontario enacts as follows :

1. Each member of the College shall pay to the Registrar, toward the general expenses of the College for the current year, an annual fee of the amount of two dollars ($2 00), pursuant to the provisions of Section 27 of the Ontario Medical Act.

2. And it is hereby declared and enacted that Clause 41a of the Ontario Medical Act has been in force from the 1st of June, 1886, and is now in full force and effect.

Adopted in Committee of the Whole.

G. M. SHAW,
Chairman Committee of Whole.

Adopted in Council.

A. F. ROGERS, President.

———

BY-LAW No. 76.

Whereas the Council of the College of Physicians and Surgeons of Ontario has power to make rules and regulations, or pass by-laws governing the Council in its proceedings and times of meeting ;

And whereas it is expedient that By-law No. 39 be amended ;

Therefore be it enacted, and it is hereby enacted, that the first clause be amended by striking out the words " second Tuesday in June " and substituting the words "first Tuesday in July."

Adopted. ·   GEO. LOGAN,
Chairman Committee of Whole.

A. F. ROGERS, President.

PROCEEDINGS

Meeting of the Medical Council of Ontario

JUNE, 1896.

MEDICAL COUNCIL BUILDING,

TORONTO, June 9, 1896.

The Medical Council of the College of Physicians and Surgeons of Ontario met this day, Tuesday, June 9th, 1896, at 2 o'clock p.m., in accordance with the by-laws of the Council.

The President, Dr. Harris, in the chair, called the Council to order.

The Registrar called the roll and the following members of the Council answered to their names : Drs. Armour, Barrick, Bray, Britton, Brock, Campbell, Dickson, Emory, Fowler, Geikie, Graham, Hanly, Harris, Henderson, Henry, Logan, Luton, Machell, Moore, Moorhouse, McLaughlin, Reddick, Rogers, Rosebrugh, Sangster, Shaw, Thorburn, Thornton, Williams.

Dr. HARRIS then addressed the Council as follows :

Members of the College of Physicians and Surgeons of Ontario :—I am very glad and proud to welcome you all back to our session at this our thirty-first annual meeting ; I am sorry the political necessities and the discharge of his duties call for the absence of our friend, Dr. Roome. I do not come before you, gentlemen, prepared with any written speech ; I do not think it is necessary I should, but there are a few points I wish to bring before you, a few matters that have arisen during my incumbency of office. During my year of office my time has been very fully occupied with matters of mutual interest pertaining to the welfare of this Council and of the profession. As you all know, I, with the Toronto members and the members of the Legislation Committee and Executive Committee, have been before the Legislature, and there have been meetings of the Executive Committee and many other matters to occupy the attention of your President. One of the important things brought forward, and one in which we are all interested, is the examinations of the Council. The Council examinations have been successfully and thoroughly carried out, I can assure you. I am in a position to speak with knowledge on this subject, because I acted as Chairman of the Board of Examiners both last fall and this spring. I am very pleased to be able to tell you that the assessment levied last year has been largely responded to, 1,129 members having paid ; the Treasurer's receipts from that source amounting to $7,200.00 to date. The payment by these members and the continued default by others make it quite plain to me, and I presume it must to you, gentlemen, that it may be necessary to bring Section 41a of the Act to bear upon the delinquents. Prosecutions have been carried on as vigorously as the funds at the disposal of the Prosecutor would permit. There is a point I wish to call specially the attention of the Printing Committee to, and that is, I think that the Announcement might be divided into three parts, the first to contain say the curriculum, examination papers and list of candidates, the second giving minutes and by-laws combined, and the third part minutes alone. I only offer this as a suggestion of a method by which we might reduce the cost of our printing and not as a hard and fast rule for publication of our Announcement. I am moved to make this suggestion by the fact that in the experience of the Registrar, and in my experience during my term of office as President, and to some extent prior to that time, it rarely happens that anyone applying for the Announcement desires the whole combination. On the subjects of the recent legislation as to matriculation and so on, the reports of the Executive and Legislation Committees will be submitted and will give you full information. I think these reports will pretty thoroughly cover the ground, for I understand that Dr. Thorburn, as Chairman of the Legislation Committee, has in his report gone very fully into the matter ; and the Executive Committee's report also contains information in a brief and concise shape. It is gratifying to us to know that as a profession we stand second to none on this continent, or perhaps in the world, so far as our educational requirements are concerned.

As I stated when I rose to address you, I have not prepared any written address. I have been in ill-health for some time and have been very busy, for I have not only had my own professional work to look after, but also, as you all know, considerable work to do for this Council. I do not wish to occupy your time further than to avail myself of this opportunity to thank the members of this Council most heartily for the kindness and courtesy each and every member has shown me, and the assistance they have rendered me in carrying out this work. The man who assumes the office of President of this Council, the highest position in the gift of the profession in the Province of Ontario, needs no little help, but I must say that the members of this Council have not been in any sense reluctant to aid me in fulfilling the duties of my office, and in every way in their power to prevent my work from being onerous. Again thanking you for your kindness and countenance, and for the honor you have done me, I will now retire from the chair, and ask you, gentlemen, to elect a President for the ensuing year. (Applause.)

Dr. BRAY—I have very great pleasure in moving that Dr. A. F. Rogers, the present Vice-President, be elected President of this Council for the ensuing year. It is not necessary for me to make any remarks in support of Dr. Rogers' nomination, because you all know him.

Dr. LOGAN—I take much pleasure in seconding that nomination.

The President called for further nominations.

There being no further nominations,

Dr. MOORE moved, seconded by Dr. BRITTON, there being but one person nominated for the office of President, That Dr. Bray cast one ballot on behalf of the members of the Council for Dr. Rogers.

The President read the motion.

Dr. SANGSTER—Mr. President, I beg to call your attention to Section 3 of By-law 39, which says, "The election of President shall be by ballot. A majority of all the votes of the members present shall be necessary to an election." I do not approve of the mode of procedure that has been followed by this Council in the selection and election of their Presidents, and I object to that by-law being departed from. It is not competent for this Council to alter a by-law in this way ; a by-law can only be altered or amended by another by-law, and as there has been no by-law amending By-law 39 in that particular, I, as a member of the Council, object to any departure from our by-law. I do not think that any thoughtful, independent man can approve of the mode of procedure that has been adopted by this Council in the election of their President, a mode of procedure that practically renders the presidency the reward of subserviency to any section or combination of sections in this Council. I have no wish to go back into the past when ruling power in this room had no opposition ; but I claim that under existing circumstances a system which rotates the office of President among the different sections of the Council, conferring it in turn upon each individual member of his section, provided only he has not placed himself on record as being insufficiently ductile, is a pernicious system, and one that is utterly fatal to all independence and freedom in debate. I can conceive that under a more rational plan the presidency of this Council might be and would be a most distinguished and most honorable position within the reach of any member of the profession in the Province, and that the most exalted members of our ranks might be emulous of filling it. But a system of rotation which seldom or never confers the office twice in succession to the same gentleman, no matter how worthy thereof he might have proved himself to be, and which is open even to the suspicion that manly independence is no part of the qualification for its occupancy, is a mischievous system, purely evil in its tendencies, and so derogating from the dignity of the office as to make it worthless in the estimation of right-thinking men. The President's chair has been filled in the past, and more than once, by a really eminent man. It has at times been filled —not on many occasions—by men who by the general claim of the profession would have been declared worthy to fill it. But your unhappy system, while it does not in any case raise the actual man to the level of the position, does in every case lower the position to the level of the actual man. I claim, therefore, that in selecting a gentleman to fill the chair of this Council, the most eminent, the most respected, the most distinguished of our members, or one of the most, should be selected and placed there, one whom the general feeling of the profession would acknowledge as such ; and I claim, moreover, that once a proper man has been placed in that chair, although our Act requires us to elect a President annually, he should be expected to fill it during——

The PRESIDENT—You must allow me to stop you, Dr. Sangster. I cannot permit you to throw out any insinuations against any gentleman who has occupied the chair.

Dr. SANGSTER—I am not throwing out any insinuations against any gentleman who has occupied that chair. I have said that at times it has been filled by really eminent men, and there is no insinuation in that.

The PRESIDENT—I am referring to the latter part of your remarks. I am only stopping you to caution you, because you are transgressing.

Dr. SANGSTER—I claim that without proper reason a member should not be interrupted when speaking. I was about to remark that I think your system is vicious, inasmuch as it does place a premium upon a general pliability to the wishes of the dominant sections in this Council. I was remarking when you, Mr. President, stopped me, that I thought the most eminent man in our ranks should fill that place, and he should be expected to fill it from year to year during the life of the Council, or better still, during the lives of several successive Councils, as long as he remains a member of this body. I think everyone will agree with me in that respect ; and I think, further, that a ballot should be placed in the hands of every member of this Council, and that he should be required, in accordance with your by-law, to cast it. However much we may esteem and admire Dr. Rogers in his private personality or as a member of this Council, as a candidate for the office of President he is not *persona grata* to a section of its membership ; such being the case, we cannot permit his election to be declared unanimous. I am not saying this from any spirit of hostility to Dr. Rogers ; I have no doubt he deserves the position, and has done much to earn it in the work he did last year. In reference to the imposition of the tax, he certainly displayed a great deal of zeal, and a great deal of even exalted eloquence, in that respect. I am moved to these remarks, and I desire to say that I have no wish to see one of my friends in this chair, because we have unanimously decided that until we have secured the reforms which in the interests of the profession we are seeking, our place in this Council is upon the floor of this chamber, and we have not concealed from ourselves the fact that in placing ourselves in opposition to the mode of procedure that has been adopted in the Council we have made ourselves, individually and collectively, presidential impossibilities. I claim that a ballot should be passed.

Dr. CAMPBELL—I will just say that the by-law requires that these officers shall be elected "after nomination, by ballot," and there is one nomination, I believe.

Dr. McLAUGHLIN—Surely you don't claim you are prepared to override the by-law which declares that "the President shall be elected by ballot." Do you propose by resolution to override a by-law ?

Dr. REDDICK—The by-law not only requires that the election shall be by ballot, but it requires a majority of the votes of the members present to elect a President.

Dr. WILLIAMS—The decisions of the Council in the past have been that the method pursued was in accordance with this portion of the by-law. The word "nomination" being put in there is intended to imply that there shall be one or more nominated. If there are not two nominated it is expected to imply that there is no opposition to the man who is nominated in the first place. The question has been discussed before and it was considered it would save time simply to put in one ballot ; it is not because there is any disposition not to pass the ballot around and let everybody vote, but the belief was that only one nomination taking place and one ballot being put in, that complied with the law, that if any other persons wished to vote differently they would have made a nomination. The Council had no thought in the past, when adopting this course, that they were overriding that by-law at all.

The PRESIDENT—I have one motion before me and I will put it to the meeting——

Dr. ARMOUR—I rise to a point of order. As I understand it, it is provided in this by-law that it is necessary, even though there is only one nomination, to take the sense of the meeting and be sure by the ballots that a majority of the Council favors the election of the nominee. I understand, Mr. President, that you have ruled against that, and that you propose to put the motion to the meeting and ask that one ballot be cast and that that will suffice for the election of the President. I appeal against the ruling.

The PRESIDENT—I have not given any ruling yet ; you don't need to appeal.

Dr. McLAUGHLIN—The point of order is made that you are not able by that motion to overcome the by-law. That by-law declares that the President shall be elected by ballot and the motion is that he shall not be elected by ballot, but by one individual. I ask you for your ruling.

Dr. BROCK—I would like to ask for more information before we are asked to support your ruling, or the contrary.

The PRESIDENT—I have been present ever since this by-law was first introduced in the Council, and there has never been a ballot taken in the way suggested by Drs. Sangster, McLaughlin and Armour for the office of President ; the ballots have never been passed around but once, and that was for the office of Vice-President on the occasion of my election to that office. It has always been customary in this Council for some one to move, as has been done to-day, that some member, perhaps the gentleman who made the nomination, should cast the ballot. It has been customary to conduct the business in this way, but if Dr. Sangster would move a resolution in amendment to this, or if he would nominate some other member for the presidency, we would take a ballot. My ruling is that this motion is perfectly in order and I shall put it to the meeting.

Dr. ARMOUR—I desire to appeal to this Council, and I will tell them my reasons, because I want them to endorse my appeal. We have a by-law here which has evidently been overlooked, which has been ignored in the past as a matter of custom, but it is here, and I think it is properly here——

Dr. WILLIAMS—Excuse me, it has not been overlooked in the past,

Dr. ARMOUR—This meaning of it——

Dr. WILLIAMS—A different interpretation was put upon it, and the course taken was supposed by the Council to be in acccordance with the meaning and spirit of that by-law.

Dr. ARMOUR—This is the point I want to call your attention to and on which I want to get the sense of the Council : the by-law requires that the President shall be elected from among the members of the Council after nomination by ballot, and a majority of the votes of the members present shall be necessary to elect him. Now, Mr. President, I appeal to the Council to endorse and maintain their own by-law.

Dr. SANGSTER—Mr. President, I wish to point out that your ruling is defective on this ground : It may be there is actually a section in this Council that would fail to nom-.inate some other gentleman to that position, they are not unaware that the matter has been cut and dried beforehand and they know that as far as electing a man is concerned they are powerless, but they object to being placed as unanimously consenting to the election of the gentleman who has been nominated ; and I claim that the only way in which we can protect ourselves is to claim the right, the inalienable statutory right, of casting a ballot whichever way we please.

The PRESIDENT—I have ruled that this motion is in order ; Dr. Armour has appealed from the ruling of the chair. Shall the ruling of the chair be sustained ?

The President declared the ruling of the chair to be sustained.

Dr. McLaughlin called for the yeas and nays.

Dr. GEIKIE—I am in favor of putting things right ; I think there should be a ballot.

The Registrar took the yeas and nays as follows :

Yeas—Drs. Bray, Britton, Brock, Campbell, Emory, Fowler, Harris, Henderson, Logan, Luton, Machell, Moore, Moorhouse, Rogers, Thorburn, Williams.—16.

Nays—Drs. Armour, Barrick, Dickson, Graham, Hanly, Henry, McLaughlin, Reddick, Rosebrugh, Sangster, Shaw, Thornton.—12.

Dr. Geikie declined to vote.

The President put the motion as follows : "Moved by Dr. Moore, seconded by Dr. Britton, That as there has been but one person nominated for President, Dr. Bray cast the ballot." And on a vote having been taken, declared the motion carried.

Dr. Bray then cast a ballot, and on the ballot being examined by the President he declared Dr. Rogers elected President of the Council for the ensuing year.

Amid very hearty applause, Dr. Rogers, the President-elect, was conducted to the chair and addressed the Council as follows :

Dr. ROGERS—Gentlemen of the Council, I have not come to this meeting prepared with any set speech to represent the feelings I have of appreciation for the honor which has been. conferred upon me in electing me to the position of President of the Council of the College of Physicians and Surgeons of Ontario, an honor which I realize is one of the highest in the gift of the profession in this Province, one of the highest, perhaps, in the gift of the profession in Canada. I thoroughly appreciate the honor, and I ask you all, individually and collec-tively, to give me that support which you have given my predecessors in this office. I crave heartily the good will, and the esteem, if I can get it, of every individual in this room, of every member of this Council ; and l can assure you that while I occupy this position I will always endeavor to fill the duties to the very best of my ability, and to always act as fairly in every ruling I am called upon to give as it is possible for a man to do. While I regret the little discussion that has occurred, I hope that any little irritation which may have been felt will be forgotten, and that you will unite together in promoting the business of this. Council as expeditiously as possible.

The President called for nominations for the office of Vice-President.

Dr. HARRIS—I beg to move, seconded by Dr. BRITTON, That Dr. Thorburn be Vice-President of this Council for the ensuing year. In the past year, while filling the office of President of this Council, I have come very closely in contact with Dr. Thorburn as Chair-man of the Finance Committee, and I have also been brought in close contact with him prior to that time during the many years he has been chairman of that committee, and I know that he has been a hard-working member of this Council, and has devoted a great deal of time to their work, not only in our Council meetings and as Chairman of the Finance Committee but also as Chairman of the Legislation Committee, particularly during this past year ; and I do not think that to-day in this Council there is any man more deserving of the position than Dr. Thorburn.

Dr. GEIKIE—I beg to move, not from any opposition to Dr. Thorburn—in fact I had no idea he would be nominated for this office, and I intended to have made this motion first, if I had been quick enough—That Dr. Henry, who is an old member of the Council, should be Vice-President for the ensuing year.

Dr. WILLIAMS—I beg to move, seconded by Dr. CAMPBELL, That Dr. Rosebrugh be Vice-President for the ensuing year. I do not know that I need make any remarks on this subject, because you all know Dr. Rosebrugh as well as I know him, and he comes before the Council on his own well earned reputation.

The President declared the nominations closed.

Dr. McLaughlin—I want to congratulate you and the Council on the fact that we are very likely to have an officer now. It is as clear to me as the sun shines that we have no President.

The President—Order. You must withdraw that.

Dr. McLaughlin—I believe there is a by-law that states that the majority of the votes of the Council must be cast for President and Vice-President ; one vote, and one vote only, has been cast, and in my judgment we are without a President, and I am very glad we are to have a Vice-President.

Dr. Harris—We have more than one nomination this time, and we may have a ballot.

Dr. McLaughlin—The President ought not to be in the chair ; he is there by one ballot, which is not within the by-law.

The Registrar then passed the ballot.

The President—The ballot has been cast and I find that neither one of the gentlemen named has received a majority of the votes of the members present, consequently this vote will have to be taken over again.

Dr. Machell—The lowest man should drop out.

Dr. Williams—I do not think that that is necessary.

Dr. Geikie—Give us the result.

The President—The ballot shows Dr. Thorburn to have received twelve votes, Dr. Henry ten votes, and Dr. Rosebrugh seven votes, of the twenty-nine present.

Dr. Moorhouse—Let the lowest vote drop out.

Dr. Campbell—To be strictly in accordance with the by-law, as that seems to be a very necessary thing, we shall have to keep on balloting until one has the majority, unless some one of the three chooses to withdraw of his own accord.

The President—The ballot will again be passed to be taken on the three nominees for the office of Vice-President.

Dr. Sangster—May I ask, while the ballots are being cast, whether it is not usual in bodies as grave and important as ours is, to have scrutineers to examine the ballots ?

The President—It has heretofore been the custom to have the Registrar count the ballots, and I am now following that custom.

The Registrar then passed the ballot.

The President—The ballot has again been cast and neither one of the nominees has received a majority of the votes. The votes stand now, Dr. Thorburn twelve, Dr. Henry eleven, Dr. Rosebrugh five.

Dr. Rosebrugh—I see plainly the choice is not likely to fall on me, so I beg to retire from the contest and leave it between the other two gentlemen.

The Registrar again passed the ballot.

The President—I find on the last ballot taken that Dr. Thorburn received eighteen votes and Dr. Henry eleven votes. I have much pleasure in declaring Dr. Thorburn duly elected Vice-President of this Council for the ensuing year.

Dr. Thorburn then said—Mr. President and gentlemen, I thank you very much for the honor you have conferred on me, and if I ever have occasion to be in the chair I have no doubt I shall receive the same loyal, royal support you have given me to-day. I will do the best I can in the high office you have elected me to.

The President then called for nominations for the office of Registrar.

Dr. Campbell moved, seconded by Dr. Bray, That Dr. R. A. Pyne be elected Registrar for the ensuing year.

There being no other nominations, the President put the motion, which was carried unanimously.

Moved by Dr. Britton, seconded by Dr. Harris, That Mr. B. B. Osler, Q.C., be appointed the Council's Solicitor for the ensuing year.

The President put the motion, which was carried unanimously.

Moved by Dr. Bray, seconded by Dr. Machell, That Dr. W. T. Aikins be Treasurer of the Council for the ensuing year.

The President put the motion, which was carried unanimously.

Moved by Dr. Williams, seconded by Dr. Harris, That Mr. Alex. Downey, C.S.R., be appointed Official Stenographer for this Council for the ensuing year.

The President put the motion, which was carried unanimously.

Moved by Dr. Williams, seconded by Dr. Shaw, and resolved, That the following gentlemen constitute the Committee to Nominate the Standing Committees : Drs. Logan, Moore, Dickson, Machell, Brock, Sangster, Barrick, Henry, Moorhouse, Thorburn, Bray, Harris, Reddick and the mover.

The President put the motion, and on a vote being taken declared it carried.

Moved by Dr. Harris, seconded by Dr. Campbell, That the Council do now adjourn for half an hour to enable the Committee to Strike Standing Committees to meet and prepare their report for submission to the Council.—Carried.

On the Council resuming, Dr. WILLIAMS presented the report of the Striking Committee, naming the various Committees as follows :

Registration Committee.—Drs. Rosebrugh, Campbell, Dickson, Barrick, Hanly, Roome and Shaw.

Rules and Regulations.—Drs. Emory, Hanly, Luton, Reddick and Machell.

Finance Committee.—Drs. Dickson, Armour, Bray, Brock and Henderson.

Printing Committee.—Drs. Luton, Emory, Henry, Barrick and McLaughlin.

Educational Committee.—Drs. Britton, Fowler, Graham, Harris, Logan, Moore, Moorhouse, Sangster and Williams.

Property Committee.—Drs. Emory, Barrick, McLaughlin, Machell and Thornton.

Complaints Committee.—Drs. McLaughlin, Armour, Reddick, Henry and Geikie.

Moved by Dr. WILLIAMS, seconded by Dr. BRAY, That the report of the Committee to Strike Standing Committees be received. Carried.

Moved by Dr. WILLIAMS, seconded by Dr. BRAY, That the report of the Committee to Strike Standing Committees be now read and adopted.

The President read the motion.

Dr. McLAUGHLIN—I see that I am put upon three committees here of considerable importance, and I would be very glad to be relieved from one of the three. I see that I am put upon the Printing Committee, Property Committee and Complaints Committee. You all know that I am a miserable man with complaints, and I wish to be taken off of that committee, and I would be glad if some person would name a substitute.

Dr. MACHELL—I notice that Dr. Shaw's name, by oversight, appears only once on the committees. I beg to move, seconded by Dr. MOORHOUSE, That Dr. Shaw's name be substituted for Dr. McLaughlin's name on the Complaints Committee.

The President, having asked for and obtained the consent of the Council, put the motion, and on a vote having been taken declared it carried.

Moved by Dr. WILLIAMS, seconded by Dr. BRAY, That the report of the Committee to Strike Standing Committees as amended be adopted.

The President put the motion, and on a vote being taken declared it carried.

NOTICES OF MOTION.

No. 1. Dr. EMORY—For the appointment of a special committee to take into consideration the question of the examinations of the Council, with a view to make them a more equable and genuine test of the attainments of the candidates.

No. 2. Dr. BRITTON—That tenders be forthwith advertised for for the printing required by the Council ; that no part of any agreement entered into by the Council shall provide for the publishing in any journal of a report of the Council's proceedings or for the issuing of a free journal ; that the profession be kept fully informed by a verbatim report of the proceedings, published in the Announcement ; and that the accepted tenderers be required to furnish security satisfactory to the Finance Committee for the proper fulfilment of the contract.

No. 3. Dr. SHAW—To introduce a by-law to amend By-law No. 70.

No. 4. Dr. WILLIAMS—To amend By-law No. 39 in its 31st clause.

No. 5. Dr. BROCK—That all the accounts of the College of Physicians and Surgeons for the past five years be examined by a chartered accountant, and a full report presented to this Council as soon as possible.

No. 6. Dr. CAMPBELL—That it is expedient to amend the by-law levying an annual assessment, by providing that members of the College of Physicians and Surgeons resident in Ontario who are not engaged in practice and members not resident in Ontario be relieved from the payment of assessment.

COMMUNICATIONS.

The Registrar then read a number of communications, which were referred to the various committees.

ENQUIRIES.

Dr. SANGSTER—Mr. President, I have an enquiry or two I desire to make. I believe at the present moment the College of Physicians and Surgeons send, or profess to send, to every member of the profession in Ontario a monthly journal. It may not be within your knowledge that there was no journal furnished to the profession during the month of April. Is there any assignable reason for that omission ?

The PRESIDENT—I can only refer the matter to the Registrar ; I do not know of any reason.

The REGISTRAR states that he does not know of any reason.

Dr. SANGSTER—On the last journal issued, at the top of the page, there is a charge made of one dollar per annum, though this Council profess to send to every member of the profession in Ontario a free journal. Is it the intention of the Council no longer to supply that journal free ?

Dr. THORBURN—There has been a notice of motion given bearing on that subject.

Dr. SANGSTER—There is another point which I suppose will come up for discussion afterwards. It is broadly stated that the Council did send that journal to every member of the profession in the Province free, and then to place a professed charge of one dollar per annum on the cover is a simple attempt to defraud the post-office revenues. If that is the case, I, as a member of the Council, object to the Council being placed in the humiliating position of being in any sense a party to a fraud of that kind.

Dr. BRITTON—I gave notice of motion a few minutes ago that I think will cover this matter referred to by Dr. Sangster. I feel perfectly satisfied that that motion of which I gave notice will be carried almost unanimously. It is not our fault that anything of the kind spoken of by Dr. Sangster has appeared upon the pages of the journal. I, perhaps, have been more opposed than any other member of the Council to the issuing of a free journal ; but I never noticed on the cover of the journal that one dollar is mentioned as the subscription price, or I would have objected to it. However, this Council cannot be called in question in regard to the matter, because the placing of this price on the journal is only a recent occurrence, and as we have had no opportunity of considering it, and if the matter had been allowed to remain over till to-morrow it would have been settled forever, without the necessity of interference with that journal.

Dr. WILLIAMS—That price may apply to people outside of this Province. As a matter of fact I saw that journal in Prince Edward Island last summer, and had a read out of it there ; and I saw it in Nova Scotia. That dollar may, as I say, apply to the other Provinces, because the journal goes to Manitoba, to British Columbia and elsewhere throughout the Dominion, and while the Council furnish it free to the members in the Province of Ontario it does not follow that it is free to all outsiders, and I think in that sense the dollar is legitimately put on there.

Dr. SANGSTER—I think that merely confirms the view I take. It is well known that that journal has been sent, without paying postage, to every member of the College, and the post-office has to that extent been mulcted in proper postage, and I claim that this Council, not only this year but in past years, have been made a party to that by permitting their name to be on it as sending it to the members of the College of Physicians and Surgeons of Ontario.

Dr. HENRY—I want to know what induced the Honorable Mr. Ross, Minister of Education, to interfere with our matriculation and to threaten to introduce a bill to take the power of the matriculation examination out of the hands of the Council.

The PRESIDENT—I will answer Dr. Henry's question by stating that that matter will come up in the report of the Committee on Legislation and the Executive Committee's report and be fully dealt with by them.

REPORTS OF THE SPECIAL AND STANDING COMMITTEES.

None.

CONSIDERATION OF REPORTS.

None.

UNFINISHED BUSINESS FROM PREVIOUS MEETINGS.

None.

On motion the Council adjourned to meet at ten o'clock to-morrow. The committees in the meantime to organize and prepare their reports for presentation.

SECOND DAY.

WEDNESDAY, June 10, 1896.

The Council met at 10 o'clock a.m., according to motion for adjournment.

The President in the chair.

The Registrar called the roll. Present—Drs. Armour, Barrick, Bray, Britton, Brock, Campbell, Dickson, Emory, Fowler, Geikie, Graham, Hanly, Harris, Henderson, Henry, Logan, Luton, Machell, Moore, Moorhouse, McLaughlin, Reddick, Rogers, Rosebrugh, Sangster, Shaw, Thorburn, Thornton, Williams.

The minutes of the preceding meeting were read by the Registrar.

Dr. GEIKIE—I desire to move a slight amendment to the minutes, namely, that my name, if I am not mistaken, is mentioned as being on the Committee on Complaints, and I wish to move that the minutes be amended by the exclusion of my name, for I decline to act on the committee. As a representative of Trinity Medical College, one of the largest, if not the largest of our Ontario medical colleges, the only committee on which

I have a claim and the committee on which, perhaps, from my several years' experience as a teacher, I might have been most useful, was the Education Committee. I may say that I do not personally regret my exclusion from that committee, inasmuch as excluding me means a great saving of labor on my part and a great saving of my time ; but on the other hand, I feel that, as the only representative on this Council of Trinity Medical College, it is my duty very strongly to object to this omission, and I would be derelict in that duty did I not make a strong objection to the exclusion of that body in me from all share, for this year at all events, in the deliberations of the Education Committee. Some may think that perhaps the representative of Trinity University is our representative——

Dr. ARMOUR—I rise to a point of order. We are now considering the adoption of the minutes, which must be adopted as they were put down at the last session ; we have no power to amend them at this stage, and Dr. Geikie is out of order in discussing that matter now.

Dr. GEIKIE—I am speaking on a question of privilege ; I move that the minutes as read be amended.

The PRESIDENT—I will have to rule you out of order, Dr. Geikie, for the present. After the minutes are adopted you can move to have this matter rectified.

On motion the minutes were confirmed as read.

Dr. GEIKIE—As to the question of privilege, I will ask to be heard for a few minutes. Some of the members may think the representative of Trinity University, my friend Dr. Harris, is our representative, but he is no more so than is Dr. Williams, Dr. Thorburn, or Dr. Moore ; the relations existing between Trinity University and Trinity Medical College being one of affiliation only. We are a distinct corporation, having a distinct Act. Our Act gives us the legal right to be represented here and gives us other rights in connection with the Council besides. The exclusion of the representative of the College, whether intentionally or otherwise—and I do not say it is intentionally—is unfair and I regard it as a wrong to the entire faculty of our College and to every former student who is now practising in Ontario or elsewhere, and I am perfectly sure it will be so regarded, not only by us, but by the teachers and graduates of other Colleges as well as our own, for I have reason to know and am proud to know that the colleges co-work and that each one regards a wrong inflicted on another as though it were inflicted upon itself——

Dr. SANGSTER—I again rise to a point of order. If the rules of order of this Council are to be transgressed with impunity by one, they must be transgressed by all. There is a proper time for this discussion, and I claim your ruling, Mr. President, that the order of business shall be maintained.

The PRESIDENT—On the question of privilege, Dr. Geikie is in order.

Dr. SANGSTER—I thought the proper time was under the head of Miscellaneous Business.

The PRESIDENT—No, under our rules a member may rise to a question of privilege at any time.

Dr. GEIKIE—I have been here for twenty years, and should be familiar with the orders and rules of the Council. I felt, even before your ruling, Mr. President, that my remarks were in order. I regret, as far as this Council is concerned, that this wrong has been done. I know that in the Council it is the body that inflicts without cause a wrong on another, and not the body on which that injury is inflicted, that really suffers ; and for the sake of the Council I do say that I very, very deeply regret that this has happened. I am sure that it will cause very, very widespread feelings, easy to create but difficult to allay, and which that ordinary sense of fairness and justice which I think is to be looked for in all learned bodies like this should have rendered absolutely impossible. I may say that since I have come to the Council this morning I have been informed that it is some idea with regard to my views as to matriculation that led to my exclusion ; with regard to that I maintain that no views that I could hold, or that I could not hold, should have militated to the exclusion, not of myself personally, but of the representative of that great college which I have the honor to represent ; and I have to say that the idea is utterly wrong, my views were those of the Legislature, those of the Minister of Education, views the adoption of which has now been made absolute by the Legislature upon the Council, and which, I think, are founded on common sense and on nothing else, and which should not have been taken as a reason either for the exclusion of the representative of Trinity College or any one else from any committee of this Council.

NOTICES OF MOTION.

No. 1. Dr. ARMOUR—That the advice of Mr. Christopher Robinson, Q.C., be had on the following : 1st. Had the Medical Council at the annual session of 1895 a legal right to assess an annual tax on the medical profession for the years 1893 and 1894 as enacted in Clause 3 of By-law No. 69 ? 2nd. To what proportion of the arrearages of the annual tax which are outstanding at various dates from 1874 to the present time can Section 41a of the

Medical Act passed in 1891 be legally applied for their collection ? 3rd. Are there any members of the medical profession, as it now exists, exempt from the operation of Section 41a ? Also that Drs. Williams, Henry, Campbell, Sangster and Armour be a delegation to wait on Mr. Robinson to secure the above advice.

No. 2. Dr. SANGSTER—That it be an instruction to the Registration Committee to carefully examine the credentials on which registration has been granted to such persons as have become members of the College during the twelve months preceding the second Tuesday of June of each year, and to report thereon to the Council during the current and succeeding sessions.

No. 3. Dr. HANLY—That the opinion of our Solicitor be obtained regarding the possibility and probability of removing malpractice cases from juries and placing the decision in the hands of the Judges, and also how security for costs can best be secured.

No. 4. Dr. GEIKIE—To have his (Dr. Geikie's) name struck off the Committee on Complaints.

COMMUNICATIONS, PETITIONS, ETC.

Communications were received from Mr. Foster and from Dr. F. H. Young, which were referred respectively to the Complaints and Finance Committees.

MOTIONS OF WHICH NOTICE HAS BEEN GIVEN AT A PREVIOUS MEETING.

Dr. EMORY moved, seconded by Dr. WILLIAMS, That the following be a committee to take into consideration the question of the examinations of the Council with a view to make them a more equable and genuine test of the attainments of the candidates, and to report on the same to this Council at this meeting : Drs. Harris, Moore, Sangster, and the mover and seconder.

The President read the motion.

Dr. EMORY—It is not necessary for me to detain the Council but a moment in speaking to this motion. Having but a few years ago the honor of being appointed by this Council to serve upon the Board of Examiners, and having so served I had opportunities of seeing what seemed to me some points which could be improved upon ; and I have thought of the matter since then, and during the past examinations I visited the hall during the oral examinations. I do not know that it is necessary at this time to go into the particulars which seemed to me might be improved upon, but if a committee is appointed they will no doubt enter fully into the consideration of the case, and when the matter is considered by them and reported upon by them and the report brought in it can be fully discussed in Council.

The President put the motion, and on a vote being taken declared it carried.

Moved by Dr. BRITTON, seconded by Dr. MOORE, That the Printing Committee be instructed to advertise forthwith for tenders for the printing required by this Council ; that no part of any agreement entered into by the Council should provide for the publishing in any journal a report of the Council's proceedings, or for the issuing of a free journal ; that the profession be kept fully informed by a verbatim report of the proceedings in the Announcement ; and that the accepted tenderers be required to furnish security satisfactory to the Finance Committee for the proper fulfilment of the contract.

The President read the motion.

Dr. BRITTON—I do not know as it is necessary for me to say much in regard to this motion. I feel confident there will be very little discussion on it and it will pass in the Council without any opposition. The matter has been under discussion for many years. On the first occasion when it was discussed, there were only two of us who opposed the method of printing that has been adopted recently, that is, by a journal publishing company ; and there were only two of us who, I think, opposed the issuing of a free journal. On the next occasion it came up I stood solitary and alone. I mention this to indicate to you the strong convictions I have had upon the matter, straight through, from first to last. Last year there were quite a number who stood beside me in this matter, and when I moved a resolution almost identical with this I think it had a good many supporters ; and it would be only taking up the time of the Council unnecessarily to go into the merits of the case, because I think the resolution shows upon the face of it, and the changes that have taken place in the personnel of our journal—I call it our journal by way of courtesy, although I disclaim any responsibility for anything that has been stated in that journal at any particular time—and the succession of events that have taken place during the past few years, are quite sufficient to warrant this Council in doing their business in a businesslike way, like any corporate body, like any private individual, or like any wholesale or retail dealer in the City of Toronto. I have to pass some reflections upon what was formerly done. I am not going to find too much fault with the members present who were opposed to me formerly ; they certainly did what they believed to be right, at the same time I think they were guilty of errors of judgment. I have had no conversation with any member regarding this matter excepting two—I think the matter came up between two individuals and myself—and I do not know definitely what the feeling of the Council is in the matter. ·

Dr. WILLIAMS—I think Dr. Britton is rather premature in assuming that the Council are willing to come to his views in one jump after, as he says, the year before last he himself voting alone, and on previous years with a very slight support. I think he is wrong also in assuming that this Council's position was governed by the personnel of the parties publishing the journal. I think there is a stronger motive at the back of publishing the journal——

Dr. BRITTON—Excuse me, I am afraid Dr. Williams drew a wrong inference from what I said. I intended to say there has been an entire change, not only as to the caption of the journal, but in addition to that, the parties who at present are responsible for the fulfilment of that contract took rather peculiar views formerly regarding this Council. That is what I referred to. I made no reference to the gentleman who was awarded the contract, nor had I at any time thought that the personnel of the publisher had any influence upon this Council in securing the contract. The error arose from my speaking briefly, not wishing to take up time.

Dr. WILLIAMS—To the balance of the resolution I would offer no objection, and would agree with it ; but to assume, as Dr. Britton seems to think, that we would continue the parties now doing the work is unfair ; to assume as well that because the personnel of the journal that we have been publishing is changed, that therefore we do not think it necessary to have a journal sent out at all is wrong altogether. (Hear, hear.) My recollection of the object of having that journal sent free to the different members of the profession is that it was to keep the profession in touch with the Council. (Hear, hear.) It is true you can get to them through the Annual Announcement, but that Annual Announcement won't get there till next fall. They know the profession is meeting now in the early part of the year. Is it fair to keep them from any information until next fall ? Now is when they want to be in touch, when the matter is a live question, when it is up ; and to put it in the Announcement and send it next fall at a time when it won't probably be read at all, is not just what we want. Another thing I desire to draw your attention to is—it is within the experience of every member of this Council—and I do not hesitate to say the members here will admit it, that when the Announcement comes it is too big a thing to look at, and they throw it aside to be looked at when they have time. Generally the time don't come. While if a medical journal comes it is likely to be read for its medical information, let it be good or bad, and it is read for that purpose, and, being read, it brings under their notice the proceedings of the Council, and the profession is kept in touch with the proceedings of the Council as it cannot be by any other method. Another thing, the profession are getting but a small thing when you send them a journal free. They, to a large extent, have appreciated that. In my own division I have taken occasion, at least twice, to go largely over my division, and have entered into conversation with the medical men throughout the riding, and I found that the medical men appreciated getting the journal, and looked upon it as a means by which they were kept informed of the proceedings of the Council and what was being done. Now, I think, under these circumstances, inasmuch as it costs almost nothing above what our ordinary printing would cost, to send a journal, it would be most unwise to stop that means of keeping the profession well informed of what is being done in the Council. We got into difficulty before we had an association spring up that called itself the "Defence Association." Why did that occur ? It occurred simply because the profession were not kept informed of what the Council were doing. We could not expect the daily newspapers to publish our proceedings fully ; our medical journals would not do it, and the profession were therefore in absolute ignorance of what the Council were doing, and hence there was the ground to grow up a suspicion of the Council and the belief that the Council were not acting fair and proper. Under these circumstances I hold the Council would be taking a radical backward step and doing itself a gross injustice, and injuring the profession as well, in not keeping them informed of what is done. I agree with the balance of Dr. Britton's resolution, that we should take tenders and come to an understanding what journal is going to publish it, and have proper security. That is perfectly right, I do not object to it ; but when you have done that, do not say by a vote of that kind that we are going to take a retrograde step and not keep the profession properly informed of what the Council are doing. If we want our Council matters to progress satisfactorily we must do our business above board, and do it in such a way that we are not ashamed. Not only that, but we will take pains to have the profession acquainted with what we do. Having done that we can hope to stand well with the profession, but we cannot hope so outside of that.

Dr. McLAUGHLIN—I no not intend to discuss this at length. Probably Dr. Williams would suggest how the profession has been kept in touch with the actions of the Council during this last year. The journal started out at a jolly gait to publish a little of what was done here, but he fell off his bicycle into the ditch before he got half way through. and went no further. That is the way the touch has been kept between the Council and the profession by this journal. I am disposed to think that the members of this Council are perfectly competent to select their own journal and get what information they please. I do not wish to advocate the idea that this Council should get a journal and send that journal gratuitously to members of the profession. The profession are perfectly competent to pay for their own journals, and I think they ought to do so. I think the first part of Dr. Britton's resolution unnecessary, for, if my memory serves me correctly, I think Dr. Thorburn brought in a motion about the close of last session that no contract for the expenditure of the money of this Council should be entered into for any purpose whatever unless it was by tender ; that would cover what the first part of our friend's resolution covers, and I think would do away with the first portion of this resolution. With the second part of the resolution I entirely agree. I think that satisfactory bonds should be given by every person who enters into a contract to do certain work for money for this Council, just as would be done in any ordinary transaction.

Dr. THORNTON—Mr. President, I think the first copy of the journal we had issued last year should be a sufficient lesson to any of us with regard to the propriety of engaging further in this journal publishing. I have not a copy here in my hands, but it is not necessary to read the exact wording. We all remember the efforts that were made to secure the printing and issuing of that journal in the manner decided upon at the time ; and a reference by any member of the Council to the first pages of the journal will show the impressions that were conveyed in its publication. I contend that those impressions were entirely misleading, and there is always a danger that they will be misleading. A matter of that kind is very apt to perpetuate friction. We had an unusually long sitting last year, and the conclusion to be drawn from the first pages of that issue of the journal was—I say this without qualification, because I do not think that anyone will disagree with me—that the prolonging of the session was entirely owing to the addition of a certain number of members to the Council ; I say this is misleading. We had an unusually long session, but it could not have been a very short one when some of the committees did not bring in their reports until the time that every previous session of the Council had closed its sittings. There was a source of irritation conveyed by that journal at once, and to get rid of this I think the motion that Dr. Britton has made is a very businesslike motion, and it will obviate further friction of that description.

Dr. HANLY—I think, with Dr. Britton, that we should use ordinary business methods in having our work done ; that if we have such a journal as we have had it does not serve the purpose it should, that is, to keep the profession in touch with what is being done, because it has done that. I had no knowledge of some of the changes until I received a private letter from the Registrar informing me the Announcement had not been sent out as it should have been. I was at a meeting of the Medical Association in my district, and about fifteen of the members present stated that they did not receive the Announcement.

Dr. BARRICK—I quite agree with the motion as it is now before the meeting. •

Dr. ARMOUR—There is one respect in which I think it may be advantageously amended by adding to it. I believe there is nothing in the resolution that removes the present journal from being, or commands it not to be, the journal of the medical profession. It is now published as the official journal, I believe, of the medical profession, and I think there should be an addition to the motion nullifying that, if there is a reason for it. I do not propose to go into the discussion of the matter further, because this matter was pretty thoroughly discussed last year. But I do hope that Dr. Britton's view that there will be few to oppose his motion at the present time may be correct. I may also say that I think Dr. Williams has formed a rather false estimate as to the value of that journal to the profession and to some views held by the members of this Council. I can assure Dr. Williams that instead of quieting that feeling and those views that led to the organizing of the Defence Association, those views are stronger in the profession to-day than ever before. When he says that it had removed those, as he called them, erroneous views, I think he is altogether mistaken with regard to them.

Dr. BRAY—As regards what Dr. Armour has said about putting an additional motion to discontinue the journal, I submit that there is no necessity for that. The contract only calls for a year, and the contract has expired now, so that Dr. Armour's suggestion is not necessary at all. As to the publication of the journal, I think that it is almost absolutely necessary that the proceedings of this Council should be published in some journal ; whether it is wise to give that monopoly to one journal and send that journal free to every member of the profession, is a question I am not prepared to answer by saying it is in the interests of the profession that it should be so sent. That is a question for our consideration. Dr. Britton has been a little bit mistaken in saying that he stood alone, because while I did not express any very strong opinion in the matter, I did say that I did not believe that we should have a journal sent out unless we had full control of that journal and sent it out under the lines of the British Medical Association's journal. I said if we were strong enough to do that, then I was perfectly willing that that should be done ; and we should hire a man who would be responsible to this Council to do so, and let all remuneration coming from advertisements, and so on, in that journal go to increase the revenue of the Council. But I was and am opposed to the way the journal has been conducted, and I am on record to that effect. At the same time, I agree that it would be very nice and a very proper thing to do if we could make some arrangements with the existing journals, as they come out every month, to publish our proceedings, so that the members of the profession throughout the country would see through the journals what the Council were doing. I agree a good deal with what Dr. Williams said about the Announcement. The Announcement comes very late in the year, when it has lost its interest ; the time has gone by ; people want to see what is going on without waiting three or four months to do so, and I think if we could have those proceedings published in a journal it would be a very great advantage. But I am not prepared to say whether or not such an agreement could be come to. I do think, under the existing circumstances, that it is better for the Council to drop the journal under the present management, at any rate.

Dr. WILLIAMS—I understood you to say a moment ago that the contract terminated with the year, that it is terminated now ; therefore you have no contract, and it would be with some journal that you would make a contract.

Dr. BRAY—The contract with the present journal is done—it has terminated. I do not . say that a contract should be made ; but I think if there was some arrangement come to by the existing medical journals whereby the proceedings of this Council should be published, they would reach every medical man. I think that it is certainly very much against the interests of the existing journals for this Council to send a journal free ; at the same time, that free journal has been appreciated by the profession ; the members of the profession in my constituency were almost unanimously in favor of having a free journal sent to them. I think, however, if the journal could be sent in the way I suggest, under the control of the Council (edited by somebody hired by this Council), so that none of these advertisements would appear which are to be seen in the journal which published our proceedings during the past year. I do not think there should be any advertisements in the report of the Council's proceedings ; I think the report should be devoted entirely to the Council's business, and if that can be accomplished I would hold up both hands for it. But I am opposed to such a contract as we have had.

Dr. GRAHAM—I concur very much with Dr. Britton's resolution, but I think that there is part of it unnecessary. If I understood the printing contract of last year, I understood that it was no part of the contract to issue this journal free. When I went back to my constituency it was mentioned, and I said it was not our official journal. I wrote to an authority on that subject, and he repudiated the idea of it being the official journal, and I think he was right. I do not remember that phase of the thing entering into the contract at all. That part of the resolution is, I think, entirely unnecessary ; otherwise, in the resolution I agree with Dr. Britton.

Dr. CAMPBELL—I think the Council at large is quite in accord with the first part and the last part of the resolution, that there should be tenders got, and so on ; the second part of the resolution is one on which there may be reasonable differences of opinion as to whether the Council shall send a copy of a journal, or of several journals for that matter, to the members of the profession without charge, in order, as Dr. Williams says, that they shall have the proceedings of the Council at an early season, when they can become acquainted with it and with its work, and when they can have some interest in its work. That is a matter about which I think there may be reasonable differences of opinion. The journal that has been sent in the past has not been one that has contained very much reading matter in which I myself was personally interested ; but I have heard of quite a number of physicians in my own neighborhood who found a great deal of interesting matter in it—I mean outside of Council questions altogether—on medical subjects and were very much pleased with receiving the journal in that shape, and looked upon it as some return for the assessment which they were called upon to pay. So far as I am personally concerned it is a matter of indifference to me ; I could get along without a copy of a journal of that description being sent to me ; but I think there is ground for a difference of opinion on that point, and if Dr. Williams would make a motion to amend Dr. Britton's resolution by striking out that particular part, I would be pleased to support it, in order to leave that an open question. Striking out that portion of Dr. Britton's resolution will not commit the Council to adopting the plan of sending a journal or several journals to the profession. It will leave that, so far, an open question, which may be decided on the lines suggested by Dr. Bray by an arrangement with several journals to have it printed and sent to the members.

Dr. SANGSTER—I am fully in accord with Dr. Britton's motion. I do not believe that this Council had better go, into the printing and publishing business. It went into real estate once and burned its fingers badly, and I think it had better keep out of all such transanctions and proceedings. The objections to Dr. Britton's motion seem to turn upon two points : first, that there is a prevailing wish in the profession to obtain a free journal ; next, that there is a prevailing wish in the profession to get a knowledge of the proceedings of this Council at an earlier date than the Announcement furnishes them. With regard to the last, let me say I see no reason, if our proceedings are published by contract with reasonable expedition, why the profession should have to wait more than a very short time after the close of our session before the proceedings are put in proper form before them. I think we could reach the profession at as quite an early date through the Announcement as we do at present, and much more profitably than we do through the medical journal. Then, with regard to the prevailing wish to obtain this medical journal, let me say that at present there is another medical journal published and sent free to every member of the profession ; and a short time ago there was a second one, and a little while ago we had three free journals all sent to the members of the profession in this Province. I do not think the profession is so dying, as might be inferred from remarks here, for information supplied through the columns of medical journals ; and I do not think that they are not able and not willing to pay out of their own pockets for any information of that kind that they may desire. There is one other point I want to suggest before I sit down, and it is this : if there is a desire on the part of the profession to obtain access to the proceedings of the Council through a journal, I should think in these days of sharp business enterprise that the proprietors of the different medical journals would themselves, of their own motion, publish the proceedings of the Council gratuitously at as early a date as they could issue them. I really can see no force made in the different objections that have been urged against Dr. Britton's motion ; on the other hand, I could, if I dare venture on your time, point out a score of, as I think, very strong and valid reasons why this Council should not only in the present cut themselves free from any connection with any medical journal, but they should carefully refrain from forming any such connection in the future.

Moved by Dr. WILLIAMS, seconded by Dr. HARRIS, That the resolution be amended by striking out the second part, "That no part of any agreement entered into by the Council shall provide for the publishing in any journal a report of the Council's proceedings or for the issuing of a free journal."

The President read the amendment.

Dr. BRAY—When Dr. Williams spoke I was just going to explain that by voting for Dr. Britton's resolution, which I favor to a great extent, it takes away the power of the Printing Committee, the committee which this resolution will go to, and it is in fact an instruction to them not to do this. Now I think a committee is the proper place to discuss the pros and cons of any question, and after due deliberation they make a report to the Council, and the report would and should have more weight, and should be more intelligible than if there was free discussion going on now, because the committee will go into the matter thoroughly and their report is the thing that should be here discussed. But if Dr. Britton's motion, as it is now, is carried, it cannot be discussed ; it shuts off discussion on that part of it entirely. That is the objection I have to that portion of Dr. Britton's motion ; the other part I quite agree with.

Dr. WILLIAMS—If Dr. Britton's resolution is carried as it stands it prohibits the Printing Committee from ascertaining or not if a reasonable contract can be made with any journal. It prohibits as well the sending of the journal to members of the profession. I object strongly to that, because before the committee have had an opportunity to ask for tenders for printing, and when they might get what would be very satisfactory offers for doing this work, the Council have been committed. If that printing can be done and the publication issued to the profession free, without incurring any material increase in cost to Council, I think there are few members of the Council that would not be willing it should be done. That the journal that gets the printing contract should be considered the official journal of this Council is certainly no part of this Council's business. The Council do not undertake to establish an official journal, and it is only a business representation made by that paper for which we are not responsible in any sense whatever ; and if it becomes necessary that we shall place a veto upon the person getting that contract to prevent him doing that we can do so in an agreement—we can easily do that. "As we do not accept this as our official journal, and we are not responsible for it, therefore you shall not on that journal make a statement setting forth that it is the official journal of this Council." That is a mere matter of detail that is easily carried out. Then, there have been some objections raised on the ground that the contracts during the last year have not been satisfactorily carried out by the journal we were dealing with. As to that, while we may have failures with one journal, perhaps because of some unfortunate business arrangement, it does not vitiate the entire system ; it simply says that so far as that particular journal is concerned it is not wise to enter into a contract with it unless they can give some satisfactory proof that they are going to have better business management. It does not say anything against the system whatever. The statement has been made that I have said, or was understood to say, that this journal had done away with the feeling that there was among the profession. I did not intend to say that. What I did say was that if the profession is kept thoroughly and properly informed of the doings of the Council as they proceed, it should have confidence that we do our business in such a way that the profession should be satisfied ; and I think it is the right of this Council to see that the profession is kept fully informed of what the Council are doing, and unless that is done the profession are not in a position to judge of the Council's business. Within the last year I had a letter from a gentleman in my own division who was one of the strongest opponents that this Council could have, and he wrote me stating that he had had the journal and had read up the proceedings carefully, that he had read the Announcement and had completely changed his mind,' and had sent in his fee ; and that he considered it an honor to belong to such a body and to have the privilege of paying his fee, while previously to that, when I was there, he had expressed the very strongest possible opinions in the other way. I hold it is the right and duty of this Council to take steps to keep the profession regularly and well informed about every step they take ; and when they have done that they have done their duty and nothing less. The question then comes up, if that is their duty, which is the best way to go to work to accomplish it ? I believe there is no more efficient way than having a publication in a medical journal so that it reaches every man in the entire Province. On that ground I object to Dr. Britton's resolution, because it ties our hands and prevents the Printing Committee from asking for tenders that would carry out that idea in any shape whatever.

Dr. McLaughlin—I only rise to call the attention of the Council to what I said a little while ago, namely, that we discussed the propriety of having our printing done by tender. I have advocated it time and again here and it was advocated by other members of this Council. And on the twenty-seventh day of June last, Dr. Thorburn moved, seconded by Dr. Machell, that in future before any contracts are made involving any expenditure of money, tenders for such expenditure be asked for and, all things being equal, the lowest tender be accepted. Dr. Britton will see, therefore, that the next part of his resolution is unnecessary, because it is already provided for by a general resolution of the Council. Only one word in reply to Dr. Williams. Neither Dr. Williams nor any other man of this Council has pointed out or can point out why we should not have a report of our proceedings in the hands of the profession as quickly as we would have it dribbled out month by month in the journal ; and if this Council are desirous of having their proceedings in the hands of the profession as rapidly as possible, the proper way is to print the whole thing as quickly as possible and send it to the profession, and not have, as last year, a little dribble sent one month and a little dribble another month and finally have it disappear.

Moved by Dr. Brock, seconded by Dr. Logan, in amendment to the amendment, That this Council postpone discussion of this matter until the reports of the Printing and Finance Committees are received.

The President read the amendment to the amendment.

Dr. Brock—I will not take up the Council's time very long, but I have had a good deal of experience about journal business, and I think after this Council get a report from the Printing Committee we shall find it is quite possible to have the proceedings of this Council published without any expense to the Council. Medical journals have been published which have given the proceedings of the Council so long ago that I do not wish to go back that distance ; but it is possible to publish the proceedings of this Council and the proceedings of our Association by the medical journals if they wish to do so. There is not a reporter here this year from the daily papers, and (though last year we had three or four) there will consequently be no report of the proceedings going out this year in the daily press that will be at all satisfactory to the profession. I think the Printing Committee can give us a report that will be satisfactory to this Council and that will settle the question, and Dr. Williams' arguments are sufficient to my mind to say that the amendment to the amendment should carry ; he uses the arguments I would use myself.

Dr. Machell—Dr. Pyne informed me two months ago that this Announcement could be printed in from four or six to eight weeks at the very longest. Heretofore the proceedings of the Council have not been printed in the journal in anything less than from two to three months—two to three months is the shortest time. Now, if this Announcement could be got out and in the hands of the profession in from two to six or possibly eight weeks it is the simplest way to do. Last year I was not in favor of giving the contract to any particular journal and I am still of that opinion, I have no reason to change my opinion.

Dr. Logan—The only point I wish to make in connection with the amendment to the amendment is that if Dr. Britton's motion as amended by Dr. Williams is carried by the Council it will then become the opinion of the Council, and if you refer it to any committee that committee are debarred from changing the opinion of the Council ; or if the committee see proper to make a change in the resolution you send to them, and it is brought back to the Council, the Council cannot go back upon their previous opinion and would debar themselves in that sense from changing their own opinion. I see the necessity of this or other similar questions being placed before the committee to which it is properly assignable first, and then if the committee suggest any change in the matter, the Council have a right to consider it, to be consistent and to carry out their opinion.

Dr. GEIKIE—Would it not simplify the matter to give the committee an instruction that the Registrar shall see that the Announcement is published and mailed to practitioners not later than the 1st of August in each year ? Our last Announcement came to the profession in the end of the month of February of this year. Its encyclopædic character probably explains this, and we may not have such an Announcement again. If our Announcement were in the hands of the profession in August, it would keep everyone in touch with what was going on.

Dr. ARMOUR—I am opposed to Dr. Brock's amendment for the reason that if we entertain the amendment and refer this first to the Printing Committee, we will not have an opportunity or time to advertise for tenders and utilize them during this session ; for that reason, if for no other, I think it should not be entertained. I desire to refer again to Dr. Williams. He seems to think I misapprehended his meaning in regard to his views of the effect of this journal, though I think in his reply to me he practically reaffirms the views I apprehended he insinuated here. I have in my hand the *Ontario Medical Journal* for last June, and I desire to read you a brief portion of an editorial contained in that number, and to show you the undesirability of perpetuating a journal of this kind, and I will be very much surprised if after hearing this that even Dr. Williams will approve of a repetition of this kind of work in the name of the Medical Council. The article is as follows : " When the idea of increasing the number of members was promulgated, our voice [that is, the *Journal's* voice] was against it ; and now the wisdom of our stand is clearly evidenced. There was more breath used, more trouble caused, and more money spent this year than ever occurred in the history of the Medical Council. Useless bickerings, unparliamentary methods and language pervaded the meeting from beginning to end. We may be asked why this was so, but we only need to point to the fountain-head, with its three attached spouts, which unfortunately has been foisted on the Council by the misjudgment, and in many of the cases by misrepresentation, from the elected to the electorate [whatever that means]. A letter which is public property, in that it can be produced at any time, states, and that forcibly, that one of the new members got most of his votes by promising to help insist on the immediate payment of all back assessments owing by the medical profession of the Province. And yet he gets up in his place in the Council chamber and asserts that he never canvassed for a vote, and, to add to his record, proceeds to vote against the reinstatement of the clause dealing with the annual assessment. Truly we will be sorry for this gentleman when his words and actions are reviewed by his constituents on the production of the printed report of the proceedings. All thought that this wonderful Defence Association would surely be able to send good, strong men to represent them, but their actions proved straight from start to finish that the composition was principally wind, after the style of what the lay people call water-brash—bitter." I will not proceed further—that is enough to show you the style that that journal has been carried on in, in the name of the profession. I would be surprised that any member would approve of such writing, such references, such misrepresentations as are contained in this article.

Dr. HENRY—I just rise to say that this matter was discussed last year, and we had the expressions of this Council on this very question that has been under discussion so long this morning. I am strongly in favor of Dr. Williams' amendment. I think this Council never did an act that gives such satisfaction to the medical men in the country—I speak of my own constituency—as the sending of a free journal ; and I think it would be a very unwise thing to dispense with that journal. It has given universal satisfaction. We have spent the whole morning discussing this thing that was threshed out last year, and the expense of this discussion will be very nearly that of the printing ; and we are also wasting time discussing what was discussed thoroughly last year, and I do not think this Council wants to stultify itself after what was said last year.

Dr. THORBURN—I thoroughly agree with a great deal of what has been said in regard to the action of this Council on this matter, but I think it has been before the members every session, and perhaps there is no subject so thoroughly discussed, with more or less satisfaction, or dissatisfaction. I think it is a very important thing, and before any action is taken I think it should be submitted to the committee as suggested by Dr. Brock's amendment to the amendment, and let the committee discuss it and bring in their report, and then let the matter come up for discussion in Council.

Dr. EMORY—You have a Printing Committee here whose duty it is to bring in a recommendation to the Council, and I am in favor of Dr. Brock's amendment that it is left to that committee for a report, and on that report a proper discussion may come up. Dr. Armour has just told us if the amendment to the amendment carries it will be too late to call for tenders. I submit that in pursuance of the resolution carried last year, which Dr. McLaughlin read to us, the Printing Committee must immediately advertise for tenders, they have no option in that matter, that is their duty, their instruction ; and when those tenders are received I think they will be in a position to bring in a recommendation which will save a great deal of time and discussion. As one gentleman has said, the discussion has cost us as much as the whole printing would cost.

Dr. BARRICK—I will just say that in dealing with this matter one objection I have to referring this to the Printing Committee is that we are now dealing with a principle, and I think the Printing Committee have other duties to perform than the deciding of a principle, and especially a principle that has been before the Council for a number of years. The principle is, shall or shall we not have a free journal? If that matter is settled then the committee know exactly what they are doing ; and I think it is the place of this Council now, when this resolution is before the meeting, a resolution which has been before the Council for some years, to settle this and let it be an instruction to the Printing Committee to act thereon. We expect to have a short session, and we have to get tenders for the printing and present them and have it all settled in a few days ; but if that committee is to take up their time in discussing a principle which has been discussed and threshed out by this Council for a number of years, I think there will be very little time to get tenders and get the business done properly. While this is up now, it seems to me we should have the matter settled and have a tender for this printing, as called for by Dr. Thorburn's resolution of last year. But, are we to send out and get tenders from the various journals for the publishing and sending of a free journal to the profession ? What Dr. Williams has said is perfectly true, that we want to do the business of this Council above board, and we want to do nothing here but what we want the profession to know, and we want the profession to know what is done here as soon as possible ; but Dr. Williams' argument that in sending a free journal we do get this communication to the medical men sooner is not borne out by the facts. I am sure that scarcely any member of the profession could be satisfied with the little dribble we got last year, waiting on for six or seven months before the medical profession knew what was done by this Council. Let us drop altogether that free journal business and direct the efforts of the Printing Committee to the speedy publication of our proceedings, and also urge on the people who take the contract for printing and publishing and sending this Announcement to the practitioners. As Dr. Machell has said, this can be done within four or six weeks ; even if it takes two months we would then have, as Dr. Williams desires, the report of our proceedings in the hands of the profession while it is fresh, and before it gets old and stale, as our Announcement of last year was when it came to the hands of the profession. I can see no reason why, if we leave alone the publication and sending of a free journal, we cannot place in the hands of every medical man in this Province the proceedings of this Council in the course of at least two months (and that I think would be far more satisfactory than the method adopted in the past) and let us cut loose from this publishing business altogether. I think it is derogatory to this Council to have any journal posing itself as the official or quasi-official organ of this Council. I do not think we should go into that business at all. Let us now, while we are here, settle this principle, shall or shall we not continue to perpetuate the sending of a free medical journal to the practitioners of this Province ?

Dr. SANGSTER—I have only a few short remarks to make ; I wish to say that I thoroughly agree with what Dr. Britton has been saying. It appears to me that there is a tendency here, as on other occasions, to put the cart before the horse, and the impression seems to prevail that it is the business of the Committee on Printing to instruct the Council, but I think it is the business of the Council to instruct the committee ; and I think it would be absurd to let this go to the Printing Committee and then come back here, wasting all the time we have already devoted to it, and have us go *de novo* over the whole business again. I claim it would be a great loss of time, and I hope, therefore, that Dr. Brock's amendment to the amendment will not be entertained, and that we may be permitted without further loss of time and consequent expenditure of money to proceed to a vote upon the question.

Dr. BRITTON—After having listened to the discussion that has taken place, my convictions regarding the propriety of issuing a free journal have not been changed one particle.

Dr. WILLIAMS—Nobody could expect it. It has been your stand for years.

Dr. BRITTON—Yes, but I do not think I have been prejudiced at all in the matter. I would not feel very much inclined to take credit to myself for changing my views year after year, although anybody should feel free to change his views when he feels he is incorrect. As I said before, I have not changed my views in regard to the advisability of issuing a free journal. I might give a good many reasons for that. I know in the discussions that have taken place, in the public press especially, there has been a good deal of reference to the remarks made in the journal published by the company that did our work ; and no matter how much we may disclaim responsibility in connection with those utterances, we cannot throw them from our shoulders completely ; that is an utter impossibility, for the reason that part of the contract entered into between the Council and those who did the printing for the Council was that a free journal should be issued and sent to the profession throughout the country, which constituted it at least a quasi-official journal. We have absolutely no control over the utterances of this journal ; we do not know who may be the editor of next month's journal, and we do not know what sub-editor may edit the following issue ;

we do not know what his views may be ; we are not consulted ; there is no committee appointed by the Council to be consulted by the editor of the journal, yet we forsooth are held responsible for what that journal may say. In addition to that, I take it, it is an unbusinesslike way to do things, and it is unfair. In having a free journal issued and our business transacted in that way, we do not do as straighforward business men ordinarily do ; it is not a straightforward business transaction. We are entering into a sort of speculation, and that certainly is derogatory to this Council. We are also guilty of an act of unfairness towards vested interests ; there are other journals published in addition to the journal that may be doing our work, and some of those other journals have worked in the interests of the profession for many, many years. It has been said that the medical journals have not taken sufficient interest in the proceedings of this Council to publish them ; but, sir, I know that for many years a full report was given—that is, a report of the minutes—and it was only when the special circumstances arose which made it appear necessary, some years ago, that the profession should know every word that transpired in this Council chamber that a resolution was introduced that a stenographer should be employed and the profession be given full information as to what the Council were doing. We for many years were utterly ignorant and oblivious to the fact that there was occasion for the profession to know all that we did ; yet we have blamed those journals, blamed all the journals, because they did not do what we did not think was necessary to be done. It is only a few years ago that we thought it necessary to do this, and that was on the occasion when a radical change was being made in the curriculum, and I think it was Dr. Bergin who introduced the resolution. It is very necessary the profession throughout the country should be in close touch with the Council ; everybody will admit that ; just as necessary as it is that the public at large should know fully the proceedings that take place in our local Legislature or in the Federal House at Ottawa. There is no necessity for having the proceedings published in any journal, and there is no objection to having them so published ; but there certainly is an objection to entering into an agreement with any journal that our proceedings shall be published. Let the journal publish the proceedings if it desires. If the proprietor of any journal thinks it is going to magnify his journal in the eyes of the medical community and render it more interesting, he is at liberty to publish them ; but we have no right to allow that to be part of an agreement, because if that be part of the agreement, that means we are paying something for it. It may be represented in a certain way that it costs him more to do the printing than we are paying him for it ; he may say that, and he may make it appear so, therefore the publishing of the proceedings in the journal is really a gratuitous matter, and the issuing of a free journal also is gratuitous, in a way ; that is, we are paying nothing for it. But I say, so long as those two items form part and parcel of the agreement equitably, we must say we are paying for it in some way. I think myself that perhaps it would be a mistake to refer this to the Printing Committee, unless the Printing Committee will report in a very short time, say to-morrow. If that can be done, I think there would be no great objection to referring the matter to the Printing Committee, because that committee knows pretty well, I think, what the views of the Council are ; and when the recommendation comes from the Printing Committee, if there is necessity for further discussion, I suppose it can be discussed then. As there appears to be a diversity of views regarding this matter, and the three or four or five gentlemen who comprise that committee in the space of an hour's session can discuss the matter fully among themselves, therefore I have no objection to referring my motion to the Printing Committee, provided that the Printing Committee be instructed to report to-morrow morning.

Dr. BROCK—I claim my right, as mover of the amendment to the amendment, to reply to Dr. Sangster. No one has claimed in this Council a greater right of full and free discussion before this Council than Dr. Sangster himself. Dr. Sangster used the argument that after this report returns from the Printing Committee if we commence discussing it, it will take a great deal of time, but I think the common sense of this Council will recognize we have discussed it pretty fully at present and any resolution which may be brought in will be very quickly settled. I think it was very bad taste in the first place to place ourselves on record that no matter what the evidence may be before the Printing Committee they should be debarred from bringing in a report which is their opinion, and not only their opinion, but an opinion based on the facts presented. There are certain facts that may be presented to that committee ; the possibility is that tenders may be submitted ; the journals in this city may be prepared at once to give us full satisfaction with regard to the publication of the discussions in this Council immediately ; if so, the Printing Committee will be able to direct us in such a way that we can settle the question immediately. In my amendment to the amendment I have the words " the Finance Committee's report ; " that can be amended by leaving out the words " Finance Committee." But I think it is very important for us to know how we stand financially. We were in a very bad position this time last year, but we may be in a much better position this time this year and we may be able to spend a little more money in having our report sent out. I think it would be well that the amendment to the amendment should be carried.

2

Dr. BRITTON—I would suggest that it should be referred with instructions to the com-mittee to report to-morrow morning or, at all events, as soon as possible.

Dr. WILLIAMS—I want to say a word or two to the amendment to the amendment. That is simply passing over the principle for the time being, and it leaves it, after the committee reports back to the Council, to be re-discussed. It is doubling time on the work ; when it comes back it will take no less discussion probably than it has taken to-day, and I agree with the remark made by Dr. Sangster that the Council should settle the principle.

Dr. BARRICK—Hear, hear !

Dr. WILLIAMS—And then, when it goes to the committee, the committee simply carry out the details. I think that is the correct principle, and of course, believing that, I shall have to vote against Dr. Brock's amendment, because I believe the Council must settle the principle in any case and the committee only the details. Under these circumstances I stand by my resolution that I think the Printing Committee should have an opportunity to ascer-tain what the cost will be, and when they have done that and reported to the Council, to say we will either continue that or we won't ; but let as settle the principle now.

The President put the amendment to the amendment, and on a vote having been taken declared the amendment to the amendment lost.

The President then put the amendment, and on a vote having been taken declared the amendment lost.

The President then put Dr. Britton's motion, and on a vote having been taken declared the motion lost.

Moved by Dr. SHAW, seconded by Dr. HENRY, That the by-law to amend By-law No. 70 be now read a first time. Carried.

The by-law received its first reading.

Whereas power hath been granted to the Medical Council of the College of Physicians and Surgeons of Ontario to fix the amount to be paid its members and officers, under Sections 12 and 13 of the Ontario Medical Act, be it therefore and it is hereby enacted :

That Clause 1 of By-law No. 70 be amended by striking out the words "$12.50 per diem for days necessarily absent from home," and inserting in lieu thereof the words "$10.00 per diem for each day's actual attendance at the Council during the annual session."

Moved by Dr. SHAW, seconded by Dr. HENRY, That the Council do now go into Com-mittee of the Whole for the purpose of the second reading of the by-law to amend By-law No. 70.

The President read the motion.

Dr. SHAW—It will be within the recollection of several of the members of the Council that last year when this question came up I expressed disapproval of the by-law, as then introduced ; and it will also be remembered that when it was brought before the Council it was referred to a large and representative committee of this Council. In now venturing to bring it before your notice, I realize fully that when a question of this kind has been referred to as important a committee as it was referred to last year, composed of some of the oldest and ablest members of the Council, and they having given it their careful con-sideration, their consideration should not be lightly questioned. I do not propose to make a speech ; I can't do that, but I think I will be able to give you some reasons why the by-law should be amended in the lines I have proposed. In the early days of the Council, up to the year 1874, the members of the Council received the small allowance of $5.00 per diem ; in the year 1874 and up to 1880 it was increased to $8.00 per diem ; and in the year 1880, when the Council were becoming possessed of a little more funds, and about the time the site was purchased on which this building stands, the amount was increased to $10.00 per diem with a reasonable amount for expenses ; and you are all aware that about 1887 that amount was again increased by an allowance of $3.50 for hotel expenses. Now, Mr. President, in discussing this question, it is somewhat interesting to note the practice that prevails in other bodies having powers and duties similar to the College of Physicians and Surgeons of Ontario ; and while we should not be guided entirely by the practice that pre-vails in these bodies, yet the information which we obtain may be of advantage in enabling us to come to a correct decision on a question of this kind. I have taken the trouble to look into the allowances paid to the members of the various medical councils of the Provinces of the Dominion ; and beginning with the Province of Manitoba, having duties and powers very similar to our own, I find there the members living in the country, not residing in Winnipeg, are paid $5.00 per day while in attendance at the Council and an allowance of ten cents per mile one way, and the members residing in Winnipeg are not allowed anything. We heard last year a good deal said about the New Brunswick Act. It was cited in the strongest possible terms as a reason why we should impose the annual dues. Now, if we take up the New Brunswick Medical Council Act we find that their powers and duties are very much the same as our own, and we also find that the members of that Council residing out of Fredericton, where the Council meets, receive no indemnity, no sessional allowance whatever, but simply the mileage travelling to and from their places of residence. We find the same practice prevailing in Nova Scotia. The members residing out of Halifax, where the Council meetings are held for the transaction of business, receive a mileage allowance with no per diem gratuity. The same thing precisely prevails in Prince Edward Island. I do not know that I should have gone outside of our profession to obtain cases in support of my contention but for the example which was set us last year. But I feel that I may take up the same bodies that were taken up last year in the Council in bringing another matter before us. I refer you to the Pharmaceutical Association, an old established body, very much better off than we are, with assets in round figures of sixty thousand dollars and a debt of only ten thousand dollars, its business carried on by eight or ten members (I am not sure, perhaps it is thirteen), meeting in session twice a year for three or four days each session ; and we find they carry on their business very much less expensively than we do, although they are in a much better condition financially. The members of their Council for the first twenty-five years of their Council's existence received only $3.00 per diem, with an allowance of four cents per mile for travelling expenses each way ; and last year the allowance was increased to $4.00 per diem.

Dr. MOORE— What association is that ?

Dr. SHAW—The Pharmaceutical Association.

Dr. MOORE—Surely you don't compare them with doctors ?

Dr. SHAW—I didn't compare them with doctors, nor would I have referred to the matter at all if the argument had not been used last year.

Dr. MOORE—When the members of that Council are attending its sessions their shutters are not up on their places of business, but their business goes on as usual.

Dr. SHAW—If it be supposed their time is not so valuable as that of medical men, and if we should not have compared them at all, let me refer to another society, of which the time of its members, I think you will all agree with me, is quite as valuable as the time of members of this Council ; I refer to the Benchers who are elected to represent the Law Society of Ontario. The Law Association of Ontario is conducted by an organization called " The Benchers of the Law Society," all elected, with the exception of two or three members. Their powers and duties are quite as onerous as ours, in fact, more so. They have to deal with the standard of matriculation, the period or term of study, the examinations, the amount of fees that shall be paid by students entering their ranks, and they have in addition to our duties a Law School, to which the Benchers have the duty of appointing the professors to give lectures, they have the appointing of instructors ; they have care of a part of the library at Osgoode Hall; and care of a portion of Osgoode Hall ; and their duties, I understand, are by no means light. As I have said, they are nearly all elected, all with the exception of two or three, and they are composed of some of the most eminent men in the Province of Ontario, and I think that they are quite as representative a body as the Medical Council of the College of Physicians and Surgeons of Ontario ; in that body there are perhaps more eminent men than in the Medical Council. Now, what are they paid for their services or for all the work which they do ; and I am told the work which many of them do is a very large amount of work ? They do not even get any travelling expenses in attending the sittings. They meet from twenty to twenty-five times a year—true, their sessions are comparatively short, and they receive not one cent for all their services in connection with managing the affairs of the Law Society of the Province of Ontario ; while here the Medical Council, managing the affairs of the profession in the Province of Ontario, have received what I conceive to be too large an allowance.

Dr. HARRIS—Perhaps we are not all as rich as you are.

Dr. SHAW—I am a millionaire ; I will admit that. Still, I am not so rich that I refused to take my indemnity last year. Now, pertinent as these arguments are to my mind why this sessional allowance should be reduced, there are other reasons stronger than these why the amount should be reduced. The most important of these is that our financial condition will not permit of us paying out so much money for the attendance at the Council sessions. I have taken a little trouble to look into the financial position, and I can submit some figures for your consideration—figures which are approximately if not absolutely correct. If you take the past five years of the Council since the imposition of the $2.00 annual dues, you will find the revenue of the Council from all sources, excluding assessment dues, is $82,931.72. For the sake of argument, supposing the penal clause had been enforced during this period and every member of the College had paid the annual assessment with the regularity of the seasons—I have excluded in the figure I have just given any assessments that were paid—and if the $2.00 had been paid by every member, it would have given an additional sum of $22,500.00, making a total of $105,431.72 for the past five years. During the same period of time the expenditure has been $103,220.36, leaving a net gain during the five years of $2,211.36, or a gain each year of $442.00. Now, Mr. President, I think we can get more correct information by making the same calculation including the past three years, because I find that during the years 1889–90, 1890–91, 1891–92 and 1892–93 the receipts from fees, and so on, were very much larger than they have been during the last three years. I had a little difficulty in explaining that away, but in talking the matter over with the Treasurer, he thought possibly it was due to the fact that in the fall of 1892—a little more than three years ago—the increased matriculation standard and the increased period of study came into force, and since that time there has been less received from fees for registration and from students, and for two or three years before that there was a very much larger amount received. To my mind, the last three years gives a more correct statement of our financial condition, and if we take those three years, we find the revenue from all sources, not including assessment dues, is $46,159.27. If to this, as I did in the former calculation, we add the full assessment dues for these three years of $2.00 on 2,250 members of the College, it then gives us the amount of thirteen thousand and some odd dollars, making a total revenue, providing that every man had paid his assessment for the last three years, of fifty-nine thousand and some odd dollars ; for the same years the total expenditure was $63,000.00. I am sorry to weary you——

The PRESIDENT—You have gone over your time allowance of fifteen minutes. You have spoken seventeen minutes.

Dr. ROSEBRUGH—I would move that Dr. Shaw be allowed a few minutes' more time to finish his discourse.

The President took the sense of the Council and granted Dr. Shaw leave to conclude.

Dr. SHAW—That would leave a balance on the wrong side of $3,370.86, or an actual loss each year of the last three years of $1,126.00. Now, if these figures are correct, and I believe they are correct, we to-day are running behind at the rate of over $1,000 a year, and I think it is time that we should economize a little more, perhaps, than we did last year ; and it is with that end in view I introduce this by-law. I do not want you to infer that I do not think our services are not worth the amount paid us ; but I think the financial condition of the Council will not permit us to pay so large an indemnity. In framing the by-law, I had some difficulty in my mind as to the amounts I should place in it. A sessional allowance of a certain amount would perhaps shorten our session to a certain extent ; but, on the whole, I have come to the conclusion that if we made it $10.00 per diem for the actual days in attendance it would remunerate us for our attendance here and prevent any actual loss. It was never intended that we should be paid the full compensation for our time and attendance here ; we were never sent here with the expectation we should receive the full remuneration. I look upon the position of a member of this Council as largely an honorary position, and there are plenty of men quite as good as we are who would be quite willing to come here and look after the affairs of the profession in Ontario for a less amount of money ; and apart from that, I think the finances of the Council will not permit of our paying out so much money. I am sorry to detain you so long, and yet there are some things more I would like to have said.

Dr. ARMOUR— I approve of Dr. Shaw's by-law so far as it goes, but the chief objection I have to it is that it does not go far enough. I think there are many reasons why the members of this Council at the present time should forego their sessional indemnity altogether——

Dr. McLAUGHLIN—Hear, hear !

Dr. ARMOUR—In the first place it appears to me that it would be adding greatly to our dignity, as members of this Council, if we were willing to forego it in consideration of the honor the profession has done us in sending us here to represent them. Emoluments of this kind are very much the outgrowth of this continent ; there are very few such in European countries, and where they exist they are very small. In the great countries of Germany and Austria their parliamentary representatives receive what would amount in our currency to from about $1.50 to $3.00 per day ; in France those emoluments vary from $3.00 to $5.00 ; in the Imperial Parliament of Great Britain and Ireland, the peer of all the representative institutions the world has known, such services are given gratuitously. In the United States, which this country and this Council to a considerable extent have copied, the representatives of the people are paid very liberally, but it is not observable that this has conduced to the dignity or the usefulness of these bodies, perhaps the reverse might be said. When you look at this proposal to wipe out our sessional allowance altogether from the view of our present financial stress, which Dr. Shaw has very properly referred to, it presents many prepossessing features. It is a strange coincidence that the cost of carrying this building during the past years amounts to about the same figure as was paid to this Council in indemnity for the last session. It cannot but be a reasonable proposition to such members as are now with us who were responsible for engaging in the enterprise of the construction and maintenance of this building as well as those who are in favor of still carrying it, for I presume they would be willing to forego their sessional allowance that they may indulge in this luxury. The retention of this building gives no satisfaction to anyone save those members here who insist on retaining it. A thorough canvass of the profession shows that it is not desired by the profession and the majority of the profession refuse to pay a tax for it. Instead of resorting to penal coercion to collect a tax from an unwilling profession, why not meet this liability in this way? It may be objected that those who have been and are willing to relieve the Council of its costly maintenance by its prompt sale should not be asked to make the sacrifice in favor of its maintenance; but it may be that those members constitute the most generous part of the Council, for I believe every one of them will vote, not only for this by-law, but for a by-law to wipe out the sessional indemnity altogether in order that penal coercion Acts and the consequent calamitous effects may be avoided and peace and concord reign among us. I will not detain you longer, but I hope when it comes to a test that this by-law or one going even very much further will be carried.

On motion of Dr. Williams, seconded by Dr. Brock, the Council adjourned to meet at 2 o'clock p.m.

AFTERNOON SESSION.

The Council met at 2 p.m. in accordance with the motion of adjournment.

The President, in the chair, called the Council to order.

The Registrar called the roll and the following members were present: Drs. Armour, Barrick, Brock, Campbell, Dickson, Emory, Fowler, Geikie, Graham, Henderson, Henry, Logan, Luton, Moore, Moorhouse, McLaughlin, Reddick, Rogers, Sangster, Shaw, Thorburn, Thornton.

The minutes of the preceding meeting were read by the Registrar, and confirmed, and signed by the President.

NOTICES OF MOTION.

By Dr. GEIKIE—That it be an instruction to the Educational Committee that the Annual Announcement of the Council shall be got ready and mailed to the members of the profession in Ontario not later than August 1st of each year.

COMMUNICATIONS, PETITIONS, ETC.

The Registrar, Dr. Pyne, read several communications, which were referred to the committees.

MOTIONS OF WHICH NOTICE HAS BEEN GIVEN AT A PREVIOUS MEETING.

Moved by Dr. GEIKIE, That the by-law amending By-law No. 39, page 1. be amended by adding after the word "election" on the third line from the top, the words "and in every case each member present shall be furnished with a voting paper for such election."

Dr. GEIKIE—My object in moving that motion is very, very simple. I hold that ballot papers or voting papers should certainly be furnished and a regular ballot gone through with in the election of our officers. It will not take more than two or three minutes to do this, and then no one can find fault with the method of our election; and if the future President has the vote of every man so much the better for him. I have not brought this motion to cause any discussion, because it is so simple and plain that I do not think there can be two views on the subject.

Dr. WILLIAMS—I have a notice of motion bearing upon the amendment of the same clause in the by-law, and I have also a by-law prepared for the purpose of such amendment. I think it will be well to deal with both Dr. Geikie's motion and mine at the same time, and that it would save time to do so.

Dr. CAMPBELL—It is evident there are going to be two or three motions in regard to this matter, and it is possible there may be some others. It seems to me the proper course is to refer it to the Committee on Rules and Regulations, from whom this by-law originally emanated, and let that committee consider it. I therefore move that it be referred to the Committee on Rules and Regulations.

Dr. GEIKIE—On the understanding that it does not mean its death and burial.

Dr. BROCK—I will second Dr. Campbell's motion to refer it to the Committee on Rules and Regulations.

Dr. McLAUGHLIN—It does seem to me in a Council like this, where we are pressed for time, that we should not be asked to undertake any work of supererogation, and if there ever was a work of that kind it seems to me it is this. If you can get a few words of the Queen's English that will indicate more clearly what we are to do than the words we have in our by-law I would like to see them. The third clause on page 1. reads as follows: "The President and Vice-President shall be elected from among the members of the Council, after nomination, by ballot, and a majority of the votes of the members present shall be necessary to an election." How can you put in the English language better and more clearly that in electing the President and Vice-President of this Council they shall be balloted for, and that a majority of the ballots and votes of the members present shall be necessary for election?

Dr. GEIKIE—We saw yesterday somebody didn't understand it.

Dr. DICKSON—The only advantage I see in the amendment to the by-law proposed by Dr. Geikie is that the members shall not be required to furnish their own paper.

Dr. McLAUGHLIN—Looking a little further on in the book at Section 14 I see, "A motion must be put in writing and seconded before it is stated by the President, and then shall be disposed of only by a vote of the Council, unless the mover, by permission of the Council, withdraws it. Every member present shall vote unless excused by the Council." I think the previous clause is perfectly clear that a ballot is to be taken, and that the majority of those present must vote, and that for election a candidate must receive the votes of the majority of those present. If a by-law was to be brought in, a sort of Remedial Bill, to relieve us of our difficulty, we not having a President, in my judgment, and by that remedial bill or by-law you would clothe our friend in the chair with authority to act as President, I would be very glad to harmonize with a movement of that kind, but, as I understand Clause 3, the language seems to be perfectly clear.

Dr. HARRIS—I presume these remarks are directed against me particularly. You, Mr. President, are charged with not being properly elected to the presidency of this Council. If you are not properly elected now, then I presume that I was not properly elected last year ; and I presume, if the last speaker goes on, that we will find that we have had no President for years, simply because we did not comply with his reading of that clause. I do not agree with him. I maintain that yesterday we conducted our election strictly according to the method laid down in our rules and regulations when you were elected to the presidency of this Council. A ballot was taken, though Dr. McLaughlin said no ballot was taken. If there had been two members nominated for the office then there should be a ballot taken all round, as was done in the case of the election of Dr. Thorburn to the office of Vice-President. But we never had yet a contest for the presidency, never had yet to pass ballots around to elect a member to that office ; it has never been required. The method followed yesterday has obtained in this Council over and over again, and I maintain that the method is perfectly right. If Dr. McLaughlin wished to object yesterday when a motion was put that Dr. Bray cast a ballot, why did he not get up and nominate some other member ? No, he would not do that, he just simply arose to obstruct—perhaps it is unparliamentary to say that he rose to obstruct the business, but it nevertheless was obstructing business all the same, and he should not have done it.

Dr. SANGSTER—I rise to a point of order. I object to any gentleman using the word "obstruct" in a case like that. Dr. McLaughlin got up in order to make the business conducted in this Council conform to the method in which the business of similar bodies is conducted——

The PRESIDENT—What is your point of order ?

Dr. SANGSTER—My point of order is, it is not in order for any member to get up and charge another member with obstruction.

The PRESIDENT—Dr. Sangster's point of order is well taken, and I think Dr. Harris will withdraw the objectionable word.

Dr. HARRIS—I do not think Dr. McLaughlin is an obstructionist, and I do not think I should have used that word, and I will withdraw it, for while it did rather annoy me at the time, I do not now think he did it intentionally at all. However, I do think that our course yesterday was perfectly right, that our President is properly elected to the chair, and that my ruling yesterday also was perfectly right ; and I also want to say that I do not think our by-law needs amending at all.

Dr. SANGSTER—Mr. President, I would like to ask a question through you of Dr. Harris, just in order to put before you what is my view upon the matter. Supposing things had been so that I had attended that caucus the night before last, and I was apparently cordially en rapport with the other members there present, and I agreed with those present that Dr. Rogers should be in that chair, and supposing that I, having in my heart animus against you, got to my feet and moved that you should be President, as Dr. Bray did, and then, in accordance with what is said to be the usage of this Council you had deputed me to cast a ballot ; and supposing that I had cast that ballot against the nominee, as I presume I would have a right to do, because you have no right to know positively how I am going to cast a ballot, what would be your position under those circumstances ?

Dr. HARRIS—Do you ask me the question ?

Dr. SANGSTER—I am speaking to the President.

The PRESIDENT—You ask me the question, and I suppose I will have to answer it. The answer must be this. You have one nominee, and if Dr. Bray in this case had cast a ballot for a person who was not nominated, that would not be an election.

Dr. McLAUGHLIN—Supposing he had marked "nay" instead of "yea ?"

The PRESIDENT—I say in that case if Dr. Bray had cast a ballot for any other person than the one nominated it would not have been a ballot, and there would be no election ; the ballot would have to be cast over again. That is the answer to that question.

Dr. WILLIAMS—The change I wish to make in the clause is a little different one to the one taken up, and I think would settle the point we are dealing with effectually, while I am getting at it for a different purpose. The amendment I want to put in is to strike out the words "after nomination" and put in "without nomination ;" that would be my amendment. If "without nomination" were put in there, it would make it absolutely clear that a ballot must be taken all round in every case. I think it would have another very material advantage and that is, that the man who wished to be President would not be put in the humiliating position of being obliged to ask somebody to nominate and second him. By my amendment, if you put in the words "without nomination," it allows every member of the Council to vote for just whosoever they please, and whoever gets the majority of votes comes to the front. That, I believe, would be the correct solution of the case, and would be the proper amendment. I think if we went into Committee of the Whole on Dr. Geikie's amendment and mine together, we would effectually settle the whole matter in a few minutes.

Dr. GEIKIE—My reason for proposing my amendment is, there is a question in my mind that I cannot answer now satisfactorily, it is this : Can any one member of the Council casting a ballot be regarded as the Council giving a ballot ? I do not think so.

Dr. HARRIS—I think it can be done in that way. If the Council by resolution directs a member of this Council to cast a ballot for the Council, I think that is the Council giving a full ballot.

Dr. MOORE—When we are at this ballot business I think we had better fix it so as to have no more trouble. What is the object of a ballot ? Is the object to have a secret ballot ? If we use a ballot such as we have now, we might just as well have no secret vote, but hold up our hands in the ordinary way. I voted against this ballot years ago and had it staved off for one year, and I think now if we are going to have a secret ballot, we should have a ballot box and vote with white or black balls. What is the use of writing a name on a piece of paper and sending it up to your scrutineers or your Registrar ? They know how you are voting, if they know your handwriting. Let us have a ballot box and then we can vote secretly if we want to.

Dr. McLAUGHLIN—The motion of Dr. Williams covers different grounds from those I anticipated it was going to cover, and it will meet the difficulty. It seems to me that if we discussed this further we would still have different views ; the late President would still think he is right, and I would think I am. I think we had better adopt Dr. Williams' motion and have this discussion ended.

Dr. CAMPBELL—I am not satisfied with either the proposition of Dr. Geikie or that of Dr. Williams. I would like to have our by-law amended in this way, " Provided that where only one candidate is nominated, he shall be declared to be elected by acclamation." That is the way I would like to have it. There are two propositions already in, and you now have mine, and I think for that reason it would be well to refer them to the Committee on Rules and Regulations and let them report, when we can adopt their recommendation or vote it down.

Dr. THORBURN—I quite approve of the action of the President, Dr. Harris, yesterday. I have for a number of years attended meetings of public institutions where votes have been taken for the election of the presiding officer, sometimes where there have been hard expressions used and where there has been strong opposition ; but invariably, where only one candidate was nominated or proposed, it was held to be in the power of the meeting to appoint some person to cast a single ballot. It was quite in order to nominate another person, and then a vote would be required. I know that the mode adopted yesterday is the universal usage, and I am almost surprised that Dr. McLaughlin, a man who is well posted in these things, should object to it ; for, while he may prefer his own view, he knows that this is the way it is done.

Dr. SANGSTER—Where everybody wishes it.

Dr. THORBURN—There might be strong objection to the candidate, but these persons objecting had not proposed another name, therefore a single ballot was considered quite sufficient. I do not like the idea Dr. Williams suggests, that we should mix up and every man put down a name without some consideration ; we might name ten or fifteen men, and prolong the election or nomination for an indefinite period. I think the suggestion of Dr. Campbell is the correct one, but I do not see any necessity of altering our method of casting a ballot at all.

Dr. GEIKIE—You would have no caucus ?

Dr. THORBURN—That is universally the case, I think.

Dr. REDDICK—The rules and regulations provide that there will be a nomination, and they also say very plainly that the President and Vice-President shall be elected by the votes of the majority of those present. Suppose that some other person had got a motion in ahead of the motion that Dr. Bray should cast the ballot, that some person else cast that ballot, and suppose that person cast that ballot against what was generally understood to be the majority of the Council, what would be the result ? I have not the least objection to the election, but I wish to have this cause of difficulty removed, because it looks to me like child's play. I have never seen it in any societies where they pretended to do things according to strict rule or according to anything like rational rule. While I have not the least doubt but that the wish of the great majority of the Council would be sustained, I do think there should be some provision made that if only one candidate is nominated he should be the elected candidate.

Dr. THORNTON—I think the views expressed correspond in a great measure with the experience of the majority of the Council, and I quite agree that we should have a ballot in every case. One of the reasons I had intended to mention has been mentioned by Dr. Reddick, namely, as to the party that is to cast the ballot ; a difficulty might arise as to the person who should cast the ballot for the Council. With regard to the experience of the members of the Council, to get us all of one mind, we would require to make a change, and the representatives of the schools on this Council be sent out into the territories and the rest be appointed, and then we would be all on the same footing. Some of the members of the Council may think objection is taken to this merely for the sake of taking objection. No such thing. When we go back to our constituents, they say, "You voted so-and-so." We reply, "No, that was not my idea at all." "But," they answer, "the thing was unanimous ; there was only one way for you to vote." Then, in this point Dr. Reddick mentions the whole matter hinges on the particular individual that is appointed or voted by the Council to cast the ballot. Those of us that represent territories—I am not casting any reflection on anyone—have a lot of questions to answer and a lot of questions to get round, and sometimes all the ingenuity that we can make use of is required to get around them, and I do not care to have them covered up. I think in every case we should follow the plain reading of our rule, and that the President and Vice-President should be elected by ballot and by a majority of the members present, and that we should take a ballot in every case.

Dr. BROCK—As seconder of Dr. Campbell s motion, I wish to say that I think it would be well for us, as we ask, to refer this matter to the Committee on Rules and Regulations, for the simple reason that if there are any evils connected with the election of the officers, if the caucus system is dangerous to the independent action of the members of this Council, it would be well to have a report from the Rules and Regulations Committee, considering this question and providing some means of getting rid of that evil.

The President put Dr. Campbell's amendment to refer to the Committee on Rules and Regulations, and on a vote having been taken declared the amendment carried. Dr. Geikie's motion was also referred to the Committee on Rules and Regulations.

Moved by Dr. WILLIAMS, seconded by Dr. HARRIS, That the by-law to amend the third clause of By-law No. 39 be now read a first time.

The President read the motion.

Dr. WILLIAMS—This is dealing with exactly the same clause but in a different manner to that proposed by Dr. Geikie.

The President put the motion, and on a vote having been taken declared it carried.

Dr. Williams read the by-law a first time.

Whereas power hath been granted to the Medical Council of the College of Physicians and Surgeons of Ontario to make by-laws establishing rules and regulations to govern the conduct and proceedings of meetings of the said Council, .

And whereas By-law No. 39 makes provision for this purpose,

And whereas it is expedient that Section 3 of the said by-law be amended,

Therefore be it enacted, and it is hereby enacted, that Clause 3 be amended and made to read as follows :

"The President and Vice-President shall be elected from among the members of the Council without nomination, by ballot, and a majority of the votes of the members present shall be necessary to an election ; provided that in case of a tie the election shall be decided by the member representing the greatest number of registered practitioners."

Moved by Dr. WILLIAMS, seconded by Dr. SHAW, That the Council do now go into Committee of the Whole on the by-law to amend By-law No. 39.

Moved in amendment by Dr. CAMPBELL, seconded by Dr. BRITTON, That instead of the Council going into Committee of the Whole, the by-law be referred to the Committee on Rules and Regulations.

Dr. HARRIS—I think, inasmuch as Dr. Geikie's motion has gone to the Rules and Regulations.Committee, perhaps Dr. Williams might let his by-law also go to that committee, to be dealt with and reported on by them. I agree with Dr. Campbell that that committee is the proper place for it.

Dr. ARMOUR—I wish to say that I approve of Dr. Williams' by-law. We are all conversant with this matter, and are as well prepared to vote on it now as we would be if it were threshed out in committee for the next week. For that reason I disapprove of the amendment of Dr. Campbell, and I hope that Dr. Williams' by-law will be referred to Committee of the Whole and passed on by them, and have done with it.

The President put Dr. Campbell's amendment, and on a vote having been taken declared it carried.

Moved by Dr. CAMPBELL, seconded by Dr. WILLIAMS, That it is expedient to amend the by-law levying the assessment by relieving from its operation members of the College of Physicians and Surgeons of Ontario resident in this Province who are not engaged in the practice of medicine, and those members not resident in the Province ; and that the Solicitor of the Council be instructed to prepare the necessary amendment.

The President read the motion.

Dr. CAMPBELL—Mr. President and Gentlemen, you will notice I have put this in the form of a simple resolution in order that the opinion of the Council might be obtained upon the matter involved in the question, for the reason that if it is approved it should go to the Solicitor to have the amendments properly prepared, so that no person may take undue advantage of the provisions of the by-law, while on the other hand, if the sense of the Council is against it, the matter will of course drop, and there will be no expense in preparing the proposed amendment to our by-law. It seems to me that the proposition I have made is one that would commend itself to the sense of fairness and justice of the members of the Council. As I understand, the object of having an assessment at all is based on the theory that certain expenses have necessarily to be incurred in the carrying out of the Medical Act, and those people who receive the benefits of that Act are assessed a certain amount to pay. Whether that is a sound theory or not—whether it is right and proper to collect an assessment or not—is a matter not necessarily involved in this proposition. The ground I am taking is that if an assessment be collected, then it does seem to me there are certain classes of persons who ought to be relieved from the operations of the law assessing them. There are those who have retired from the practice of medicine, some few who have gone into other occupations, some who from chronic disease or from the misfortunes of old age are incapacitated from active work, and who are not practising medicine themselves (though resident in the Province), and are not receiving the benefits of the Medical Act. They are not interfering with anybody else in the practice of medicine. Then there are also those who have removed from the Province, either for a time or permanently, and it does seem advisable that the parties included in these three classes should not be cut off the Register, so that they should remain there and be relieved from the payment of assessments ; that seems to me only a matter of justice. I will admit there is another class I would like to see brought under the same law—some, possibly not many, I hope not many—who have become old, not incapacitated for work, but who have found themselves superseded in the race for business by other more energetic and possibly more competent men, and they are unable to make a living, the little amount they do is a trifle. These men appeal to our sympathies ; they are good men, but men morally capable but physically incapable of doing a certain amount of work. I would like to have seen certain individuals of that class, of whom I am told there are some—for I have no personal acquaintance with any, but I believe there are some few men in the Province of that class—relieved from this assessment, for I believe that upon them the imposition of this assessment really comes as a burden. I understand, however, from the opinion obtained from the Solicitor, that the Council have no power to relieve persons of that class, and that men who are actually practising in the Province must pay the assessment—that if any pay, all must pay. But we have power to relieve the classes spoken of in my motion, and I presume there will not be any objection on the part of the members to offering them this small relief.

Dr. SANGSTER—I concur in what has been said by the last speaker, but I think his resolution scarcely goes far enough. There is a class of practitioners, I do not think a large class, who have been out of the Province for a certain number of years, and who have returned to it, and by the retroaction of our assessment they are held liable for their whole arrearage. In one particular case that I know of, not in my own constituency but in the far east, a man who was out of the Province for fifteen years, returned, and he thinks it a great hardship that during that fifteen years, while he had no benefits from this Council, received no Announcements, no documents, no privileges of any kind, he should now be held liable for the fifteen years' assessment. I think that that is a class that may as well and quite as properly be considered as those that have been named.

Dr. WILLIAMS—Mr. President, in seconding this motion, I beg to say that it is one that fully harmonizes with the views that I have entertained for some time, but I did not believe that the Council had power by a by-law to effect this purpose. I was under the impression that it could only be brought about by getting an amendment to our Medical Act giving the Council optional power by which they could deal with cases of this kind ; but I am informed the Solicitor states we can by by-law deal with these cases. If that is correct, and I have no reason to doubt it, then I fully harmonize with what Dr. Campbell has said. There is a class of practitioners, too, on which Dr. Campbell has not laid much stress—has only spoken incidentally of, and I think it is because of his kind feeling that he did not wish to mention them —I mean the class who are incapacitated by physical infirmity, and there are a few, unfortunately, of that kind, though there are none in my own division, that I have felt exceedingly sorry for. I think of one practitioner who lost his eyesight and is now unable to practice, and is left in rather straitened circumstances. I think that if the Council have the power, as we are advised we have, to adopt a by-law of that kind, it is only right and fair that we should do so. With reference to the class that Dr. Sangster refers to (those that have returned after being absent from the country for some time) it is, in a measure, though not entirely, covered by one of the classes mentioned by Dr. Campbell, that is the class of persons absent from the country; they should not be expected to pay, and should not be stricken from the rolls because of non-payment while absent. Of course, in order to reach the class Dr. Sangster refers to we would have to make the clause retroactive, so that those who have returned after being absent for some time should not be called upon to pay the full assessment. I have no doubt the details can be worked out so that these different classes can be fully and effectually covered.

Dr. SHAW—I was just going to rise before Dr. Sangster did to speak of the class to which he alluded. I know from personal knowledge that there are some practitioners resident in Ontario who are in the position he states. They have lived out of the Province of Ontario and have been members of other bodies, in which they have had to pay an annual fee; and they think it is rather unfair that, while living in another Province or another country, after their return to Ontario after an absence of fifteen or twenty years, they should be obliged to pay the Council dues during the interval. I quite endorse Dr. Sangster's remarks on that class of practitioners, and I sympathize fully with Dr. Campbell's motion in regard to the others.

Dr. BRAY—Mr. President and gentlemen, I quite agree with Dr. Campbell's motion, though he rather forestalled me. I was going to bring in a motion of a similar nature. I think all the classes mentioned deserve consideration, including the class Dr. Sangster named, and I think the by-law should be made retroactive to cover these. There is another class of practitioners who live out of the Province that we must make a discrimination against. For instance, there are registered practitioners who have large practices in Detroit and Buffalo and all along the border who come over here and practice occasionally; that class should be made come over here and pay their fees. I know of my own knowledge there are a good many registered practitioners living in Detroit, who are registered here, who often come over and practice here. I think you will all agree with me that those persons should not be included in that class that has been mentioned to-day. That matter came up before the Lambton Medical Association two weeks ago, and I promised that Association to enquire into the matter, but Dr. Campbell forestalled me, and I am very glad it was he who did, for he is much more capable than I am of bringing in a by-law of that kind, and I want to support him, because it is a matter that should be dealt with.

Dr. MOORE—I heartily agree with all that has fallen from the lips of Dr. Williams and Dr. Campbell and the other speakers; but I want to refer to a class spoken of by Dr. Sangster: those who go to the country to the south of us and come back again. I want to know, for instance, in the case of a man who goes over there and stays for six months and comes back again, are we only going to charge him $1.00, or shall we charge him $2.00? He may go there and stay for a year, and then claim to be exempt for that year. I think we should put some limit on it, because in the case of an absence of ten years or five years it would seem a hardship; but if they are to be exempt if only absent for one year or so, it would entail a great deal of work being done by our Registrar. I think that our by-law should state the time that practitioners must be out of the country before this exemption will apply.

Dr. ARMOUR—I fully agree with the object of this by-law, but it appears to me it might be accomplished in another and a better way. Dr. Moore and Dr. Bray have raised objections that may arise out of any general by-law we might pass which would have a great many provisions and conditions in it; I think it would be better, and I know it is usually customary in cases of this kind to move to remit the tax, that the members of the profession in indigent circumstances, or members who have been living outside of the Province, may ask for a remission of the tax when the Council is in session; then the Council may pass a resolution to remit those taxes from year to year. I believe the object would be better accomplished in that way.

Dr. McLAUGHLIN—Would it not be better to leave all these minor details for consideration when the by-law comes in.

Dr. CAMPBELL—I have a letter from the Solicitor addressed to Dr. Harris. I submitted this question to Dr. Harris and I presume he did not wish to take the responsibility of answering that himself, so he submitted it to Mr. Osler, in order that we might know the exact power of the Council. I will read the letter.

William T. Harris, Esq., M.D., Brantford.

MY DEAR DR. HARRIS,—I have your letter of 30th ult., and have read Dr. Campbell's letter and the questions propounded by him.

Having regard to the provisions of 56 Vic., Cap. 27, Sec. 6, empowering the Council to modify Sec. 41a of the Ontario Medical Act, I am of opinion that it is in their power to pass a by-law providing for the remission of fees in the case of a practitioner who is absent from the Province, or who has entirely ceased to practice during one year ; and further providing under certain conditions that Sub-sec. 5 of Sec. 41a shall not apply to such cases.

I am of opinion that the Council cannot make distinctions in individual cases, that is to say, that it is not within the power of the Council to determine that by reason of partial disability, or other circumstances, that it is reasonable that a member of the Council should be relieved from the operation of the section in question.

The result is, in my opinion, that if a practitioner ceases entirely to practice in the Province, he may be relieved of payment of fees and of penalties for not taking out certificate ; but if he practices he must take out certificate and pay the fees.

Yours truly,
B. B. Osler.

Toronto, June 2nd, 1896.

The President—That places the matter before the Council in a very clear light.

The President put the motion, and on a vote having been taken declared it carried unanimously.

Moved by Dr. Hanly, seconded by Dr. Emory, That the opinion of our Solicitor be obtained regarding the possibility and probability of removing malpractice cases from juries and placing the decision in the hands of Judges ; also, how security for costs can best be secured.

The President read the motion.

Dr. Hanly—This is a subject, I think, on which we will not differ much and on which we may be somewhat unanimous, and I also think it is of a good deal of importance, especially to those unfortunate persons of our membership who have been in that boat, and I thoroughly sympathize with them. It is well known to you that juries give verdicts often in direct contradiction to the facts. I am not acquainted with the procedure, but I think there are some classes of cases in our country that are now not placed before juries, but that the Judges are empowered to decide. What called it to my attention was this : In my own neighborhood there is a fellow practitioner who was prosecuted for failure of a result in the case of a broken thigh-bone, and that case has been three times before the Assizes, and is now, I think, under appeal, and the expense to the practitioner has almost ruined him. I do not wish to say much about this question, nor to occupy much time, but I want to open the subject and see if anything is to be done, and get an opinion, and, if possible, make a further movement in the matter to try to secure some satisfactory result.

Dr. Williams—This would have to be done by an Act of the Legislature. The point as to obtaining security for costs has been brought up before. When some of the amendments to the Medical Act were obtained, application was made to the Government to have that matter covered by the amendments to the Act. But the Government objected in the strongest terms ; they said that an Act of that kind would appear like legislation in favor of the class, that is, in favor of the doctors ; and that an action for damages in that way must stand upon the same basis as every other action for damages, and that there could be no special Act put through and justified upon that basis. I fear nothing can be accomplished in that way.

Dr. Moore—I think there is no doubt whatever about that. As Dr. Williams has stated, this matter was brought before the Legislature and the Hon. C. F. Fraser, now dead, took very strong grounds against it because it would be class legislation. It is true, I believe, that at the last session of the local Legislature some cases have been taken out of the hands of juries, such as cases brought against corporations, which I believe are now tried by Judges. I am afraid we would not be able to accomplish anything of that kind even if we went before the Legislature ; when we were before them, very strong opinions were expressed by the Government.

Dr. McLaughlin—I think the introduction of a bill into the House for the purpose of accomplishing that would secure its rejection ; I think it would be quite impracticable to succeed on that line. I think a great many of our practitioners are at fault in not thoroughly guarding themselves against actions, though I admit it is not always possible to do so. I have set many a fracture, and I think the longer I live the better I am able to treat them, but the longer I live the more I am disposed to call in two or three practitioners to have their testimony to the correctness of my treatment and to assume responsibility. I think if practitioners, through the country especially, where little, miserable jealousies prevail, were to live and work in harmony together and cast aside those petty jealousies—not to combine against the public, because if bad work is done the man ought to suffer, but we ought to guard ourselves against people who are not seeking what is just but what is often very unjust. I have no doubt the case referred to by my friend Dr. Hanly was very well treated, but I think the solution of the difficulty is for the medical men of the country to guard themselves by having consultations, and in that way they will not be so liable to have actions brought against them.

Dr. GRAHAM—I would move that the motion of Dr. Hanly be referred to the Legislation Committee when one is formed.

Dr. HENRY—Before that motion is put I wish to know what the question is for ; is it to get the opinion of counsel ?

Dr. HANLY—That is what is asked for.

Dr. HENRY—If what you ask for cannot be got without legislation it would be better to refer it to the committee ; we cannot get an opinion from Mr. Osler without paying $15.00 or $20.00 for that opinion.

Dr. HANLY —The question as to security for costs has not been touched on now.

Dr. McLAUGHLIN—That question has been up and has been discussed in the newspapers and by others, and they have not been able to effect anything in respect to that.

Dr. CAMPBELL—I think if we refer the matter to the Solicitor for advice it will show that the Council realizes that injustice has been done, and that we are anxious to do all we can. Then if the Solicitor informs us that we cannot do anything, there is no harm done, and we have shown that we are anxious to relieve practitioners who are suffering in this matter.

Dr. HANLY—I bring this forward at the solicitation of the Medical Association of my district. I am satisfied that the question should be referred to the Legislation Committee for them to take such action as may be deemed proper.

Referred to the Legislation Committee.

The PRESIDENT—Dr. Geikie gave notice of motion to have his name taken off the Committee on Complaints.

Dr. GEIKIE—That is not a motion ; it is simply a request that my name be struck off the Committee on Complaints, for I shall not attend the meetings of that committee.

ENQUIRIES.

Dr. SANGSTER—I desire to know whether any member of this Council received during, or subsequent to, our last meeting, opportunities of revising and correcting the speeches that were delivered by him in this Council chamber last year.

The PRESIDENT—I am not aware that any did.

Dr. SANGSTER—Did you yourself have any opportunity of revising ?

The PRESIDENT—None whatever.

Dr. SANGSTER— And I understand no gentleman present had any such opportunity ?

The PRESIDENT—I can't say as to that ; that would be a personal matter between him and Dr. Orr.

Dr. SANGSTER—I suppose I may take silence to be a negative answer to my question.

Dr. HARRIS—Perhaps I, as retiring President, might be expected to answer that. So far as I am personally concerned I had no opportunity to do anything of that kind, and did not do anything of that kind. Does Dr. Sangster mean statements taken down by the stenographer and published in the report?

Dr. SANGSTER—Yes ; I mean opportunities to correct the speeches made.

Dr. HARRIS—So far as I am aware I do not know of a single case where any member of the Council had an opportunity to revise his speeches. As Dr. Sangster will remember he asked me the question, Had the Printing Committee or any one else the power to instruct the stenographer to cut out or change anything, and I answered that no one had that power but the Council. I am not aware of any single case where anyone went to the stenographer and asked him to make any changes, and I am sure, as President of the Council, that I did not do so.

REPORTS OF STANDING AND SPECIAL COMMITTEES.

Dr. HARRIS presented and read the report of the Board of Examiners.

To the President and members of the Medical Council of the College of Physicians and Surgeons of Ontario :

GENTLEMEN,—I beg leave to report that as President of the Medical Council and chairman of the Board of Examiners, I inspected the Examiners' and Registrar's schedules, and I therefore report on the result of the professional examinations held in Toronto in September, 1895, and in Toronto and Kingston in April, 1896.

For the Primary examination in September, 1895, 38 candidates presented themselves, of whom 19 passed and 19 failed, the percentage being 50 per cent.

For the Final examination in September, 37 candidates presented themselves, of whom 23 passed and 14 failed, the percentage being 62 per cent.

In April, 1896, 133 candidates presented themselves for the Primary examination, of whom 79 passed and 54 failed, the percentage being 60 per cent. passing.

For the Final examination 123 candidates presented themselves ; of this number 88 passed and 35 failed, 72 per cent. passing.

The number of each candidate with the number of marks obtained on each subject will be found in the schedule of the Registrar, the number of marks in each case being taken from the schedule of the Examiners. The Registrar's schedule so prepared has been inspected by me and certified correct.

The examinations were as practical as possible. In Anatomy, wet and dry preparations were used of the whole human body; the viscera, bones and models.

In Pathology, Histology and Therapeutics, microscopic and gross specimens were used.

In Chemistry, practical work was required in the laboratory.

In Medicine and Surgery, clinical examinations were held in the General Hospitals in Toronto and Kingston.

In Midwifery, Medical and Surgical Anatomy, the subject, models and instruments were used.

The members of the Board of Examiners have been requested to submit any recommendations or suggestions they might be disposed to make in connection with the examinations, and no response has been received.

All of which is respectfully submitted.

WILLIAM T. HARRIS, Chairman Board of Examiners.
June 9th, 1896.

Dr. SANGSTER—I would ask Dr. Harris if the Examiners in marking the papers put the value of each answer in red chalk on the margin, thereby fulfilling the requirement made by the Committee on Education at the last meeting.

Dr. HARRIS—I have referred the matter to the Registrar and he informs me that the Examiners marked according to instructions, giving the number of marks in red chalk in every instance, and that they were furnished with pencils specially for that purpose.

Dr. SANGSTER—Is there any means by which the Registrar could, without any serious labor, give us an intimation of how many were registered during the year outside of those who were registered through the examinations.

The REGISTRAR—There has not been one put on the Register this year except those that took the examinations.

Moved by Dr. HARRIS, seconded by Dr. BRITTON, That the report of the chairman of the Board of Examiners be referred to the Committee on Education. Carried.

UNFINISHED BUSINESS FROM PREVIOUS MEETINGS.

The PRESIDENT—Dr. Shaw's motion may now come up.

Moved by Dr. SHAW, seconded by Dr. HENRY, That the Council do now go into Committee of the Whole for the purpose of reading a second time the by-law to amend By-law No. 70.

Dr. GEIKIE—Is it in order to move an amendment?

Dr. ARMOUR—A motion to go into committee can not be amended.

The PRESIDENT—I will rule that under our rules a motion to amend can be made.

Dr. GEIKIE—I move in amendment that the by-law settling the allowance be so changed as to allow nothing to members of this Council, wherever they live or wherever they come from, in the shape of expenses or anything else ; that they shall do the work absolutely gratuitously.

The PRESIDENT—That is not an amendment, and I cannot accept it.

Dr. GEIKIE—I think it will increase the dignity of the Council before the public.

The PRESIDENT—That is not an amendment ; the motion is that the Council go into Committee of the Whole.

Dr. GEIKIE—I would not have done it, but you gave me permission ; that is my motion and I will move it at the proper time.

Dr. WILLIAMS—This is a motion to go into Committee of the Whole. There are two ways of dealing with it ; you may vote it down here, or you may vote to go into Committee of the Whole and then amend as the Council decides ; but if you are wholly and totally opposed to it the way is to vote it down now ; if not, go into Committee of the Whole, when you may amend it as you see fit.

The President put the motion and called for a vote.

Dr. MCLAUGHLIN—Do I understand that if this is negatived it puts an end to this motion?

The PRESIDENT—Certainly.

Dr. MCLAUGHLIN—In that case I wish to ask liberty to say a few words before you submit the motion. When corporate bodies or private individuals find their financial condition is not very safe, if they are wise and hope to live through any financial depression, they must begin to curtail expenses. The Council are going back year by year, they are not going forward, and if we are actuated by wisdom in my judgment we ought to do something to cut down this enormous increase in expenses in connection with the sessional indemnity or payment of the members of this Council, which this last year has almost doubled anything that existed in previous years. I think, Mr. President, we would not act wisely if we go on during this session and take out of the funds of this Council, if the money is to be found there, another $4,189.49, or possibly more. I do not harmonize with the by-law ; I agree with Dr. Geikie personally, and I want to be understood as meaning exactly what I say. There are men possibly who may say—I do not know that there may be found any in this Council, but possibly some outside—that this is simply claptrap, and that I am making this proposition for the purpose of securing popularity in my division or in the country. That you may understand that that is not true I want to tell this Council that I have no intention of being a candidate for re-election. I was brought out contrary to my wishes by the unanimous voice of the people of my division, so unanimous that when a gentleman entered the field to oppose me—the returning officer appointed by this Council— he was unable to get twenty names in that whole division, to be nominated. I have given my friends notice that I have no desire to return to this Council ; I would rather retire to private life and to the practice of my profession. Therefore, what I am now saying is not claptrap, and I mean exactly what I say when I express my opinion that every member of this Council ought to render his services during the present financial depression gratuitously to his profession. It is an honorable thing to be a representative of a noble profession like ours, and I am perfectly willing to do it free of charge. If that cannot be done my next proposition would be, and I am not willing to go beyond it, to grant to each member an indemnity of $50.00 per session. I think that would enable us to have a little remuneration and to cover our expenditure ; and if we did that the figures would work out something like this : there are thirty members in attendance here, or may be when Dr. Roome is with us—that would be $1,500.00. The railway expenses last year were something over $500.00 I believe, covering two rates, to and from the city. I think if we manage our time economically we may not have to go home, and therefore the expenditure in connection with travelling may be limited to $250.00, making together $1,750.00. Last year the session cost $4,189.00. Deducting this $1,750.00 from that sum we have a saving to the Council of $2,439.00. I claim it is the bounden duty of this Council to economize in every direction. The city of Toronto here is in debt and running into debt, or running behind, and what are they trying to do ? I do not say how far they are succeeding, but there is an effort on the part of the City Council to curtail expenses. And, go where you will, you see the same tendency on the part of all corporate bodies where they are acting wisely. Banking concerns are finding they have difficulty to make both ends meet ; and all over the country they are endeavoring to curtail expenses, and the number of their employees is being diminished, and I say the Council ought to make an honest effort to reduce their expenditure. Therefore I say the motion to go into Committee of Supply should carry in order that we may give this by-law a careful consideration, and if goes into Committee of the Whole I shall move to have it amended either for us to do away with the sessional indemnity altogether or, if that should fail, to give to each member $50.00 of an annual indemnity.

Dr. SANGSTER—I strongly disapprove of killing a proposition in that way, because the effect would be to kill, too, a proposition that aims at the reduction of the expenditure of the Council. I do not like the by-law as it is proposed, although I think it is a step in the right direction ; it reduces, or attempts to reduce, the per diem allowance to what we proposed it should be last year. But I personally am opposed to a per diem allowance ; I would very much prefer a free service on our part, as Dr. McLaughlin suggests, or a sessional indemnity, say of $50.00. A sessional indemnity of $50.00 would cover our incidental expenses of being here and would leave a margin of some kind, but l do not think under the circumstances that prevail now we should expect or accept more than that. The Council's strong box is troubled with an aching void ; there are several leaks in its bottom, from which things are escaping——

A voice—Fistulæ.

Dr. SANGSTER—Yes, there is not only a main vent emptying into this corner lot, but there are several fistulous openings surrounding ; one running into subsidized journals, another into too expensive examinations, another into very large per diem allowances, another into large salaries, into extravagance, into $300.00 speeches, and several other fistulous openings of that kind. Propositions looking to the closure, or partial closure, of any of these exhaustives by knife or ligature or any other process seem not to command the attention of the Council ; they do attempt to plaster over the openings by words, but they are only to be stopped by deeds, and I think the time has come when a stoppage of some kind is necessary. Some of our friends say that our constituents do not want us to do the work for nothing, and I have heard others say if the profession is not prepared to recoup them for the outlay in time and money they are quite willing to resign and let some others take their places. I do not think, under the circumstances, that the profession would be probably very fastidious about accepting our services for nothing, especially in the present empty condition of the treasury, and considering the services we render the profession are practically not of much value. It may be questionable how far the profession could assign any substantial value to the services we render to the profession in this Council as at present conducted ; and if any of us were unwise enough to resign because of too low remuneration being received, or because of the absence of all remuneration, I do not think our constituents would meet with any great difficulty in getting, in any constituency, a dozen or a score of men quite as able as we are who would be perfectly willing to do the work for the honor and for nothing beyond it ; for it is an honor to represent a hundred and fifty or two hundred of our fellow practitioners in this Council, and I think we should not only esteem it an honor but should show we esteem it by showing a willingness to reduce the money we receive. I do not suppose any of us came to this Council under the impression that we would receive any pecuniary advantage from doing so. I know that we, not resident in the city, all understood that our acceptance of the position would result in financial loss. I do not conceive that we are going to have as short sessions in the future as we have had in the past ; our membership is one-fifth larger, and the Council is no longer a mutual admiration society, as it was when every meeting of this body was a love feast, and taffy pulls were the order of the day, and the presidency was the glittering prize to the most amiable and least long-winded and least tenacious, and personalities and long speeches were at a discount.

Dr. BRAY—I wish they were now.

Dr. SANGSTER—At that time the whole business, or the main business, of the session consisted in preparing and applying a strong atropine collyrium to the eyes of the profession so as to enable it to properly see the real estate and tax business, and perhaps manufacture a new solution of cocaine and apply it to its conscience whenever it becomes restive on the questions of coercion, and extravagance, and overcrowding. Now, to use a trite saying, *nous avons change tout cela*, we have here a somewhat lively opposition troubled with a pestilent itch to dip beneath the surface of things and to know why things are as they are in this Council and not as they ought to be. We have a small but a very stalwart opposition which may not be hypnotized and cannot be coaxed, or whispered, or coerced into line. We have a number of men here endeavoring to correct what we think is done wrong in the interests of the profession, and we know our rights and mean to maintain them ; we are quite content to keep within the limits of rule and regulation, but we insist that we shall be permitted to express ourselves moderately and correctly and rationally on any subject that may come up. When there was no opposition in this Council, when it was all government, there was no real fighting, there may occasionally have been a sham battle, but it was with button foils ; but now, if I may so express myself, we are fencing with sharpened points, and we mean business, and business means the consumption of time, so that it is vain to expect you are in the future going to limit your Council sessions to five days. You may count upon a session of seven days at the very least, and seven days with the intervening Sabbath—because we were told distinctly last year that if you had to sit over Sunday the members would expect payment for that day—would mean eight days, and eight days' session would cost the Council, at our present rates, in addition to two travelling expenses, $3.000.00 ; while, on the other hand, a sessional indemnity of $50.00 a member would make the whole coast $1,500.00, so that if we can go into it and amend the by-law to that effect, if we do not amend it so that we should give our services gratuitously, we shall at least save this Council annually $1,500.00 and if the session is prolonged much, as it would inevitably be prolonged if the government is as long winded and tenacious as it was last year, the saving to the profession would be twice or thrice $1,500.00. We know profession is cheap, but it has been customary for the members of this Council at times to profess a great deal of anxiety to relieve the profession from the annual tax, which is regarded by so many of us as vexatious and odious, and unconstitutional and unnecessary. Now, here is a practical mode of reaching the difficulty ; we do not expect to carry our friends the appointees and the homœopaths completely in our attempt to change the mode of paying the members so as to reduce the expense to a half or a third of what it is at present, but it certainly will be a curious thing to see how the elected members vote so as to keep this matter from going into committee, and in that manner to choke it off and stifle it. While I think the arguments in favor of the proposed movement to make it a sessional indemnity instead of a per diem allowance, or to make the service free, are strong on the ground of economy, yet there is another reason which appeals to me very strongly on behalf of supporting that contention ; I conceive that either free services or a sessional indemnity would largely conduce towards thorough debate and well-considered legislation. All through last session whenever discussion tended to touch any of the special privileges of certain classes in this body, so as to remove or tend to remove customs that were expensive or otherwise, a very determined effort was made to choke off discussion on the plea of expense, and if that failed then an attempt was made to place the odium of continuing the session, and thereby increasing the expense, upon the opposition. We are quite content to allow our constituents to judge us in that matter. We know, as I have said, our constitutional rights, and we mean to insist upon their being observed. We intend to express ourselves on every question that comes up, and we are not going to be prevented from asserting our claims by any threat that upon us will be thrown the onus of continuing the length of the session and thereby increasing its expense. We do not propose to have any of our number fed upon starch for a month and being deprived of any opportunity of obtaining *taka diastase*, which would digest the starch and prevent flatulence, and then come to this Council pregnant with a gentle zephyr which, for want of vis-a-tergo, took five mortal hours for delivery ; but while we keep within the limits of the fifteen minutes we claim to be heard——

The PRESIDENT—You must also keep within the lines of debate ; you are away from the subject before the chair.

Dr. SANGSTER—I bow to your decision, but my opinion is I am speaking within the subject. I will not speak much longer ; I will close with one remark. If there is any reality, if the members of this Council are sincere in their expressions and desirous of lessening the expenses of the Council, they should give practical evidence of that desire by helping us to go into Committee of the Whole and pull down the annual expense of the session. If the members of the Council are not willing to do that, cannot see their way clear to do that, the only other alternative will be to be less tenacious themselves and not to place a premium on flatulence.

Dr. HARRIS—I want to say this, and I think the majority of the members of the Council feel as I do, that we have had this subject up long enough and it is pretty near time we took a vote on it. This playing to the grand stand, to use a baseball or lacrosse expression, by gentlemen getting up here and putting themselves on record before their constituents, posing here as great economists, we all understand. It is done because it goes in print and is circulated about ; they are endeavoring to make it appear that we are the men who are putting the profession to expense. But who put the profession to expense last year ? These very men who have spoken for this motion are the ones. Who are doing it now ? These very men. I would be ashamed to stand up here in this Council, as Dr. Sangster has, and occupy the time of intelligent members by taking as he has talked and yet has said nothing ; there is nothing in it at all. We all know that and I trust you will take a vote on it and not allow this motion to go to Committee of the Whole.

Dr. BRAY—I believe Dr. Sangster was a member of the committee that considered this subject last year and took up a great deal of time and brought in a unanimous report which this Council adopted towards the close of last session, and now at the very commencement of a new session, Dr. Sangster and those with him try to upset this work that has already been done. I would ask who was responsible for the expenditure of this money in connection with the last session ? Who was responsible for all the long-winded speeches that Dr. Sangster speaks of ?

A voice—These men.

Dr. BRAY—They had a good representation on that committee, and they did not take exception to amount to anything, yet this year, almost at the very commencement of the session, they try to undo what we did last year, and I maintain that that is squandering money for no good at all. Dr. Sangster says, What will our constituents think ? I can tell him what my constituents think. My constituents have told me that we are not paid half enough, and that they were willing to pay us a great deal more. I feel satisfied if I were to vote for this by-law or any by-law to reduce the indemnity of the members I would be voting contrary to the wishes of my constituents. Dr. Shaw may be perhaps in a little different position because he is of the opinion that his services are not worth $10.00 a day, and perhaps he fears his constituents have the same view as he has on this matter. I am very sorry to see any member of this Council put such a low estimate on his time and attainments, because just as we value ourselves are our constituents apt to value us. Gentlemen, I do think that a great deal of the discussion we have had is nonsense, and for my part I do not intend to occupy your time further than to say I think it is childish to endeavor at the opening of this session to undo and negative what it was last year unanimously decided upon to do.

Dr. THORNTON—With regard to this matter of indemnity, speaking for myself, I do not propose for one moment, although I am in favor of economy, to do anything that would virtually disqualify the poorest member of the profession from representing his fellow practitioners in this Council (hear, hear), and I say if we have to come here to do the work of the profession for nothing there are many of us that certainly would be in all justice and all reason disqualified. (Hear, hear.) On the other hand, I am in favor of all reasonable econ-

(To be continued.)

omy and I have always thought that a sessional indemnity was the only way you could get at the matter. (Hear, hear.) Further than that, on the other side of the question, the idea that certain parties on this side of the House are, or a section of this chamber is to be held responsible for the prolongation of the session of last year I resent at once, though I will admit that we were here last year an unreasonably long time and we incurred a fearful lot of expense—I felt it at the time and expressed myself on it. But why did we go home from this Council chamber to return at a future date? It was because the committees had not reported, and we could do no further work in this Chamber until the committees reported. Go back to the position of those committees and you will see that in every committee the parties alluded to as prolonging the session were not only in a minority, but they did well if they had a single member on any committee ; therefore they did not control those committees and consequently Dr. Harris' remarks with regard to the prolongation of last year's session are entirely out of place.

Dr. HARRIS—I do not think so.

Dr. BRITTON—The charge has been made that certain committees were responsible last year for the prolongation of the session, for our going home and returning at the end of a week or ten days.

Cries of "Question, question."

Dr. BRITTON—I rise to a question of privilege——

The PRESIDENT—You have a right to speak.

Dr. BRITTON—As I said before, the statement has been made that the session of last year was prolonged, and unnecessary expenditure incurred because the committees had not done their duties——

Dr. THORNTON—No. I said a great amount of expenditure. I didn't say, "unnecessary expenditure."

Dr. BRITTON—The inference would be drawn by any reasonable or sensible man that that was what you meant ; one could draw no other inference ; you were not speaking in a conversational, but in a criticizing tone.

Dr. THORNTON—No ; I was speaking to Dr. Harris' remark.

Dr. BRITTON—I speak regarding my own committee, the Educational Committee. I think it must be acknowledged by every member that was on that committee last year—and the personnel this year is very much the same—that there was more work brought before that committee than had been probably in the last fifteen years (hear, hear) and I think it will be endorsed by certain members who are called by themselves the "opposition"—I do not wish to use that term—I think Dr. McLaughlin and Dr. Sangster will both corroborate me when I say we had an immense amount of work to do, and my co-laborers worked hard and well to get the work through ; and I know that I sat up to two and three o'clock almost every morning through the session of that committee and in the interim of the week or ten days ; and this year, for that very reason, anticipating possibly the same amount of work, and knowing it was too much for one person to do, no matter what his physical capacity was, I declined the position of chairman, until it was very kindly suggested by certain members of the committee that a sub-committee should be appointed to assist me in doing this work. It must be obvious to all present that it was a very unfair charge for a member to make so far as the Educational Committee were concerned, and I think the other committees carried forward the work as well as they could. I do not know that I have stated heretofore, but I will say it now, that there were certain members in this room who were given to carping and speaking on little technicalities that did not amount to as much as a tinker's curse. I could name one of those members, a gentleman that raised a row here that lasted for half a day, and there was so much done in the way of scavenger work that eventually it was an open secret that those who acted as the scavengers were glad enough to go, or propose to go to certain of the leading papers in this city to suppress the language they had used and to keep it hidden, that they had done what was an imprudent and unwise thing.

Cries of "Names, names."

Dr. BRITTON—I am not called upon for a name. Every member of the House will know who I mean.

Dr. McLAUGHLIN—Is that parliamentary language?

The PRESIDENT—I think Dr. Britton will withdraw the words "tinker's curse."

Dr. BRITTON—I will use the words "tinker's condemnation." I do not want to take up your time, because it costs us $70.00 or $80.00 an hour for our discussions here (I perhaps have spoken ten minutes) and I am not going to speak any further, for I think I have exonerated myself and my committee ; and I think I was perfectly justified in standing up for my own honor, dignity and integrity.

Dr. SANGSTER—I rise to a point of privilege. We have been charged here with being the cause of the length of last session. The charge was openly made by Dr. Harris that our speeches were the long speeches of the session ; and in anticipation that Dr. Harris or some other body might make that charge, I have made a calculation which I will state, and which is open to verification by any member of the Council who has the Announcement before him. If you will take your Announcements and count the lines appropriated to the speeches of the five Defence men, Drs. McLaughlin, Armour, Thornton, Reddick and myself, and take the speeches made by the present President of the Council, by Drs. Britton, Williams, Moore and Campbell, you will find that the aggregated speeches of the five Defence men come to rather less than 4,400 lines, while the aggregated speeches of the five gentlemen named come to 4,800 lines, or one-eleventh more. I hope Dr. Harris will take note of this and feel rather ashamed of what he said.

Dr. HARRIS—I do not retract anything that I have charged, and I believe it to be true that they obstructed the Council right through the session last year.

Cries of " Question, question."

Dr. McLAUGHLIN—There have been some very hard words used by four or five of us here, and I rise to a question of privilege. I want to express my extreme regret that these unkind words should have been introduced into the chamber ; I am sorry we should spend, this little half hour in the use of such language. So far as misconduct on my part in the last session is concerned, I cannot look back and see that I was guilty of any impropriety in the course that I pursued. I do not know that I did anything that any member could truthfully apply the word " scavenger" to. We came here to discharge a certain duty and we have endeavored to discharge that duty. You will all confess there were a good many irregularities going on in this Council before we came here that have been rectified——

Cries of " No, no."

Dr. McLAUGHLIN—I think when the profession know what we have done that such language as Dr. Britton has applied—but I won't refer to that further, because I understand he has withdrawn it, but we cannot discuss questions here openly and quietly if the use of such language as we have listened to to-day is permitted, and I hope this will be the last.

A voice –On both sides.

Dr. McLAUGHLIN—Yes, on both sides.

Dr. THORBURN—Speaking on behalf of the Finance Committee, and one or two other committees, I want to say that any cause of delay was not attributable to us. It may have been to some extent due, perhaps, to the desire on the part of one or two new members to know more about our affairs than they already knew, that made them very anxious and oftentimes delayed our meetings very much, but as far as we were concerned there was no unnecessary delay.

Dr. SHAW—I think I have a right to make a remark or two. Without any desire to delay the Council I want to say in the first place that I am exceedingly sorry if by the introduction of this bill I have created a little unnecessary feeling on the part of the members of the Council, either on one side or the other. I regret that anything of that kind should be the result of a bill introduced by me. I am aware there are many ways of reducing the expenses of the Council ; one way would be to make the Council just about one half as large as it is. Without going into details, it seems to me that is a serious question, and one which must come up at an early date. The Council is too large, it is unnecessarily large——

Dr. BRAY—That is not the question.

Dr. SHAW—When I sat down before and listened to the early remarks of Dr. Armour, I was under the impression I would get some support for my proposed amendment to By-law No. 70, but I find now that I stand entirely alone on this question. My idea is not that we should give our services entirely gratuitously, but we should have sufficient remuneration that there would be no financial, no pecuniary loss to any member of the Council by attending here. The position was always intended as an honorary one, and the amount of money is not a remuneration or fee for our services, but is simply an honorarium. I said I hoped I would get more support when I listened to the remarks of Dr. Armour, although I had no conversation with him on the subject, in one way or the other ; I hoped he would agree with the views I have referred to. I am not wedded, entirely to the terms of my by-law ; my own idea would be $8.00 per day for the days in actual attendance, with a mileage allowance as at present arranged, which in a session of five days' duration would make a saving to the Council of $900.00, and $900.00 every year is a consideration in our present financial condition, and I would be quite willing to go that far. However, I introduced the by-law in such terms as I thought would be acceptable to a majority of the members of the Council. Dr. Bray was kind enough to refer to me a little while ago, saying he was sorry to see me put so little value on my time. I do not put so little value on my time, and I think the citizens of Hamilton, if Dr. Bray desires the information, put as much value on my time as perhaps the citizens of Chatham and the surrounding country may put on his. At any rate I am not ashamed of the value which they put upon my time. My constituents have never spoken to me on this subject, but I have spoken to one or two of my constituents before coming here and told them what my views were, and I think the men who are the best men in the constituency quite agree with the idea that we should not have a full remuneration for our time here, that we should simply accept an honorarium. I have no desire to bring this up for the sake of playing to the grand stand. My friend, Dr. Harris, whom I have known for twenty years and more, will give me credit for something else than that, because he is an old friend of mine, and I know he would not say quite so strong words about me when he reflects. I might say now, that I am not playing to the grand stand at all, and whether the Council will give me credit or not for being conscientious in bringing this matter up, I have brought it up because I believe it is in the interests of this Council and in the interests of the profession. I believe that to begin to curtail our expenses we should begin at the fountain head.

Dr. WILLIAMS—I have not spoken on this by-law perhaps for the reason I have a great deal of sympathy with Dr. Shaw in introducing this by-law ; I am aware that last year when the Council came to what seemed to be a unanimous position on the subject that Dr. Shaw, while he did not take active opposition, did not feel at the time that he was just perfectly satisfied with the matter. When it was brought up here a good many of us thought an amendment might be brought about in some way, and it was referred to a Committee of the Whole and from them to a special committee, and after that special committee had discussed the matter from one standpoint and another they arrived at a certain conclusion, and that conclusion was finally embodied in a by-law and was adopted by the Council. While there might be certain views in that with which I do not feel harmonious myself, some that I think might be amended and might be changed, yet the committee agreed, making concessions on one side and the other, that they would come to a certain report ; they made that report to the Council and the Council adopted that unanimously, and having done so I feel disposed to stand by the position the Council took until we have the matter further investigated and see further reason why we should make some change. We have not found that reason yet ; our Finance Committee has made no report to the Council to show us in a better or worse position than we were at the time we adopted that by-law last year, and before we should be asked to change from that and take a step lower or any other step, we should know there is a good and sufficient cause for that beyond question. I do not sympathize very strongly with Dr. Sangster in the views that he has expressed, and I want to say this, that Dr. Sangster or any other member who wishes to be a reformer, and who wants to get his views to prevail in the Council, should not first have insinuated improper motives to all the other members of the Council. His correct method, if he wishes to make a success and to be a reformer, is to put his views in such a reasonable and plausible way that they will commend themselves to the whole of the members of the Council. There are gentlemen here that are quite as anxious to further the interests of the Council as Dr. Sangster is ; but when he gets up and makes one insinuation after another, attributes one evil motive and another evil motive in rapid succession, he cannot hope that the Council will willingly accept what he suggests as an improvement. I object in the strongest terms to Dr. Sangster or any other member of the Council using insinuations of that kind. I hold, no matter who the man here is, we have a right to treat him as though we believed he was honest in his motives, and I do not think that when the doctor uses such terms as that a member was "insufficiently ductile," and terms of that kind, he is using the proper expressions to members of this Council. (Applause.) I object in the strongest terms, and I think if reforms are sought they cannot be secured in that method, but I believe that, as some of the leading politicians in this country say, you can secure by mild methods what you cannot drive out of the Anglo-Saxon. I do not propose to consider this question any further, for the Council have had it discussed in various ways. I may say frankly that if you went into Committee of the Whole I might be prepared to vote for some change that might be brought about in that by-law ; but it is a question now whether it will ever get to the committee. It may get to the committee, but the way to get it to the committee is not to attribute wrong motives to the Council ; that is the means by which it will be killed, and every time you want to kill a resolution you must get up and insinuate that other members of the Council are not acting honestly and fairly. I do not know that Dr. Sangster intends always when he uses strong language to be particularly harsh in it. Sometimes a man may do that without knowing that he is putting so much spice into his remarks. I will excuse such a man. I admit that sometimes when I get just the least shade warm myself I may put items of spice in that were stronger than I thought, and perhaps Dr. Sangster does the same ; and if he does I think if some of his friends, some whom he believes to be his friends, would call his attention to it he might make it a little more mild ; and if he did so the points he suggests would find a great deal more favor with men who are constituted after the ordinary type of human nature. (Loud applause.)

Dr. Moore—Mr. President and gentlemen of this Council : This discussion has lasted quite a long time, and I think it has now cost the Council about $282.00 for this little folly, this little explosion of wind.   While I have no desire to find fault with the generosity of members of this Council, yet if Dr. Shaw's conscience is pricking him because he has taken $4.50 a day too much last year——

Dr. Shaw—No.

Dr. Moore.—Surely he can refund it and then his mind will be free again ; and if my friend Dr. Armour finds that the $112.00 and better which he got last year is pricking his conscience, he can refund it and go on this year and not take anything for his attendance. I do not see why, if a man finds he is rich enough, and he is generous enough and loves the profession enough to give his services free, we should find any fault with it ; and if Dr. Armour sees fit to give his time for nothing he is at perfect liberty to do so, and I am satisfied the Council will not find any fault with it.   Dr. McLaughlin can act in the same way.   Dr. McLaughlin says he is not playing to the grand stand, but he also tells us he is not coming back again.   Dr. McLaughlin will be only two sessions longer here, and he is also in a better position than some of us because he has his practice, and besides a nice little office that brings him in a little something while he is away, while with the majority of us "the shutters are up."   Dr. McLaughlin, under these circumstances, could very well afford to do for two sessions without the little indemnity.   But my friend, Dr. Sangster, likes an indemnity, a little indemnity : $50.00 will do him.   I want more than $50.00.   I think everybody wants more than $50.00.   I do not think the profession expect us to come here and sit here for one or two weeks without being paid.   I say if these gentlemen want to give their services free let them give them free, but the rest of us that do not feel like that can vote as we see fit on this motion.

The President here put the motion, and on a vote having been taken declared it lost.

Dr. Sangster called for the yeas and nays.

The Registrar took the yeas and nays as follows :

Yeas—Armour, Dickson, Hanly, Henry, Machell, McLaughlin, Reddick, Sangster, Shaw and Thornton—10.

Nays—Barrick, Bray, Britton, Brock, Campbell, Emory, Fowler, Geikie, Graham, Harris, Henderson, Logan, Luton, Moore, Moorhouse, Rogers, Rosebrugh, Thorburn and Williams—19.

MISCELLANEOUS BUSINESS.

Dr. Williams—I have a proposition written out in the form of a notice of motion, that I would like to be permitted to put in as a notice of motion, so that it will go to the Educational Committee.   I do not think it will take any time or cause any discussion.   It is that it be an instruction to the Educational Committee when revising the Announcement, to omit the names of all matriculates and the names of those who have a first, second or third year or primary standing, and also the names of those who have obtained their membership through examination, and to substitute in lieu of those the names of all who have become registered since the publication of the last Register.

Moved by Dr. Bray, seconded by Dr. Moorhouse, That the rules be suspended to allow this to come in as a motion.   Carried unanimously.

The President read the motion.

Dr. Williams—You have heard the motion read and I will explain what the purpose is in a few minutes.   What I want to accomplish is this.   You have here a long list of matriculated students, followed by a list of names of first year's standing, and a list of second year's standing, some in the third and then the primary standing ; and then you turn over and find a list of those who have become practitioners by examination.   I conceive that those names in the Announcement serve no good purpose whatever, and it is my suggestion that those be all eliminated from the Announcement, and that in their place we should put in the names of those who have become registered after the last Register was issued, so that in our Announcement we would get a full list of all the registered practitioners after the date of the last published Register.

Dr. Barrick—This motion appears to me to be so reasonable that we ought to pass it without any further discussion.   It would be an advantage to the Printing Committee in getting their tenders if they could relieve the person tendering from putting all those names in.

The President—Should this not be referred to the Printing Committee rather than to the Educational Committee, Dr. Williams ?

Dr. Williams—The Educational Committee deal with the Announcement, and if this passes here it becomes an instruction to the Educational Committee, and the other committee know about it, it becomes a matter of knowledge to them, so it doesn't matter which committee gets it.

The President put the motion, and on a vote having been taken declared it carried unanimously.

Dr. CAMPBELL—I would ask permission to introduce a matter at this stage which could be referred to a committee at once, and it is something that does not commit the Council to anything. I did wish to give notice of motion, and when the matter came up for consideration ask that it be referred to a committee, but my idea now is if there is any objection to it from the Council, that it be referred to the committee now. It is to amend By-law No. 39, by adding to Rule 3 the following : " And provided further that should there at any time be only one candidate in nomination, he shall be declared elected by acclamation." I wish to move the reference of this to the Committee on Rules and Regulations, that they may consider it when considering the other matters referred to them which have a bearing on the same subject.

Dr. DICKSON—You might further add, in the event of three being nominated, that after the first ballot the one having the least number of votes should be dropped.

Dr. CAMPBELL—I will do that. If there is no objection I would like it to go to the committee.

The President put the motion, and on a vote having been taken declared it carried unanimously.

Dr. McLAUGHLIN—I do not want it to be understood that I am agreeing with the principle.

The PRESIDENT—No. This is simply referring it to the committee.

On motion of Dr. Armour, seconded by Dr. Harris, the Council adjourned to meet at 10 o'clock to-morrow morning.

THIRD DAY.

THURSDAY, June 11, 1896.

The Medical Council met at 10 o'clock a.m. in accordance with motion for adjournment.
The President, Dr. Rogers, in the chair, called the meeting to order.
The Registrar called the roll, and the following members were present : Drs. Armour, Barrick, Bray, Britton, Brock, Campbell, Dickson, Emory, Fowler, Geikie, Graham, Hanly, Henderson, Henry, Logan, Luton, Machell, Moore, Moorhouse, McLaughlin, Reddick, Rogers, Rosebrugh, Sangster, Shaw, Thorburn, Thornton and Williams.
The minutes of the previous meeting were read by the Registrar, confirmed, and signed by the President.

NOTICES OF MOTION.

Dr. GRAHAM—That a committee consisting of Drs. Campbell, Moorhouse and Reddick be appointed to furnish regular and daily reports of the proceedings of the Council to the public press.

Dr. CAMPBELL—To submit a by-law amending By-law 69, in accordance with the resolution on that subject adopted by the Council on the 10th inst.

Dr. GEIKIE—That for the remainder of the session, in order to enable the Council to finish all necessary business by Saturday next and thereby reduce the cost of the session, members will be restricted on the time of speaking to ten minutes, and the introduction of matters irrelevant to the discussion will be considered out of order, and therefore not permissible.

Dr. GEIKIE—That it be an instruction to the Educational Committee to amend Clause 9, Section 3, page xi. of the Annual Announcement by substituting the word " fifty " for the word " sixty " in the first line of the said clause ; also to change the pass percentage in chemistry, theoretical and practical, from fifty to forty, so as to enable students to devote more of their time to the study of anatomy, physiology, histology and materia medica.

COMMUNICATIONS.

The Registrar read a communication from Dr. O'Reilly, Superintendent of the Toronto General Hospital, inviting the Council to visit that institution ; and a communication from B. H. Lemon, who was erased from the Register for unprofessional conduct some five years ago, asking to be reinstated on the Medical Register.
The latter communication was referred to the Discipline Committee.

MOTIONS OF WHICH NOTICE HAS BEEN GIVEN AT A PREVIOUS MEETING.

Moved by Dr. ARMOUR, seconded by Dr. SANGSTER, That the advice of Mr. Christopher Robinson, Q.C., be had on the following : 1st. Had the Medical Council, at the annual session of 1895, the legal right to assess an annual tax on the medical profession for the years 1893 and 1894, as enacted in Clause 3 of By-law No. 69 ? 2nd. To what proportion of the arrearages of the annual tax which are outstanding at various dates from 1874 to the present time Section 41a of the Medical Act can be legally applied for their collection. 3rd. Are there any members of the medical profession as it now exists exempt from the operation of Section 41a ? Also, that Drs. Williams, Henry, Campbell, Armour and Sangster be appointed a delegation to wait on Mr. Robinson and secure the above advice.

The President read the motion.

Dr. Armour—Mr. President, we had thought, after the legislation of 1893 changing the functions of this Council and placing the penal and coercive measures entirely under the control of the elected members, that one of the chief objects for which the Medical Defence Association was constituted had been remedied ; but the occurrences of last session will make it imperative on us to still take active measures in defence of what we believe to be the common interests of the profession. Then a majority of the territorial representatives came here, I understand, pledged to their constituents against supporting or approving of the penal clauses of the Medical Act ; but so successfully was the matter manipulated in the Council last year that the alternative was placed before them of either foregoing their sessional indemnity or voting for those clauses. It occurred that there were only five territorial members that succeeded in withstanding this pressure at that time, and the result was that the penal clause was re-enacted, the sessional indemnity was forthcoming, and the well-known wishes of the great majority of the profession were ignored. It should be the first duty of those who desire to apply this penal coercion against their fellow-practitioners to know that this Council is acting within its legal rights in making the application of those penal clauses. After the many humiliations to which past Councils have been subjected for illegal acts, I cannot believe that even the most ardent coercionist can desire that there should be a repetition of the former trials and troubles——

Dr. Brock—I rise to a point of order. Is it right for members to read their speeches ?

The President—No. But I think Dr. Armour is not reading ; I think he is speaking from notes.

Dr. Armour—I am not reading; I am refreshing my memory from notes. I was saying that before attempting to execute their penal coercion they should be willing to learn from the best legal authority that they have the right, or to what extent they have the right to do so. It looks absurd to suppose that, when given power by the Medical Act to assess a tax for the current year in which it is assessed, this Council could legally assess a tax for years when the transaction of affairs was in the hands of another Council. There is nothing contained in the suspending clauses of 1893 that would warrant such a presumption. There are important legal points involved in the application of the penal clause, and the Council should not be satisfied with anything but the best legal advice as to their legal right to use it, before attempting to coercively apply it to a rebellious profession. There are many of those who entered the profession before the existence of the Council who believe they are exempt from the tax and exempt from Section 41a. And there are many who believe it cannot be retroactively applied, that is to accounts that existed before the clause was enacted. It may be that it cannot be legally applied to accounts that would, in the ordinary course, be outlawed. The medical men of the Legislature who were induced to consent to its passage did so with the understanding that it would not be so applied, and I understand that the opinion of the Attorney-General was that it should not be applied to accounts of more than six years' standing. It is only reasonable to assume that it is the duty of this Council to procure for the profession the best legal opinion on these questions. And when the members of the profession are assured of their legal responsibility, I am confident it will do much to restore the harmony between them and this Council which it is desirable to have. While it may suit the needs of our treasury to procure funds regardless of the means, it should be beneath the dignity of this body to stoop to means which may be put on a level with blackmailing by others, using penal enactments for the collection of the accounts where such could not legally apply. I trust, Mr. President, there will be no objection to securing this advice and that this motion will pass unanimously.

Dr. Williams—I have listened with some considerable interest, though I admit with some little surprise, to the remarks of Dr. Armour. I think it is within the knowledge of every man in this Council—I must be mistaken, because apparently it is not within the knowledge of Dr. Armour—that Mr. Osler's special advice was taken on this subject and that Mr. Osler wrote out the by-laws under which this Council was to act. (Hear, hear.) Now, Dr. Armour says we want the best possible legal advice; well, gentlemen, it is an open question whether Mr. Osler's or Mr. Robinson's is the best possible legal advice. I will say this, my own conviction is Mr. Osler stands second to no man in this country in his legal opinions (hear, hear) and in his standing in the profession. Now, under these circumstances, Mr. Osler himself, in his own office, having prepared the by-laws for this Council and having sent them up under his special directions, I think there should be no question in the mind of any man here as to whether or not we were within our exact legal authority or right. My opinion is that if there is any person who thinks we are not within our legal right, who thinks we are taking some money from him to which we are not entitled, and who wishes to pit the opinion of some other man against that of Mr. Osler, the chance is open for him. But when we have secured the advice of one who is recognized as one of the best counsel in this country and have got his opinion, I think we ought to be satisfied with that opinion and not take a certain percentage of the money of this Council and cast it away for another opinion which may put us in a divided position, so that we do not know exactly what we are going to do and do not know where we stand. It is notorious that doctors differ ; it is equally true that sometimes lawyers will present things in different shapes, and it may leave the client somewhat in a muddle. Dr. Armour has said that a majority of the territorial men came here pledged against the penal clause. I am not aware whether that is true or not, but I am one of those territorial men, and I know this, that while I saw the majority of the men in my division I did not pledge myself to any position, but I took the position that "whatever becomes necessary that I am prepared to do and take the responsibility. If it is necessary to have a penal clause, then that penal clause shall go in with my sanction." I said, this is necessary and this must be carried out, that if one man pays his fee every other man practising the profession must pay or else stand aside. (Hear, hear.) I hold that it is unjust and unfair, it is dishonest, to take the fees from one part of the profession and allow the other part to go scotfree. If there are some men who are so mean that they will not come forward and pay their fee honorably there should be a law in such a way that they cannot take advantage of the upright men who do stand by their profession. And I hold that to make an insinuation that members of the Council after they came here were hoodwinked is an insinuation that is altogether too strong against the members of this Council and ought not to have been made by a fellow member. (Hear, hear.) Dr. Armour says the present Council cannot assess for debts or collect fees that were due under the previous Councils. Now, I think in this respect Dr. Armour is under a serious misapprehension ; he seems to suppose that this Council terminates every time an election comes about, or possibly every year. I do not think a much greater fallacy could exist ; I think this Council stands exactly in the position that a council does in a municipality, or that a school board does ; it is never dead, it is continuous from year to year ; the succeeding Council is always responsible for the acts of its predecessors and it is a continuous body ; it does not terminate with the end of the session or with the election of new members. That view, as implied by Dr. Armour's expressions, is entirely a mistake. Furthermore, if that was not a mistake we have the Solicitor's opinion on that point, for he himself drew the clause bearing on that special subject. And are the Council going to take upon themselves authority to act in direct opposition to what the Solicitor told us we had a right to do in a matter of that kind ? By acting in opposition to that we would be doing a dishonest thing to those members of the profession who had paid their way all the time and allowing those who had kept their money down quietly in their pocket and enjoyed the benefits of membership to go scotfree, or at the most, as Dr. Armour says, only collecting for the six years, they forsooth wanting to take the benefit of the Act which would allow them to escape by saying this debt is six years' old. Gentlemen, would members of this profession stoop to so mean a thing as that under these circumstances? I think not. Then, it is insinuated that it is something like blackmail, that it shall be beneath the dignity of the Council to blackmail members who are owing for a period of over six years. Gentlemen, I have yet to learn that you can justly charge it as being blackmail when you make a man pay his own statutory debt that has run for longer than six years. (Hear, hear.) If that term can be applied it is a kind of blackmail that is just and honest in this country and ought to go on for all time and make those men who seek to shirk their honest debts, by getting the length of the law, bear their share of their honest debts and responsibilities the same as others do. I think it is unfair to say you will accept the fee from one man each year right along, and use that for the benefit of the profession, and allow other men to lag behind, and then when six years have elapsed, tell them that it is blackmail to make them pay. Gentlemen, that is a morality in the profession that I for one do not believe in. I believe in every one of our members being placed exactly on the same platform, and if I pay my fee year after year, and you pay yours there is no reason why every other man should not do exactly the same thing, providing it is right and proper under the Statutes by which we are governed. Under these circumstances I do not favor Dr. Armour's proposition ; I hold we have got the best legal opinion we can get (hear, hear), and until we have good reason to believe that that is wrong I do not propose to change from it and I will, so far as my vote can, prevent the change. (Hear, hear.)

Dr. GEIKIE—Dr. Williams has very very ably stated in his excellent speech a great many reasons why every man should be treated alike in this matter. I would not think of going over the same ground, although I endorse most thoroughly every position he took, and I am glad to hear him take the stand he has taken. There is another position that struck me since the subject was brought up, and that is, the injurious effect it has outside of this Council chamber to have doctors talking about and trying, apparently, to get out of the little payment of $2.00 a year as an assessment for the maintenance of what is necessary to the dignity and good conduct of the profession. I have had occasion to mention the matter casually to lawyers of good standing ; I have done it just to draw them out on the subject ; and in every instance there was an unconcealed expression of contempt for the smallness of those who, in a profession such as ours, would meanly haggle and wriggle about the payment of a dollar or two a year for the maintenance of the profession. I have no sympathy with that sort of thing whatever. If the tax is a dollar let every man pay his dollar, and if for some reason he has not paid it for some years let him pay it up to the last as well as the first farthing. Even if it is two dollars, that is very little compared with what the lawyers have to pay and what they pay cheerfully and without a grimace, without saying a word, and without any long discussion such as seems to be threatened here, a discussion which, to my mind, is not at all to the credit of the profession.

Dr. SANGSTER—I rise to a point of order. Is it in order to discuss the general question of the payment of the fee when the question before the House is whether a Solicitor's opinion shall be obtained or not ?

The PRESIDENT—I allowed Dr. Armour to digress very very far from the point of his motion ; and I did not call him to order, although I did not think he was right ; therefore having allowed one member the privilege I am per force compelled to allow the same privilege to others.

Dr. SANGSTER—I do not think it should be allowed on the part of any one.

Dr. BRAY—Dr. Sangster thinks this now after Dr. Armour has got his remarks in.

Dr. GEIKIE—I claim I am perfectly in order and that what I am saying is perfectly relevant. I have a feeling of intense shame that a committee of this Council should go regarding such a petty matter and ask either Mr. Osler's opinion or the opinion of Mr. Christopher Robinson. I do not like the idea even of one medical man stooping so as to ask any lawyer, do you think we ought to pay our little annual assessment or not ? Or, if we have not paid it, do you think we ought to be forced to pay it or not ? Pride makes me feel that is an ignominious position for this Council to sanction on the part of even one of its members. (Hear, hear.)

Dr. McLaughlin—It seems to me this question is not a proper subject for discussion, but you cannot allow one member to discuss it without giving the privilege to all.

The PRESIDENT—I granted the privilege to Dr. Armour, who introduced the motion.

Dr. McLaughlin—Yes, and you have allowed other speakers to discuss it, and it is therefore open to others ; that being so, I will say a few words. I regret that a question of this kind cannot be discussed without bringing passion in and charging people with dishonesty—

Dr. MOORE—And blackmail.

Dr. McLaughlin—Yes. I do not approve of any of those expressions ; I am free to admit that. I think in this Council we ought to come up to a fair dignity and discuss questions purely on their merit ; if there is merit on one side and merit on the other let them be discussed fairly and squarely without the introduction of these miserable terms, charging every man who does not pay up his two dollars with dishonesty as has been done ever since we came to the Council. I am just as honest as any man in this Council, and I do not think it is proper to apply this unpleasant epithet ; and I say there is no argument in saying a man is not honest ; that is merely a wild assertion that has no force whatever. In regard to the relative merits of the two lawyers, because that has been brought up, I want to say that no one esteems Mr. Osler higher than I do ; he is a personal friend of my own, and in his own branch in law no man I think can touch him ; but Mr. Osler is not what you might call a constitutional lawyer ; he is not one of those lawyers who pry down into knotty questions such as may be involved in the interpretation of Statutes ; that is not his line at all ; he is a criminal lawyer, and in that line he is without a peer in this Province. Mr. Christopher Robinson, on the other hand, is a gentleman to whom such questions are constantly referred ; he is the one, above all others, who is consulted upon all knotty questions arising out of municipal law, more so than any other counsel. While I make that distinction between the men I make it honestly, because I have had reason to consult on matters of that kind and I know that lawyers in the country go to Mr. Robinson when they want to get the interpretation of such laws as this as well as of municipal laws. I say nothing against Mr. Osler ; I say he is, in his particular line, without a peer in this Province. Coming to the question involved, that is the right of payment of this money or not, the two gentlemen who spoke on the other side characterized the refusal to pay two dollars a year as a mean, little, miserable, nasty thing. If that was the only question involved I thoroughly agree with these men ; if it was only the payment of a couple of dollars it would be a contemptible thing for us to waste one minute of time of the Council in discussing it. I have said before, and I say now, if this assessment is based on principle, based upon sound statutory grounds, I am prepared to support it. I am prepared to do more than give $2.00, to give $20.00 if necessary, to sustain our Council and profession in an efficient manner. You and I have read with more or less disgust, I am sure, during the last six months of the occurrences in the Transvaal ; we have heard there of the Parliament governing and ruling a people without the people being represented in that Parliament ; that the men who pay the taxes in the Transvaal are the most responsible men, the best men intelligently, the most useful men to that country ; and Mr. President, you to-day occupy an analagous position to President Kruger. President Kruger does not represent the people he rules over, neither do you represent the members of the profession of this Province ; you are there not by the votes of the profession of the Province at all but you are there in that chair to-day because of the votes of men who do not represent the profession. This Council is represented in part by territorial members ; these members truly represent the profession, but all the others do not. It is upon this anomalous ground that I have objected to this tax from beginning to end. If the profession of Ontario levied this tax, if they alone had control of the money and the distribution of it, then I would submit to any tax they put upon us. You, Mr. President, last year, and other members of this Council, referred to other bodies such as the Pharmaceutical Society, the Law Society and to other medical societies throughout the Dominion ; but we stand alone in this anomalous position of being non-representative of the profession. True, in the Law Society there are four or five members who are ex-officio members of the Society who never attend, but the great mass—I think thirty-six or thirty-eight members—of that Law Society, the Benchers, are elected ; these others of whom I spoke, the Minister of Justice and some of the Judges, are ex-officio members. Practically, the Law Society is self-governing. The trouble with us is the profession is not self-governing, and so long as this Council remain not self-governing I object to this Council taxing the profession or doing anything with the taxes of the profession ; and I claim that if we tax the profession the profession must have full and plenary power to say what shall and shall not be done with the taxes of the profession, that they shall have exclusive power. That is my ground. If we had that in this Council then I am entirely with you. But the gentlemen who represent the schools, and our homœopathic friends (who only represent a constituency of some fifty or sixty members of the profession while each one of our rural members represents 130 to 150) come here and dispose of this money, take it themselves, and vote it for other purposes. I say that this is not in harmony with the age in which we live ; the age in which we live demands if there is taxation there must be full representation ; and it is upon that principle I have objected to this tax all along. Let us have representation of the entire profession in this Council, and only representation of the profession, and then I will go with Dr. Williams, and I will go with my friend, Dr. Geikie, I will go with this whole Council and say, " levy upon the profession, let the profession levy upon itself as much money as you think proper in order to carry on the affairs of the Council efficiently and carry them on economically." That is my ground. Am I a dishonest man because I stand on sound principle and refuse to submit to these matters I have just objected to ? Will my friend, Dr. Williams, not allow me the right of judgment ; will he not allow me the right to say that that is a sound principle and upon that principle I stand ? The sum of money called for from each individual member amounts to nothing. You say it is only $2.00. I do not care if it was only two cents ; I stand on a sound principle, the violation of which belongs to the dark ages and belongs to President Kruger, a man in the Transvaal, and should not find a place in the Province of Ontario.

Dr. GRAHAM—I do not wish to say anything offensive about Dr. McLaughlin, because he is an old friend of mine, but it appears to me he is laboring under a mistake in regard to this tax being unconstitutional ; he is applying the constitution of Ontario, perhaps, or the constitution of the Federal Parliament, to our constitution. What is the British constitution ? Of course it is the laws that have been enacted for all time, and will be enacted for all time. I consider our constitution is the Ontario Medical Act. The constitution may not be just, it may not be right, but according to our constitution the tax is right. As I say, our constitution is the Ontario Medical Act, and any by-laws that we pass in the meantime. I may be wrong, but I have always thought that Dr. McLaughlin was wrong in applying other constitutions to our constitution. I do not mean to be harsh at all, but I contend if he thinks that this tax is iniquitous, he must go further back than that and change the constitution, and I think he should say no more about the constitutionality of the tax until he tries to change the constitution. (Hear, hear.)

Dr. MOORE—Just a word or two. I do not intend to detain the Council very long. I am going to stay, I think, within bounds—I will stay at all events in Toronto and not go over to the Transvaal ; and I will try and stay with matters concerning this Council and not with matters concerning any other sect or society. The part of this resolution that appears to me the most offensive is the gratuitous insult we offer to Mr. B. B. Osler, whom we have elected year after year as our Solicitor. That resolution asks us now to go outside to Mr. Christopher Robinson, a gentleman for whom I have every respect. If we did that we would be ignoring our own Solicitor, who is the peer of any lawyer in the Kingdom of Great Britain, a man who stands deservedly high, and whose name is a household word all over this Dominion of ours. To offer this gentleman a gratuitous insult is something this Council ought to be above, and I only wish that this motion and the whole discussion concerning it could be obliterated, that our profession and the world should not see that we have had such a resolution brought into this Council, offering a gratuitous insult to the man who has honored us by accepting the position of our Solicitor, a position he did not accept for the emoluments of the office, but because of the respect he had for the profession ; and I tell you he has enabled us to rid this profession of quackery and to raise the standard of and benefit our profession, and the public at large. To say that this man is not able to interpret his own Act seems to me simply ridiculous, and is an insult to the ability and genius of this man whose transcendent ability is acknowledged all over this continent. So far as the constitutionality of this portion of the Act is concerned, we are acting under an Act given to us by the local Legislature, and if our Act is unconstitutional we should go back to Sir Oliver Mowat and the Government and ask them to make it right ; tell them it is not constitutional. We are acting within the Statute, and there is not an act we have performed where we have gone outside of the powers given us by that Statute. I am sorry to see such a resolution as this before this Council, and I am sorry also that such a gratuitous insult should be offered to a man of the ability of our Solicitor ; and I say this idea was born in ignorance, conceived in malice, and I don't know hardly what I should say it was delivered in, if it was not in want of good common sense. I trust that this will be voted down, as it ought to be voted down, and I ask you, gentlemen, to vote it down and not thrust an insult in the face of so eminent a man as Mr. B. B. Osler.

Dr. SANGSTER—Mr. President, is it in order for a member of this Council to say that any act on the part of a fellow member in an argument upon a point of interest to all is conceived in malice ?

Dr. MOORE – I will say "in ignorance."

The PRESIDENT—I do not think it is exactly in order, but I might say in answer to Dr. Sangster's question, that I allowed a great deal of latitude in language here, more perhaps than I ought to have allowed. But I want it understood from this time out that I propose to stop all personalities. (Hear, hear.) Every word that I believe comes within the range of our by-laws as personalities I shall call upon the member uttering it to withdraw. And I am going to ask the members to keep entirely and strictly within the parliamentary rules of debate, and to use no word which may be construed as offensive to another.

Dr. SANGSTER—Mr. President, is it your ruling that the word "malice" is not unparliamentary ?

The PRESIDENT—I will rule from this time onward that it is not parliamentary.

Dr. SANGSTER—Do you rule that it is unparliamentary as to this ?

The PRESIDENT—No, because I have allowed you to use similar words.

Dr. MACHELL—When Dr. Armour commenced to read his motion I felt rather inclined to support it, but before he had finished I felt he had made a great mistake in introducing it at all, and I shall certainly vote against it. I think it would be a deliberate insult to Mr. Osler, and I fancy he would consider it as such, and I am not very certain but Mr. Osler would say to us, "Take your Council matters elsewhere, I do not want to have anything more to do with them."——

Dr. MOORE—He would be quite right.

Dr. MACHELL—He would stand very much in the same light that a medical man does who has been attending a case for weeks and weeks, and whose patient has got on fairly, and then without any reason some person else is asked to step in and make a diagnosis or prognosis, which you will all agree with me would not be fair to the medical attendant ; and for that reason I do not think it is quite fair to Mr. Osler, and I think he would probably resent it. I shall certainly vote against the motion.

Dr. SANGSTER—Mr. President, with regard to the remarks that have fallen from Dr. Machell, I beg to say that if Mr. Osler were to give up the Solicitorship of this Council, I do not think the Council would necessarily be stranded thereby. However, I will touch upon that before I am through, probably. Dr. Graham is evidently a little at sea. He said that what we should attack in this matter is the constitution that we are under, and that while we are under that constitution we must accept all that it involves. I do not think that at all. Constitutions are reformed and remodelled. Our constitution may be such that we cannot approve of it, and it is our duty and our place as rational beings to seek its repeal by constitutional means. That is what we have been doing from the outset in this Medical Defence Association ; but it does not appear to have got through Dr. Graham that that is what we are at. That is the only point for which the Medical Defence Association was formed and for which we have been striving throughout. Now, I am somewhat surprised that this resolution does not commend itself to the members of this Council. I think the concession that it asks for is a reasonable one for this Council to grant, and that, to my mind too, without any loss of dignity or prestige ; and that by so doing it will show a spirit of compliance and conciliation that could not fail to be appreciated by the profession, and which would therefore make for peace. I do not attach any importance to the argument that has been urged on the score of economy. The economy of this Council is so one-sided, partial and spasmodic that it cannot be genuine. It is only when information is sought in the interests of the profession that we are treated to platitudes on expense and histrionics on economy. When it is with the object of bolstering up the very debatable acts of the majority and their obstructive votes that legal opinions——

Dr. BRITTON—I rise to a point of order. Is it correct to use the term "obstructive" vote ?

The PRESIDENT—Dr. Sangster, will you be kind enough to withdraw the word ?

Dr. SANGSTER—Yes, I will withdraw the word. When it is a question about bolstering up the very debatable contentions—the word "debatable" is not out of order—of the majority in this Council by legal opinions of doubtful validity and by $20.00 quasi-legal letters not touching one point of law, but merely tendering to the territorial members in this profession instead impertinent advice as to how they should conduct their business in the interests of their constituents, then the gentlemen who are now so loudly and suddenly eloquent about economy are perfectly dumb. I do not suppose the whole sum involved in obtaining that opinion now asked for would reach $100.00, and it would perhaps not reach $50.00 ; and, under the circumstances, I think that might be money profitably and well expended. We heard last year and on other occasions expressions dropped by members of this Council which showed that the Council have, as a whole, a just dread of law suits and their incidental expenses. Now, it is well known there is a great deal of angry feeling in the profession regarding the points which this opinion is intended to cover. That feeling of irritation has not been allayed ; it has been strongly intensified by the acts of the Council last year in reinstating the coercive clauses of the Medical Act ; and whenever your preliminaries regarding erasures from the Register shall have ripened into deeds, in all probability this Council will have to face not one but many actions at law ; and even though the decisions of the courts should be, as they may be—I am not lawyer enough to determine—favorable to the position of this Council, and if the courts decide that all the Acts and by-laws reviewed were *intra vires* of the Legislature and *intra vires* of this Council, any one of such affirmative decisions, founded as it would be on an action at law, would cost the Council many times $100.00. I think, therefore, provided you are sure of your ground, as you profess to be, it would be a wise thing to obtain this opinion, and to thus stave off possibly some very vexatious and costly law suits by satisfying those concerned that in resisting the tax they have not, legally speaking, a leg to stand upon. I do not sympathize with the remarks made that in seeking this opinion we are offering any mark of censure or want of confidence to Mr. Osler. I conceive that Mr. Osler is out of the case in this matter. The object concerned is not to support, not to confirm the unwavering faith of the Council in Mr. Osler, but to satisfy the unbelieving, to convince the sceptical who are disputing the legality of this tax in some or all of its aspects that they are wrong and that the Council are right. This Council, or rather the older members of this Council, have fixed upon Mr. Osler the paternity of the coercive clauses of the Act. That being the case, that partiality which all parents show to their offspring, especially to their brain progeny, renders Mr. Osler a prejudiced and therefore an incompetent witness ; he is in the position of a juryman who has not only formed an opinion of the case about to be tried, but who has repeated it publicly over and over again, and is therefore on that subject very properly ruled out of court. At any rate, it is clear to all that he is not likely, under the circumstances, to be anxious to pick flaws or to find holes in his own workmanship. If the opinion of Mr. Christopher Robinson were obtained, and it confirmed Mr. Osler's opinion, as very possibly it might do, it would greatly strengthen that opinion. You profess you are quite sure that Mr. Osler is quite right, and therefore I cannot understand why, in order to remove a bone of contention from the profession, you refuse to expend the small sum that is asked for so as to carry the matter outside of the present deadlock that seems to exist between the profession and the Council. I have nothing to say disparaging to Mr. Osler's great ability ; I acknowledge his great eminence in his profession, and I believe that in his own line, as my friend Dr. McLaughlin remarks, he stands unapproached ; but at the same time, I may remind you that it is by following Mr. Osler's advice that Section 41a was obtained, and that this Council provoked and have promoted a rebellion that will never be allayed until it eventuates in revolution. Moreover, I may proceed to say that in legal matters this Council have been in the keeping of Mr. Osler for ten years past, and during the whole of that time they were also forensically brooded over with watchful care by a very distinguished territorial representative who, on account of his eminent legal attainments and knowledge of law, I believe was commonly known in this chamber by the sobriquet of the "Chief Justice" of the profession, and yet, notwithstanding their double legal guardianship and legal nourishment from without and from within, this Council—(not this Council, but the last Council and their predecessors)—were suffered to go on year after year. Council after Council arose, were elected, lived, blundered and died in blissful ignorance of the fact that every year of their existence they were breaking their own by-laws and grossly overriding the several provisions of the Medical Act. Now, I claim that a legal gentleman who did not notice or did not object to the many breaches in those respects that were committed by our predecessors can scarcely feel insulted if intelligent and interested men refuse to swallow his legal opinions, *holus bolus*, without any question. I do think it would make for peace, that it would remove the trouble with most of those who are non-payers if you can obtain from a perfectly impartial and independent source an opinion that the Council are right on these matters. It is well known that among many eminent lawyers the opinion prevails that it was not *intra vires* of the local House to make an Act overriding the Statute of Limitations, especially in the face of the fact that the Legislature consented to that Act in 1891, and consented not to repeal that Act in 1892 upon the distinct assurance—as we have Mr. Meredith and other members of the House in evidence—that there was no intention on the part of this Council to make that principle retroactive in its application. There are many lawyers who deny that a certificate, a diploma, a license to practice medicine purchased thirty or forty years ago, paid for and secured unconditionally from the Dominion authorities, over the signature and seal of the Governor-General, can be revoked and made of no effect at the will of a body created by a local and provincial Parliament. There are many of us who believe that Section 3 of By-law 69, passed last year, was *ultra vires* of the Council. Here is my own feeling about the matter—— I notice you are looking at your watch, Mr. President ; is my time nearly up ?

The PRESIDENT—You are one minute over time.

Dr. SANGSTER—I will sit down at once. I do think you should have called Dr. Geikie to order when he began to encroach on that subject ; he is not technically out of place, but he is in reality, because the Act of 1893 decided that university representatives should have no voice in the reinstitution or the suspension of those by-laws. Last year we suffered Dr. Britton and one or two university representatives to express themselves both during the time that by-law was being considered and before, but I do not think it was good taste for them to do so. The matter is purely within the purview of the territorial representatives.

A voice—That is for voting only.

Dr. BRITTON—My good sense has been called in question just now as to my act of last year when I spoke in favor of the assessment ; and I must say a few words. It is very true that the amendment of 1893 to our Act (as I said last year) paralyzed my arm and I cannot vote in favor of an assessment, but I am very glad that I have an opportunity of saying a few words, and in this connection I think I am not out of order ; I am speaking now on a question of privilege.

The PRESIDENT—You are quite in order.

Dr. BRITTON—It is quite in order for me to go backward a little to see how it came about that I and the representatives of the different universities and schools were deprived of certain privileges which we had formerly ; I shall go as far back as the time that we had a joint committee. The origin of that committee was this, in this Council it was resolved that a committee be appointed for the purpose of conferring with a committee to be sent by the so-called Defence Association. The initiative was taken in this Council, so far as I know ; and in accordance with that a committee was appointed by the Defence Association, and we met in this room. I need not go over the deliberations that took place on that occasion, but I will say this, that it was stated by one member of that committee, after all efforts had been made that could have been made for conciliation by the committee of the Council, that the efforts of the Defence Association would not cease here. This gentleman spoke in a very excited manner, and he used threats ; I think that the threats that he used were corroborated by other members of that committee—I would not say that positively, but at any rate their acts subsequently went to show that they quite approved of these threats. The threats were of this nature, that the Legislature would be approached, that they had already been using their private influence with members of our local Legislature, that they would continue to do so ; that this body was not constitutionally organized because the representatives of the schools should not have any voice in the disposition of the funds of this Council nor in the collection of the funds necessary to carry on their work. I do not think that that gentleman, nor any other gentleman who was a member of that committee, will deny that that course was pursued ; what we saw from time to time, week in and week out, year in and year out I was going to say, in the public press is quite sufficient to convince anybody that that was the line of procedure ; and I know as a matter of fact that members of the Legislature were approached in that way. As I say, the threat was made that the public would be appealed to, that the efforts would not be limited to trying to convince the members of the profession, but that their efforts would be extended in other directions ; that is, to convince the public, and, as I said, to convince the legislators by speaking to them privately. The charge, if not already made, was made very shortly after that, that the School men had managed to attach to them a sufficient number of territorial representatives, and that they had whipped the homœopaths into line, so that they were able to control the deliberations of this body. The School men were an obnoxious class here, they had no right to be here, they were not sent here by those who were paying any fees, and, therefore, they should not even sit here—that the profession should be governed by those elected by the profession itself alone. Now, I say that statement (and I am within parliamentary rules when I say it) that the School men were controlling the deliberations of this body, and leading by the nose respectable men, men of intelligence, men who knew just as much as they what the profession required, men who were looked upon as respectable men in the community, was without a foundation or tittle of truth. That was the representation made to our legislators. I say, then, by unfair means, by using an argument which was not truthful in any sense of the word, certain legislators were influenced, and the result of it was the School men were deprived of using their franchise in the way of determining how much funds it was necessary that this Council should have for the purpose of conducting their affairs in the proper way, and how those funds were to be raised. I say that was unfair, I say it was unjust, and I say it is unfair to-day that the representatives of the universities and colleges have not an opportunity of voting on a question of that kind, no matter what certain few men may think regarding it. I do not know that those men have ever thought of it; possibly they have; if they have, they will pardon me for repeating what they already know. I wonder if it has ever struck them that the large proportion of funds used by this Council for their purposes comes from the students of this country? It has been said by them that I represent the members of the medical faculty of the University of Toronto. I deny any such imputation. What do I come here for? Do I come here for the purpose of looking after the interests of the few individual men, members of that faculty, or looking after the interests of the faculty itself? Do I not come here for the purpose of looking after the interests of the students of the University of Toronto? I say I do; that is my business here. It is my business to see that a proper curriculum is formed; it is my business to see to it that the provisions of the curriculum are observed; it is my business to see that no favors are granted to any other institution; it is my business to see that no special favors are granted to the University of Toronto; and it is my business to stand here and see that justice is done between the schools, and to see that men are properly educated; and I say that the argument of those gentlemen that I am not a representative tax-payer—I will use that term—falls entirely to the ground. This tax is only a small affair compared with our complete and total revenue; it is a comparatively small affair compared with what has come in from the students even during the present year. During the present year we have received from students coming up for the fall examination $1,410.00, and from those who went up for the recent spring examination, $8,505.00, making a total of $9,915.00, and the amount of assessments paid during the year is $7,083.00 as against over $9,000.00, nearly $10,000.00, paid by the students; and forsooth, then, I must not even be allowed to say a word, because I am the representative of a university. I know the ultimate end and aim of those gentlemen who have taken this ground in opposition to the representation of the schools, because they have stated it. When they first started out on their campaign they stated it,—that they would not rest satisfied until the profession was properly represented, and until the schools had no voice in this matter. I am correct, I think, when I make this statement, and I am satisfied it cannot be successfully confuted. It has been stated time and again—it was stated in their original manifesto—it was stated certainly by one of their exponents in some of the letters, that that was the ultimate end and aim——

Dr. SANGSTER—May I just put Dr. Britton right on one point on which he is a little astray? The claim was that the representatives of the universities had a right in this Council so far as education and examination went, but their right to meddle with the government of the profession was what was attacked.

Dr. BRITTON—Mr. President, is my time nearly up?

The PRESIDENT—You have two minutes more.

Dr. BRITTON—Of course I must endorse what has been said by others regarding Mr. Osler's ability. We have had no reason so far to find fault with Mr. Osler's acts in relation to this Council; he has done his work well, and I, for one, can not vote for any measure which would cast a reflection upon a man who is worthy of our confidence. We have a solicitor that I think is the peer of any. No matter what litigation I should be at any time forced to enter upon, I would be perfectly satisfied to put my case in the hands of Mr. Osler, and I think this Council should likewise be satisfied to do so. We have no right to pass over him, and to do so would be really offering him an insult. I can not vote for the motion. There is one other matter on which I wish to speak. I wish to make a correction in the speech, I think, of Dr. Sangster. I inferred from what Dr. Sangster said that Mr. Meredith—the present Chief Justice, Sir W. R. Meredith—manifested opposition to any enactment in this Council which would be retroactive in its character. I happened, not as a member of the Legislation Committee, but on the invitation of Dr. Thorburn, who at that time was the chairman of that committee, to be present at an interview which was held with Sir Oliver Mowat and other members of the Government in relation to the Meacham Bill, which was then before the committee appointed by the House. I recollect very well that Mr. Meredith was present, and that he said very little. Mr. Meredith did say, "Gentlemen, is this thing necessary, or is it not? is this money required, or is it not? Two dollars a year is a very trifling matter; if it is necessary then of course it ought to be paid." But he never took any exception to the fact that we were seeking to collect what had been due, never said a word against it. I have something more to say, too. Mr. Meredith was in opposition, as we all know. I had a long conversation regarding the matter with a leading member of the Government, and he concluded the conversation by saying, "Well, Britton,—(I know him very well)—all that I have to say is that it is a very picayune matter;" and he used some rather forcible expressions, quite as forcible as that.

Dr. ARMOUR—Would you name the member?

Dr. BRITTON—No; I do not name the member. You should be satisfied to take my word. I believe I am an honest, truthful man.

Dr. ARMOUR—I am not questioning your word; I want the information. Do you refuse it?

Dr. BRITTON—I do refuse it.

Dr. McLAUGHLIN—I think it is a matter of customary usage that men shall not make statements and base arguments upon them if they are not prepared to give names.

The PRESIDENT—I shall rule on that matter that it is not necessary for Dr. Britton to give the name. It is not parliamentary practice to give the name, but the practice is contrary to that entirely.

Dr. BRITTON—The subsequent acts of the Government, I think, will fairly convince us that the opinion expressed by that individual member of the Government was also held by his colleagues. I am not going to call anybody names, but I do want to say that I should be ashamed to accept the privileges granted by the corporation of the College of Physicians and Surgeons and to be a member and get all the benefits and pay nothing for them. I pay my $2.00 as a matter of principle and as a matter of self-protection, and as a matter of right to myself. I pay it individually outside altogether of my constituents, and as far as I can, I shall insist upon it, with the exception of those for whom we have consideration as shown in the resolution introduced yesterday by Dr. Campbell, as far as my humble voice goes, that every member of the profession in this Province will pay his honest debts and make a fair recompense for what he receives.

Dr. SANGSTER—I rise to correct some statements made by Dr. Britton with regard to myself personally. Dr. Britton rose to show that I had made a mis-statement with regard to Mr. Meredith, but I do not think he did show it in the least. I agree with Dr. Britton that Mr. Meredith was in favor of Section 41a, and that I heard him in committee say that if the money had to be collected that was the only way to collect it. I am frank enough to say what I heard, but it seems to me Mr. Meredith and other members of the House are in evidence in the reports of the debate to the effect that it was understood that that clause was not to be made retroactive in its application.

Dr. THORBURN—I rise now merely to corroborate what has fallen from the lips of Dr. Britton in reference to the committee at the House. Not only did Mr. Meredith express himself in that way, but nine-tenths of the profession as represented in the House were of that opinion. I also want to say that I quite agree that it is a most contemptible thing to object to a small contribution paid to the support of our profession. There is no other profession in existence that is a corporate body, the members of which do not contribute something to its support; even the mechanic and the laboring man have organizations, and they contribute something to the support of those organizations. I shall vote against the measure.

Dr. BARRICK—I have a very strong feeling against this Council or against anybody spending the time of one session to legislate and the time of the next session to undo what they have done the session before (hear, hear); it was upon that ground that I voted against Dr. Shaw's resolution that he brought in and spoke to yesterday. Last year we settled that matter, and I think it would be a very unwise expenditure of the money of this Council to upset the work we did last year. I am one of the territorial representatives that came to this Council unpledged in any way at all. Every one knows that there has been a bone of contention before the profession for a number of years; every one knows that that bone of contention has been placed under the nose of nearly every practitioner in this Province, until the odor of that decaying bone has been such that every medical man really got disgusted with it. (Hear, hear.) I was very sorry last year to find that this bone had been brought before this Council, and I acted last year in the way I did with a view to having this bone buried, and I was very glad to follow my friend Dr. Williams, and my friend Dr. Bray, in an effort that promised to restore peace and harmony to the profession, and to secure what I fondly hoped would be the last burial of this bone of contention. Last year we said it was right and proper that we should have this clause, but we were willing that the penal clause should be held in abeyance for one year in order that we might restore the good feeling and harmony of the profession, and to see the results thereof, and to be guided by the results of our action in re-instituting this section of the Act. I am gratified to see in the collections last year, amounting to $7,083.00, ample proof and testimony that the course we adopted last year was the proper course to pursue, but I am very sorry to find the bone that we thought was buried last year has been resurrected this year. I cannot give my consent to this motion, but I shall again take the position I did last year and endeavor to keep the bone buried as long as it is possible to do so. Dr. Williams, in his able speech, and the other members who have spoken, have stated the case most clearly, but the strong ground I take is that we should not in one session undo what we have done the session before, but should let it stand for a few years and see how it works out, and I am satisfied if we do so the sore will get less, but if we do not the constant irritation will be sure to make it worse. The only object I can see in getting another opinion upon this matter would be to do what we had to do in the city of Toronto ; we had to bring an expert engineer from England to settle a difficulty here that seemed so plain that everybody thought it was an unnecessary expenditure of public money. Now, if every man in connection with this Council will solemnly pledge himself to bury that bone forever, if Christopher Robinson's opinion is in harmony with what we have done, that is the only reason I can see, and the only good I can see. But if Christopher Robinson's opinion is given, I am just as satisfied, if it is in harmony with what we have done, there will be other members who will want some other opinion next year, and have the same bone resurrected again next year. The only advantage in getting that opinion that I can see would be for every man to pledge that he would be bound, and that he would never again bring that bone before this Council, if Christopher Robinson says the imposition of the fee is right.

Dr. THORNTON—I only want to say a word or two in regard to the nature of the discussion. It seems to me we may discuss this subject to any length on the lines on which we are going and yet accomplish nothing whatever. The first question to my mind is, Are we loyal in our support to this Council ? I, for one, declare my loyalty to the support of this Council. Then the next question that arises is, How are we going to get the necessary funds to carry out our aims ? If we find in the transaction of our business we are incurring losses—you may think I am entirely out of order, but I see no other way to get at it—that necessitate a certain amount of money being in our treasury, the question will arise, Can these troubles be obviated or not ? I twice or three times said last year in this Council that we were continually keeping the cart before the horse. We are doing the same thing now, and it seems to me we are going to have to put our heads together before we ever get it turned round. We may wander all over the field, we may discuss the matter in every shape we like, but unless we settle the one question as to the necessities of this Council first, and the necessary expenses to carry on their undertakings, we will never get the other point settled. Dr. Barrick has talked a great deal about burying this bone of contention ; there is not a member more anxious to bury every bone of contention than I am. I say, and I say positively, that this Council have never buried the bone of contention with a decent burial ; they have undertaken to bury it, but invariably have left one end of the bone sticking out, and until we get away from that mode of procedure I do not see how we are going to settle this trouble.

Dr. HENRY—I regret very much indeed that this resolution has been brought before the Council this morning. I thought last year, after the discussion and the time and attention given to the subject, we would never hear it moved again. I think what Dr. Armour asks for—a special committee to consider this question—is quite unnecessary. We have had, and acted upon, the opinion of Mr. Osler, and in that opinion I have every confidence. More than that, I may say that through the country where I live I find the constituents I represent do not object to the payment of a small fee, but they do object to the coercive character of Section 41a, and that I myself object to strongly ; as I objected to it years ago, so I am prepared to object to it to-day. But I maintain that every gentleman who is a member of the College of Physicians and Surgeons of Ontario should be honest enough and manly enough to pay his $2.00 a year, and I think it would be a great injustice to the men who have paid year after year to get an opinion from another lawyer in the city of Toronto that would let other gentlemen escape. I say every man should pay, or if they will not pay, then those that have paid and have been loyal to the Council should get their money back. I hope the resolution will not carry, and I am sorry we have wasted the whole morning at an expense, I suppose, of $250.00 or $300.00. It is perfectly absurd to talk of economy, and then indulge in such a long-winded discussion as this has been. We have talked about going home on Saturday night, but it seems to me the way we are going we shall be here two weeks, and the Council will have another $4,000.00 to pay, and I leave it to you to say where the money is to come from.

Dr. DICKSON—I have preferred to keep my seat rather than take the floor since I came here, because I have observed that much of the time occupied has been really of no value either to the Council or to the profession. When this matter was brought before the Council this morning it seemed to me that we have been beating about the bush, and are yet very far away from catching the bird. It has occurred to me the wisest course to pursue would be to allow a test case to be brought up ; it would not be necessary that every man in arrears should be at once pounced upon and an action instituted. If a test case were brought up it might be that Mr. Christopher Robinson would be selected to defend, and the probability is that we would thus be able to determine the question finally and certainly ; and the Council, I think, have sufficient good judgment if we lost in that case to refrain from any further action of that kind. It seems to me that is the only practicable way in which we could reach a determination in this case, and it certainly would be a more sensible course than to quietly sneak off and ask an opinion from another solicitor, when we have a solicitor who has been engaged and who, so far as I can learn, has given the utmost satisfaction in the past. There is another point in reference to the remark that fell from Dr. Armour to, which I must offer some reply, and that is, that most of the territorial members, if not all of them, came here pledged to——

Dr. ARMOUR—I said a majority.

Dr. DICKSON—I thought you said all the members.

Dr. ARMOUR—I said I understood a majority.

Dr. DICKSON—I thought Dr. Armour said they were all pledged to vote against the penal clause. I do not know what the other territorial representatives did, but I know that I for one came here perfectly free in that matter. I stated in my circular to the electors (for I was unable to see them all personally, and I had to approach them by means of circular) that so far as I could see it would not be a thing that was likely to be an objection at all ; if it were found that it was necessary to impose a fee that it would not likely be objected to, but to my mind it would be really necessary to impose a fee from year to year.

Dr. SHAW—I rise only to say that it appears it is quite necessary that an assessment on the members of the profession should be made ; and I quite agree with the idea that every member should pay his $2.00 a year. I think it would be quite time for us to take up this matter when a case is brought before the Council, then the Council would be prepared to get a solicitor to defend them, and it is not necessary until then that they should move in the matter. I am prepared to vote against the motion.

Dr. BRAY—I want to say in the first place, I take exception to Dr. Armour's statement as to how I came here, pledged or unpledged. I have always endeavored since this difficulty has arisen between the members of the profession to conciliate, if possible ; and it was I who moved a resolution in this Council for that purpose. Since some of these gentlemen have come into the Council I personally tried to conciliate them, but apparently they will not be conciliated. I have consulted my constituents, and they have approved of my course not only in this matter but in the votes I have given in this Council. Before I came down here last year I laid the matter of the imposition of this tax before them ; and they said to do so ; and I brought a resolution from one of the societies authorizing me to do so. I met that same society a short time ago and they said, "We very much approve of your action in that respect, excepting in one particular, and that is, we believe that every man should pay his fees, and if they do not do so you must put into effect the clause that has been suspended, and unless you do that we will have to send somebody else to the Medical Council." That is the opinion of my constituents, and that being the case I must abide by that, and as a consequence must vote against this motion. My constituents are perfectly satisfied with the method to be used in collecting these dues ; they are satisfied it is necessary and they are perfectly willing to pay it. Under those circumstances I must certainly vote against the motion.

Dr. BROCK—As all the territorial representatives are protesting, I rise also to make a statement ; I never heard a medical man yet object to the payment of that fee ; the only thing I have heard is that they are wondering at our not putting in force Section 41a ; they believe we should take every measure possible, and, as I stated at the last session, that we should leave nothing undone to collect that money immediately ; if we had done so at the last session we would have had all our money in. The discussion in this Council reminds me of a case that was brought before a judge, who when he saw that there was going to be a good deal of discussion, and a great deal of time taken up, and consequently a great deal of money expended on both sides, asked the amount of money at stake, and when he was told it was one dollar, he pulled a dollar out of his pocket and settled the case at once. I think this case could be settled by asking our people to pay down their dollars or have the Defence Association pay for them.

The President put the motion, and on a vote having been taken declared it lost.

Dr. Sangster called for the yeas and nays.

The Registrar, Dr. Pyne, took the yeas and nays, as follows :

Yeas—Drs. Armour, Hanly, McLaughlin, Sangster and Thornton.—5.

Nays—Drs. Barrick, Bray, Britton, Brock, Campbell, Dickson, Emory, Geikie, Graham, Henderson, Henry, Logan, Luton, Machell, Moorhouse, Rogers, Rosebrugh, Shaw, Thorburn and Williams.—21.

Moved by Dr. GEIKIE, seconded by Dr. GRAHAM, That it be an instruction to the Printing Committee that the Annual Announcement of the Council shall be got ready and mailed to the profession as early as possible in August of each year.

The President put the motion, and on a vote having been taken declared it carried.

On motion, the Council adjourned to meet again at 2 o'clock p.m.

AFTERNOON SESSION.

The Council met at 2 o'clock p.m., in accordance with motion for adjournment.

The President, in the chair, called the Council to order.

The Registrar called the roll, and the following members were present : Drs. Armour, Barrick, Bray, Britton, Brock, Campbell, Dickson, Emory, Fowler, Geikie, Graham, Hanly, Henderson, Henry, Logan, Luton, Moore, Moorhouse, McLaughlin, Reddick, Rogers, Sangster, Shaw, Thornton and Williams.

The minutes of the last meeting were read by the Registrar, confirmed, and signed by the President.

Moved by Dr. BRAY, seconded by Dr. MOORHOUSE, That, instead of going into the order of business, the Council do now adjourn, in order that the committees may meet and prepare for the evening session. Carried.

The Council adjourned to meet at 8 o'clock p.m.

EVENING SESSION.

In accordance with motion for adjournment, the Council met at eight o'clock.

The President, Dr. Rogers, in the chair, called the meeting to order.

The Registrar called the roll, and the following members were present : Drs. Armour, Barrick, Bray, Britton, Brock, Campbell, Dickson, Emory, Fowler, Geikie, Graham, Hanly, Henderson, Henry, Logan, Luton, Machell, Moore, Moorhouse, McLaughlin, Reddick, Rogers, Rosebrugh, Sangster, Shaw, Thorburn, Thornton and Williams.

The minutes of the last meeting were read by the Registrar, confirmed, and signed by the President.

NOTICES OF MOTION.

No. 1. Dr. HENRY—For the formation and establishing of a medical tariff for the Province of Ontario.

No. 2. Dr. GEIKIE—In any examination covering four subjects, only candidates passing one-half or more of these shall be credited with the subjects passed. Where the examinations comprise more than four subjects, candidates must pass three or more of these at one time in order to receive credit for the same.

COMMUNICATIONS, PETITIONS, ETC.

None.

MOTIONS OF WHICH NOTICE HAS BEEN GIVEN AT A PREVIOUS MEETING.

None.

ENQUIRIES.

Dr. SANGSTER—It seems to me I have something to enquire about, but I don't know what it is. I will not be brought to a close for want of something, so I will make an enquiry, at any rate. To how many members of the College has the Registrar, since the last meeting, sent a certificate of having paid the annual fee as required by law ?

The PRESIDENT—The Registrar informs me that he has sent to 1,131 members.

Dr. SANGSTER—Were the certificates sent in every case ?

The PRESIDENT—Yes, as a receipt.

Dr. SANGSTER—At our last meeting, the Registrar, I believe, was instructed to enquire as to or to take the necessary steps to procure, if possible, the seals and documents belonging to the old Eclectic and Homœopathic and Provincial Boards of Examiners. Have any steps been taken in that matter ?

The PRESIDENT—The Registrar informs me that he wrote several communications to Dr. Hall, the ex-Secretary of the Eclectic Board, and registered one communication to him,

but has not received any reply.   That is all that has been done in regard to the Eclectic
Board.

Dr. SANGSTER—And in regard to the Homœopathic and Provincial Boards ?

The PRESIDENT—The Registrar informs me that he has not done anything at all with
reference to those, because he does not know who to write to, unless he wrote to the representatives in the Council.

Dr. SANGSTER—Then we are just where we were last year.

The PRESIDENT—I presume it is a very difficult matter indeed to get information
about.   If any member of the Council has any information now which he can furnish, or
has heard of any information and would furnish it to the Registrar, it would help to forward
the matter.

REPORTS OF STANDING AND SPECIAL COMMITTEES.

Dr. BRAY presented and read the Report of the Discipline Committee.

To the President and Council of the College of Physicians and Surgeons of Ontario :

GENTLEMEN,—Your Committee on Discipline beg leave to report that they have had
under consideration the cases referred to them at the last meeting of this Council in June,
1895, viz. : Those of Dr. Parsons, of Coehill, Ont., Dr. J. F. Danter, of Toronto, and Dr.
H. O. Martin, of Toronto.

In reference to the former, although every effort has been made by your committee and
the Detective to serve Dr. Parsons, we have so far been unable to do so.   Your Detective
has visited various places where the said Dr. Parsons has been heard of, only to learn that he
had gone to some other locality, and he finally discovered that he was in Manitoba.   Your
committee did not deem it advisable, owing to the enormous expense it would entail, to have
the Detective visit Manitoba in order to personally serve him.   Consequently no action has
been taken in this case further than to consult our Solicitor in regard to the evidence now
in our possession, which he informs us is sufficient to warrant your committee in going on
with the trial so soon as Dr. Parsons can be served.   Acting on his advice, we have decided
to wait until an opportunity occurs to accomplish this without any great expense to the
Council.   Your committee learned through the Detective a few days ago, that Dr.
Parsons had returned to Ontario, but they did not instruct him to issue a summons for him
to appear before your committee, as there was no time to hear the case before the present
meeting of the Council, it being necessary to give him two weeks' notice.   Your committee,
however, will have him served, and go into the investigation at as early a date as possible.

2.   After examining the evidence and considering all the circumstances in connection
with the cases of Doctors Danter and Martin, we would recommend that no action be taken
at present, in view of the fact that these parties are not now, nor have they been for some
time, acting in an unprofessional manner so far as your committee are aware.   But this
report is not intended in any way to convey the idea that no action shall be taken on the
original charges should your committee deem it advisable to do so, or circumstances arise
making it necessary to proceed with the investigation.

3.   With regard to the following resolution referred to your committee, viz. : "That the
Discipline Committee consider whether or not it is possible to arrange a method whereby
the cost of trials of members of the College charged with infamous conduct can be reduced
without in any way interfering with the efficiency of said trials, and further, that the said
committee shall report to this Council at their next session [1896] whether or not they can
suggest any means of reducing the cost of public prosecutions, and that they confer with the
Attorney General if necessary,"

Your committee beg leave to report that they have considered the matter of Discipline
trials in all its bearings, and have consulted with the Deputy-Attorney-General with this
result ! That it is impossible in our opinion, under the present Act, to lessen the expense
connected with such trials to any appreciable degree.   Mr. Cartwright went thoroughly
into the question with us, and that gentleman could suggest no better or cheaper way of
conducting those trials than the one your committee has always adopted, having due regard
for efficiency ; and he further said that he was doubtful if any amendment to the Act could
be made that would insure the desired result as economically and perfectly, and in his
judgment the present Act could not be improved upon.

4.   In the matter of the public prosecutions of unregistered persons, we put the
question to the Deputy-Attorney-General as to whether or not the Government would take
upon itself to conduct and pay the cost of such prosecutions.   His reply was that he would
not undertake to answer that question in the absence of Sir Oliver Mowat, as it was one of
policy.   But he did not believe that the Government would entertain any such proposition,
as the fines in such cases went to the College.

Your committee have sought information wherever it could be obtained, hoping to be able to suggest some scheme whereby the expenses of these prosecutions could be materially lessened, and at the same time satisfy the general profession by ridding the Province of unlicensed quacks, and in seeking this information we have found that no action of the Council is so much appreciated by the practitioners as the thorough carrying out of this portion of the Act. It has been suggested to us by Mr. Wasson that a committee be appointed with whom he could consult and to whom all evidence could be referred, and that this committee take upon itself the responsibility after considering the evidence in each case, whether or not a prosecution should be instituted, and should they deem it advisable to instruct him to prosecute, then all the costs connected with such prosecution should be borne by the Council, he to be responsible and under the instructions of such committee. Your committee are not prepared to say whether under this plan the expense to the Council would be lessened, but we are of the opinion that the work would be more efficiently and satisfactorily performed than under the present system, and would recommend this suggestion for your consideration.

All of which is respectfully submitted.

JOHN BRAY, Chairman.

Adopted as amended by Committee of the Whole.

J. P. ARMOUR,
Chairman Committee of Whole.

Carried. A. F. ROGERS.

Motion to amend Discipline Committee's report:

It was moved by Dr. MACHELL, seconded by Dr. DICKSON, That the committee mentioned in No. 4 clause of this report be composed of the following members, viz. : Doctors Barrick, Emory, Thorburn, Britton and the mover. Services to be gratuitous. Carried.

The report was received.

Dr. THORBURN presented and read the report of the Property Committee.

To the President and members of the Medical Council of the College of Physicians and Surgeons of Ontario:

GENTLEMEN,—Your Committee on Property beg leave to report that the building is in a fair state of repair.

The instructions received by your committee from the Council in June, 1895, have been carried out.

The building and property was advertised for sale last year in the months of September and October, 1895, in the daily *World, Mail* and *Evening Telegram,* published in Toronto, and in February, 1896, in the daily *Globe, World* and *Evening News,* in Toronto, and I may say that every endeavor was made to find a purchaser. A number of enquiries were received from capitalists and others, but up to the present time no definite offer has been received.

Your committee feel, however, that the time is fast approaching when the building may be sold at a fair price. It was the opinion of several real estate men that it was not a good time to offer the building for sale. They also oxpressed the opinion that the property was a good one and would be one of the first properties to sell as the real estate market increased.

You will find attached to this a report of an inspection made of the boilers, elevator and machinery, and a report on the condition of the building by the Caretaker, with some recommendations as to cleaning, alterations and repairs which are thought necessary if your Council see their way to do the same.

Your committee ask that in the event of the property not being disposed of, that they be empowered to re-arrange the loan, as on the first of November, 1896, the existing mortgage can be paid off. We are of opinion that if this power is granted, a substantial reduction of interest can be secured, and are of the opinion that the money can be had for 4½ per cent. if not for 4 per cent.

The revenue for the year's rents amounts to $3,215.16, nearly $400.00 more than last year. This, of course, is not taking into account our own premises or any allowance for the same.

We are pleased to say that we look for a larger revenue from rents next year, as a great portion of the vacant offices will be rented. The number of vacant rooms has been reduced to six.

Our supplies, such as fuel, etc., have been purchased after receiving tenders for the same.

All of which is respectfully submitted.

JAMES THORBURN,
Chairman Property Committee.

Adopted. A. F. ROGERS.

To the President and members of the Medical Council of the College of Physicians and Surgeons of Ontario:

GENTLEMEN,—I beg leave to lay before you my report on the Medical Council building.

1. The boilers have all been inspected and found in good order. I have had them all cleaned and painted.

2. The lavatories are all in very fair order ; we require one particularly for ladies.

3. The elevator wants a good overhauling and some of the ropes replaced.

4. The walls, ceilings and stairways require calsomining or painting, as they are in a very bad state.

5. The woodwork of halls and stairs requires painting or varnishing.

6. Several of the offices require calsomining, repapering and varnishing.

7. Babcock's or some other fire appliances are required in all the halls.

All of which is respectfully submitted.

·THOMAS WASSON.

TORONTO, June 1st, 1896.

REPORT OF INSPECTION OF ONE PASSENGER ELEVATOR.

Situate at south-east corner of Bay and Richmond Streets ; owned or controlled by the College of Physicians and Surgeons; date of inspection, April 18th, 1896; name of inspector, F. Idenden.

Car or platform, good. Safety apparatus, good. Shipping apparatus, good. Cables, hoisting, good. Cables, counterweight, good. Cables, shipping, good. Hoistway, car and counterweight, guides and counterweight, good. Counter-shafts, none. Overhead sheaves, timbers and bearings, good. Automatic stop, good. Belts, none. Brake and connections, good. Pulleys, tight and loose, none. Machine bearings, good. Thrust bearings, none. Keys and set screws, good. Cylinders, good. Piping, good. Pump, none. Valves, good. Pressure and discharge tank, none. Doors, gates or other guards to car, good. Doors, gates or other guards to hoistway, good. Annunciator good. Gas or electric wire cable? Gas. Lighting in car, good. Elevator attendant, apparent age, 27 years. Is he competent to run elevator ? Yes. Is there an inspection sign suspended in car? None.

Remarks.—This elevator is clean and well oiled.

Liability Department, the Travellers' Insurance Company of Hartford, Conn.

INSPECTION REPORT.

The Boiler Inspection and Insurance Co. of Canada, To R. A. Pyne, Esq., M.D., College of Physicians and Surgeons, Toronto:

We beg to inform you that the two steam boilers insured under Policy No. 2715 were inspected with steam "off" on the 19th inst. and as far as could be ascertained, found in the following condition :

Both boilers were fully examined and found quite clean inside. No leaks at any of the rivetted joints and no sign of any overheating.

There is some corrosion around the back hand-holes and care should be taken to make these joints perfectly tight.

The brickwork is all in good order. The steam gauges were tested and set right, as they were a little heavy.

Boilers had better have some compound or soda put in them and then be filled up entirely full of water.

GEO. C. ROBB, Chief Engineer.

TORONTO, May 27th, 1896.

The report was received.

Dr. THORBURN presented and read the report of the Legislation Committee.

To the President and members of the Medical Council of the College of Physicians and Surgeons of Ontario:

GENTLEMEN,—As convener of the Committee on Legislation, I beg leave to report that I personally watched all proposed legislation at the last session of the Legislative Assembly, and had the Registrar assist me in the supervision of all medical matters likely to come before the House, and kept myself in constant communication with the medical members of the House and others.

After consultation with prominent medical men and others in the Assembly, and the chairman of the Executive Committee, it was deemed necessary to call the Legislation Committee together and also the Executive Committee. The chairman of the Executive Committee, who was familiar with the situation, gave instructions for the Executive Committee to meet, and they will no doubt report the result of the Executive Committee meeting.

Your committee met on the 27th of March, 1896, the following members being present : Drs. Thorburn, Barrick, Emory, Sangster, Williams, who were joined by Drs. Harris and Rogers of the Executive Committee, the following members of the Council also being present : Drs. Britton, Geikie and Machell.

The local House appointed a special committee composed of the following members of the House to consider the bills to amend the Medical Act, namely : Hon. Mr. Hardy, Hon. Mr. Ross, Drs. A. McKay and J. McKay, Meacham, Ryerson, Willoughby, Messrs. Biggar, German, Haycock and St. John.

Mr. German's bill was first discussed and a compromise arrived at, the Executive Committee agreeing to carry out a certain understanding ; the bill was withdrawn.

Hon. Mr. Ross' bill was then considered, and after a lengthy discussion in which all the members of the Council present took part, contents of the bill were agreed upon, Mr. Ross undertaking to withdraw the bill on the distinct understanding that the Medical Council at its next meeting would carry out the principles of the bill, and agreeing to " clean the slate," as the Hon. Mr. Ross said, re all applications for registration as matriculates down to 1st November, 1895.

Mr. Haycock's bill was not considered before the committee, as it had been decided by the House upon the moving of the second reading.

The three bills, with the understanding arrived at regarding matriculation, as per Hon. Mr. Ross, are appended hereto.

All of which is respectfully submitted.

JAMES THORBURN,

Adopted. A. F. ROGERS. Chairman Legislation Committee.

No. 136.]   BILL.   [1896.

An Act to amend the Ontario Medical Act.

Her Majesty, by and with the advice and consent of the Legislative Assembly of the Province of Ontario, enacts as follows :

1. Sub-section 1 of Section 23 of the Ontario Medical Act is hereby repealed, and the following sub-section substituted therefor.

(1) Notwithstanding anything in this Act contained, any person holding a medical or surgical degree or diploma of any University or College of Physicians or Surgeons of England, Scotland or Ireland, entitling such person to register in Great Britain or Ireland, shall be entitled to present himself for the Final examination prescribed by the Council for Ontario candidates for registration, and upon passing the said examination, and paying the same fees as are payable by such last mentioned candidates, he shall be entitled to registration.

BILL.

An Act respecting Matriculation in Medicine.

Her Majesty, by and with the advice and consent of the Legislative Assembly of the Province of Ontario, enacts as follows :

1. (1) Notwithstanding any by-laws or regulations which may have been passed by the Medical Council under the Ontario Medical Act, any person who presents to the Registrar of the Medical Council a certificate that he has passed the examination conducted by the Education Department on the course prescribed for matriculation in Arts and approved by the Lieutenant-Governor in Council, shall be entitled, on payment of the lawful fees in that behalf, to registration as a medical student within the meaning of Section 11 of the Ontario Medical Act, being Chapter 148 of the Revised Statutes of Ontario, 1887.

(2) Any person who before the passing of this Act has not passed the examination in all the subjects prescribed for matriculation as aforesaid, shall be entitled to registration as a medical student on submitting to the Registrar of the Medical Council a certificate that he has completed such examination by passing in the remaining subjects of such matriculation, including Chemistry and Physics.

(3) Any student in medicine who submits to the Registrar of the Medical Council certified tickets that he has attended not less than two courses of lectures at any chartered medical school or college in Canada, shall be entitled, on the payment of the lawful fees in that behalf, to take the Primary examination or the examination of said Council taken by students at the end of the second year, provided that the standing obtained at such examination may not be allowed until such student presents to the Registrar of the Council the matriculation certificate prescribed by this Act.

(4) A certificate from the Registrar of any university in Canada that the holder thereof has passed the examination in Arts prescribed for students at the end of the first year, shall entitle such student to registration as a medical student under the Ontario Medical Act.

2. Any by-laws or regu'ations of the Medical Council for determining the admission or enrolment of students varying the examinations for registration hereinbefore mentioned, shall not be valid or binding unless and until approved by the Lieutenant-Governor in Council.

Memorandum respecting Matriculation in Medicine, containing the conclusions arrived at with the members of the Executive and Legislation Committees of the Medical Council at the Parliament buildings, on the 27th day of March, 1896.

1. Any person who presents to the Registrar of the Medical Council a certificate that he has passed the examination conducted by the Education Department on the course prescribed for matriculation in Arts, including Chemistry and Physics, and approved by the Lieutenant-Governor in Council, shall be entitled, on payment of the lawful fees in that behalf, to registration as a medical student within the meaning of Section 11 of the Ontario Medical Act, being Chapter 148 of the Revised Statutes of Ontario, 1887.

2. Any person who before the passing of this Act has not passed the examination in all the subjects prescribed for matriculation as aforesaid, shall be entitled to registration as a medical student on submitting to the Registrar of the Medical Council a certificate that he has completed such examination by passing in the remaining subjects of such matriculation, including Chemistry and Physics.

3. Any student in medicine who submits to the Registrar of the Medical Council certified tickets that he has attended not less than two courses of lectures at any chartered medical school or college in Canada, shall be entitled, on payment of the lawful fees in that behalf, to take the Primary examination or the examination of said Council taken by students at the end of the second year, provided that the standing obtained at such examination may not be allowed until such student presents to the Registrar of the Council the matriculation certificate prescribed by this Act.

4. A certificate from the Registrar of any chartered university conducting a full Arts course in Canada, that the holder thereof matriculated prior to his enrolment in such university, and passed the examination in Arts prescribed for students at the end of the first year, shall entitle such student to registration as a medical student under the Ontario Medical Act.

5. Any person who on or before the first day of Nevember, 1895, has passed the examination of any university in Canada for matriculation in Arts, or the matriculation examination conducted by the Education Department entitling to registration in Arts with any university in Canada, or an examination entitling to registration with the Medical Council when the said examination was passed subsequent to July 1st, 1888, shall be entitled to registration as a medical student.

Commencing from 1st July, 1888, to 1st November, 1892, second class non-professional certificate, with Latin.

Since 1st November, 1892, the junior matriculation certificate, with Physics and Chemistry, as prescribed by the Education Department of Ontario.

No. 105.]   BILL.   [1896.
An Act to amend the Medical Act.

Her Majesty, by and with the advice and consent of the Legislative Assembly of the Province of Ontario, enacts as follows :

1. Notwithstanding anything contained in the Ontario Medical Act, or any amendment thereto, the Council of the College of Physicians for Ontario shall not have power to impose any greater fees or charges upon any person being a candidate for admission to practice medicine, surgery and midwifery in the Province of Ontario, and for registration under the said Act, than will amount in the whole to the sum of fifty dollars ($50.00), which shall include fees for registration certificate and all examinations required to be passed by such person for admission and registration.

The report was received.

Dr. HARRIS presented and read the report of the Executive Committee.

To the President and members of the Medical Council of the College of Physicians and Surgeons of Ontario :

GENTLEMEN,—The Executive Committee met on the 9th of October, 1895, for the purpose of fixing the name of the matriculation, as proposed by the Council in June, 1895, so that it would harmonize with the name fixed by the Education Department, to read as follows : "The Junior Matriculation examination as conducted by the Education Department of Ontario," and to take the place of the name as indicated by the Council at its last session, namely, "The Pass Art Matriculation," as it was found to confuse intending candidates, and it was necessary to rectify the same.

We also considered the applications of persons for registration, and the Registrar was instructed as to the same.

We recommend that the special case of W. C. P. Bremner, B.A., University of Toronto, who asks for registration and a three years' course under special circumstances, be granted by the Council. This application will appear before your body at this meeting.

Your Committee again met on the 27th of March, 1896, after the co-joint meeting of the Legislation Committee and Executive Committee at the Parliament buildings, and gave your Registrar instructions in accordance with the understanding arrived at between the Hon. Mr. Ross and the special committee of the Assembly, which are appended to this report.

All of which is respectfully submitted.

WILLIAM T. HARRIS,

Adopted. A. F. ROGERS.   Chairman Executive Committee.

Moved by Dr. Rogers, and resolved, That the Registrar be and is hereby instructed to admit all candidates applying for Primary examination who present two courses of tickets in medicine, whose matriculation is not completed, on the following conditions : " The Matriculation examination is to be completed before the Primary examination shall be allowed, even if successful in passing the examination of the primary subjects." Carried.

WILLIAM T. HARRIS, President,
Chairman Executive Committee.
A. F. ROGERS, Vice-President,
C. T. CAMPBELL.

Moved by Dr. Rogers, and resolved, That the Executive Committee of the Council, having had a consultation with the Hon. G. W. Ross, Minister of Education, in regard to the Council's matriculation standard, and upon the request of the Minister of Education and the Government amounting to a demand, therefore the Executive Committee hereby instruct the Registrar as follows :

" That any person who on or before the first day of November, in the year eighteen hundred and ninety-five (1895), had passed the examination of any university in Canada for matriculation in Arts, shall be entitled to registration as a matriculated medical student on submitting to the Registrar of the Medical Council a certificate to that effect signed by the proper officer in that behalf, and paying the fees for registration as a matriculant."

WILLIAM T. HARRIS, President,
Chairman Executive Committee,
A. F. ROGERS, Vice-President,
C. T. CAMPBELL.

Re the case of Dr. Young, who applies as a British licentiate for leave to take the Final examination, and if successful to be registered, moved by Dr. Rogers, and resolved, That inasmuch as the case of Dr. Young presents special features, that the Registrar be and is hereby empowered to permit the said Dr. Young to present himself for the old Final examination (which is practically the same as the Intermediate and Final examinations at the present time), and upon passing the same and paying all fees ($100.00) he shall be allowed to register.

WILLIAM T. HARRIS, President,
Chairman Executive Committee,
A. F. ROGERS, Vice-President,
C. T. CAMPBELL.

March 27th, 1896.
The report was received.

CONSIDERATION OF REPORTS.

Moved by Dr. BRAY, seconded by Dr. HENRY, That the Council go into Committee of the Whole to consider the report of the Discipline Committee. Carried.

Council in Committee of the Whole.

Dr. Armour in the chair.

Dr. Bray read the preamble and clauses 1, 2, 3 and 4, and on motion the said preamble and clauses were respectively adopted as read.

Dr. Bray read clause 5 and moved its adoption.

Dr. BRAY—Before this is adopted I wish to say that this is an important matter, and perhaps it would be as well to refer this clause of the report to the Finance Committee or whoever is dealing with the matter of prosecutions.

Dr. ROSEBRUGH—We have a Discipline Committee, and I do not think any committee could be formed which could more properly deal with this than that Discipline Committee, who have a very great deal of information connected with each case.

Dr. BRAY—This is not the business of the Discipline Committee ; this clause refers to public prosecutions of unlicensed practitioners, while the Discipline Committee have to deal with licensed practitioners.

Dr. WILLIAMS—I think if that clause is read over again, till we all get the pith of it through our minds, perhaps we can give a vote on it now and decide whether it is satisfac- tory or not as well as at any other time ; each member can form his opinion in a very short time, I think, if the clause is read over again.

Dr. Bray reads 5th clause of report.

Dr. WILLIAMS—Have the Discipline Committee given any thought to where this com- mittee should be located, or anything as to the practical carrying out of the suggestions ?

Dr. BRAY—Yes, we have thought of that ; we have talked it over a good deal and have asked the opinion of others ; and it has been suggested that it should be placed in the hands of some committee, and it was suggested (not by any member of the Discipline Committee) that the Discipline Committee were the proper committee to deal with this for two or three reasons ; the first reason is that they will, in all probability, have to meet on purely disci- pline business, and when so meeting, the Prosecutor could gather up a number of cases and present the cases to the committee without any extra expense to the Council ; another reason is that perhaps the Discipline Committee are more familiar with this part of the business of the Council than almost any other members of the Council. It was also sug- gested that the committee for this purpose should meet four times a year, and it was after- wards suggested twice a year. In reference to that, my opinion is that there should be no time fixed for the meetings of this committee, but that they should meet as seldom as possible, and only when meeting for other business ; that is, if you give it to the Discipline Committee. If you give it to some other committee, it will entail more expense than if given to the Discipline Committee. Do not think, however, that the members of the Discipline Committee are looking for any more work or honor ; we are not. We are making these suggestions purely with a view of lessening the cost of these trials. I dare say you all have seen the Prosecutor's report—I think it was put on the desk of everybody here. You will notice in that report that while there has been about twenty-five cases where convic- tions have been got and fines paid, the larger number of cases where no convictions have been got, and a number of cases where convictions have been got and the parties have gone to jail in preference to paying the fine, have been a source of expense to our Prosecutor, and he has derived no revenue from them, and I am told that this year he is $400.00 behind. I think, perhaps (not reflecting on Mr. Wasson), he has not used quite as much discretion in some of those cases as a committee of this Council would use. I think if a committee were appointed that the committee would go over the evidence and instruct the Prosecutor and curtail his expenses as much as possible. I think, myself, if the prosecutions are to con- tinne, that something of this kind must be done ; and I certainly think the prosecutions must be continued, because if we allow the prosecutions to drop, no matter what the funds of the Council are, for one year, we will be over-run with those unlicensed quacks. One reason why Mr. Wasson is so much behind is that these quacks are becoming very sharp ; where, three years ago, he would have had no difficulty in convicting a good many, now, when they have been up a couple of times before, their wits are sharpened ; and it is in such cases I think a committee would be valuable ; the Prosecutor would obtain reliable informa- tion from all sources he could, and submit that information to the committee, who would, if necessary, submit it to the Solicitor, and on being satisfied proceed with the case, but would not allow the Prosecutor to go to any unnecessary expense before he obtained the necessary evidence.

Dr. MACHELL—When the members of the Property Committee were going over the building this afternoon, or after we had gone through the building, Mr. Wasson spoke to two or three of us very much in the same strain that he evidently did to the members of the Discipline Committee. Bearing that in mind, I wrote out a motion after I came here this evening, very much on the lines that Dr. Bray has spoken on, with one exception. I will read it and then give my reasons for it : "Moved by Dr. Machell, seconded by Dr. Dickson [one of those Mr. Wasson was speaking to], "That a committee, composed of Drs. Barrick, Emory and the mover, be appointed, with whom the Official Prosecutor shall consult before instituting legal proceedings for infractions of the Medical Act." I selected the three names I have mentioned because we are three men here in Toronto, whom the Detective might call up at any time, and this would be a committee that would entail absolutely no expense to the Council, though of course it would be a committee that would not be able to give the same legal opinions, or opinions bearing perhaps as good legal value as the Discipline Committee would ; but it would, on the other hand, have the advantage that it would not be a committee which would have to be called together from different parts of the Province ; it would be a committee which could be called on a few minutes notice ; and while the Discipline Committee, meeting four or five times a year, would be sufficient for the purposes Dr. Bray spoke of, I think there are circumstances where action might have to be.

taken within a few days or within a short time, in order to catch a man before he got out of the particular town where he would be practising illegally. I do not know that I intended to go quite so far as Dr. Bray did, that is, committing the Council to all the expense of the prosecution after the Prosecutor once had the sanction of this committee ; that was not my intention. The Prosecutor said there were a number of instances in which medical men wrote in from the country saying that such and such a man was practising illegally, and asking to have the Prosecutor sent out. In such a case as that if he were not sent out it would look as if the officers of the Council—Dr. Pyne and probably the Prosecutor—were not doing their duty. But if the Prosecutor could say to any party writing him in that way, the committee did not approve of or did not sanction this prosecution, it would relieve the executive officers of the Council of a certain amount of responsibility, and it was more for this reason that I suggested the formation of this committee.

Dr. BRAY—I may say that we thought over this matter and that what Dr. Machell speaks of was suggested, and I think perhaps that may be a better suggestion. I do not wish it to be understood that when I suggested the Discipline Committee I meant we were going to meet four or five times a year specially for the purpose of dealing with these matters, because we might receive the information by letter and conduct our deliberations by letter ; letters might be written to each member of the Discipline Committee by the Prosecutor, conveying to them the information on which they could advise him ; and it would not follow that the committee would actually meet to consider these matters ; it was not the intention of the motion that the Discipline Committee should meet to consider this class of prosecution except when meeting on Discipline Committee business. I would be very glad indeed to have this work taken off the Discipline Committee ; there is nothing would please me better, and I quite fall in with the suggestion of Dr. Machell, if it is agreeable to the rest of the members ; I am agreeable to any method by which this matter can be efficiently and cheaply dealt with. I know very well, as Dr. Machell has said, that there are cases where the offender is only a few hours in a place, and prompt action is necessary to secure his conviction. I have been written to, and I have no doubt each of our territorial representatives has been written to, to send the Detective at once, without giving us any evidence. Another point to be noted is that doctors throughout the country will write to their representative, or to the Registrar, or to the Prosecutor, saying "we want the Prosecutor sent up ;" and then when he gets there he cannot get one word of information out of these very gentlemen who wrote asking for his assistance ; they do not want to have their names mixed up with the prosecution, and do not seem to want to give any information to the Prosecutor. I think this matter should not be considered hastily, but should be considered thoroughly, in order to bring about the results we desire.

The PRESIDENT—Do I understand that no prosecutions can go on unless sanctioned by this committee ?

Dr. BRAY—No ; I do not mean to take away all responsibility from the Prosecutor ; there are lots of little cases where he is sure of a conviction, but I have reference partienlarly to doubtful cases and cases where there will be likely a lot of expense. Our Prosecutor has informed me that there is one case in Dunville that has cost about $200.00 ; that is the kind of case the committee might deal with. I do not mean that we should take away all discretion from Mr. Wasson ; and I do not mean that the Council should be responsible except for a case where this committee advised a prosecution. My idea is only to provide for difficult or doubtful cases ; and my object is not only to endeavor to ensure success, but to control the expenditure.

Dr. MOORE—As a member of the Discipline Committee, I am very much pleased to hear Dr. Machell's motion ; I am glad to know that he is willing, and that other members of this Council, resident in this city, are willing to take upon themselves this duty. So far as I am personally concerned, I shall be very glad to be relieved from it, but it is to my mind very necessary that we should have such a committee ; it is also very necessary that the committee should be as inexpensive as possible. One reason this committee is necessary is, the Prosecutor is notified by some medical gentleman within the Province that there is some man practising medicine without a license in his neighborhood ; our Prosecutor goes to the place indicated and prosecutes this man, and the offender is convicted and fined $25.00 or $30.00 or $40.00, as the case may be, but he prefers in lieu of payment to take a month in jail ; he takes the option of the month in jail, and the Prosecutor is out his expenses ; and at the end of the month your unlicensed practitioner gets out of jail and in two or three days is back at his old tricks again. Then the Prosecutor, we will say, follows him up again and has him convicted and fined ; as before the offender goes back to jail again and pays his fine by being housed and fed at the public expense for another thirty days, and at the end of that time is set at liberty and goes on with the old work again. Our Prosecutor gets a salary of only $600.00 a year, and is entitled to whatever he can make out of these prosecutions. The Prosecutor, as a matter of fact, is $400.00 out this year. We cannot expect him to go on in this way ; and he himself says he cannot go on, and we know as business men that he cannot. It seems to me that any case submitted to this committee, in which the committee decide to prosecute, the Council should pay the expense, provided there is a loss. If that were decided upon, I think more efficient work might be done and in that way our public Prosecutor would not be out of pocket. We can hardly expect him to go on next year and prosecute where there is any doubt, especially as he has met with a financial loss of $400.00 this year. We talked this subject over in the Discipline Committee, and thought we might probably make the experiment of approaching the Legislature at its coming session, although we are timid about applying for further legislation ; and we thought it well to state our views to the Council so that the Council may form their judgment and act as they deem best. We know that if a man sells liquor without a license, he may be fined $50.00 for the first offence, with the addition of a month or two months in jail ; on the next conviction there is no option of a fine, he has to go to jail for three months ; and if he is found guilty a third time, he has to go to jail for four months, without the option of a fine ; so that you see in this case the punishment is progressive. But the punishment is not progressive under our Act ; and really a designing man with a little capital could put this Council to a very great deal of expense. If we can only obtain from the Legislature the same law as that which applies to liquor sellers, we then would be enabled to put the unlicensed practitioners and quacks to flight to a moral certainty. We spoke to Mr. Cartwright, the Deputy-Attorney-General, on this subject ; and Mr. Cartwright thought as we had a precedent in the license law we might safely go to the Legislature and probably get an amendment to our Act. I am making this statement now merely as a suggestion for the information of the Council. I shall be very glad, indeed, if this matter is handed over to such an able and representative committee, as has been suggested by Dr. Machell, in this city. I am very much in favor of Dr. Machell's resolution and I shall vote for it.

Dr. Dickson—As seconder of the resolution and in answer to Dr. Rogers' remark I wish to say I think that every case should be referred to this committee. I think the Prosecutor should have no option, because it might be that in many cases he would feel from the evidence he received almost certain of securing conviction which to the committee might not perhaps seem just likely to be an accomplished object. The members of this committee proposed by Dr. Machell live in the city and are easily reached by telephone. For those reasons, I think every case should be brought before this committee.

Dr. Brock—This report and Mr. Wasson's proposition have a bearing on the Finance Committee's report. I find that in the Finance Committee we are about considering this question. We examined the vouchers and looked over the report of the Registrar and over Mr. Wasson's report, and we were also endeavoring to find some recommendation by which we would be enabled to save this Council the enormous expense of these discipline trials. I think if any member of this Council would personally examine the vouchers he would see at once the great leakage which we have had ; I have noted one case, that of the Rose trial. This matter was receiving our serious consideration, and I think it was because it was receiving our serious consideration that Mr. Wasson probably has made this proposition. I think Dr. Machell's motion will settle the whole question most satisfactorily. It will remove a great deal of the expense and will prevent Mr. Wasson acting on his own responsibility and leading this Council into expenses that we do not know anything about.

Dr. Bray—I think Dr. Brock has misunderstood the position of affairs. Dr. Machell's motion suggests a committee for the public prosecution of unlicensed practitioners, a work the Discipline Committee have nothing at all to do with. I take it for granted that Dr. Brock means that Mr. Wasson in doing any work for the Discipline Committee should submit all his evidence to the Discipline Committee before he goes on. Do I understand you aright, Dr. Brock ?

Dr. Brock—Yes.

Dr. Bray—You have got the two things confused. This motion and our discussion have been in reference to the prosecution of unlicensed persons, a work which the Discipline Committee have nothing to do with. The Discipline Committee have only to do with registered practitioners who transgress. I quite agree with Dr. Brock's suggestion that it should be an instruction of this Council to the Prosecutor to submit everything of this kind to the Discipline Committee before he goes on. It has not been done heretofore and I think it should be done just the same as he would submit to the committee Dr. Machell suggests anything in ordinary prosecutions. But I am very much afraid if Dr. Dickson's suggestion, that every case should be presented to the committee, was acted on they would have a great deal more work than they bargained for ; but if they are willing to do it, I am quite willing they should.

Dr. Britton—There is just one point in connection with this I wish to refer to. It has already been suggested that it could be arranged in this way, that the Prosecutor could be allowed to proceed with cases in which he was pretty sure he would secure conviction, but cases about which there was even a shadow of doubt he might submit to the committee, and even though they appeared to be doubtful cases, if the committee recommended he would prosecute and then the Council should assume the responsibility of paying any expenses in connection with such prosecutions. I think, therefore, it would be unwise to have a resolution framed in such a way as to direct that all cases, doubtful and otherwise, should be submitted by Mr. Wasson to the committee. If some such provision as has been recommended be not adopted I think it would be very difficult to make an arrangement with Mr. Wasson for the coming year in view of his report that he has lost $400.00 during the past year. I think it would be far better that he should be allowed his discretion to proceed where he is satisfied of success, and in cases where he is doubtful to refer all the evidence to the committee named by Dr. Machell. That committee could determine, before instructing Mr. Wasson to proceed with prosecution, whether or not the merits of the case would warrant them recommending the Council to assume the responsibility of the expenses.

Dr. CAMPBELL—While Dr. Bray was speaking, explaining that clause, the idea struck me it would not be expedient to have the Discipline Committee attend to the work for the reason he had mentioned himself, that they could only attend to it at great expense except during their meetings, which meetings would be only occasionally. I think the appointment of a committee composed of some of our members resident in Toronto, if they were willing to serve, would certainly be the wisest plan ; and I thought the four members mentioned by Dr. Machell, the two territorial representatives, Dr. Emory and Dr. Thorburn, the Vice-President of the Council, would be gentlemen in whom the Council would have such confidence that if they advised the Prosecutor to go on with the work we would all back them up in the action that they had taken. The general sentiment of the Council seems to be that something of the kind proposed is necessary and that the committee suggested by Dr. Machell would be the best ; and now I would simply suggest to Dr. Bray to amend the clause of the committee's report, that a committee consisting of these four gentlemen be appointed, and then it will not be necessary to bring it up by a separate motion to-morrow, but settle it now and save time.

Dr. HENRY—Do we understand that the proposed committee is not to be a spending committee, that those gentlemen will do the work without expense ? I do not see anything to prevent the Discipline Committee from attending to that duty of advising the Prosecutor ; I think it is part and parcel of their duty. I know, of course, it is the duty of the Discipline Committee to look after regularly licensed practitioners, but there is nothing in the Act to say they could not advise the Detective in dealing with unlicensed parties. Of course there is the difficulty that they are at different ends of the Province, but that difficulty can be easily obviated ; we could have them all in Toronto, where I think they ought to be. However, I have no objection to the formation of this committee provided there is no expense.

Dr. BRAY—The Discipline Committee does not want the job. We are very happy indeed to think there are gentlemen in Toronto who are willing to undertake this arduous duty.

Dr. MACHELL—I have just a word or two to say in explanation. If you will look at the writing in the motion, you will see that my original intention was that "the Prosecutor may consult this committee," but my seconder thought that we had better put in the word "shall." My intention originally was that in doubtful cases the committee should be consulted, but where, as Dr. Britton suggests, the Prosecutor had no doubt about his case, it would not be necessary for him to consult the committee. I named Dr. Barrick and myself as territorial representatives, and named Dr. Emory, but did not name Drs. Thorburn and Britton for the reason that I did not want to make the committee too large. As Dr. Thorburn's name, however, has been suggested, I would also like to add it with Dr. Britton's, and then the committee would include the whole of the Toronto members, and in that way would divide up the responsibility.

Dr. BRITTON—Mr. Chairman, I would like to see the committee as small as possible. I think that three men who are possessed of good judgment would be quite a sufficient guarantee to this Council that the advice given would be the best. So far as I am personally concerned, I think it would be unwise to add my name to those already mentioned as members of the committee ; it would be far better the committee should consist of three or four at the outside than of five or six, unless the members of the committee are disposed to do the work gratuitously.

Dr. MACHELL—That is what we want to do—to work gratuitously on this committee.

Dr. BRITTON—If that is the case I am perfectly willing to have my name put on. (Hear, hear.)

Dr. DICKSON—When I expressed the opinion that the word "shall" should be put instead of "may," I understood that Mr. Wasson's proposition was that he should receive a salary as heretofore, and that the fines should go to the Council and the Council should bear all expense where fines were not secured. Of course, in the event of the present arrangement being adopted, I clearly see it would be desirable to allow the Prosecutor in such cases as he felt he could secure a conviction to go on, and only in such cases as he was doubtful of, and where the possibility was he might not succeed, to consult with the committee proposed before taking any steps or incurring any expense. After having received further light on the subject from the discussion, I am quite willing that the word "shall" should be changed to "may."

Dr. THORBURN—I think this committee is a very important one. The expenses in connection with prosecutions are something alarming, and one sometimes asks, Is it worth the shot? Isn't it waste of money? Perhaps it is to our advantage that quacks should go on and treat the public. We are doing this work of prosecution as much for the public as for ourselves. Another point I wish to mention is, I think a small committee is a more effectual one than a large one. Where there are quite a number of men on a committee they reason with themselves in this way, "I cannot go, but there are plenty of other fellows there;" while if you name a smaller committee, each man feels that the thing cannot go on without him. So far as remuneration is concerned, while I am as fond of money as most men can be, if it is thought desirable I shall be happy if you choose to put my name on and keep it on to give my services gratuitously. But I do not see why we should as a committee be different from other committees altogether. There is a good deal of work in this thing, and a good deal of bad feeling is oftentimes created, and I would like if possible that the Discipline Committee should undertake this duty, but I see difficulties in the way. Calling them to Toronto from different parts of the Province would be attended with a very great deal of expense. I think the committee proposed would be of very great advantage to the Council.

Dr. McLAUGHLIN—There is no doubt the enforcement of any law that is calculated to punish scamps is environed with a great many difficulties; and even if you appoint this committee I have not the slightest idea you are going to overcome these difficulties. In my judgment a good, sharp detective, who has had experience in failures, ought to be able to suggest as much wisdom as to future action as any one else, more particularly one of a judicial mind or one who has had judicial experience in such cases. If any of our members here were magistrates and had to deal with the enforcement of the License Act, they would know how difficult it is to enforce that Act, and there you are dealing with men a good deal like the rascals we are trying to reach with the Medical Act for the benefit of the public. I agree with Dr. Machell. I think it is well, if we have a committee at all, that they should be in Toronto, where their labors should not be attended with much expense to the Council, and I think this committee would be able to give as good advice as the other committee proposed, and they certainly should say to Mr. Wasson that he should not run to all parts of the country when he gets a little hint that something is wrong, that he ought not to go until some medical man or some person in that locality assumes the responsibility of placing, as far as he can, substantial evidence in his hands in order that a prosecution might proceed, and when that has been obtained I think it is well that it should be submitted to this committee. Whilst I quite agree with the motion to have the committee, I do not look for a vast improvement upon prosecutions in the future over the past, because I say if you attempt to get hold of those fellows they are a class of men always, I think, who will not scruple to make a statement, after kissing the Bible, that is not in harmony with the truth, and they won't scruple to do anything to get others to do the same in order to relieve them of the punishment that is likely to be inflicted upon them. I agree with the suggestion of Dr. Moore that the Act should be altered so that the punishment should be progressive as it is under the Liquor License Act. I think under the Liquor License Act the punishment for the first offence is $25.00 to $50.00, the next $50.00 to $100.00, and the punishment for the third offence is imprisonment without fine, and a surrender of license. These are my views. I concur in the appointment of this committee, and I hope good will come out of it.

Dr. BARRICK—There is just one thing I wish to be perfectly clear upon; I am not sure whether I understand this motion right. Is it the understanding that in all cases where the Prosecutor assumes the responsibility himself of taking proceedings that he himself is responsible for the expenses of those proceedings, and he gets the fines in those cases?

Dr. MOORE—That is correct.

Dr. BARRICK—And that any case where he is doubtful, where he might say, "Here is a case in which I am not sure whether the fines will pay me for my trouble," he will submit to this committee, and if this committee undertake to recommend the prosecution, then this committee commit this Council to the expense of those prosecutions and the Council will get whatever fines come from them?

Dr. MOORE—That is our idea of what the understanding should be.

Dr. ARMOUR—You are under a misapprehension as to how it is at the present time. We now pay our Prosecutor $600.00 a year salary, and if his fines do not amount to sufficient to cover his expenses, then he must meet them out of that salary.

Dr. BARRICK—That is what I say. I understand he gets $600.00 a year apart from prosecutions altogether.

Dr. ARMOUR—And he pays his own expenses.

Dr. BARRICK—He gets $600.00 a year and he must bear the expense of these prosecutions, but he gets the proceeds of the fines. This proposition is that he shall do the same thing, only where he is doubtful and thinks he is going to fall short, and it would not be safe for him to assume the responsibility, he will then consult the committee, and when the committee once decide that they shall prosecute they make the Council liable for that particular prosecution, and the Council get the benefit of the fine, if any.

Dr. ARMOUR—That is the intention, I understand, of this proposition.

Dr. CAMPBELL—Of course, that would have to be afterwards definitely arranged in the new contract entered into by the Prosecutor. The adoption of the report and the amendment will not, of course, definitely fix that.

Dr. WILLIAMS—I think there is one advantage in having a committee, whether it results in cheapening the matter or not. This Council have a responsibilty as to the kind of cases that are prosecuted, and when it goes into the newspapers that the Prosecutor has had some person up and fined, the Council of the medical profession are held responsible. Under these circumstances, I think that we should have a committee which would pass judgment on the cases before they are prosecuted, and should know whether or not they are proper cases to take before the public. There are sometimes cases that seem to be vexatious more than anything else and that the profession would be ashamed to have prosecuted, and would prefer that they were not interfered with. I heard of one case, I think in the neighborhood of Barrie, where information was laid and the Council were urged to have a prosecution pushed against a man who was not a registered practitioner, because he had used a syringe. The ground was taken that it was a surgical operation, and that under the Act he was open to prosecution. To my mind, that sort of case would be very vexatious to the public, as well as to the profession. And sometimes prosecutors, in their zeal, might take some kind of cases that we would rather, for our own reputation and for the pleasure of the public, were left alone entirely ; and I think it is a good thing that a share of those cases should be submitted to a committee before they are put before the public on the responsibility of the Council.

Dr. SANGSTER—I agree with a good deal that has been said, and I do not agree with much more. I am not second to anybody in my desire to see those who are breaking the law prosecuted ; I think they should be prosecuted condignly ; but, as I have already stated, I think this Council is not the body that should have the responsibility of prosecuting them. I know, from much conversation with members, that the great reason why the medical profession is just now so unpopular in our Legislature is due partly to our public prosecutions, partly to our tariff or attempts at a tariff, and partly to a—I do not know what else to call it—pure cussedness on the part of the Patrons and others in the House. I think that when we have a public Prosecutor, and it is understood he prosecutes at his own risk, he is merely like a bloodhood sent through the country by this Council to hunt its prey. If he does that under the ægis and sanction of a committee, I think the public will hold this Council much more directly responsible for those prosecutions even than it does now. And I submit that the law is wrong in that matter. I do not care what the feeling of the House is, or what the expressions of Mr. Cartwright may be on the subject, if proper representations were made to the Legislature, and the whole matter was placed properly before the Legislature so as to show that these prosecutions are made not in the interests of the profession, but in the interests of the public, and that it is police work that belongs not to this Council, but to the Attorney-General's office or to some other office. I cannot conceive that we should fail to obtain justice in the matter. I ask you to imagine what would be the condition of the lawyers throughout the country if they were in the same condition ? Suppose the lawyers obtained an Act (which they have been too wise to do) authorizing them to appoint a public prosecutor to go through the country and to haul up and fine every township and county clerk and every broker who ventured to draw deeds or to write wills, would the lawyers not in a very short time have as great a howl against them on the part of the ignorant public as the doctors have now ? I do think it is and has been a great weakness to this Council that they ever assumed those prosecutions ; and I do think that under happier auspices the work might have been placed at first, as I think it might yet be placed, where it properly belongs—not in the hands of this Council, or in the hands of a committee of this Council, and not in the hands of a prosecutor appointed by this Council. I would like to see steps earnestly taken, taken with a firm determination to push them to the end, to place the matter properly before the Government ; and I am quite sure that if the Government were convinced that the prosecutions were in the interests of the public, as I am confident they are, steps might be taken to relieve us of what is a very unpleasant and very expensive duty.

Dr. BRITTON—I would like to know before the vote is taken upon this motion, whether this work is to be done gratuitously, because if it is not, it would be far better if the committee consisted only of three members.

Dr. ROGERS—I think you had better add to Dr. Machell's motion that the work of the committee shall be done free of charge.

Dr. SHAW—We should not be willing to ask a committee to do a lot of work for nothing when we are not willing to do our work in the Council for less than we were paid last year.

Dr. MACHELL—It was my intention we should do the work free because we live here, but I have not spoken of the matter to Dr. Emory or Dr. Britton.

Dr. MOORHOUSE—Is it the intention of the committee to visit outside places?

Dr. MACHELL—No.

Dr. MOORHOUSE—I do not see, under those circumstances, what expense they may be put to ; they may have to meet for half an hour, but that is all the mover intended.

Dr. BRITTON—There might be half a dozen cases submitted at once, and a lot of evidence to be gone over that would take half a day.

Dr. MOORHOUSE—The Prosecutor will be given authority to undertake certain work on his own responsibility ; I think the intention of the mover of this amendment was that the committee should not be put to any great. expense or loss of time. I think if they are they should certainly be paid.

Dr. EMORY—The first intimation I had of the proposition was when Dr. Machell read his motion. I for one am quite willing for this year to give my services on that committee gratuitously. It is largely an experiment ; we may have nothing to do, but if we find the duties so onerous as to interfere with our professional duties, I am sure that next year the Council will relieve us of them. (Hear, hear.)

Dr. BARRICK—I would like it made perfectly clear in that resolution whether it is just those cases that the Prosecutor does not wish to undertake himself will be submitted, or that all cases will be submitted.

Dr. SANGSTER—I would like to know whether the public Prosecutor has, under existing circumstances, and whether it is intended he shall have under this committee, unlimited power to prosecute and pay for solicitors or counsel in these prosecutions?

Dr. ARMOUR—That is not covered in this resolution. Subsequently it might be arranged, but if this is to be a final disposition of the matter possibly it would be better to add something further to this resolution.

Dr. THORBURN—When the Finance Committee's report is taken up there will be an opportunity given for discussing that.

Dr. BRITTON—I should think the committee would control details of that kind in its conference with the Prosecutor. I think he would be expected to act in all respects under the instructions of that committee when the committee is called on.

Dr. BARRICK—I think the point raised by Dr. Sangster is a very important one. Suppose this committee say, " we think that is a proper case to go on to prosecute," does that give the Prosecutor *carte blanche* to employ counsel and to go into any expense he may see fit, and run this Council into perhaps more expense than ever before? The point is, what control the committee would have in respect to controlling the expense that might be gone into?

Dr. CAMPBELL—It strikes me we had better leave that open now, and on consideration of the report of the Finance Committee, or whatever committee deals with the engaging of a Prosecutor, fix all the details and terms.

Dr. DICKSON—It was the intention of the seconder, and, I think, of the mover, that the Prosecutor should receive all his suggestions in these cases from the committee.

The CHAIRMAN put the motion as follows : "Moved by Dr. Machell, seconded by Dr. Dickson, That the committee mentioned in the fourth clause of the report be composed of the following members, viz.: Drs. Barrick, Emory, Thorburn, Britton and the mover," and on a vote having been taken declared it carried.

Moved by Dr. BRAY, seconded by Dr. MOORE, That Clause 5 as amended be adopted. Carried.

On motion, the committee rose and reported the adoption of the report as amended.

The committee rose, the President in the chair.

Moved by Dr. WILLIAMS, seconded by Dr. BRAY, That the report as amended be adopted.

Dr. SANGSTER—I want to ask the Committee on Discipline whether they have received any communications or taken any action on any communications re Dr. McCully, who is under suspended sentence by this Council. He is, I believe, at present in Milwaukee. Some months ago I was almost deluged with marked newspapers sent from the city of Milwaukee, containing portraits of Dr. McCully, and large advertisements in which he flourished the fact that he was "none of your doctors that were ex-flunkeyfied,"—or some such word—" by the Medical Councils, and I would like to know what Dr. McCully's standing is with this Council now, or if he is to be suffered to travel through the United States as a member of this College, and to flourish that fact in connection with his advertisements. If such is the case, then the sooner the Discipline Committee revoke his suspension the better. I have just now been handed by the Prosecutor one of his advertisements in which Dr. McCully says after the most flourishing heading, " Young men, have you sapped your vitality by vicious habits, is your manhood almost gone, your nervous system nearly wrecked, is your memory bad, your brain dizzy, and are you on the verge of self-destruction ? Then, apply to the greatest specialists. We warrant our work in every case. Old men, have you burned the wick of life at both ends—is your sexual life gone ? We bring it back ; we guarantee our work," and so on.

Dr. MOORE—I made a motion that the report be adopted as amended, and Dr. Sangster's remarks seem to me to be quite irrelevant.

Dr. SANGSTER—I may be out of order in reading this, and if so, I will sit down. I merely wanted to enquire whether that man was to continue to travel through the United States as a member of this College.

The PRESIDENT—Dr. Moore, as a member of the committee, might give you some information.

Dr. MOORE—I am glad to say I have never received any of those papers, and I did not know he was touring the United States in this manner ; but I suppose he has a right to tour the United States as he pleases ; he is out of our jurisdiction. He is under suspended sentence, and if he comes back here I presume he will be taken in hand right away (the sword is over his neck), and probably at the next meeting of the Council the full penalty of the law will be meted out to him. But at present he is out of our jurisdiction ; we cannot follow him to Milwaukee.

Dr. MOORHOUSE—I wish to remark that I do not think we as a Council, in the face of this proof that Dr. Sangster has just read, should allow this man to go abroad under our cover or protection. True, he is under suspended sentence, but I think that this is a fresh proof that the old Adam is still operating in him as lively as ever. I think we ought to strike him off the Register, or he will be back here, no doubt, before long. I think we have been long-suffering enough and that he ought to be stricken off without further delay.

Dr. DICKSON—Does not suspended sentence mean that he must commit another offence before we can take further action ?

Dr. MOORE—No.

Dr. DICKSON—Then cut him off.

Dr. SANGSTER—Certainly, if another man is brought up under the report of the Discipline Committee and it is pleaded we should allow him to go under suspended sentence, in view of the fact that he can go and travel through the States, though under that suspended sentence, and circulate foul stuff of that kind, then the Council will be very loath indeed to let him off under suspended sentence.

Dr. MOORHOUSE—Is the discussion of Dr. McCully's character before the chair on that report ?

The PRESIDENT—No, it is out of order.

Dr. McLAUGHLIN—Can we not amend that report by instructing the Discipline Committee, if they are still alive, to strike Dr. McCully's name off the Register ?

Dr. THORBURN—Does his name appear in that paper as a licentiate of this College ?

Dr. SANGSTER—Yes.

Dr. BRITTON—When Dr. McCully's case came before the Council for consideration, I was one of those who pleaded that he might go under suspended sentence, notwithstanding he had acted in such a way as to humiliate and disgrace this profession largely in this country, and notwithstanding I had to say on that occasion, he was, amongst all sinners against decency and propriety, one of the greatest—at the same time because of the promises he made and because I had a certain amount of confidence in his word that he would keep those promises, I pleaded for him. Now I feel just as strongly the other way. We have dealt with the matter very patiently ; and I am not very certain whether—supposing we pass that resolution as an amendment to that report, and instruct the Discipline Committee to have his name taken off the Register—we would not be acting *ultra vires* ; and it might be that an appeal from our decision to a higher court would be sustained. I will move that the Discipline Committee be instructed to get the advice of our Solicitor as to the speediest and best method of proceeding for the purpose of removing Dr. McCully's name from the Register.

Dr. MOORE—This man is out of our country and out of our jurisdiction entirely. He can commit what crimes he has a mind to in a foreign country, and while he remains there we cannot punish him here for what he does there. Dr. Sangster has read an advertisement, but we do not know, as a matter of fact, that Dr. McCully instigated that advertisement. We have no proof whatever that Dr. McCully authorized anybody to put that in the paper ; and for us to take from a man his license and erase his name from the Register upon an advertisement appearing in a paper, without any proof that it was upon his authority or at his instigation, seems to me would be an action totally unwarranted. And I also wish to point out that the Discipline Committee have no power to strike a man's name off the Register ; they simply take the evidence and report to this Council. It is only this Council that can strike a name off the Register ; and to ask this Council to-night or to-morrow to strike a man's name off the Register simply because we find an advertisement with his name attached to it—not his signature—to my mind would be a very dangerous course to pursue.

The PRESIDENT—I think so, too ; I shall have to rule the matter out of order.   There is a motion before the House to adopt this report.

Dr. MOORE—I have no desire to defend Dr. McCully ; my only desire is that we shall not in our haste, or by any rash act do something whereby we might put ourselves in a very awkward position

The President put the motion, and on a vote having been taken declared the report adopted as amended.

Dr. Britton asked leave to introduce a motion at this stage without formal notice.

The President took the sense of the meeting, and granted leave to Dr. Britton to introduce his motion.

Moved by Dr. BRITTON, seconded by Dr. THORBURN, That the case of Dr. Samuel Edward McCully, now under suspended sentence, be referred to the Discipline Committee.

The President read the motion.

Dr. McLAUGHLIN—The question is, Has Dr. McCully's crime been such that we can strike his name off ?   I agree with Dr. Moore, that we have not a tittle of evidence against S. E. McCully on which to erase his name from our Register.

Dr. WILLIAMS—My view harmonizes with the remarks made by Dr. Moore, that we really have no ground to proceed against this man at the present time at all ; and I believe, as long as he is in the United States and is not interfering with us here, we would bring ourselves very much into disrepute if we took action against him and struck his name off. I do not think he is harming us—he is not harming the practitioners of the Province of Ontario, and whatever he may say in the United States I do not think is any material business of ours.   And I think if we trouble ourselves to follow all over the United States people who are not just what they should be, we will incur an unreasonable amount of expense and, what is still worse, a considerable amount of censure, and my conviction would be we would deserve the censure.   I think we should be perfectly satisfied that Dr. McCully has got out of the country, and so long as he will stay out we should let him alone.   When he comes back to Ontario, I think, is time to take prompt action and deal with him, provided we have something against him ; but I do not think it is reasonable, after you have let him once out on suspended sentence, to bring that matter up again and erase his name unless it is shown that he is not keeping the contract entered into.

Dr. CAMPBELL—I think there can be no objection to passing Dr. Britton's motion.   It does not commit the Council to anything, and the Discipline Committee have to report to the Council before anything is done.

Dr. MOORE—Except to add to the motion that the Discipline Committee should not act.

Dr. WILLIAMS—I agree with Dr. Campbell that it should be added that they do not act or incur any expense.   I would like added to the end of the motion, " With instructions to take no action until he enters Canada "

Dr. BRITTON—I would not like to add that, because in case the taking of his name off the Register be advised by our Solicitor, if that addition be made it would strengthen his case on appeal.

The President put the motion, and on a vote having been taken declared it carried.

Moved by Dr. THORBURN, seconded by Dr. MOORE, That the report of the Property Committee be adopted.   Carried.

The PRESIDENT—There is another report which Dr. Reddick has which we might consider now and get out of the way, but it has not yet been presented.

Moved by Dr. EMORY, seconded by Dr. MOORE, That the rule be suspended to allow Dr. Reddick to present his report.   Carried.

Dr. REDDICK presented and read the report of the Committee on Rules and Regulations. The report was received.

REPORT OF COMMITTEE ON RULES AND REGULATIONS.

To the President and members of the Council of the College of Physicians and Surgeons :

Your Committee on Rules and Regulations beg leave to report as follows :

With reference to some suggestions as to amending of Rule 3 relating to the election of President and Vice-President, your committee beg leave to recommend that no change be made in the rule.

R. REDDICK, Chairman Committee.

Adopted without amendment.   A. F. ROGERS, President.

Moved by Dr. REDDICK, seconded by Dr. MACHELL, That the report of the Committee on Rules and Regulations be adopted.

The President read the motion.

Dr. REDDICK—The committee discussed the several suggestions that were made, also the by-law suggested by Dr. Williams which repealed the old rule and provides that the President and Vice-President shall be elected from among the members of the Council present, without nomination, by ballot, and that a majority of the votes of the members present shall be necessary to an election, and provided that in the case of a tie, the election should be decided by the members representing the greatest number of registered practitioners. That is practically the same as the old rule with the change that there is to be no nomination. It provides that there shall be a ballot without nomination. Then Dr. Campbell's suggestion, which was the one I was favorable to, so far as my own opinion went, was an addition. A sub-section added to Rule 3 providing further that "should there be only one person nominated, he shall be declared elected by acclamation," and that when there are more than two candidates in nomination, after a ballot the one receiving the smallest number of votes shall be dropped. The committee do not recommend any change at all. After discussing it we thought it was well to leave it alone.

Dr. WILLIAMS—It is perfectly clear from this year's work, and I think in some years previously, that the present reading of the rule is not above misunderstanding and not above dispute. I think it is not free from considerable objection. The objection to me is that it requires some person to nominate a candidate who is in the field for election, and I think it is humiliating to a man who wishes to be a candidate to ask somebody to put himself in the position of nominating him. I admit that so far as I personally am concerned I would not like just to have to ask some one to nominate me. And I think further, that the objection to open nomination is that it offers opportunity to persons who may be desirous of doing a little wire-pulling. It is quite well understood that if one man is nominated it is rather an unpleasant thing for some other person to get up and nominate another man, and because of this you sometimes hesitate to nominate the man whom you think is best fitted for the position against some other person because of the feeling of unpleasantness that might arise. I think that could be entirely avoided and the work facilitated just as well by doing away with the nomination. Let each person vote by ballot, and when they vote by ballot the person whom they want to be elected very speedily comes to the front. My experience in County Council work where it is done that way, is that in the election of Warden the first ballot may get scattering votes, but the second time it takes form, and the third time, and often before the third time, some person is elected. You do not have to say the last man shall drop out, or anything about it, because immediately the votes take form the man you want will come to the front.

I move in amendment, seconded by Dr. SHAW, That the report be referred back with instructions to strike out the words "after nomination," and to substitute therefor the words "without nomination."

Dr. THORBURN—I beg to take exception to Dr. Williams' views in the matter. I do not think it is at all desirable to do away with the nomination. Among thirty of us here perhaps there would be sixteen or seventeen men whose names would be put in the ballot, and we would have to go on for an indefinite time to arrive at a correct conclusion. I will give you an illustration of it. Not many years ago in Ontario—I do not want to be more definite than that—at a church meeting the names of two very prominent men were mentioned for an elevated position, and there was a third party nominated by the ballot, and he got one vote, and in consequence of the two prominent candidates not appearing this man who originally started with one vote was elected at the head of his church. I think it better to go on just as we have been doing heretofore, and if there is any objection to a candidate for a position, it is quite competent for those who object to suggest the name of somebody else.

Dr. MOORHOUSE—I quite agree with Dr. Thorburn's remarks. I remember the case myself to which I think Dr. Thorburn refers, and similar cases are in my mind now, where the attention of large bodies has been taken up for whole days in a fruitless effort to arrive at a conclusion by ballot; and from what has taken place in the last two or three years in this Council chamber, I think we would be in the same sort of turmoil. I think it is always more manly and dignified in an assembly of this kind to set the various names openly before the Council for election, and things will come to a termination more speedily and more satisfactorily than by an informal ballot. The ballot always seemed to me to be a most undignified way of conducting business, and to be a way quite beneath the dignity of an assembly of this kind. And it is not open and fair; it is a sort of stabbing in the dark. Whenever a ballot is asked for I always think the man or men who ask for it want to keep their hands hidden. Therefore I would oppose this motion of Dr. Williams'.

Dr. LOGAN—Some years ago when this matter was introduced and we changed from the old way I was opposed to the secret ballot. I wish to state now my views on that matter, and to say that I am still entirely opposed to the secret ballot in any form in which you choose to introduce it. It may be necessary for politicians; I believe it is. There is a large section of our people in this country who are dependent upon some others, and if the manner

5

in which they voted were made known to their employers it might result in their losing their situations. That makes it a necessity for politicians to use the secret ballot. But, gentlemen, is it necessary for us to resort to measures of this kind when in this Council? Is it necessary for honorable men and educated men to have a secret mode of expressing their opinions upon matters relating to the medical profession? I think it is an undignified—I think it is an unmanly thing, and therefore I am decidedly opposed to this method of giving expression to the opinions of the Council, not merely upon the election of President, but upon any other matter, and I am glad to have had an opportunity of expressing my disapproval of the secret ballot, whether in the manner indicated in Dr. Williams' amendment, or in any other way.

Dr. CAMPBELL—I have opposed the ballot in the past, and I am opposed to it now, but the Council operate in this matter by ballot, and therefore, when the question came up the other day, I submitted a proposition to this effect, that if we are to have a ballot then we should add to our rule a proviso, that, if at any time only one candidate is nominated he shall be declared elected by acclamation. That gets over the necessity of having a ballot when there is only one candidate nominated. And further, when there are more than two candidates in nomination, after each ballot the one receiving the smallest number of votes shall be dropped. It might happen, if there is not a provision of that kind, with three candidates in the field you might keep on balloting all day, and for several days. Of course it is not likely, but such a thing is possible. If we are to have a ballot it seems to me that my proposition is the best way to get over the difficulty. If anybody chooses to bring in a motion to amend the clause by providing that we have no ballot at all I am quite willing to vote for it; but, as it stands now, we have a ballot, and therefore I wish to move that the report be referred back to the committee with instructions to report to the Council the amendment I have proposed. But, as I say, while that is my amendment, I am quite willing to have the ballot struck out altogether.

Dr. MOORHOUSE—I will second Dr. Campbell's motion; it is quite in accord with my views. I am not opposed to the ballot, but only to the informal ballot, such as Dr. Williams proposes. I think it would be beneath our dignity to adopt an informal ballot in an assembly of this kind.

Dr. EMORY—As a member of the Rules and Regulations Committee, I beg to state that the reasons which prompted us in suggesting no change should be made were that the present by-law had worked satisfactorily, and we could see no reason for making any change, and we thought our recommendation would be adopted without any discussion, and thus save the time of the Council; but if we are going into amendments, and amendments to the amendments, and amendments to the amendments to the amendments, we are not saving the time of the Council.

Dr. SANGSTER—I, like Dr. Logan, do not like the ballot. I think it is anomalous that in this Council the President and Vice-President are the only officers that are elected by ballot. The cases of these officers are the only instances in which the by-laws recognize the ballot. I would prefer an open, square vote. If you alter this at all, you will have to alter it by a formal by-law, as it is part of one of your existing by-laws, and I will gladly second a motion by Dr. Logan, or anybody else, to the effect that when that by-law is amended, it shall provide that, like all other votes in this Council, the votes for President and Vice-President shall be open votes.

Dr. CAMPBELL—My present motion is the proposition I submitted in Council and it was referred to the committee. It was to amend Rule 3 by adding to it, "and providing further, that if there shall be at any time only one candidate in nomination, he shall be declared elected by acclamation; and further, when there are more than two candidates in nomination, after each ballot the one receiving the smallest number of votes shall be dropped."

Dr. LUTON—As a member of the Committee on Rules and Regulations, I raised an objection to Dr. Campbell's suggestion in that committee, because, if there are three individuals nominated to any position, the first vote is taken with a certain result, and for the person that receives the smallest number of votes to drop out and have no further chance in the election is unfair to that man. Many times when elections are carried on in the way suggested by Dr. Williams, the man that on the first ballot would have the lowest number of votes and would consequently be dropped, as per Dr. Campbell's motion, is finally the man selected. I think that shows that in a case of this kind it would be an unjust thing to drop out the man that happened on the first ballot to get the lowest number of votes, and I think that objection would be fatal to Dr. Campbell's suggestion. Again, with reference to the suggestion of Dr. Williams, reducing these things to practice, I remember quite well in the county of Elgin, when they proposed that everybody should have the chance of nominating as many as he had a mind to propose, ten or twelve councillors of the township or county would be nominated for the position of Warden; and I remember very distinctly it took two days under that system to elect a Warden; that is how it worked

.in practice there, and it might work that way here. I think the committee considered all these things fully, and, so far as I am able to judge of it, I think the best results will follow by just leaving the by-law as it is.

Dr. REDDICK—It must be understood that any suggestions or motions that have to go in would have to be made, as Dr. Sangster said, by by-law ; that was one of the reasons why we did not suggest any change, but we might better have done so, and have saved all this trouble and discussion. After discussion the committee thought it better to let it go as it was and save time, as any instruction given to us must only be an instruction to recommend a by-law. If you want to change one iota or one word, there must be an instruction to the committee to bring in a by-law.

Dr. WILLIAMS—If that motion is referred to the committee to make a change then it is true a by-law necessarily follows. There have been some remarks made about this method being very much below the dignity of a profession like this, but I do not know that it is, I do not know that there is any very great amount of lowering of the dignity of a man to write a ballot and put it in. Perhaps it may be thought so by some people who have very exalted notions of human nature ; but I do not want to be of that class. I believe there are members of the Council who will stoop to infinitely lower things than merely writing the name of some man they want for President. I think it is a lower thing to ask a man to vote for you or to nominate you ; I think it is infinitely worse to do anything of that kind than to write a name quietly on a ballot and put it in for the man you want. As to the practicability of this matter, I served quite a good few years in the County Council where there were between thirty and forty members, and the vote by ballot was always taken without nomination, and I never saw any difficulty whatever in coming to an election for Warden in a very short time ; the Warden's election was the only one carried on in that way. No person's feelings were hurt ; it is the method by which you prevent one member having hard feelings to another, and you all know, I do not need to tell you, there are men for whom you have a warm friendship, yet in your right-down honest judgment in your heart you feel "that is not the best possible man to put in the chair." I would not like to give him a little slap in the face by getting up and nominating somebody else or perhaps by openly voting against him. I would infinitely prefer to have the thing pass off quietly and smoothly, and not disturb friendship in any way. Sometimes these disturbances of friendship interfere with the workings of business afterwards. Isn't it better all round in securing the best men for the place, and in preventing irritation and ill-feeling, to quietly put in your ballots without any talk about it, and let these be counted. I do not take very much stock myself in people talking about the ballot being un-British, and all that sort of thing, because the British people themselves vote by nomination. You may think it is very British to hold up your hand and run your head against a stone wall, if you like, but I do not want to be of that class of people ; and I believe it is infinitely better to pass along smoothly and comfortably without irritating people and disturbing things than it is to do the other way, and I, for one, prefer the ballot in the quietest possible way it can be got.

Dr. BARRICK—I think that either of the ways that have been suggested would lead to less friction than we had this year on the ballot as it is. I am quite in favor of Dr. Williams' resolution ; I think it would lead to less friction and lead to less ill-feelings than any of the others. There is no doubt, as he has stated, that the man that seems to be the choice of the Council would gradually work his way to the front without much loss of time. We want to adopt some plan that will lead to less friction. There is a tendency in this Council to keep rubbing up old sores and making friction.

Dr. MCLAUGHLIN—Dr. Williams objects to the present by-law because it is a very undignified thing to be nominated.

Dr. WILLIAMS—No. It is undignified to have to ask some person to nominate you.

Dr. MCLAUGHLIN—I quite agree with you, but surely a man who is fit to occupy that chair will get a nomination without asking for it. (Hear, hear.) I certainly think it is a most undignified act on the part of any person to go round begging that he shall be nominated, and I hope that has not been done at this meeting or any other meeting. If that is Dr. Williams' only objection, there is no objection in it, as far as I can see—it is invalid, for to be nominated is an honorable thing. In a few days 215—yes, twice 215—430 men, and more than that, for there are triple and quadruple contests in some places, will be nominated in this Dominion.

Dr. MOORE—A thousand.

Dr. MCLAUGHLIN—Yes, probably a thousand ; it is not undignified.

Dr. WILLIAMS—It is not undignified.

Dr. MCLAUGHLIN—Then Dr. Williams' argument must fall to the ground, because I cannot think that this Council will ever assemble here without feeling that "there is a man who would be fit to be President." My friend, Dr. Williams, does not object to the ballot because it is British ; the British people do it. But they do not do it under circumstances such as this. In the British House of Commons there is no ballot for their chief officers, nor in the Legislature ; an open nomination is taken and an open ballot in all cases except where the election is by acclamation.

Dr. WILLIAMS—Those are party votes.

Dr. McLAUGHLIN—It is all party ; there are two parties here ; one party thinks the man is fit and the other party thinks he is not. Personally I would be in favor of having no ballot at all ; not for the reasons that have been assigned altogether, but because every member of this Council is sent here as the representative of some body of men, be it large or small, and I hold we ought not to put ourselves in any position where our constituents will fail to find out what we have done. I think all our acts in this Council should be open to the gaze of those who send us here ; so that, if we seek re-election, all our acts will be open and above board, and will be before those who selected us once, in order that they may see whether it is a proper thing to select us once more. That is my principal objection to the ballot. I would like those who sent me here to know every act I have performed and hear every word I uttered, and upon that ground I would prefer having this election conducted by an open vote ; and, so far as this Section 3 is concerned, it seems to me it is as plain as A B C how our election should be conducted, and I think next year we will not have any difficulty in understanding it.

Dr. GRAHAM—It seems to me there is not so much trouble about the section itself ; it is more about the interpretation. To decide upon the interpretation of this clause would facilitate matters, and it appears to me that could be done without a by-law.

Dr. McLAUGHLIN—I would suggest that the President submit the whole clause to the Attorney-General and I would be willing to be bound by it.

Dr. MOORE—I think we had better get on. We have wasted $45.00 to $50.00 in wind over a few words.

The President put Dr. Campbell's amendment to the amendment, and on a vote having been taken declared it lost.

Moved by Dr. LOGAN, seconded by Dr. SANGSTER, in amendment to the amendment, That the report be referred back to the committee with instructions to amend the by-law by striking out the words " by ballot."

The President put Dr. Logan's amendment to the amendment, and on a vote having been taken declared it lost.

Moved by Dr. GRAHAM, seconded by Dr. HENRY, in amendment to the amendment, That the proper interpretation of said clause be that the ballot be passed to each member of the Council in the case of one or more nominations.

The PRESIDENT—That is not an amendment to the main motion nor to the amendment.

Dr. HENRY—That is what we have been discussing here to-night ; we want to get this Rule 3 thoroughly interpreted. That is what it was referred to the Committee on Rules and Regulations for.

The PRESIDENT—The main motion is to adopt, the amendment is to amend, and this motion now is to interpret—an entirely different thing, and I cannot accept it as an amendment to the amendment.

The President put Dr. Williams' amendment, and on a vote having been taken declared it lost.

The President put the main motion, and on a vote having been taken declared it carried, and the report adopted.

On motion of Dr. Moore, seconded by Dr. Thorburn, the Council adjourned to meet again at 10 a.m. on Friday, the 12th June, 1896.

FOURTH DAY.

FRIDAY, 12th June, 1896.

The Council met at 10 o'clock a.m., according to motion for adjournment.

The President in the chair.

The Registrar called the roll and the following members were present : Drs. Armour, Barrick, Bray, Britton, Brock, Campbell, Dickson, Emory, Fowler, Geikie, Graham, Hanly, Henderson, Henry, Logan, Luton, Machell, Moore, Moorhouse, McLaughlin, Reddick, Rogers, Rosebrugh, Sangster, Shaw, Thorburn, Thornton, Williams.

The minutes of the proceedings were read by the Registrar, and confirmed, and signed by the President.

NOTICES OF MOTION.

No. 1. Dr. CAMPBELL—To introduce a by-law appointing a Discipline Committee.

No. 2. Dr. CAMPBELL—That after the adoption of this motion no new business be introduced without unanimous consent.

COMMUNICATIONS, PETITIONS, ETC.

The Registrar read a communication asking that the writer be placed under the four years course. Referred to Educational Committee.

MOTIONS OF WHICH NOTICE HAS BEEN GIVEN AT A PREVIOUS MEETING.

Moved by Dr. HENRY, seconded by Dr. DICKSON, and resolved, That in the opinion of the Medical Council there should be established a medical tariff for the Province of Ontario in order that the reasonable charges or fees of the registered medical practitioners may have a legal status in all courts of law in this Province; that such medical tariff should be framed and sanctioned by this Council, but it should only come into legal force when it has received the sanction and approval of three Judges of the Supreme Court of Judicature of Ontario; that such medical tariff when it comes into legal force as aforesaid, may be printed and copies of it distributed to the registered medical practitioners of Ontario, and such copy, having the seal of the College and the signature of the Registrar attached thereto, shall be received in all courts of law in lieu of the original tariff; that such copies of the said medical tariff shall be a scale of reasonable charges within the meaning of Section 39 of the Medical Act.

The President read the motion.

Dr. HENRY—I just rise to say that in introducing this motion I think I am carrying out the wish and desire of my constituents, some of whom have expressed the opinion to me that they have felt the want of such a tariff. I know that under the old tariff many a vexatious suit was avoided and many a time has a medical man been relieved from a disagreeable position : the tariff has settled many a case that would have been very disagreeable because the plaintiff would have been forced to bring other medical men into court to give evidence on his behalf ; and I believe it will be a move in the right direction if we can get legislation, though I feel like the rest of the gentlemen of the Council, that perhaps it would be a very bad thing to approach the Legislature while they are in the temper they are in at present. I think if we had a provincial tariff that would give satisfaction. The great objection before was to the great multiplicity of tariffs. But if we had one that applied to the whole Province it would give universal satisfaction ; and if the Legislature is going to be approached at the next session for some legislation in connection with medical matters, I think it would be well and wise to have this thing brought up and considered by a committee before.

Dr. WILLIAMS—This matter was up before the Council last year, and a resolution was passed authorizing the members of the Council to obtain information from their constituents so far as practicable on this subject. Dr. Henry's resolution now does away with my taking any action, and we can listen to the opinions of the members of the Council in so far as they have been able to get them from their constituents and themselves, under Dr. Henry's motion as well as if it had been introduced specially. Personally I entertain no different views from those expressed last year, and that was the conviction that at the present time we are better without a tariff and better without approaching the Legislature, than endeavoring to get a tariff. And in fact we could not get one unless we consented to that tariff being submitted to either the Judges or the Governor in Council for approval. I understand that some members of the Council take the ground that if we have a tariff it should be a tariff like the legal tariff, covering the entire Province. When I look at that it seems to me an impracticable thing. For instance, the prices that are charged in the city of Toronto are considered very reasonable and fair, but if you applied those in some of our back country constituencies they would be considered outrageous ; I do not hesitate to say that they would be regarded by the public as being outrageous charges, and a tariff of such charges could not there be carried out at all. It is not possible, I think, under the circumstances to have a tariff that is applicable to the whole Province, and I think I may say that the Attorney-General is of the opinion that it should apply to the whole Province. I do not think it wise to ask the Government to put through any such tariff at all. During the last year I have written to a good many of the leading men in my own constituency, and I got back responses from a great part of them, and among them I did not get one answer favorable to our making a move to get a legalized tariff ; our members seemed to be of the opinion that it was better to leave things for the present as they are ; that they were getting along satisfactorily. After writing a great many letters and getting answers, I did not get one single one that advised us to go on and secure legislation upon that subject ; that being the case, I shall, of course, vote against Dr. Henry's resolution, and in favor of leaving the matter just as it is at the present time.

Dr. McLAUGHLIN—I am of the opinion that we have no power to pass any tariff ourselves and submit it to the Judges and have it become law, without going to the Legislature——

Dr. WILLIAMS—No ; that is conceded.

Dr. McLaughlin—I think it would be quite useless and likely to do the profession more harm than good in the present temper of the country to go near the Legislature just now. I would suggest that Dr. Henry, if he wished to get the consensus of the opinion of the representatives in the Council as to what a general tariff might be, he might do that and then have it put into the journals and have it circulated through the Province. But to proceed further with this now would be quite useless ; we have not the power, and we would have to go back to the Legislature to get the power, to establish such a tariff; and I know pretty well the temper of the Legislature, and I can assure you in the interests of the profession, we will be far better to let them alone at the present time. I hope Dr. Henry will withdraw the motion, or we shall have to vote it down.

Dr. Williams—I think we should get the opinion of the Council on it now.

Dr. Henry—There is an idea through the country that the old tariff is still in existence ; in fact, almost every week I receive a communication from some of my constituents at Walkerton and other places I might mention, asking for a copy of the tariff, and I believe one half of the practitioners do not know that the tariff has been abolished, though Dr. Williams' constituents apparently do know it.

Dr. Williams—I have made it my business, in writing, to call their attention to the pages in the Announcement where they would find a debate had taken place on the subject in the Council, and ask them to read those pages and give me their views, as well as the views of their immediate neighbors. •

Dr. Henry—Speaking of the tariff being made to suit the whole Province, I no not see that there would be much difficulty. We can have a minimum charge for the poorest parts of the Province, and a maximum rate fixed for the cities ; I cannot see any difficulty in that. The only difficulty I can see is the Legislature. I think the Legislature are in a pretty bad temper at present, and after the way they have clipped our wings recently, I would not like to go myself, though I do not know what we have done that we should lose our wings. I think, however, it is better to have this matter disposed of and get the expression of opinion of the Council.

Dr. McLaughlin—If you go to the Legislature again, you will be apt to come away without any wings at all.

Dr. Thornton—When this discussion came up last year, I determined to be in a position to know something about the feeling of my electorate and to be able to speak with that knowledge at this meeting of the Council, so I made it my business to enquire from a number of members of the medical profession in my division, and I think in only one instance did I get a decided opinion. In the majority of cases I got an interrogation to the effect, "In what way are we suffering for want of a tariff?" This came to me in nearly every instance, and I found it was totally impossible to get a definite opinion from the electorate at the present time. I fully concur with what Dr. Williams said, that, for the time being, we had better leave it alone.

Dr. Dickson—As seconder of the motion, I beg to say that I have had some opportunity of learning from my constituents what their views are on this subject. The effect of the information I have gained is that it would be desirable to have a provincial tariff; and, for my own part, I cannot see why the tariff should not be made provincial ; I think the services rendered in the extreme north, at Pembroke, are quite as valuable as services rendered in the city of Toronto ; services of a like character I think are worth quite as much. It is true that we do not perform many of the capital operations that are performed in the city of Toronto, and for that reason we do not charge anything for them, but any operations we do perform, I think are well worth being paid just as much for ; and as far as my own experience is concerned, I have no difficulty in getting the same remuneration in Pembroke as practitioners in Toronto for the same operation. I think the difficulty that exists in other localities is simply because gentlemen have not insisted on being paid full value for their services. My constituents think a tariff would be desirable for some sections of the field, for all parts do not enjoy the same fees we do in Pembroke—in some parts of the division these are smaller, but that has apparently pretty well grown from the competition. And they would be glad now if a provincial tariff were established in order that they might have authority for going back again to reasonable prices ; and, therefore, in order to satisfy my constituents, I would vote for the resolution.

Dr. Graham—In accordance with the resolution passed by the Council last year, I took a good deal of pains in order to elucidate the opinion of the most prominent medical men in my constituency ; and I had an opportunity of meeting a great many personally and having conversations with them on this point, and I have also communicated by letter with a great number ; and although they thought that it would be a very good thing to have a legalized tariff, they consider they would be perfectly willing to leave it in abeyance for several years, on account of the very irritable condition of the temper of the Legislature at the present time, and in no case did any one insist on having a legalized tariff at the present time.

Dr. SANGSTER—I also have conversed very extensively with my constituents, as far as I could meet them, on that point ; and the result of my investigation in that direction is to the effect that there exists in the profession itself a very great deal of apprehension as to what the tariff is designed for. I understand, from what was said last year, that the tariff is not, and never was, designed as a tariff of fees that all the medical men in a certain section should adhere to, on account of the congestion and over-crowding of the profession, and the loss of morale in the strife to live, and the lowering process of one under-bidding another. A great many men in the constituency would desire a tariff, if it could be obtained, that would compel all to stick to the same fee ; but I understand that this is impossible, and a tariff in that sense is entirely out of the question. As soon as medical men generally are made to comprehend that the tariff is merely to serve as a guide in courts of law, as to what charges are reasonable and proper to collect, they say, we don't care tu'pence about that, we are not suffering in any way for a tariff. I have no sympathy with the idea that Dr. McLaughlin and others have advanced, that if we have a real grievance, as I think we have or shall have in the near future, that we should be afraid to approach the Legislature to demand anything that can be shown to be right and just for the profession, and not adverse to the interests of the public. (Hear, hear.) I believe the medical men of this Province, once they are aroused to a consciousness of the danger that confronts them, and of the necessity of combined action on their part, can bring an influence to bear upon the individual members of the Legislature in their constituencies that will carry all before it ; and I claim, therefore, it is puerile, it is cowardly, on our part to say we are afraid to approach the Legislature to ask for what we know to be our rights and what is just and proper. I am at present very firmly of the conviction that we should not approach the Legislature on the subject of tariff, because that has been one of the sore points in the House. I was riding in the cars a short time ago with a member of the Government—Mr. Hardy—and in speaking of it, he told me of some unfortunate case—of course he ridiculed it—where a practitioner had a charge of $50.00—so the Patrons put it—for setting a broken thumb, that had been brought up and brought up in the House until they were all sick and tired of it. Of course, Mr. Hardy said, everybody knew it was false ; that, if such a charge was made, it was made because it became necessary to have attendance in consequence of the broken thumb ; but he said it was put as the charge for setting the broken thumb.

At the request of the President, Dr. Thorburn, the Vice-President, took the chair.

Dr. ROGERS—This motion was introduced to-day by Dr. Henry at my request ; and for your information I have come from the chair to address you for a moment on the points which I think are of importance, not only to the profession in Ontario, but points which I think my constituents demand. I am strongly in favor of a provincial tariff ; I am strongly in favor of a tariff of some kind, a legal tariff ; and I am very much gratified at the way Dr. Sangster grasped the reason why the tariff was first originated, and why those sections of the Act were put there. The intention never was to frame a tariff for the purpose of compelling medical men to all charge alike ; and if you will turn up Section 39 of the Medical Act, you will find it says : " Every person registered under the provisions of this Act shall be entitled, according to his qualification or qualifications, to practice medicine, surgery, or midwifery, or any of them, as the case may be, in the Province of Ontario, and to demand and recover in any court, with full costs of suit, reasonable charges for professional aid, advice and visits, and the cost of any medicine or other medical or surgical appliances rendered or supplied by him to his patients." Then turn back to Section 16 : " The said Division Association may from time to time submit to the Council a tariff, or tariffs, of professional fees, suitable to their division, or to separate portions of their division ; and upon the said tariff, or tariffs of fees, receiving the approval of the Council, signified by the seal of the College and by the signature of the President thereof, being appended thereto, such tariff or tariffs shall be held to be a scale of reasonable charges within the meaning of Section 39 of this Act for the division or section of a division where the member making the charge resides."

Dr. McLAUGHLIN—That was repealed.

Dr. ROGERS—I am aware of that. But the object was that you should have the right in a court of law to collect reasonable charges ; the section says " the right to frame a scale of charges which shall be held to be a scale of reasonable charges." That was the object. It was held it was best to have some scale or tariff of charges so that a Judge, when a case came before him, would have this to show that it was a scale of reasonable charges. We lost the right of having a tariff for two reasons ; first because there were twelve tariffs in Ontario, yes, more than that ; secondly these tariffs were not framed properly, all the copies of them were not signed by the President of the Council, with the seal of the College attached, and they were utterly useless, they were so much waste paper. I maintain that at the present time our charges have no legal status at all, you cannot collect in a court of law to-day one dollar, unless the Judge feels inclined to give it. He may take the evidence of a dozen doctors, but he is not compelled to do so. Your fees have no legal status at all to-day, and I maintain that in taking off Section 16 the Government of this Province not only did an unjust thing, but they took away certain vested rights we obtained when we became members of this College. When we passed our examinations and became members of the College and paid our fees, we did it because we were to have a legal status; and I say again, that in taking that section away, the Government have taken certain vested rights of the College of Physicians and Surgeons of Ontario; and in fact not only that, but I claim in doing it without consulting this Council and the medical men of this Province they have violated every principle of justice towards the medical men of this Province; and I want to say that I would be ashamed to get up and say, I am afraid to go to the Legislature. When the time comes that the medical men of this Province dare not go to their servants, the Legislature, then it is time to say, Gentlemen, wipe away the Medical Act altogether. (Hear, hear.) It is not for us to sit here as members of a profession which, I believe, without using extravagant language, is composed of the most eminent and prominent men in the Province, and say that we dare not go to our servants and ask what is right and what is just. Dr. Henry in his speech honestly stated that there was a grievance, but he says he does not think it is right for us to go to the Legislature at the present time. I think it is right for us to go to the Legislature at the present time; I think we have got a very serious grievance. For the last three years we have not gone there, but has not the Medical Act been tampered with? And has not there been attempted legislation every year? Certainly there has. There was last year, and there was the year before. Did we go and ask for that? Not at all. Even the Government introduced a measure last year which meant to dictate to this Council and others what we should do, as if we were a lot of boys. I claim the Medical Council is just as capable of conducting their affairs as the Hon. Mr. Ross is capable of conducting the affairs of the Government, and I say it was an outrage to introduce a measure which would take away from this Council the right of controlling matriculation. That was a Government measure, but it was not a very creditable thing for the honorable gentleman who introduced the measure, to allow every man who had passed the poor miserable examinations in the Old Country to come out here and register by passing our last or final and clinical examination. While I am a little out of order, I am strongly of opinion that the medical men of this Province should be given back their vested rights and should have a right to have a scale of reasonable charges, so that if Dr. Fowler, or Dr. Moorhouse, or Dr. Barrick, should unfortunately have to go before the court, the court cannot say to him, "Doctor, I will give you nothing," as I heard a Judge in my own division say to a member of our profession, who came before him with a charge of $40.00, and a most reasonable charge it was, "I need not give you a cent," notwithstanding he had three doctors there to prove the charge was reasonable.

Dr. ARMOUR—Will you tell us who that Judge was?

Dr. ROGERS—Judge Mosgrove. The Judge claimed he was not bound by any Act of Parliament, when they have taken away that tariff, to give one dollar; it is for him to say. And there is no appeal from Division Courts; the Judge stands there with autocratic power, able to say, "Dr. Sangster, I will not give you a dollar." And you cannot compel him to.

Dr. SANGSTER—I do not want to interrupt you, but I know there is a decision in the English courts rather adverse to what you say and yet really emphasizing what you say; it has been held in the English courts for years back, that a doctor's advice and attendance was not a marketable commodity, but whatever medicines he gave his patients he could claim a fair price for.

Dr. ROGERS—Thank you. I forgot that. The decision on that point is that for medicines you have given you can claim the actual marketable value for, and the Judge shall allow you for it, but so far as the English courts are concerned you cannot claim anything for your fees. We stand in this position to-day. We have come here and passed our examinations and paid our fees and complied with all the laws of the Province and of the College of Physicians and Surgeons, and, for my part, when I did these, I did it on the ground that I would have a tariff of fees by which I could go to a court of law with a right to demand my fees for my work. The Legislature have taken away that tariff and my vested rights. I am ashamed to stand here in this Council to-day and hear it said that we dare not go to the Legislature. I say we can go to the Legislature, and go with the certainty of getting anything we ask that is right and fair, but I would not go without a petition being signed by the medical men of the Province. I am sure if we get a petition signed asking for what is right and fair, the Government will listen to us and will grant our request. I am sorry that this matter was not brought up in the last session and that it was not brought up earlier in this. And if you go to the Legislature and get power to have a tariff, you should first ask for a provincial tariff, and then ask, after that tariff is framed and sanctioned by this Council, that before it becomes law three Judges of the Supreme Court of Ontario— that is, the Court of Appeal—shall have sanctioned it and that after it is so sanctioned it becomes a legal tariff for all courts of law. That will take away the strongest argument of the ministers that our tariff was framed by doctors and sanctioned by doctors, and that no one else had anything to do with it. If we get the sanction of three Judges, three of the most honorable men in this Province, surely the public and the courts of law would have confidence in that tariff, and we would in this way satisfy those members of the Government who have been opposed to our having a tariff. Is there any reason why we should not have a provincial tariff? Has it not cost a medical man living in Muskoka as much for his education as Dr. Barrick's cost him, and is not his education just as good as Dr. Barrick's in Toronto, and is he not just as capable of performing an operation as Dr. Barrick would be? Then why should he not have the same fees? There is no justice in saying that a practitioner's fees should not be quite as large simply because he happens to live in the backwoods. If, for instance, I live in the backwoods, and my education and attainments professionally were just as good as those of men living in Toronto, why should I have less fees? Do they have different fees in the Law Society? No. The man in the small village does not have different fees from those which would be taxable by a lawyer in a large city. He gets five dollars for drawing a deed in the country village, the same as though he lived in a large city. Why should the medical men be different? There is no reason why medical men in a country place should receive smaller fees because their expenses of living are a little less. We are not mechanics, but professional men, and we should have a professional tariff. The object of a tariff is to establish a fair reward for our professional services, it makes no difference where that professional service is rendered. If this Council thought it would be wise to have two rates, one for the rural portions and one for the cities, there is nothing in the resolution to prevent it ; but I would personally urge the Council to have one tariff and to make the fees as low as possible, and then we would have something so that the Judge could not say, "I will give you nothing for your services." These are the reasons why I advocate the passing of this resolution. It is simply an expression of opinion on the part of this Council that we ought to have a tariff ; it does not say we are going to have one, but it says if we go to the Legislature and if we get power we are willing to take a tariff on those lines. I think it is a fair resolution, it will disgrace no one ; and it will be a credit to the Council because lots of the medical men understand we have no tariff. I can speak very strongly on this point on behalf of some of my constituents, and the reason I am speaking strongly to-day is because some of my constituents have spoken strongly to me, and therefore I advocate the passing of this resolution, and ask you before voting for it to lay over to think whether it would not be well to put on our proceedings the record of having passed a resolution of this character.

The President resumed the chair.

Dr. CAMPBELL—I do not think, Mr. President, there would be any harm done in passing the resolution, for as you have just said, it is simply the expression of opinion in favor of a provincial tariff, and to that I think there can be no objection. So far as the opinion of practitioners in my section is concerned, if I may be permitted to speak for that section, as the representative of the division is unavoidably absent, there is no particular enthusiasm one way or the other ; they seem to be comparatively indifferent ; I have not found any one who is anxious to have the matter so definitely fixed by law, and they are quite willing to let it rest as it is. I hardly think myself, that we are in so very bad a position as you have stated, Mr. President, because the section of the Act under which we have power to collect reasonable charges remains, I believe, still unrepealed ; Clause 16 of the Act which gives the power of fixing a tariff has been repealed, but the same power and the same vested right we had before of collecting in a court of law reasonable charges, I think still remains. When the tariff was there, when the divisions had their different tariffs, many Judges acted on their own discretion, and though the tariff was laid before them, they preferred to take their own ideas as to what were reasonable charges in any particular case. The old English idea, of course, always was that a physician did not receive any pay, he might receive an honorarium, but that was a matter between him and his patient ; he could only receive pay for the actual material he gave his patient, but for his services as a gentleman he could not receive pay. That feeling, however, I think is dying out in England ; I doubt if it has ever been in existence in Canada, and I am pretty sure to-day no modern Judge who is not so completely fossilized as to be fit for superannuation, would think for a moment of saying that a physician should not receive pay for his services just the same as a lawyer would, even though there was no tariff by which a scale of charges was fixed. I do not think any harm can be done by passing the resolution, but at the same time I do not think we need worry ourselves very much or fear that our rights have been greatly diminished by the acts of the Legislature in taking away that clause of the Act.

Dr. LOGAN—While most medical men are in the habit of sometimes disagreeing, I take it that we all agree about getting our pay, and as much of it as we possibly can. I fancy there is very little difference of opinion among us as to the propriety of having a tariff, provided we can accomplish it in our own way. The point I wish to make is not in that direction ; it is that after our consenting to the desirability of a tariff, the next thing to consider would be the propriety of presenting ourselves at this time to the Legislature. I have had a little experience with our Legislature, and I find they are somewhat erratic ; and I think it absolutely essential, if we go to the Legislature that we should go united ; if we express a difference of opinion here amongst ourselves, for instance this very discussion, if it is made public, will destroy the probability of our securing a tariff. I think, then, it is absolutely essential, if we make up our minds to go to the Legislature, that whatever resolution is adopted, we should be unanimous. That is the only point I wish to make. (Hear, hear.)

Dr. SHAW—Mr. President, as the resolution instructed the territorial representatives to gather a little information on this question during the interval between the present and the last session, I, with many of the other members, endeavored to get as much information in the city of Hamilton as I could before coming here ; I took the trouble of advising with the majority of the practitioners there ; and my experience was to the effect that, with one or two exceptions, they were not aware that we had no legalized tariff, and they had not felt, therefore, they were in any unfortunate position. The majority of them, while thinking we should have a legalized tariff, were of opinion that it would be more useful as a guide to our charges in our professional work than of use in our courts of law—perhaps we are less inclined to go to court there than practitioners in other parts of the Province are. Though I have been practising there for eighteen years, I have not been in a court of law at all, so that personally I have not suffered ; and I am not of the opinion that we will suffer if we do not have a tariff. I took the trouble, however, to write to many of my constituents in the counties which I represent, and in every case, with one exception, their replies were to the effect that they thought we should have a tariff, but that they were under the impression that now was not the proper time to approach the Legislature with that object in view.

Dr. BRAY—Mr. President, as a territorial representative, I have taken very much the same course as Dr. Shaw has, with reference to my constituents ; but I find that they were better informed than the gentlemen in Hamilton, for they all knew that we had no tariff ; my constituents think there should be something to guide the Judges in giving decisions in the event of medical men having to come into a court of law ; and when I said to them that it was proposed to have a provincial tariff, they said that would be all right if it was on a sliding scale. I take a little exception, or at least, I differ a little from some of the gentlemen who have said that services are worth as much in one place as another, for there are certain services that are perhaps not worth as much and in other cases you have got to be guided by the financial standing of your patients, and if we had a tariff that was pretty elastic, as a sliding scale, I think it would be very popular in the profession. I cannot see any harm in passing this resolution because we cannot get this tariff until we go to the Legislature ; because if we really want a tariff it will give us a great deal of help towards it, and I would like to see it passed unanimously, as Dr. Logan has said. There may be a difference of opinion as to what time we should go to the Legislature, but that is a matter for consideration later. I am going to give a notice of motion when it comes to miscellaneous business, on this subject, which I will explain later on, as I think this Council should pass this resolution because it is not committing us to anything, and I know it would be gratifying to our constituents to know we are endeavoring to put them on a legal standing so far as collection of fees is concerned.

Dr. ARMOUR—I cannot agree with Dr. Bray. I think it would be a great mistake to pass this resolution unanimously, or in any other way ; if you pass this resolution unanimously, it would naturally lead to some further action being taken by the Legislation Committee should a Legislation Committee be appointed. Some members of the profession may have a grievance with regard to this matter, but that grievance is not very widely extended throughout the members of the profession of this Province. We had a right, for many years, to establish tariffs in the different territorial divisions of the Province, and I believe I am right in saying that several of those divisions never utilized that right ; this, I think, is proof positive that the grievance spoken of is not very widespread among the members of the profession. I will not detain you longer than to say, I hope the resolution will not carry.

Dr. Bray asked permission to again address the Council.

The President granted Dr. Bray's request.

Dr. BRAY—The tariff was utilized and utilized to a very great extent ; I do not think there is a county in the Province of Ontario that had not a medical tariff. I do not mean to say they had a divisional tariff, but they had a city tariff or local association tariff of the town or village, and most of them, nearly all of them, were sanctioned by this Council, but they were not appreciated for their legal value so much as they were as a guide ; for instance, if a patient wanted to know if a practitioner had any authority or any guide for making a charge, all that was necessary was to show the tariff and say, this is our tariff, and in that way the tariff obviated a lot of friction and prevented many law suits. As an illustration of how this tariff was of use, in the town of Paris a couple of years ago there was a suit brought against the Grand Trunk Railway for some operations that were performed there, and the Medical Officer at Montreal wrote to me for the tariff for this Province. I told him there was no such thing as a tariff for this Province, that the divisions of the Province had tariffs of their own ; he then asked me to send him the tariff of my division, and I did so, and they were guided by that tariff. I was sent for as a witness to go to Paris to testify to the correctness of the tariff, and I did so ; and the plaintiff recovered because of that tariff, and he would not have recovered if that tariff had not existed.

The PRESIDENT—I have just asked the Registrar how many tariffs there were, and he tells me there were ten in the Province, and there were only twelve divisions.

Dr. ARMOUR—Will you just allow me to correct you about that. For instance, in the division I live in there was a tariff endorsed by the Council, but it only applied to one county in the division, the county of Brant ; the other three counties connected with the division have never had a tariff, and no doubt that is the way it has been throughout the Province.

The President put the motion, and on a vote having been taken declared it carried.

Moved by Dr. CAMPBELL, seconded by Dr. BRAY, That By-law No. — to amend By-law No. 69, be read a first time. Carried.

The by-law was read a first time.

Moved by Dr. CAMPBELL, seconded by Dr. BRAY, That By-law No. — be referred to Committee of the Whole and read a second time.

The President read the motion.

Dr. CAMPBELL—I find on consultation with the President and Registrar that they are of opinion that there is some conflict between the by-law as submitted and the other by-laws of the Council, and rather than waste any time in discussion I would ask permission to have the motion stand for the present, and with the permission of the Council I will withdraw the motion.

Leave granted and motion withdrawn.

Moved by Dr. GEIKIE, seconded by Dr. MOORHOUSE, That it be an instruction to the Educational Committee to amend Clause 9, Section 3 (Examinations) page xi. of the Announcement by substituting the word "fifty" for the word "sixty" in the first line of said clause ; also to change the pass percentage in chemistry, theoretical and practical, from fifty to forty, so as to enable students to devote more of their time to the study of anatomy, physiology, histology and materia medica.

The President read the motion.

Dr. McLAUGHLIN—I submit that this motion is irregular, because in a motion of that kind you do not put in any reason you assign in favor of the motion, the reason should be part of Dr. Geikie's speech. It would be just as regular to put in "in order that the boys may kick their heels," as to put in "in order that they may devote more time to histology" or anything else ; it has nothing to do with it.

Dr. GEIKIE—Dr. McLaughlin is very regular, I know, but if it is come to this that the Council will not submit to a motion then the sooner the Council is blotted out the better.

The PRESIDENT—I rule that Dr. Geikie's motion is in order.

Dr. GEIKIE—I should think it is. My reason for submitting the motion is a very simple one ; your standard on all subjects is 50 per cent. Take the Primary, in which there are four subjects ; a man who makes 50 per cent. on each of the four makes a total of 200 marks, but by the existing by-law if he should happen to fail however little in one of these four subjects and doesn't reach his 50 per cent. he gets no credit ; for example, this is an actual case, a student gets in anatomy 59 per cent., physiology 59 per cent., 59 per cent. in histology, and 59 per cent. in materia medica, but in chemistry he gets 49 per cent., one short in chemistry, he gets no credit at all. In the case of the man making 50 per cent. on each of his four subjects, he makes 200 marks ; the other man makes 226 marks. Here are three cases I noted where the marks run as follows : 68 per cent. in anatomy, 54½ per cent. in physiology, 50½ per cent. in materia medica, and 26 per cent. in chemistry ; that candidate is above the percentage required in three, but he is below in the one subject, and instead of giving him credit for the three, because he doesn't reach 60 per cent. in two of the three, he gets no credit at all ; then I have another case where the marks are, anatomy 70 per cent., physiology 59½ per cent., materia medica 59½ per cent., chemistry 49 per cent., just one below, and he gets no credit. You will pass a man who obtains 200 marks, but this man gets 238 marks and no credit is given him. Let me give you another case : Anatomy 65 per cent., physiology 60 per cent., materia medica 50 per cent., and chemistry 43 per cent. ; no credit given although he passes largely above the standard in three branches and has 218 marks, 18 marks more than the pass man whose average of 50 per cent. takes him in. One does not need to give reasons in support of this motion, it is simply a matter of common sense ; the regulation has always ruled that if a man makes 50 per cent. in three branches on Primary, Intermediate or Passing, he gets credit for the same. I am not particularly tenacious with regard to the last clause, it is simply asking to let chemistry rate at 40 per cent. instead of 50 per cent., which you very properly make the pass for anatomy, for physiology, and for materia medica. The reason I suggest this is not that I do not think chemistry is important, but you have chemistry as a requirement for matriculation, and the man who passes that examination passes a good drilling in chemistry ; that is all right ; after that he has to take two courses of general and one or two practical in his medical college, and that is all right. But I maintain that whereas anatomy and physiology are the foundation of materia medica they are important for the physician, while a very wide knowledge of chemistry, such as would fit him to be a professional chemist, is not necessary, and therefore I think 40 per cent. would be a fair proportion to rate chemistry at, as fair as it is to rate anatomy and the others at 50 per cent. I am not tenacious with regard to this last clause, but I think it is common sense, and the reasons I have been able to give the Council I hope will carry weight. I forbear making any further remarks because I know that time is precious, and I hope the Council will see fit, with very little discussion, to adopt the motion.

Dr. SANGSTER—I am not going to discuss that motion now, because I think that, in accordance with the usages of the Council, as that alters the whole basis upon which the Educational Committee has done its work in the past, it would be better to boil our discussions down by letting it be referred to the Educational Committee, and I move that it be so referred.

Dr. FOWLER—I am in sympathy with a good deal of what has been said in regard to this motion, but I object to a hard and fast order being given to the Educational Committee to do a certain thing. If Dr. Geikie will alter his motion and say that the Educational Committee shall consider the propriety of doing it, I have no objection. But the Educational Committee, by his motion, is directed to do a certain thing, as if they were mere machines ; they would have nothing to consider at all, but merely to follow the direction given in the motion.

Dr. SHAW—This question came up before the committee yesterday. By-law No. 9 says every candidate must make 60 per cent. in three or more subjects in the Primary examinations. There are four subjects in the Primary and eight in the Final. If he fails in one subject in the Final examination under 50 per cent., he must take 60 per cent. all round to enable the Examiners to give him the stand, whereas in the Primary examination he has merely to take 60 per cent. on three subjects ; if he fails in one, two or three or all the rest, the Final man is allowed his stand on taking 60 per cent. on three subjects out of eight, just the same as the Primary man must take 60 per cent. on three out of four. It does seem to some extent a hardship on the Primary man as compared with the Final man.

Dr. BRITTON—Don't you mean as compared with the Intermediate man ?

Dr. SHAW—No, the Final.

Dr. BRITTON—I think that Dr. Shaw has overlooked the fact that in the Final examination there are but four subjects, as in the Primary. The Intermediate has seven or eight.

Dr. SHAW—It is the four years course, the Intermediate and Final—the old Intermediate ; it is the examination on which the students this year are getting their registration. I must confess I should like to be a little more posted on this before I get through with the Council. There is a clause which says the values awarded by the individual Examiners to the answers of candidates are not to be subject to revision except by an appeal by the candidate to the Council when special cases of hardship may seem to have occurred. It does seem to me it is perhaps a little harsh to a Primary man. There was one case where a man took 70 per cent. in one subject, $59\frac{1}{2}$ in each of two others, and 49 per cent. in another ; according to the by-law and interpreting the instructions technically that man must be rejected, and that does seem a hardship, though I think the provision I have read is a sufficient loophole for the Council to enquire into a case which may be one of hardship such as I have just mentioned ; and I think, while I to some extent sympathize with the motion, that as this clause has been working such a short period of time we should allow it to stand a little longer till we have an opportunity of seeing better how it works.

Dr. BRAY—I think we should not have these discussions on these things having to go to the Educational Committee to be threshed out there. I will second Dr. Sangster's motion.

The PRESIDENT put the motion as follows : "Moved by Dr. Sangster, seconded by Dr. Bray, that the motion be referred to the Educational Committee ;" and on a vote having been taken declared it carried and the motion referred to the Educational Committee.

Moved by Dr. SANGSTER, seconded by Dr. THORNTON, That it be an instruction to the Registration Committee to carefully examine the credentials on which registration has been granted to such persons as have become members of the College preceding the second Tuesday in June of each year, and to report thereon to the Council during the current and succeeding sessions.

The President read the motion.

Dr. SANGSTER—Mr. President, the organic functions, I take it, of this Council in the past have been first the regulation and control of all education, primary and final ; and secondly, the registration of practitioners. The former of these functions, so far as it relates at least to primary education, has practically been struck off the list of what we can insist upon ; at the instance of the medical schools the Government have practically cut the ground from under our feet in the matter of primary education, but the Council still retain, and, I suppose, purpose to hold——

Dr. GEIKIE—I wish to correct a mistake that the speaker has just made in reference to medical colleges. I know the action spoken of was not taken at the instance of the medical schools.

The PRESIDENT—Order ; you must not interrupt a speaker.

Dr. SANGSTER—Because the ground of preliminary education has been struck from under the feet of the Council at the instance of the medical schools, I think it is the more important that we should conserve and maintain in its integrity, as far as we can, the only remaining function that pertains to this Council, that of supervising the registration of practitioners. I think, therefore, that under existing circumstances the Registration Committee is the most important supervisory committee that is left to this Council. I am aware that the Council by by-law committed the duty of looking strictly into the requirements that are set forth for matriculation to the hands of an officer appointed for that purpose, and I have no doubt whatever that our present Registrar strictly and zealously and faithfully performs his duty ; I have never heard the first breath of suspicion to the contrary ; and yet through looseness or laxity on the part of somebody, before the appointment of our present Registrar, for I am quite convinced there have been no irregularities of that kind since Dr. Pyne has filled that position, or if there have, the responsibility rests with the Council and not with Dr. Pyne himself. It is believed by many that irregularities have existed in the past, and that not a few of the members of the College have found their way into it through back doors and side entrances, and that the documents by which some at least have gained entrance to this College would not bear investigation. Of course, when the Legislature steps out of its way, intervenes, and foists upon us, by some back gate, a man who is unable to get in by our front gate, we have no alternative but submission ; but I claim that this Council ought to be protected by the Ontario Government from irregularities of that kind. And I claim that if it occurs often, that if it now and then occurs even that some particular individual, because he is a relative *in posse* or *in esse*, to Judge this or Professor that or Senator somebody else, is to be granted special favors over his fellows there ought to be some way of marking the recipient of such favors in our Register so that his entrance should be marked in some way or other as an irregularity. I have said I believe there are gentlemen who have obtained registration upon fictitious qualifications. I myself know personally of several such, and I doubt if there is a man in this room who could not recall instances that he knows of, or suspects, in the past—perhaps the long past—of men having obtained entrance into the College by means of that kind. There was a gentleman whose name was presented in this Council last year, and by the consensus of opinion of those who looked into his case (the Discipline Committee and others) it was openly stated here he had no right to the registration he claimed ; and in the discussions of this Council the year before last there appears a case of a gentleman who applied for registration and was defeated, but the fact came out in the discussion that there were precedents for it ; and it was broadly stated that there was a gentleman who had been registered but who had no right to registration. I claim that it should not be possible for these things to occur. Since I gave notice of my intention to move this resolution I have learned that the irregularities took place in the old times when the Executive Committee undertook of their own motion on several occasions to introduce men into the profession through one of these side entrances. I think that thing should not exist. Every time a man is foisted upon the profession it is an irregularity ; and an injury is done to the public and a gross injury is done to the profession, and the value of every diploma that has been honestly earned and hardly won by the members of this Council is thereby deteriorated. It is not my intention that this committee should interfere with the work of our Registrar or in any way lessen his responsibility. It was pointed out very properly last year in regard both to the Treasurership and the Registrarship that just when these positions were filled by gentlemen of undoubted trustworthiness, gentlemen who possess the entire and unlimited confidence of the profession, was the time for investing the position with any checks or precautions or safeguards that might be thought desirable, but which were and are confessedly unnecessary with the present occupants of these offices, but which might be necessary in the cases of their successors ; and we all know that even our present Registrar, Dr. Pyne, and our present Treasurer, Dr. Aikins, much as we admire them and highly as we regard their services, are not here for a permanency. Life is short, death is certain ; and my friend Dr. Pyne, although I think he has a very good thing in the Registrarship, must know that there are better things with more emoluments and higher honors that may come within his reach in the near or distant future ; or if the Council continue in their present attitude, holding fast to "Micawber Castle," until something turns up by which we can get rid of it, the Council may not always be able to pay the income that Dr. Pyne at present receives.

In any or all of these events we should lose his services and should have to appoint to the position a new and wholly untried man ; and in view of that possibility it appeared to me that it might be well to require the Registration Committee to examine every man's credentials once a year and report the matter to the Council. I do not want to press the motion very strongly ; I am quite content to say that with the exception of the instances mentioned in the Council last year and the year before, the irregularities have taken place in the long past and were due to the assumption of powers by the Executive Committee. If there is any opinion on the part of the Council that the instructions I have asked for should not be given, I hope the resolution will not elicit discussion, but will simply be put to a vote and voted down. I am not wedded to it. It seems to me, though, that a committee of this kind should have existed from the beginning, and it may appear to you that it ought to be created now.

Dr. BRITTON—One or two matters have been brought up to which I think it is my duty to refer. Dr. Sangster has made a statement that it was at the instance, or partly, at any rate, at the instance of the medical schools that the Legislature cut the ground from under our feet as far as fixing the standard of matriculation is concerned——

Dr. McLAUGHLIN—This is a matter that will surely come up later. Would it not be better to discuss it later on, as it is not connected with the resolution ?

Dr. BRITTON—I have just a word to say. Dr. Sangster will remember that as representative of the University of Toronto I was present with the Executive Committee and Legislation Committee, and also certain members of the Council resident in the city, when we interviewed a committee of the Legislature in relation to the same matter, and I am sure that Dr. Sangster did not and could not refer to the University of Toronto, because he knows as well as I do the position I took in the matter myself. I took the strongest possible ground in opposition to the course the Legislature had proposed taking. (Hear, hear.) That is all I have to say.

Dr. SANGSTER—I admit candidly the truth of what Dr. Britton says.

Dr. HENRY—Do I understand that there were some friends of a Senator and some other gentleman that were irregularly registered through influence as students ? .

Dr. SANGSTER—I think that matter is referred to in the report of the Legislation Committee, and will come up later.

The President put the motion, and on a vote having been taken declared it carried.

Dr. Sangster asked for the yeas and nays.

The Registrar took the yeas and nays as follows :

Yeas—Armour, Barrick, Brock, Campbell, Dickson, Emory, Fowler, Graham, Hanly, Henry, Henderson, Logan, Moorhouse, McLaughlin, Reddick, Rogers, Sangster, Shaw, Thornton and Williams.—20.

Nays—Bray, Britton, Geikie, Luton, Moore, Rosebrugh and Thorburn.—7.

ENQUIRIES.

None.

REPORTS OF STANDING AND SPECIAL COMMITTEES.

Dr. BRAY presented and read Report No. 2 of the Discipline Committee :

To the President and Council of the College of Physicians and Surgeons of Ontario :

GENTLEMEN,—Your Committee on Discipline beg leave to report that they have examined the papers submitted to them in the case of one E. A. B. Rose, of Portland, and we do not consider this a case over which the Discipline Committee have jurisdiction, he being an unlicensed practitioner, and would suggest that his case be referred to the Special Committee on Prosecutions.

We have considered the petition of B. H. Lemon and others, asking that one Benjamin Lemon, whose name was erased from the Medical Register some five years ago for unprofessional and disgraceful conduct, be restored to the Register. Your committee beg leave to report that they have no power to grant this request, as it is a matter for the Council as a whole to consider.

Certain letters and advertisements which were referred to your committee re Dr. Curry, of Toronto, and Dr. A. C. Sinclair, of Port Elgin, have been examined by us, and your committee are of opinion that before any action is taken on these cases further evidence as to unprofessional conduct should be produced.

Your committee have had before them the letter of Mr. George B. Douglas, barrister, of Chatham, complaining of unprofessional conduct on the part of Dr. J. Golden, of Florence, and asking that it be referred to the Discipline Committee. Your committee consider it a case for the courts to deal with rather than the Medical Council.

All of which is respectfully submitted.

JOHN BRAY, Chairman.

Adopted. A. F. ROGERS, President.

The report was received.

CONSIDERATION OF REPORTS.

Dr. THORBURN moved the adoption of the report of the Legislation Committee.

The President read the motion.

Dr. THORBURN—I have annexed to the report the bills submitted to the House, if you wish them read.

Dr. ARMOUR—Will you read Mr. German's bill ?

Dr. Thorburn read the German bill.

Dr. THORBURN—That had special reference to Mr. Young, but it did not pass at all. It was agreed that Mr. Young should pass the Intermediate and Final examinations and submit himself to the same rules as our men do, and on paying the fees he was to be entitled then to registration. His contention was that he was willing to pass the Final. But the Final is a more practical examination ; it does not go into the more theoretical and most important subjects, namely, the practice of medicine and surgery, and so on, but just takes in work he would need in the laboratory and work of that kind. He finally agreed to pass these two examinations.

Dr. ARMOUR—Was he relieved from passing the Primary examination ?

Dr. THORBURN—Yes, he was.

The PRESIDENT—I have just asked the Registrar if Mr. Young succeeded in passing the examination, and he informs me that he has not passed ; that he took the examination, but failed on a portion of it.

Dr. THORBURN—I do not think it is fair to specify him singly in the public press.

Dr. SANGSTER—I do not think it is at all improper to state in our meeting the fact that he has failed, in the case of a gentleman who approaches the Legislature to enter by the back door, and then fails on his examination.

Dr. BRITTON—I was somewhat surprised two or three days ago when I got a copy of this circular issued by the Educational Department. I must have been very dense when we met the committee of the Legislature, because I understood the agreement was quite different from this. I understood there was a clause added to the bill to the effect that all who had matriculated in arts prior to July 1st, 1895, should be held eligible for registration.

The PRESIDENT—Certainly, that was all.

Dr. BRITTON—I am perfectly satisfied there was no reference made by any member of the committee of the House, nor by any of the councillors who were present at that time, to substitute the High School new examination with Latin—I am perfectly satisfied we did not go back as far as 1882, though I think there was something said about a second class non-professional certificate with Latin. That was a fairly high examination. This matter has come up in the Educational Committee, and a special committee was appointed to wait upon the Hon. Mr. Ross in order to see whether or not it was an oversight on his part that a circular of this kind was issued to the educationists of this country, because, as I say, these notes which Dr. Thorburn has read, which are really transcripts of those in the circular, we never expected to see—we simply thought the direction should be that matriculation in any university prior to November 1st, 1895, would be the qualification. I have tried on one or two occasions to arrange for an interview with Hon. Mr. Ross, but he is not to be home until some time to-day. It was Dr. Sangster's intention, and mine, that we should see him during recess at noon, so as to be satisfied as to what his understanding was, and to let him know that we, as members of the committee, did not understand it in the light of this circular. I want to let this House know now that we cannot conclude the discussion of this report until the Hon. Mr. Ross has been seen. For the reasons I have given it seems necessary that the Hon. Mr. Ross should be interviewed before we know upon what grounds we stand, and I think it would be better to postpone the discussion of the report until the afternoon.

Consideration of this report was deferred.

Moved by Dr. BRAY, seconded by Dr. MOORE, That the report of the Discipline Committee be adopted.

The President read the motion.

Dr. BRAY—For Dr. Armour's information I will say that I do not think the Discipline Committee have any power to make a recommendation to this Council ; it is out of their power to do so.

The President put the motion, and on a vote having been taken declared it carried, and the report adopted.

Dr. McLaughlin asked leave to introduce a notice of motion. Leave granted.

Dr. McLaughlin gave notice of motion to appoint an Auditor.

Dr. Bray gave notice of motion that a petition be prepared and presented to the Legislature, praying that no legislation or amendments to the Medical Act shall be introduced unless such amendments be asked for by members of the Council or through the Legislation Committee.

On motion of Dr. Campbell, seconded by Dr. Moore, the Council adjourned to meet again at 2 p.m.

AFTERNOON SESSION.

The Council met at 2 o'clock p.m., in accordance with motion for adjournment.

The President, in the chair, called the Council to order.

The Registrar called the roll, and the following members were present: Drs. Armour, Barrick, Bray, Britton, Brock, Campbell, Dickson, Emory, Fowler, Geikie, Hanly, Henderson, Henry, Logan, Luton, Machell, Moore, Moorhouse, McLaughlin, Reddick, Rogers, Rosebrugh, Sangster, Shaw, Thorburn, Thornton, Williams.

The minutes of the last meeting were read by the Registrar, and confirmed and signed by the President.

NOTICES OF MOTION.

Dr. WILLIAMS—To introduce a by-law to levy the annual assessment.

Dr. WILLIAMS—To appoint an Executive Committee.

Dr. MOORE—To appoint a Legislation Committee.

COMMUNICATIONS, PETITIONS, ETC.

The Registrar read a communication from Dr. Arthur, making enquiries about his university diploma, which he claims has been lost. Referred to Registration Committee.

MOTIONS OF WHICH NOTICE HAS BEEN GIVEN AT A PREVIOUS MEETING.

Moved by Dr. McLAUGHLIN, seconded by Dr. HANLY, that by-law No. — of the College of Physicians and Surgeons, regarding the appointment of an Auditor, be now read a first time.

The by-law received its first reading.

Moved by Dr. McLAUGHLIN, seconded by Dr. HANLY, That this by-law be referred to Committee of the Whole and read a second time. Carried.

Council in Committee of the Whole, Dr. Moorhouse in the chair.

Dr. McLAUGHLIN—I move the adoption of the first clause, with the blank filled by the insertion of the name of Dr. James Carlyle. Carried.

Moved by Dr. McLAUGHLIN, That the blank in the second clause of the by-law be filled by inserting "$20.00," and that the clause be adopted.

Dr. ROGERS—Has Dr. McLaughlin asked Dr. Carlyle whether he will for $20.00 perform the services required?

Dr. McLAUGHLIN—No, I have not asked him.

Dr. BROCK—I think our Registrar could answer the question and tell us whether Dr. Carlyle is satisfied with the remuneration offered by this Council.

The REGISTRAR—Dr. Carlyle, after doing the work this year, referred to the remuneration of $20.00, and said he felt it was too little altogether and asked me what he had better do about it. I said he had better represent it to the Council, and it ended in his sending a letter which is now before the Finance Committee. He does not say in his letter what he considers he should get, but from conversation with him I should say he thought the $20.00 was about the half what he should receive. From what he said I imagine he did not think that $40.00 would be an extravagant figure.

Dr. ARMOUR—We secured the services of Auditors last year without fixing the remuneration, and the bill they have sent in is $25.00. I think probably Dr. McLaughlin's suggestion of $20.00 is not very far from the mark.

Dr. BROCK—If we do not put in sufficient remuneration is there not danger that he may refuse to accept the position, and we would not have the accounts audited next year?

Dr. THORBURN—Last year and this year are scarcely parallel cases. The Auditors we had last year were called in at the last moment, and they could not give the same care and attention to it that Dr. Carlyle has been able to do. I think he has been working on this audit for several days and went over it carefully. He is a most competent man.

Dr. LOGAN—It would be better to ascertain (I suppose that can be done by telephone) what he would take and settle this matter before you commit yourselves.

The CHAIRMAN—The Registrar informs me that Dr. Carlyle was nearly a week engaged on this audit.

Dr. ROGERS—Will it be the same trouble again?

The REGISTRAR—It will be the same every year.

Dr. ROGERS—I will move that the blank be filled with $40.00.

Dr. BARRICK—I will second that.

Dr. SANGSTER—I will second that motion.

Dr. McLAUGHLIN—I will withdraw the "$20.00" and consent to the blank being filled with "$40 00."

Dr. HENRY—What was paid last year for the work?

The CHAIRMAN—$25.00.

Dr. ARMOUR—The year before last it was $25.00, and according to our by-law last year we were to pay $20.00 to Dr. Carlyle. He thinks that that was insufficient remuneration and is asking for more.

Dr. ROSEBRUGH—Is there a letter or communication from Dr. Carlyle ?

Dr. HENDERSON—There is a letter before the Finance Committee now saying the $20.00 is not adequate remuneration for the time Dr. Carlyle has spent in going over the work ; that it took him a whole week to do it. Our recommendation now is that he should receive $40.00 for his remuneration.

The CHAIRMAN—Dr. McLaughlin, is this $40.00 to be for services already rendered ?

Dr. McLAUGHLIN—No, not in this by-law. This by-law provides for the current year.

The Chairman put Dr. McLaughlin's motion to adopt the second clause of the by-law, and on a vote having been taken declared it carried.

Dr. McLAUGHLIN moved that the committee rise and report.

The committee rose. The President in the chair.

Moved by Dr. McLAUGHLIN, seconded by Dr. HANLY, That the report of the Committee of the Whole be adopted. Carried.

Moved by Dr. McLAUGHLIN, seconded by Dr. HANLY, That By-law No. — be now read a third time, passed, numbered, signed by the President, and sealed with the seal of the College of Physicians and Surgeons of Ontario. Carried.

BY-LAW No. 71.

Whereas power hath been granted to the Medical Council of the College of Physicians and Surgeons of Ontario, under Section 13 of the Ontario Medical Act, R. S. O. 1877, C. 142, to make by-laws, be it therefore enacted as follows :

1st. This Council hereby appoint Dr. James Carlyle as Auditor, for the purpose of auditing the accounts of the Council.

2nd. The remuneration to be paid by the Council to the Auditor for his services shall be Forty Dollars ($40.00).

Adopted as amended.

W. H. MOORHOUSE,

Adopted in Council. A. F. ROGERS. Chairman Committee of Whole.

Moved by Dr. CAMPBELL, seconded by Dr. THORBURN, That after the adoption of this resolution no new business be introduced without unanimous consent.

The President read the motion.

Dr. ARMOUR—Is it within the power of the Council by resolution to set aside the by-law or rules and regulations in this way ? I think not. I think it would take a by-law.

Dr. CAMPBELL—What is the by-law to which Dr. Armour refers ?

Dr. ARMOUR—Our rules and regulations lay down a mode of procedure to the Council, and you are setting this aside by this resolution for perhaps a considerable time. I know it is customary to do it just at the close of the session; but not perhaps a day or two before the close.

Dr. McLAUGHLIN—In our rules and procedures, day by day, there is one item, "Notices of Motion." That has been passed by by a by-law; and Dr. Campbell will say it is impossible to repeal that by a resolution. An amendment of that kind cannot be entertained unless introduced regularly by by-law.

The PRESIDENT—Do you ask for a ruling, Dr. McLaughlin ?

Dr. McLAUGHLIN—Yes.

The PRESIDENT—Then I shall rule that this motion to be effective must be passed unanimously. One dissenting voice can stop it being carried.

Dr. CAMPBELL—Our rules say " No variation in the foregoing order of business shall be permitted, except by the consent of the Council."

Dr. WILLIAMS—If it is the consent of the Council, the consent of the Council means the consent of a majority of the Council.

The PRESIDENT—I think the parliamentary rule is that the suspension of the rules of a body, whether the House of Commons or any other body, shall be by the unanimous consent of that body, of those present at any rate, and if there is one dissenting voice a motion for suspension cannot be carried. There is nothing in our rules bearing on it.

Dr. WILLIAMS—The rules of Parliament apply here only when our own rules do not cover.

Dr. McLAUGHLIN—You will notice that the matter you refer to is only the temporary suspension of a rule in order to introduce a motion. By unanimous consent you cannot alter your by-laws to affect the future, and I do not think the unanimous consent of the Council would allow us to pass this motion. We can suspend a rule for the time being by unanimous consent, but we cannot suspend it for future meetings.

Dr. GEIKIE—It is a pity to spend so much time about it. It has often been done before.

6

Dr. CAMPBELL—I do not want to take up time over this motion, and I will withdraw it rather than waste any time over it.

. Dr. THORBURN—My reason for seconding the motion was simply to hasten the progress of business.

Dr. McLAUGHLIN—I think the spirit of Dr. Campbell's motion will be observed by the members of the Council.

Dr. Campbell's motion withdrawn.

Moved by Dr. CAMPBELL, seconded by Dr. BROCK, That the by-law appointing a Discipline Committee be read a first time. Carried.

The by-law received its first reading.

Moved by Dr. CAMPBELL, seconded by Dr. BROCK, That By-law No. — (appointing a Discipline Committee) be referred to Committee of the Whole and read a second time. Carried.

The Council in Committee of the Whole.

Dr. McLaughlin in the chair.

The first clause of the by-law was read, and on motion adopted.

The Chairman read the second clause of the by-law.

Dr. CAMPBELL moved the adoption of the second clause.

Dr. SANGSTER—I object to that part of the by-law. I do not think it is necessary that that committee shall consist of three members. I know that the Act as it is now states that there shall be three or five members on the Discipline Committee, but I do not propose to accept a law simply because it is the law, if it can be repealed and if it can be shown there are good reasons for the repeal. Our Discipline Committee who were asked to enquire into it failed to discover any means by which the expense of that committee could be lessened, but I think there is a feasible way of lessening the expense of the committee. The Discipline Committee act merely as a coroner or assessor. The members of that committee listen to the arguments of counsel, they hear evidence, and make a report and recommendation to this Council founded on the evidence, and argument, and I think that one man can do that work as well as three. I think it would be just as inappropriate to put three judges on a bench as to put three gentlemen on that committee ; and I think it was the opinion of Dr. Day, one of the most eminent members of the Discipline Committee, that he could do the work alone and do it quite as well as, or better than, he could with three members. And I should, under these circumstances, suggest that when legislation is sought it will be sought in that direction, to reduce the Discipline Committee to a single member. We cannot at present say that there shall not be three members because the law says that there shall be, but I wish to dissent from the necessity of there being three members on that committee.

The Chairman put the motion to adopt Clause 2, and on a vote having been taken declared it carried.

On motion, Clauses 3 and 4 were adopted as read.

The Chairman read Clause 5.

Dr. CAMPBELL moved that the first blank be filled with the name of Dr. Bray, of Chatham. Carried.

Dr. CAMPBELL moved that the second blank be filled with the name of Dr. Logan, of Ottawa. Carried.

Dr. CAMPBELL moved that the third blank be filled with the name of Dr. Moore, of Brockville. Carried.

Dr. SANGSTER—No. I do not want to stop the Council ; I merely repeat my dissent that I uttered last year. As a representative of the profession, I claim that on a committee formed to try members of the profession for alleged misconduct in a professional sense, the judgment on those points should be by the peers of the members of the profession, by those who represent the profession, and not by any gentlemen appointed to represent a school or a college. I merely wish to enter my dissent from the name.

On motion, the preamble of the by-law was adopted.

Moved by Dr. CAMPBELL, That the committee rise and report the by-law. Carried.

The committee rose. The President in the chair.

Moved by Dr. CAMPBELL, seconded by Dr. BROCK, That the report of the Committee of the Whole be adopted. Carried.

Moved by Dr. CAMPBELL, seconded by Dr. BROCK, That By-law No. — be read a third time, passed, numbered, signed by the President and sealed with the seal of the College of Physicians and Surgeons of Ontario. Carried.

BY-LAW No. 72.

Under and by virtue of the powers and directions given by Sub-section 2 of Section 36 of the Ontario Medical Act, Revised Statutes of Ontario, 1887, Chapter 148, the Council of the College of Physicians and Surgeons of Ontario enact as follows :

1. By-law No. 65. appointing a Discipline Committee and passed upon the 13th day of June, A.D. 1895, is hereby repealed.

2. The committee appointed under the provisions and for the purposes of the said sub-section shall consist of three members, three of whom shall form a quorum for the transaction of business.

3. The said committee shall hold office for one year, and until their successors are appointed, provided that any member of such committee appointed in any year shall continue to be a member of such committee notwithstanding anything to the contrary herein, until all business brought before them during the year of office has been reported upon to the Council.

4. The committee under said section shall be known as the Committee on Discipline.

5. Dr. J. L. Bray, of Chatham, Ont., Dr. Geo. Logan, of Ottawa, Ont., Dr. V. H. Moore, of Brockville, Ont., are hereby appointed the committee for the purpose of said section for the ensuing year.

Adopted.

J. W. McLAUGHLIN,
Chairman Committee of the Whole.

Read a third time and passed. A. F. ROGERS, President.

Moved by Dr. BRAY, seconded by Dr. DICKSON, That a form of petition be framed and sent to every medical man in the Province by the Registrar for signatures, praying that the Government and Legislature of Ontario will not alter or amend the Medical Act, or introduce or carry through any new medical legislation, unless such legislation or new Medical Acts be asked for by the College of Physicians and Surgeons directly, or through their Legislation Committee.

The President read the motion.

Dr. BRAY—I have two or three reasons for introducing this motion; and I think and hope it will receive the unanimous consent of this body. My object in introducing this is to prevent, if possible, a repetition of the scenes we have had in the last two years in the Legislature, and to prevent having a bill introduced such as the one we heard to-day charac-terized so very strongly which was introduced but withdrawn at the last session, and to pre-vent the introduction of bills like the one introduced by Mr. Haycock last year. I think if, when the Registrar sends out the Annual Announcement, there is a form of petition framed he can send it to every registered practitioner, enclosing a stamp, and asking each practi-tioner to sign and return the petition. We will have 1,800 or 2,000 names, and if those names are presented to the Legislature of Ontario the Government will not dare to oppose such a strong unanimous representation as this would be. And I think if we had that it would pre-vent in the future repetitions of the scenes we have had and do away with the expense of keeping a Legislation Committee in attendance at the sessions of the House, because I think the Government will not allow anybody to introduce a measure of that kind in the face of the unanimous petition of the members of the profession of Ontario. Another thing is, I think it is almost absolutely necessary that we should go to the Legislature in reference to certain things, but when the profession are divided to a certain extent and there is a feeling in the House among the Patrons there that the profession are overriding everything, that we are a close corporation and so on, we might find difficulties in our way. But if we have those names to our petition and go there for some amendments not of a radical nature at all that are necessary, and we all know of some things that are necessary, I am satisfied we shall have no difficulty in getting them carried through. I have now put before you my whole object in presenting this motion, and I do not wish to take up any further time, and if any gentleman speaks to the motion I hope his remarks will be brief.

Dr. DICKSON—I beg to say that I did not read that motion sufficiently careful to really comprehend it as it has been read just now. My impression was that it asked that no legislation be introduced relative to the profession without first being submitted to this Council. As I understand it, the motion now reads that no legislation be introduced that is not asked for by the profession. To my mind that is a very material difference, and I think we are not likely to succeed in any petition of this kind. But I do think that we may succeed in influencing the Legislature not to take any action without first submitting any proposed legislation to this Council.

Dr. BRAY—As long as I can attain my object I am not very particular as to the wording of the resolution.

Dr. DICKSON—There is a material difference.

Dr. BRAY—Perhaps there is. That which will have the most influence with the Parlia-ment I want to carry, and if the suggestion of Dr. Dickson is a better one I want to adopt it.

Dr. WILLIAMS—I agree with Dr. Dickson that if the resolution is put it would be better to make it in the form he suggests. But personally I think it is almost worse than a waste of time to put the resolution at all. I do not think the Government can control that matter. I think any member of the House has a right to introduce a bill if he likes, and I think the Government will not interfere to stop that bill. The Government are dependent upon their members to keep them in power; and supposing some supporters of the Government intro-duce a bill, and there are fifteen or twenty or thirty of them bound together to get that bill through, do you think the Government are going to jeopardize themselves and offend all those men by saying you shall not put that bill through? In so doing the Government would be jeopardizing themselves. Their life depends on keeping on the right side of them and getting their support when the time comes.

Dr. BRAY—And the medical men suffer for that.

Dr. WILLIAMS—I do not think we do. I do not think it is practical in that shape to introduce it. It may be possible, as Dr. Dickson suggests, to have it submitted to the Council, so that the Council have knowledge of it beforehand. I do not think the two thousand or more names we would have from the medical men would exercise that amount of influence that has been spoken of. If those couple of thousand men could be concentrated some place and could bring their power to bear they could have some influence, but they are scattered, a few here and a few there, all over the Province of Ontario ; and a good many of these medical men have politics on the mind just as strong as anyone else, and it is just a question whether they would oppose their party and bring pressure to bear on the Government on that point. If this motion is changed, and I hope it will be changed, in the terms suggested by Dr. Dickson, so that the Council will be notified of proposed legislation, it will enable the Council to take such steps as they think wise in the matter. I do not think that this will accomplish anything practical, because we have a Legislation Committee here in Toronto, and any of these things that come up come to our knowledge very quickly ; and we have friends in the House ; we are always notified and we know when any proposed legislation affecting us is coming up. So I am inclined to think it is a mistake to pass this resolution at all, though if the Council hold different views I offer no opposition beyond expressing my opinion.

Dr. McLAUGHLIN—I must frankly confess if I have ever been surprised at anything being introduced into this Council I am surprised at this. That motion if carried strikes a blow at one of the dearest principles of fundamental government in any nation where there is civil government. I speak now of the right of the subject to approach the throne on any cause, for any purpose ; that right is not refused to any citizen in the British Empire or any other well governed country. The hope that by introducing a motion of this kind you are going to prevent medical men or men that are not medical men approaching the Legislature to get any amendment to the Medical Act, or any other Act that they please, is utterly futile, and if this motion were passed this Council would be a laughing stock to the Legislature and the country. It is an idea that cannot be entertained. I say there was not a principle embodied in Magna Charta more pregnant with importance to the citizens of the British Empire than the right of any citizen, be he medical man or not medical man, to approach the throne and petition the throne humbly for any change that that citizen wanted. I am surprised to hear this motion brought in this afternoon, and I hope our friends will be careful and not put themselves on record in favor of any proposition of this kind. I could easily understand some Rip Van Winkle who had gone to sleep some five centuries ago, when that kind of thing was done, and who wakes up now in June, 1896, and makes a motion of this kind——

The PRESIDENT—That is out of order.

Dr. McLAUGHLIN—I say it is a surprise that any man who has a knowledge of the privileges of civil liberty should bring in a motion of that kind.

Dr. BRAY—Mr. President, does Dr. McLaughlin withdraw the words which you have stated to be out of order ?

Dr. McLAUGHLIN—I will withdraw, not because it is not parliamentary, but because the President wants it withdrawn. I am perfectly willing to submit it to Dr. Bourinot, or anybody else, but I shall withdraw it because I do not want to say anything offensive. I feel keenly about a subject of this kind, because it strikes a blow at one of the most important principles that pervade the British constitution or any other constitution.

Dr. BRAY—In answer to the arguments used and to the very choice language that has been employed towards the mover of this resolution, I say that it is the most common practice that exists to have petitions coming in from large bodies of men to Parliament. Dr. McLaughlin during his term in Parliament must have noticed large petitions going in against Acts that were proposed. I do not see anything strange in the medical men in this Province uniting and sending in a petition and asking the Parliament—I will accept what Dr. Dickson says—to introduce no legislation until it is submitted to the Medical Council. I think it is safeguarding our profession, and I cannot see what strong objection there can be to such a procedure as that. I am very much surprised at Dr. McLaughlin making use of such expressions as he has done, particularly when he (Dr. McLaughlin) is taking money from that very Government to-day, and sitting here taking money from the profession——

Dr. McLAUGHLIN—I rise to a point of order. That statement is not true. I do not take a cent of money from the Parliament.

Dr. BRAY—I put it this way, that Dr. McLaughlin is here holding a Government position——

Dr. McLaughlin—I rise to a point of order. This is entirely outside of the point.

The President—That probably is outside of the discussion.

Dr. Bray—I bow to your ruling. I do not wish to offend the Council, but at the same time I do not like to be attacked in the slandering way—I can characterize it in no other way—in which the gentleman who has just sat down has attacked me. I would not have a spark of manhood in my body unless I resented it, particularly coming as it does from a gentleman holding the anomalous position which Dr. McLaughlin does in this Council.

Dr. McLaughlin—I ask the ruling of the chair. I am here by law. I occupy no anomalous position. My position as an appointee of the Government does not prevent me from being here, and therefore I am here in no anomalous position.

Dr. Bray—All I can say in answer to that is that the Government have advised other gentlemen in similar positions that it was not in good taste to do so. I will say that other gentlemen holding similar positions have been advised by the Government it was not in good taste to sit here. In regard to Dr. Williams saying a petition would be of no value, that if we could get all the gentlemen together, that would be, I maintain, that their not being together makes the petition all the stronger. We have forty or fifty medical men in every county of this Province, and it is not their own individual names alone that make the petition strong, but it is the influence they possess, and we all know that no men in the community hold more influence than the medical men. I therefore think that such a petition would have a very good effect and a very strong effect, and I can see nothing wrong in presenting such a petition to the Government, asking that any legislation to be enacted in the future, any bills brought in, should be submitted to the Medical Council before they are brought up in the House to be passed on. I think the Law Society introduces all the laws that govern that body. I never heard of any society or body of men going outside of their representative body to introduce measures in the Legislature until they had asked the body to do it. If any citizen is displeased with the action of any Municipal Council and he thinks he is wronged, he will go to the Council and ask for redress ; if the Council do not give that redress, he then will go to the Government or go to the Parliament for it, and in just the same way if Mr. Haycock or anybody else wants to introduce a bill to the Legislature, that bill should be sent in to this body for approval, and this body may then approve of it or may ask or petition that it be not carried into effect. I say that this petition asked for by my motion will have a great influence with the Government and with Parliament in the way of preventing any obnoxious bill going through.

Dr. Dickson—The amendment just proposed to the motion was simply with the view that no hasty legislation affecting the medical body should be enacted without the profession having an opportunity, through the Council, of considering it and urging proper measures. I do not think myself that the Legislature are in a position to legislate on matters medical without some advice, and I do not know any source from which they can obtain it, where our interests will be best served, other than from the representatives of the profession. My idea is simply that any legislation affecting the medical profession should be submitted to the Council. I am surprised that the Legislature so nearly reached a finality last year with so very few, either of the Council or the profession, knowing anything about it.

Dr. Sangster—Mr. President, I regret the tone that this discussion has taken. My friends, Drs. McLaughlin and Bray, are usually mild-mannered and lamb-like in their natures, and I am sorry they have departed from their usual custom and that they do not follow my own good example and never make use of naughty words in the discussion. I will sympathize with Dr. Bray in his object in introducing this resolution, for I know that recently events of a very irritating nature have transpired without the Council, as a Council, having any opportunity to prevent them. As a member of the Committee on Education, I have received a letter from the Minister of Education stating that certain propositions were under consideration by the Government, and he was communicating with each member of the Committee on Education asking for their views. I wrote to him the same day, stating that I would earnestly deprecate any action being taken in that direction, and I was quite sure the medical profession through the country would feel sore, and very sore, if the proposed action were taken ; and I asked him, earnestly asked him, not to commit the Government to it ; and said that I hoped the Government would not be committed to it until the Council had an opportunity to be heard upon the question, or at least, if they were so far committed, that the Committee on Legislation should be at once apprised of the intentions of the Government. I think we were badly used in that matter. I think legislation of that kind, as I said to the Hon. Mr. Ross in my letter, ought not to be sprung upon the profession. I keenly sympathize with Dr. Bray and with every other member of this Council, and I am confident we are almost a unit in that respect——

Dr. Williams—Wouldn't it have been worse if Mr. Ross had gone on without notifying Dr. Sangster and other members of the profession ?

Dr. Sangster—Yes. I was about to say that while I sympathize with the motives of the gentlemen who moved and seconded this resolution, I thoroughly agree with Drs.

McLaughlin and Williams that it would be impolitic, it would be highly injudicious, to attempt to accomplish what I know would be an impossibility, that of binding the Government or the Legislature to any such action as is there proposed. Of course, there would be much less objection to our asking the Government in pursuance of a policy of protection of this Council against such attacks to have legislation of that kind, as far as it could be, submitted to this Council before it was adjudicated upon, and I think a request to that effect might be made. But I do not think it is in our power to go further than that, and I agree with Dr. Williams that a petition of the kind proposed would be so much waste paper. There is a general notion throughout the country that men will sign a petition for almost anything. Why, I daresay there are men in the country who would sign a petition to hang their mothers-in-law. The Legislature and the Government are not likely to pay much attention to petitions ; but if the two thousand medical men in this country would get hold of their respective local members, and bring their influence to bear on them, and let them exert their influence in that House on our behalf, there is nothing the medical profession could not accomplish on its behalf.

Dr. EMORY—I do not wish to detain the Council one moment. I have been pleased to see the grand spirit of patriotism and defence of the Magna Charta displayed this afternoon, and I am cordially in accord with that ; but at the same time, the remarks of the gentleman would be better placed on the other side of the matter. He is upholding the right to go to the throne, and that is all we are asking ; we are simply asking that the Legislature will not introduce any matter without our knowledge. I think the remarks of the gentleman I have referred to were on the other side of the case.

Dr. MOORE—I think it is very important the profession should by some means know something about what is going on in the Ontario Legislature. I must say, I have to return my thanks to the Hon. Mr. Ross for having sent me a letter asking my opinion regarding this matter. That letter was the first intimation I had, living away in the other end of the Province, that even medical legislation had been introduced. As Dr. Williams said, we have politics on the brain, but he is on one side and I on the other. He sent me the bill from one or two or three days before it became law, and but for the Hon. Mr. Ross I would not have had any information of it at all. At the same time, if this resolution would do nothing more than show our Legislation Committee, if we have one appointed, that it would be part of their duty to inform the members of this Council of what is going on at the local Legislature, it would be a good thing ; because you will all agree with me that but very meagre reports of what is transpiring in the Legislature appear in the *Mail* and *Globe*, and one very soon gets tired of paying any attention to them. I know I do. I do not look up that matter at all, and consequently the whole thing slipped my eye entirely. I trust that it will not be offensive, and if it would be offensive in any way to the Government I would like to have the offensive part stricken out, because as we have to be beggars we cannot be choosers, and we do not want to offend in the slightest degree. I think this Council owe a debt of gratitude to the Hon. Mr. Ross for the noble way he stood by us, and I am quite satisfied he stands by us better than many of the gentlemen on the floor of that House—I am not speaking of the members of the Government. If, therefore, it will not be offensive, I think you had better let it go through, and let it be the duty of the Legislation Committee to notify the members of this body what is transpiring or about to transpire in the local House.

Dr. McLAUGHLIN—Perhaps I will be allowed a word of explanation in reply to Dr. Moore. The Government are impotent to inform the profession of what any private member is going to do.

Dr. MOORE—I do not mean the Government ; I mean our Legislation Committee.

Dr. McLAUGHLIN—Every bill introduced in the House appears in the local papers. It has to be announced three days before it receives its second reading, so that if we kept our eye on the papers we should see if any bill was introduced affecting the medical profession.

At the request of the President the Vice-President, Dr. Thorburn, took the chair.

Dr. ROGERS—Mr. Vice-President, before this is put before the Council I should like very much to say a word about it. I am sorry that a little warm feeling sprang up between two important members, my friends Drs. Bray and McLaughlin, but I hope that that has all passed away. I think if there is one thing Dr. Bray deserves the thanks of this Council for more than another this session it is the fact that he has framed this resolution and brought it before us. I do not agree with my friend Dr. McLaughlin, in claiming that this refers to or has any bearing upon the rights given to British subjects in Magna Charta ; what he says seems to me to point the other way. But be that as it may, I think the time has come and is to-day before this Council, when we must either bring to bear on the Legislature and on the Government the full weight of the medical profession, if weight they have, or sooner or later our Medical Act is either going to be lost or going to be so cut up that it is not worth having. You have either to face the difficulty to-day or before many years you are going to lose the Medical Act or have its best parts taken away. Dr. Sangster has referred to the fact that our matriculation, by the action of the Government—because you cannot call it any other action—has been so changed that we have hardly any more control over it. I ask you, gentlemen, is this Council not composed of men who are the peers of the Government in every sense of the word? In medical matters surely they know what is best for the profession, they know that better than any member of the Government. As the Council get no support from the people of the Province or Legislature, and as the medical profession pay taxes to support this Council and carry on their affairs, and as a great deal of their work is for the purpose of doing good to the people of the Province, we ought to be left as an independent body and should not be interfered with by the Legislature. I claim that if the Legislature are going to take upon themselves to allow amendments to our constitution and changes in our constitution, then the Legislature should at the same time say, We will pay something towards your support. At the last session some very important changes in the Medical Act were proposed. One was to place a limit on our matriculation, and we were forced to accept it. I must confess that at the time that was introduced I felt the strongest indignation I ever felt since I became a medical man. I had always considered before that the Medical Council here were like the Medical Council in England, and 1 defy anybody to point out where the British Government ever amended or altered the British Medical Act without first consulting the Medical Council. It has never been done. Now, that being the case, surely the Medical Council in Ontario should be treated in the same spirit. The whole gist of Dr. Bray's motion is simply to bring before the Legislature the one fact, that the medical profession of Ontario are a united body. Dr. Bray has suggested we should get up a petition signed by every medical man, and some person has said that it would have very little weight, but I can assure you that it would have a very great deal of weight. We unfortunately did show to the Legislature in 1893 that the medical profession in Ontario were not united. I think that is true. Whether it was expedient to do it, whether it was right to do it, is not the question. The medical profession did go there, and part of the profession asked the Legislature to alter the Act when the Council were opposed to it. The Legislature agreed to do what the portion of the profession asked, almost contrary to the wishes of the Medical Council. I think and hope that those sores have been healed, at least the most of them, and when the profession are becoming united again, as I believe they will, and when it is shown to the Legislature that this Council have the support of the medical men of this Province, and that the medical men of this Province are a united body, then I say you will find that medical amendment Acts will be stopped, because no member of the Legislature wants to have the enmity of three or four doctors in his constituency. For that reason I think that the portion of the motion which asks that they will not alter the Medical Act unless they first submit it to this body is only proper, and they cannot refuse to accept it, and it will have an advantage in making the members of that legislative body hesitate before they introduce such measures as that which was brought up by Mr. German last year. I thank Dr. Bray for bringing this motion before us, and I hope the members will pass it unanimously.

The President resumed the chair.

Dr. LOGAN—I just wish to say a few words. In the first place, I am fully in accord with the nature of this resolution. The point I want to make is that when we collect the opinion of the profession and have it before us ; it is not necessary and perhaps not desirable to present that to the Government, but it is far better to keep it in reserve, to keep it as a reserve power in case we require it in the Legislature. Supposing a bill is going to be introduced, having reference to our interests, we could then go before the Legislature and say, We object to that bill, it is not in accordance with our wishes. But they might say, Who are you? How many of the medical profession do you represent? Is there not a difference of opinion among you in reference to this question? Our reply would be, Your Honor, I wish to introduce you to this piece of paper, a paper containing the names perhaps of over two thousand medical men who have expressed their opinion of this particular subject, and I beg leave to ask you to be good enough to read it. It is not necessary we should shake this petition in the face of the Legislature before any legislation is introduced, because if we did that I think very likely the effect that Dr. McLaughlin has just stated would take place. But we should merely use it as a reserve force, and perhaps we need not use it at all, but when we have this reserve force behind us, I think we can go with very much greater confidence to that Legislature.

Dr. BRITTON—I am quite in accord with the remarks Dr. Moore made that we owe a debt of gratitude to the Government for the course they have taken in the past; that is, taking it on the whole. By-and-by, perhaps in the proper order of business, there will be a reference to certain matters that recently occurred which I may have to constitute an exception to the rule of things I am speaking of now. However, we all know that on many occasions there were bills introduced by private members and others, and these bills would have had the effect of really emasculating the Medical Act had they been carried through ; and last year, I think it was, we had occasion to say, or the Legislation Committee had occasion to report, concerning a certain bill that the Conservatives and Government alike stood as one man in opposition to that bill. I think that was a bill introduced by the Patrons. I am afraid that the method proposed by Dr. Logan would not be the best. Of course, we all know that before a bill is introduced there has notice to be given in the papers, but how many of us read the paper every night of our lives ? I never read mine till towards bedtime, and sometimes I have not the opportunity of reading it. Medical men are very busy men, and unless they are very fond of politics they are not likely to read the papers very assiduously·and such a notice might escape our attention, and if we kept a petition of this kind for a special occasion, for the moment to arrive when it was absolutely necessary, the mischief might be half done. It is like tying a man's artery when he is in a state of syncope from hæmorrhage. I think it would be far better to have this petition signed as soon as it conveniently can be done and presented to the Government, because the motion, or something equivalent to a motion, which I presume would be embraced in the petition, is an enunciation of a principle of right and justice ; and I say myself, as others have said, that it is a very unjust matter that any Legislature should interfere, should legislate, should dominate over a body of men who have been entrusted with the government of themselves and who have not abused their trust. From first to last, from the time this profession of ours has been incorporated to the present hour, I must say we have been proven to be the faithful servants of the Government, and as such we deserve that much consideration from the Government ; and when we present a petition or prayer of that kind it will influence the mind of the Government, so that no disasters will overtake us hereafter through hasty legislation that may pass through even members who, with all due respect to their knowledge of the public interests, are not as well able to know what is in the interests of the profession and of the public as we are. I am certainly in favor of the resolution introduced by Dr. Bray.

Dr. ARMOUR—The idea that has led to this proposition I suppose came from the successful petition that was signed by the Medical Defence Association and effectually used afterwards, but I think that is a misconception of our present condition and the purpose of the present motion ; they are not parallel cases at all. I had something to do with petitioning them and I think our course was on the right lines at that time, but as a member of this Council I have a different view of the matter altogether, so far as a petition is concerned. I know that the one hundred and fifty practitioners I represent do not want to be bothered at all with any such petition as this, but they want me to say what course they should pursue in regard to a petition of this kind——   .

Dr. BRITTON—Tell them to sign the petition.

Dr. ARMOUR—I have had some experience in this, and in my opinion the only way to get anything like a full representation of names on a petition is to send a man to every medical man in this Province. That is the only way to effectually carry that out. I am very sure when there is no special grievance to be redressed if you send a petition of that kind that there will not be one-tenth of the profession who will ever notice your petition or return it to you. I feel confident of that. Let us look for a moment at what the result is to be, what effect you require it to have. The resolution asks that this Council shall be informed before any resolution is introduced to amend the Medical Act. Now, let me ask you, Mr. President, who has the power to give us that information at any time ?

Dr. MCLAUGHLIN—Hear, hear.

Dr. ARMOUR—It is not possible to get such information. The Premier does not know who is going to introduce such legislation. No other person but the man who introduces it knows, and we can only get that information after the legislation has been introduced. Now, if it is necessary that the Council should be informed of amendments after they are introduced, and that is the only time they could be informed, that is a very simple matter. Why not make it a matter of instruction to the Registrar that he shall see during the session of the Legislature that no legislation is introduced without notifying the Medical Council ? I do not see why we should petition the whole of the profession to get at that. I think the motion is perfectly preposterous. I will not detain you longer.

The PRESIDENT—Order. Dr. Armour, you must withdraw the word " preposterous."

Dr. ARMOUR—I think it is parliamentary, but I will withdraw it.

Dr. DICKSON—I would like to ask whether Dr. Armour was aware of the legislation last year before it reached the stage when it was withdrawn ?

Dr. ARMOUR—Yes, I was. I have my member, my representative in the Legislature, and I always have him keep me informed on matters of this kind. There is no excuse for any member of this Council not knowing all about any bill that is introduced in the Legislature about which they desire to know.

Dr. BROCK—Mr. President and gentlemen of the Medical Council, the proposition made by Dr. Sangster, or a portion of it, was acted upon by myself with regard to the bill introduced by Mr. Haycock ; and as Dr. Armour states, it is the duty of the members of this Council to keep themselves so in touch with their representatives in the local House that they will know as soon as possible what legislation will be introduced in Parliament. When Mr. Haycock introduced his bill, I called a meeting of the profession and we called upon our member, who pledged himself he would use all his influence to defeat that bill. He was an influential member, a supporter of the Government, and a farmer as well—and that bill was defeated. I think the proper way is to keep in touch with the members, and if that is done we will never have any trouble of this sort.

Dr. BRAY—I do not object to that course. It is a very good course, but I do not see how it interferes with the medical profession petitioning Parliament to do a certain thing ; we are only talking of sending an humble petition to Parliament that before anything that affects the medical profession as a whole is enacted, or any existing Act is amended, the representative body of this profession shall be informed of it. I cannot see, for the life of me, what harm there is in a petition of that kind. You can use every endeavor and every influence you please on a member. I am not so fortunate as my friend, Dr. Armour ; we have a member representing my constituency, but I would not call him " my member," because I have not that influence over him that Dr. Armour seems to have on his member. I did not take this idea, as Dr. Armour suggests, from the successful petition he inaugurated.

Dr. ARMOUR—I did not say I inaugurated it.

Dr. SANGSTER—The Legislature meets in the early part of the year and adjourns in April, and this petition might imply that any legislation that was introduced by a private member, say in February, would have to be delayed until after this Council met in June. We cannot surely expect that the Government would undertake to do anything of that kind.

The PRESIDENT—In answer to that, I would say the Executive Committee occupy the place of the Council during the interim between meetings. In the second place, the motion specifies informing the Council or the Legislation Committee of the Council, which gets over that trouble.

The President put the motion, and on a vote having been taken declared it carried.

Dr. McLaughlin called for the yeas and nays.

The Registrar took the yeas and nays, as follows :

Yeas—Drs. Barrick, Bray, Britton, Campbell, Dickson, Emory, Fowler, Graham, Hanly, Henderson, Henry, Logan, Luton, Machell, Moore, Moorhouse, Rogers, Rosebrugh, Thorburn, Thornton.—20.

Nays—Drs. Armour, Brock, Geikie, McLaughlin, Reddick, Sangster, Shaw, Williams. —8.

Dr. MOORE—I would like to ask the permission of the Council to introduce a motion without giving notice.

Leave granted.

Moved by Dr. MOORE, seconded by Dr. BRITTON, That the Printing Committee be instructed to have a new edition of the Medical Register issued this year.

The President read the motion.

Dr. MOORE—The reason I make this motion is that the edition of the Register is now about exhausted. There are only somewhere in the neighborhood of between a hundred and two hundred copies, so that there is not enough probably to meet the requirements of the year ; and also, the Register was issued in 1892, so that it is practically five years old. I would not introduce the motion if the edition was not practically run out.

Dr. McLAUGHLIN—I do not rise to oppose the motion, but I fear if it is issued in 1896 it will still remain imperfect.

Dr. MOORE—I do not mean 1896, but in our year after the spring examinations.

Dr. McLAUGHLIN—I do not object to it, but it will take a good deal of time to eliminate the names that ought to be left off the Register. I know men in the United States who have been away from here for twelve years and who are still on the list. I know in my own division there are eight or ten names on the list who should not be on ; they are out of the country. Time should be given to see the list is properly revised.

Dr. CAMPBELL—I assume that every man who is registered has a right to be on the Register, unless we strike off his name for non-payment of assessment.

Dr. McLAUGHLIN—They are put on the Register as resident in places from which they have been away for years and years. The addresses should be changed.

Dr. WILLIAMS—Can the Registrar give us an idea about what it cost to publish the Register ?

The REGISTRAR—I think the last edition cost about $800 for 3,500 copies.

Dr. WILLIAMS—I think we had better hesitate before we undertake an expenditure of $800 this year. If it is imperative, and we cannot help ourselves, we must do it. We have made provision this year for entering the names of all that should be on the Register since last session in our Annual Announcement. Eight hundred dollars is quite a heavy item, and if we can possibly get over this year I certainly think we ought to do it. I do not see where the demand is to come in, and it may be that not more than a hundred will be required. I certainly would not publish it unless I was obliged to.

Dr. GEIKIE—The Register is very far behind and very incorrect, and we need one exceedingly. It would not be $800 expended this year, because it will last several years. There is no more incorrect record that you can imagine than our present record.

Dr. MOORE—I will consent to my motion being amended to read "within a year."

Dr. LOGAN—Is it understood that each member of the Council receiving the Register shall pay for it?

Dr. GEIKIE—They do that sort of thing in England. Why cannot we do it here? Even if it is only a twopenny book, they look for the twopence. We might charge 25 cents or 50 cents a copy for this Register; we might charge enough per copy to cover the expense.

Dr. LUTON—I would like to ask Dr. Moore what he means by the publication of a Medical Register? Is it to include all that is in the one we have before us now, which contains the Ontario Medical Act, the rules and regulations, etc.? Or is it simply to contain the names of all the physicians, with their post-office addresses and their titles, who are entitled to be registered in this country.

Dr. MOORE—In answer to Dr. Luton's enquiry, I would say it must include everything that should be in a Register, or it would not be perfect. It must include the Act and a perfect record. It is now a very imperfect record and an old record; and, as has been said, there are men's names there that should not be there; the names of dead men are there, men who have moved are there; and if called as a witness in court one could not say that many of the addresses given are correct addresses.

Dr. WILLIAMS—There is another reason why it should not be published this year unless it is imperative, and that is because next year is the year for consolidating the Ontario Statutes and our Act will then be in a shape to be published. I certainly think if there is any method of putting it off one year longer that should be done.

Dr. MOORHOUSE—I quite agree with Dr. Williams that it would be better to postpone it on account of the consolidation of the various Acts, and then we would have it in a more perfect form. While saying this I am quite well aware of the very imperfect nature of our present Register. There are a great many amendments to the by-laws, and many new Acts that do not appear; and a great many of the members whose names appear on this list have moved away or died; and the publication of a new Register would be a great benefit to us. I think each member should pay for the copy of the Register he receives. But I think it would be well to postpone its publication for another year, as our funds are not very flush.

Dr. MOORE—How long after the session of 1897 will it be before the Statutes are consolidated?

Dr. McLAUGHLIN—It is not likely you would have them in your hands before 1898; it takes a long time to consolidate them. But if you could postpone the publication of the Register it would be much better for us. The consolidation of the Statutes, I think, will be taken up at the meeting of the Legislature in 1897, but it will be the following year before the consolidation is completed.

Dr. LUTON—I would like to ask the Registrar about how many copies are demanded of him on an average per year, speaking of legitimate demands, not giving them out to everybody and anybody that may ask for them, so that we may form an opinion, taking a reasonable view of the matter, as to how many we could get along with in a year.

The REGISTRAR—I suppose 100 to 150 would do me, but when a Register has been printed formerly it has been sent to the profession.

The PRESIDENT—The Registrar has suggested to me that possibly we might get along by issuing an appendix.

Dr. MOORHOUSE—How many copies would be necessary altogether, Mr. Registrar?

The REGISTRAR—If it is not sent to the profession three thousand copies would not be necessary, but it has been the custom to send it to the profession.

Dr. BRAY—How much would the appendix likely cost? There would be quite a lot of names to go in that are not in the present Register, and while you get out an appendix nearly every year those appendices are lost, and it would be as well if you are going to publish an appendix to consolidate the appendix, and when you are doing that you might almost as well publish the Register.

Dr. BARRICK—I understand the motion of Dr. Williams is, that all the names that are not in the Register now be put in the Announcement to be published this year. When that is done we will then have a pretty complete list of our graduates; and if that is done this year, our funds not being very flush, would it not be as well to postpone the publication of the new Register for one year, inasmuch as the names of those who have graduated, and those who have registered since the last Register was published, will be put in the Announcement this year?

Moved by Dr. LOGAN, seconded by Dr. BROCK, That the following be added: "That when the Register is printed the Registrar be instructed to charge fifty cents for each copy."

Dr. GEIKIE—That is too much. That will affect the sale of it.

Dr. CAMPBELL—Anybody who wants it will pay fifty cents as readily as twenty-five cents. If they do not want it they will not pay anything.

Dr. EMORY—Would it be well, if Dr. Moore would consent, to empower the Printing Committee to do this if the Registrar finds it necessary during the year ?

Dr. MOORE—I will leave it in the hands of the Printing Committee.

Dr. EMORY—As an instruction to the Printing Committee ?

Dr. MOORE—Yes ; I will leave it with the Printing Committee. Dr. Logan's motion to sell the Register for fifty cents a copy had better be taken up as a separate motion.

Dr. SANGSTER—I do not know whether I am in order, but I would like to suggest, when the Register is published again, a little different process may be followed from that which has been followed in the past. There are so many inaccuracies in the Register, so many members of the College are put down to addresses that do not belong to them, and residences are put down to practitioners with no such practitioner belonging to them, that one does not know when one is right or is wrong in addressing any member in that list. I can appreciate the difficulty on the part of the Registrar in obtaining the information in the past, but I would submit that before any Register is printed the Registrar should put himself in communication with the territorial representative of each division, and get him to send in an exact and correct list of all the resident members in his constituency with their addresses.

The PRESIDENT put the motion as follows : "Moved by Dr. Moore, seconded by Dr. Britton, That the Printing Committee be instructed to have a new edition of our Medical Register issued this year if in their judgment it is necessary," and on a vote having been taken declared the motion carried.

The PRESIDENT then put Dr. Logan's motion as follows : "Moved by Dr. Logan, seconded by Dr. Brock, That when printed the new Register shall be sold for fifty cents a copy."

Dr. FOWLER—It is a very mean thing to charge for a thing of this kind. The profession are entitled to a copy of the Register, and I will vote against this motion.

Dr. BROCK—The proposition came from me for this reason : In England they charge for the Register and surely we are not in a better position than the medical practitioners there, or in a worse position, and I think there should be some charge or something done to lessen the expenses of this Council, and if that cannot be done I would propose that suitable advertisements be obtained, such advertisements as college advertisements and others, to defray at all events some portion of the cost. This Register goes to every member of the profession, it goes to all the insurance companies, and it goes to everyone who is interested in knowing the names of medical men throughout the Province and throughout the Dominion and United States. The profession are provided free and I think all other persons wanting this Register for business purposes should be expected to pay for it, because we do not supply them for business purposes at our own expense. We have already considered this in the Finance Committee and are recommending something to be done.

Dr. SANGSTER—I rise to a point of order. There is nothing before the House. The resolution to which that purports to be an amendment has been put and has been passed.

The PRESIDENT—This is a motion to add. I have read this motion as well as the main motion, and it is quite in order to have an addition to the main motion, though you can vote it down if you wish. It is not an amendment at all, but a motion to add certain words.

Dr. McLAUGHLIN—There has been no notice given of this motion. Is it the intention that members of the profession shall have it free or shall have to pay fifty cents ?

Dr. LOGAN—I am in favor of each one paying for it.

Dr. McLAUGHLIN—I do not object, but you need to be a little canny. We have been in the habit of giving this to the profession gratuitously, and I think it would be still advisable to give it to the profession, and provide that others who want it, such as insurance agents, pay fifty cents for it. It is my opinion that the profession are irritated enough now by assessments and perhaps you had better not irritate them any more.

Dr. THORBURN—I think all registered practitioners ought to have a free copy, at all events all that live in Ontario ; but I think the suggestion made by Dr. Brock a very good one, that all outsiders should pay for a copy. For instance, all insurance societies, and agents, and others outside of the profession, and in that way the expense of publishing our Register would be met to a considerable extent.

Dr. ARMOUR—I understand now that when any person outside of the medical profession gets a copy of our Register he pays for it—that is to come in in our financial report, so that there is no necessity for adding this to the motion we have passed. That is the present custom. But with regard to charging for the Register, that is another matter, a new matter altogether. I have not given that any special consideration, though it seems to me it would be no hardship to the profession, if the Council saw fit to charge fifty cents or a dollar for a Register, to make that charge.

Dr. MOORE—I think we had better go slowly about this charge. We do not know what kind of a book we are going to have, and probably when we get it nobody would give fifty cents for it. Let us wait till we get it and then put a price on it.

Moved by Dr. CAMPBELL, seconded by Dr. EMORY, That this be referred to the Finance Committee. Carried.

None.

REPORTS OF SPECIAL AND STANDING COMMITTEES.

Dr. CAMPBELL—The report of the Executive Committee was submitted last night by Dr. Harris, who is ill this afternoon I believe, and is not with us. This report of the Executive Committee might now be adopted *pro forma*, as it commits the Council to nothing, and the matters referred to are brought up particularly in the report of the Legislation Committee. There are no recommendations in this report at all, and if we adopt it we will get it out of the way.

Moved by Dr. CAMPBELL, seconded by Dr. ARMOUR, That the report of the Executive Committee be adopted. Carried.

Dr. BRITTON—The report of the Education Committee has been unavoidably delayed on account of the impossibility heretofore of having an interview with the Hon. Mr. Ross, who was out of the city, which interview was only secured at noon to-day.

UNFINISHED BUSINESS.

Dr. THORBURN—The report of the Legislation Committee was under consideration and we had got down to what we called conclusions submitted by the Minister of Education, and some gentlemen thought it was not in accord with their view, and suggested the propriety of a committee of our number visiting the Hon. Mr. Ross and getting a definite statement from him. That committee consisted of Drs. Britton and Sangster, and if they will kindly submit their report it will not be necessary to discuss this part any more. We have had so many different matriculations it is a most difficult matter to know what they mean—the Junior Departmental Leaving examination and the Senior Departmental something else—the very definition is a study that one can hardly understand ; and we have had different statements made ; and I hope that we have now had a definite understanding with the Minister of Education.

Dr. BRITTON—Mr. President, I have not a written report regarding the interview with the Hon. Mr. Ross. Dr. Sangster and I were appointed a sub-committee of the Committee on Education, because this matter came before that committee as well as the Committee on Legislation. I will now verbally report what transpired in the interview between Hon. Mr. Ross, Dr. Sangster and myself. Dr.·Sangster and I saw the Minister of Education and pointed out to him one implied, although not expressed, objection, or objectionable feature, I would say, of the circular issued by the Department of Education—at any rate it was embraced in the original bill, and it implies that no further changes of any kind .can be made in matriculation in this Council unless approved of by the Lieutenant-Governor in Council. We represented to him that that was taking from us the powers or in part the powers conferred upon us originally by the Act. He said he had not the slightest objection to that objectionable feature being removed. He said the Government would not take that view of the case, that he relied upon us to do what we thought would be right. We next called his attention to the fact that this circular is so far retroactive as to degrade very much the standard which we have now for matriculation, inasmuch as we find amongst these notes at the foot, to which note Dr. Thorburn referred this morning, that the High School Intermediate certificate with Latin taken at any time between 1880 and 1884 will qualify an applicant for registration ; and the next clause the 1st January, 1884 to 1888, the High School Intermediate, or third class professional. The result of the conference regarding these notes was that Dr. Sangster and myself agreed so far as we personally were concerned (we could not agree for the Council, or rather for the Education Committee, because we were not invested with that authority), and we thought at the same time in entering into our agreement that our action would be endorsed by the Education Committee and by the Council, that we would be willing to go as far back as 1st July, 1888. That is, that we would accept second class non-professional certificates with Latin, provided those certificates had been taken between 1888 and 1892. I believe there have been some applicants who have come forward with certificates of that kind. And I also believe that that second class non-professional examination, with Latin, was—I will not say equivalent to—but almost equivalent to the Junior matriculation with chemistry and physics included. This is the result of the conference, so that now there is no doubt, and in fact I shall make it my personal duty, if the Council approve of it, to go to the Hon. Mr. Ross and request him to issue a circular which will take the place of this one, which I think was prematurely issued, and to make these corrections in his new circular, which will make it quite in accordance with the agreement that we arrived at this afternoon. I do not think that the terms of the agreement that we acceded to compromised the Council in any respect, and I think, now the matter is very satisfactorily settled, the probability is we shall have no occasion to change the standard of matriculation for many a year to come. At the same time I am very glad to be able to say, as I said before, that the Minister of Education said that he had confidence in this Council, that he wanted the Government to work in harmony with this Council, and that the Government had respect for the Council's opinion. He as much as said we knew what was our own business pretty well and how to transact it and that he would leave it perfectly free with this Council to make any changes we saw fit in the matriculation or any other standard. He did not say the Government would not hereafter interfere, but he expressed his confidence in us, and said anything done by us would not necessarily be unlawful because we did not submit it to the Lieutenant-Governor for his approval——

Dr. SANGSTER—I want to ask whether Dr. Britton stated that the Hon. Mr. Ross only stipulated we should receive any of the applicants who had complied with the requirements between 1880 or 1882, I think, and 1888 up to the present time—whether that was not the understanding ?

Dr. BRITTON—I did not understand that, Mr. President. I understood Mr. Ross to say or to suggest the propriety of our accepting the credentials from 1882 up to the time that the second class non-professional was instituted——

The PRESIDENT—You mean 1884 to 1886.

Dr. BRITTON—Supposing somebody had already come forward with the lowest credential to prevail from 1882 to 1884, and had been registered by our Registrar on the strength of that credential, we would not interfere with him, we would not interfere with anything that has already been done ; but from this on no one will be qualified for registration unless those who took the second class non-professional, with Latin, between 1888 and 1892.

Dr. SANGSTER—That is precisely what I said.

Dr. THORBURN—That points out the necessity of having the rules thoroughly understood. Even one of the two gentlemen who were there to-day did not understand the Minister as expressing what the other says he did express.

Dr. BRITTON—Excuse me one moment. Perhaps I might amplify myself a little or utter a sentence or two more. I represented, and so did Dr. Sangster, to the Hon. the Minister of Education that the introduction of these clauses into this circular appeared to us not to be in accordance with the agreement that was entered into between our committees and a committee of the Legislature ; and Mr. Ross quite agreed with me. " No," he said, "nor did I so understand it at the time." I told him what we did understand ; that is, that the retroactive effect of the circular or of the Departmental regulation simply would provide for the accepting only of those who had matriculated in any university prior to November 1st, 1895. Mr. Ross said, "You are correct in your understanding ; so I understood it. But since that time, in conversation with certain educationists, I concluded it would be impracticable to carry it out on that line, and therefore the circular has been issued in this form." Then he immediately coincided with us in our desire that it should be as I have already said.

Dr. THORBURN—I think it is most important that the Council should receive a letter as to what was understood, because even in this last conversation that Dr Britton had with the Hon. the Minister of Education the minister seems to have changed his mind on one or two occasions. When he met some other parties he thought perhaps it was impracticable ; but still he did not call back this circular. So I think we had better have a distinct understanding from him in writing, and then there can be no misunderstanding about it.

The PRESIDENT—I think the Vice-President's suggestion is a very important one, and I would suggest that Dr. Britton would receive a letter from the Minister of Education before we go on with this report, and I think it will save us trouble to do so.

Dr. BRITTON—I have no reason to doubt his word in the matter, no reason to question it.

The PRESIDENT—It is his memory.

Dr. BRITTON—And I think his memory will be all right ; and I think there is not the slightest doubt another circular will be issued identical with the one already issued with the exception of the erasure of those three objectionable clauses. To wait for a letter from the minister now would mean we might have to defer this for two or three days, because the Minister of Education is actively engaged in political work and is away from home three parts of his time, doing good work (from my standpoint), and it is very doubtful whether I would be able to catch him.

Dr. SANGSTER—The Hon. the Minister of Education, I thought, was unusually explicit in his interview with Dr. Britton and myself, and I cannot conceive that he was under the least misapprehension in the matter, and I took his utterances as quite as final as if they had been written and signed ; and I think so did Dr. Britton.

Dr. BRITTON—I did, most decidedly.

Dr. ROSEBRUGH—Was there a memorandum of the agreement made between the parties ?

The PRESIDENT—There is a memorandum taken down here by our reporter.

Dr. DICKSON—I think there would be no difficulty if Dr. Britton has time to put his understanding in writing and submit it to the minister, who will attach his signature to it.

Dr. BRITTON—I will do that, certainly.

Moved by Dr. THORBURN, seconded by Dr. CAMPBELL, That the report of the Legislation Committee be adopted.   Carried.

Moved by Dr. CAMPBELL, seconded by Dr. BRAY, That By-law No. — to amend By-law 69 be referred to the Committee of the Whole and read a second time.   Carried.

Council in Committee of the Whole.   Dr. Reddick in the chair.

The by-law was read and adopted clause by clause.

Dr. WILLIAMS—Is there any clause covering the infirm.

Dr. CAMPBELL—In sending the by-law to our Solicitor I noted down the various suggestions that had been made in the Council in regard to the matter, and his letter in regard to the matter says : "I·am of the opinion that the Council cannot make distinctions in individual cases."   That is to say, that it is not within the power of the Council to determine by comparison of partial disability or other circumstances that it is reasonable a member of the Council should be relieved from the operation of the section in question.

Dr. HENRY—What is the result supposing a registered practitioner was in the United States for ten years and came back to practice in Canada ?

Dr. CAMPBELL—When he comes back he at once commences to practice and then he comes under whatever by-law we have in existence at the time.   If he makes application according to this by-law each year for each year he is away he is relieved from payment that year.

On motion, the committee rose.   The President in the chair.

Moved by Dr. CAMPBELL, seconded by Dr. BRAY, That the report of the Committee of the Whole be adopted.   Carried.

Moved by Dr. CAMPBELL, seconded by Dr. BRAY, That by-law No. — be read a third time, passed, numbered, signed by the President and sealed with the seal of the College of Physicians and Surgeons of Ontario.

BY-LAW No. 73.

Whereas by By-law No. 69, passed under the authority of Section 6 of Chapter 27 of the Ontario Medical Amendment Act, 1893, the Council of the College of Physicians and Surgeons of Ontario adopted Section 27 of the Ontario Medical Act, R.S.O. 1887, Cap. 148, and Section 41a amending the same of an Act passed in the fifty-fourth year of Her Majesty's reign, Chapter 26, entitled " An Act to amend The Ontario Medical Act ;"

And whereas by the said Section 6 of the Ontario Medical Amendment Act, 1893, the Council have power from time to time to vary such by-law ;

And whereas it is expedient that any member of the College of Physicians and Surgeons of Ontario who may not practice in any year should be relieved of payment of the annual fee for such year ;

Now therefore the Council of Physicians and Surgeons of Ontario enact as follows :

1. By-law No. 69, above referred to, is hereby varied as follows : The annual fee determined by by-law of the Council under the authority of Section 27 of the Ontario Medical Act, shall not be due and payable by any member of the College who, by reason of absence from the Province, or for any other reason, shall in no way practise medicine, surgery and midwifery in Ontario during the year for which such annual fee may be imposed.

Any registered medical practitioner who shall apply to the Registrar for a certificate in accordance with Section 41a of the Ontario Medical Act, claiming to have been relieved by this by-law of payment of the annual fee for any year, shall prove to the satisfaction of the Registrar that he has·not practised his profession during the year for which such fee has been imposed, and shall, if the Registrar so requires it, make a statutory declaration to that effect, and furnish such further and other evidence as may be required.

The decision of the Registrar upon such application, as to the liability of the applicant for the fee in question, shall be final and conclusive.

Adopted in Committee of the Whole.

R. REDDICK, Chairman.

Read a third time and adopted in Council.   A. F. ROGERS.

The President read the motion.

Dr. SHAW—I would like to enquire in the case of a practitioner who, having been absent from this Province residing in another country or in another Province of this country for a year or number of years, returns to the Province, whether this by-law relieves him from paying during the time he was absent from this Province ?

Dr. CAMPBELL—If he applies yearly for a certificate that certificate relieves him from payment for each year.

Dr. DICKSON—Does it not relieve him if he applies at the end of the time he has been absent ?

Dr. CAMPBELL—From this time forward I suppose he can do so, but it would not apply to past years. Mr. Osler says this bill could not be made retroactive. I suppose that that application could be made providing the name of the practitioner had not been removed from the Register, or steps had not been taken to collect his fees.

Dr. SHAW—It seems to me that a man who has been absent from Ontario for ten or fifteen years and returns should not be called upon to pay before being recognized as a registered practitioner, especially if he had been in Manitoba or elsewhere where he had to pay fees.

Dr. CAMPBELL—I agree with Dr. Shaw, but the Solicitor's opinion is that this by-law cannot be made retroactive. I had thought before obtaining that opinion that it would be retroactive.

Dr. HENRY—If he was indebted to the Council and came back he would be liable for what he owed before this year?

Dr. CAMPBELL—Yes.

Dr. WILLIAMS—Supposing he was absent for ten years and had not applied for a certificate for ten years, and on his return wishes to practice, would it be practicable under that by-law to allow him to pay from the time he commences to practise and say nothing about the past ten years if he had paid up before that ten years and is only indebted for the ten years he was absent?

Dr. BROCK—The word retroactive in the way there put would make it necessary for this Council to refund to those gentlemen who have come back here and have paid their fees. I know several who were absent three or four years and returned to this country and commenced practice, and who have paid up for the time they were absent. If you make it retroactive you must pay the money back to those who have paid.

The PRESIDENT—My impression is that under the law, under Section 41a, he has to apply each year for an annual certificate. Under this by-law if he applies for this certificate he will get it without paying any fee, but if in any year he does not apply for a certificate then Section 41a will be applicable, and the Registrar will be forced to erase his name. But, however, in such a case, when the practitioner came back if he proves to the satisfaction of the Registrar that he has been out of the Province all this time the Registrar would restore his name to the Register ; that is the operation of the by-law, I think.

Dr. CAMPBELL—Of course, that is a matter of interpretation. We might have some special cases arise. We are not lawyers and cannot decide this from our individual opinion now.

Dr. DICKSON—I am rather inclined to think the text of the by-law sets that forth.

The PRESIDENT—It affects only the future, not the past.

Dr. GEIKIE—It should be plain and clear that in the case of a man who has been in Oregon, for instance, for ten years, and then returns, he will have to pay only from the time he comes back, provided he was not in arrear when he went away.

Dr. WILLIAMS—The by-law is just as good as I expected it would be. My own convic-tion is that to put this matter right there needs to be an amendment in the Act, and I think when we are getting an amendment, some time in the distant future, that subject wants to be looked into and adjusted. The Act does not give us power to deal with this subject as fully as we would like to, and this is making the best of a bad case.

Dr. SANGSTER—The position seems rather anomalous to me. I was going to ask whether that opinion is the opinion of Mr. B. B. Osler? I ask that because we sometimes have, or have had paraded in the past, an opinion of Mr. Osler which was the opinion of the younger Mr. Osler, and not of Mr. B. B. Osler.

The PRESIDENT—This is the opinion of Mr. B. B. Osler, Q.C.

The President put the motion, and on a vote having been taken declared it carried.

MISCELLANEOUS BUSINESS.

Dr. BRITTON—I would just like to ask one question. Dr. Thorburn has presented the report of the Committee on Legislation, and I think Clause 5 of the memorandum attached to that report as to the circular issued by the Education Department requires a little correction. I will read the clause as it is, but as I was absent from the room I will first ask whether or not that report has been adopted.

The PRESIDENT—It has been adopted.

Dr. BRITTON—It is a little late in the day perhaps now, but still it is necessary there should be a certain change made. I will read Clause 5 of the memorandum as it stands : "Any person who, on or before the 1st day of November, 1895, had passed the examination in any university in Canada for matriculation in Arts, or the matriculation examination conducted by the Education Department entitling to register in Arts with any university in Canada, or any examination entitling to register with the Medical Council when the said examination was passed, shall be entitled to registration as a medical student on submitting to the Registrar of the Medical Council a certificate to that effect signed by the proper officer in that behalf." As I said before, according to the agreement entered into to-day we go no further back than July 1st, 1888, or, in other words, we include only "second class non-professional, with Latin," and we have nothing to do with the High School certificate between 1884 and 1886 ; therefore I would make a motion, if I be allowed to do so, that this change be made.

The PRESIDENT—I do not think the adoption of the report made the Council accept this at all. We were waiting until the Education Committee reported.

Dr. BRITTON—That memorandum was attached as part of the report and has been adopted.

The PRESIDENT—Yes ; but it does not make it part of our proceedings.

Dr. BRAY—If that correction is made, then there is no clerical error in it.

On motion, leave was granted to Dr. Henry to bring in the report of the Committee on Complaints.

Dr. HENRY read and presented the report of the Committee on Complaints :

To the President and members of the Council of the College of Physicians and Surgeons of Ontario :

GENTLEMEN,—Your Committee on Complaints beg leave to report that they have carefully looked into the various complaints referred to them, and as a result of their deliberation recommend as follows :

1. That the request of R. McKenzie (Primary) be not granted. (His request was to have his papers re-read and a re-arrangement of his oral marks.)

2. That the request of Duncan A. McCallum, a Primary student, cannot be entertained ; that is, a reconsideration of his examination papers.

3. That the request of R. O. Snider be granted, and that he be licensed.

4. That D. M. Anderson be allowed his Primary examination.

5. That the request of F. Porter, who desires a reconsideration of his Primary examination papers, be not granted.

6. That Wm. Henderson be allowed his Primary examination.

7. That the application of T. Bradley, who requests his Primary examination, be not granted.

8. That Chas. F. McPherson, who asked to be registered, have his request granted.

9. That A. W. Partridge, who asked to be registered, have his request granted.

10. That A. Rupert, who asked to be registered, have his request granted. (Failed one mark in Op. Midwif.)

11. That A. F. Reynar's request for a permit to practice be not granted.

12. That W. L. Silcox, who asks to be registered, have his request granted.

13. That Chas. H. Smith, who asks to be registered, have his request granted.

14. That J. B. Thompson's request to be registered be not granted.

15. That the request of Robert Moore to be registered be granted.

16. That the request of George Moore for registration be granted.

17. That the request of G. B. Mills for registration be not granted.

18. That the request of P. S. McLaren for registration be granted.

19. That the request of E. M. Hooper for registration be granted.

20. That the request of J. Honsberger for registration be not granted.

21. That the request of F. B. Elliott for registration be granted.

22. That in the matter of E. Allan, M.B., of Arthur, who asks this Council to furnish him with a duplicate of his university diploma, which was lost while in the charge of the officers of this Council,

We recommend that Dr. Britton use his influence to secure, if possible, a duplicate of the diploma asked for, and that this Council bear any expense incurred in securing the same.

This on condition that he furnish a proper affidavit.

All of which is respectfully submitted.

JAMES HENRY, Chairman.
R. REDDICK.
GEO. M. SHAW.

J. W. ROSEBRUGH,
Chairman of Committee of Whole.

Adopted. A. F. ROGERS, President.
The report was received.

The PRESIDENT—Perhaps before we consider this report it might be possible for the representative of Toronto University to explain what steps are taken for the issue of a new diploma to replace one that has been lost.

Dr. BRITTON—I do not know of any special instance where a duplicate diploma was asked for, but I have no doubt such cases have occurred. I am informed that most ample proof has to be furnished that the original diploma was lost, and that the applicant is the person mentioned in the original diploma.

Moved by Dr. HENRY, seconded by Dr. BRITTON, That the report be adopted.

The President read the motion.

Dr. ARMOUR—Before this report is adopted I want to say that although I was a member of that committee, my duties on the Finance Committee did not permit me to attend, and I would like to know from Dr. Henry how many primaries and how many finals were allowed to pass by the Complaints Committee, and under what circumstances they were allowed.

Dr. REDDICK—I think it is too bad that Dr. Armour, when he was a member of the committee, should not have made himself acquainted with these facts, but should now ask to take up the time of the Council.

Dr. SANGSTER—Independently of Dr. Armour, I, too, would like that information. I am completely in the dark as to the rule the committee adopted, and I would like to know what they did in reference to the complaints that were admittedly reported favorably on.

Dr. LUTON—I think the only way to do is to go into Committee of the Whole and pass the report clause by clause, and Drs. Armour and Sangster will then get the information they want.

Dr. HENRY withdrew his motion to adopt.

Moved by Dr. HENRY, seconded by Dr. MACHELL, That the Council do now go into Committee of the Whole to consider the report of the Committee on Complaints.

Council in Committee of the Whole.

The report was read clause by clause and adopted.

On motion the committee rose.

The President in the chair.

Moved by Dr. HENRY, seconded by Dr. ARMOUR, That the report of the Committee of the Whole be adopted. Carried.

Dr. THORBURN—At our last meeting there was a communication on registration received from Dr. Quain, the Principal of the British Medical Association on Registration, telling us they were about to republish an edition of the British Pharmacopœia, and asking us if we had any special suggestions to make that might be of use to them, dealing partienlarly with the flora of this country. As chairman of the committee I now beg to present the report.

Dr. FOWLER—Professor James Fowler, of Queen's College, is a most distinguished botanist, and I asked him to furnish me with a memorandum of the flora of Canada used in pharmaceutical preparations, and he took an immense deal of trouble in forwarding me the information asked, and I think it would be well to forward this to Professor Quain along with these recommendations.

Moved by Dr. THORBURN, seconded by Dr. FOWLER, That the report of the committee appointed, signed by Drs. Fowler, Geikie and Thorburn, be received and adopted, and that the Registrar be instructed to forward it to Dr. Quain. Carried.

REPORT OF THE COMMITTEE ON FLORA.

Your committee appointed to report on a communication received from Richard Quain, Esq., M.D., President of the General Medical Council of Medical Education and Registration of the United Kingdom, called attention to the fact that it might soon be thought expedient to issue an edition of the British Pharmacopœia, and inviting suggestions, beg leave to suggest that taking into consideration the uncertainty that prevails as to the strength of the tinctures and fluid extracts of different preparations, which is often a source of confusion, we recommend that a uniform strength should be established in the case of all such pharmaceutical preparations. Your committee also desire to append the enclosed information on the flora of Canada obtained from a well known botanist.

JAMES THORBURN,
FIFE FOWLER,
W. B. GEIKIE,
Committee.

I have looked over the British Pharmacopœia and find that the following plants used in medicine are common to this country (Canada) :

Gaultheria procumbens L. Wintergreen. Common.
Betula lenta L. Black birch. Common.
Aconitum Napellus L. Frequent in gardens.
Triticum sativum L. Wheat.
Zea Mays L. Indian corn.
Carum carui L. Caroway. Common weed.
Mentha pipenta L. Peppermint. In gardens.
Mentha viridis L. Rather common.
Cochlearia armoracia L. Horse radish. Common.
Cetraria Islandica. Common on trees.
Cimicifuga racemosa Nutt. Ontario.
Conium masculatum L. Common.
Coriandrum sativum L. In gardens.
Barley.
Papaver somniferum L. Poppy. In gardens.
Taraxacum officinale Web. Dandelion. Common.

Digitalis purpurea L. About Vancouver city.
Aspidium Filix-mas L. Male fern. Not common.
Hyoscyamus niger L. Rather common.
Humulus Lupulus L. Hop. Cultivated.
Datura stramonium L. Common.
Polygala Senega L. Seneca snakeroot. Common.
Linum usitatissimum L. Cultivated.
Lobelia inflata L. Abundant.
Juniperus communis L. Common.
Podophyllum peltatum L. Abundant in Ontario.
Prunus domestica L. Plum.
Abies balsamea Mill. Fir. Common.
Arctostaphylos Uva-ursi L. Common.
Veratrum viride L. Common.
Hamamelis Virginica L. Abundant.
Hydrostis Canadensis L. Not common.

This list gives a very imperfect idea of the number of medical plants in Canada. An examination of American medical works would show that we have a very large percentage of those used in the States.

Moved by Dr. THORBURN, seconded by Dr. FOWLER, That the report of the Committee on Flora, etc., be adopted, and 'that the Registrar be authorized to send same to Hon. Dr. Quain, President B. M. C. Carried.

On motion of Dr. Moorhouse, seconded by Dr. Bray, the Council adjourned to meet at 8 o'clock p.m.

EVENING SESSION.

In accordance with motion for adjournment, the Council met at eight o'clock.

The President, Dr. Rogers, in the chair, called the meeting to order.

The Registrar called the roll and the following members were present : Drs. Armour, Barrick, Bray, Britton, Brock, Campbell, Dickson, Emory, Fowler, Geikie, Graham, Hanly, Henderson, Henry, Logan, Luton, Machell, Moore, Moorhouse, Reddick, Rogers, Sangster, Shaw, Thorburn, Thornton and Williams.

The minutes of last meeting were read by the Registrar, and confirmed, and signed by the President.

NOTICES OF MOTION.

None.

COMMUNICATIONS, PETITIONS, ETC.

None.

MOTIONS OF WHICH NOTICE HAS BEEN GIVEN AT A PREVIOUS MEETING.

Moved by Dr. WILLIAMS, seconded by Dr. SHAW, and resolved, That Drs. Rogers, Thorburn and Campbell be and are hereby elected the Executive Committee for the year 1896-97.

The President read the motion.

Dr. SANGSTER—Mr. President, as was the case last year, I feel constrained to oppose this motion. To this Executive Committee is entrusted for fifty-one weeks out of the fifty-two weeks of the year the entire government of the profession. That committee assume, upon, I think, a very flimsy pretext, or have assumed in the past, to close the avenues of access to information respecting Council matters ; and the matters of this Council, important matters to the entire profession, come within the purview of that committee. A Legislature has given to the profession seventeen members out of the thirty that compose this Council; more than three-fifths of the Council are territorial representatives ; and I claim on behalf of my constituents and on behalf of the profession at large that that representation shall be respected in the committees, especially in the important committees of this Council ; and I therefore claim that the three gentlemen upon that committee should be territorial representatives. It will be remembered that something like this was proposed last year, and your attention was drawn to the fact that your by-law prescribes that there shall be three members elected to that committee, but owing to a suggestion that was made at that time the Council were placed in a very anomalous position, the astounding position, of carefully deciding that two gentlemen who were already ex-officio members of that committee might be elected on that committee ; that although a prescribed nine in your by-law respecting the standing committees meant nine, and a prescribed seven meant seven, and a prescribed five meant five, yet in the case of this particular committee a prescribed three did not mean three, but one. Now that, I say, is a most astounding position to assume ; and I claim that your by-law governing that matter shall not be departed from ; and I claim on behalf of the profession that three members of that committee shall be territorial representatives. And I now move in amendment, seconded by Dr. ARMOUR, That the Executive Committee for the current year be composed of Drs. Barrick, McLaughlin and Campbell.

The President read the motion.

Dr. SANGSTER—I was going to add that last year we were told it was unwise to make that committee larger than three, on account of the expense ; that was the only tangible reason that was assigned in opposition to enlarging the committee from three to five. If you look back to the financial returns as contained in the Announcement of 1892-93, you find that the Executive Committee was composed of three members prior to the year when your By-law No. 39 was formed and passed, and yet by a by-law the number was deliberately raised from three to five, as now appears in your by-law. There was nothing then said about the expense of the Executive Committee. In the first few years of the Council the Executive Committee was an expensive committee, not, I think, because of it containing a larger number of members, because, if my recollection serves me, it was a small number even then ; but I suppose it met frequently and held protracted meetings, or else perhaps it had a large monetary appetite. For some years preceding the time when this by-law was passed, your financial returns show that the Executive Committee had not cost the Council anything ; if you look under the head of Executive Committee, that after the year 1878-9, you will find that for 1879 and 1880, it cost the Council nothing ; for next year—1880-81—there was no cost again ; and then in 1881-82 and down to 1886-87 there was no cost ; then in 1887-88 and 1888-89, while this building was in process of erection, I suppose it was necessary for the Executive Committee to meet a little oftener, and there was a cost one year of $30.00, and the other year of $194.00 ; but at that time the Executive only consisted of three members. In 1889-90, the Executive Committee cost $6.00 ; and in 1890-91 to 1893-4 the Executive cost nothing ; in 1894-95 there was a small charge for the committee ; and during the present year there has been a moderate charge for the committee. In most of the years, therefore, it is plain that an Executive Committee of three cost the Council nothing, and therefore at the same rate an Executive Committee of five would cost the Council nothing. But the matter of cost is foreign to the question altogether ; an important principle is involved. This committee is the governing committee of the profession, and I claim the professional representatives should form a fair proportion of that committee. If it were an expensive committee, which I positively deny, we might consider the propriety of curtailing the number of its meetings or insisting it should come to its conclusions by epistolary correspondence, or of cutting off all pay from it at all, especially as this Council has no right to pay any of its committees one dollar or one cent. But whatever may be the position of the Council in that respect, the question of expense is merely a created one. The whole question of expense, which appears, I must say, without any evil meaning, to have been created for the purpose of defeating my contention last year, is not an excuse for our so emasculating the personnel of the committee as to make it by any possibility subservient to any special interests in this Council. I therefore repeat that on behalf of my constituents and in the name of the profession generally, I claim that that Executive Committee shall contain three members of our territorial representatives. Drs. Barrick and McLaughlin and you, Mr. President, are territorial representatives, Dr. Campbell is the representative of the homœopathists, and Dr. Thorburn is the representative of the appointed element. I claim that you should have the courtesy to give the element that I am connected with in this Council one representative on that committee. We form a third of the Council, and our constituents form a good third or over a third of the profession, and those in sympathy with us form more than half of the profession. Next year we hope to come here with a representation of two-thirds or three-fourths of the territorial men in the Council, and in that case I presume it will be just for us to ask you to give us two men on that committee ; but I hope that you will not deny the common English justice of enabling us to have one voice on that committee.

Dr. WILLIAMS—Mr. President, I must dissent from some considerable of the views expressed by Dr. Sangster. I think it is a wrong idea when we come to this Council to classify the members of this Council either as territorial men and School men, or any other kind of men. (Hear, hear.) The men who are here by statute are here in their right and here standing on a fair and equal basis ; they are not here for any one particular party. Perhaps with the exception of Dr. Geikie, who is a teacher, there is not one man here as a representative of the schools who is not a territorial man exactly as much as any other of our representatives. Dr. Moore represents Kingston. Is not Dr. Moore one of the territorial men as much as we are ? He practises at Brockville, and he represents the people in that country just as much as though he was elected for that special purpose. Then take Dr. Britton, who is a practitioner right here in the city of Toronto, and I ask you, are not his interests identical with those of every other practitioner in the city of Toronto ? Has he any special interest to single out Toronto University ? I think not. Here are representative men of the profession, and when they come here under their proper rights by statute, they stand here upon equal footing with every other man present, and when we come here and undertake to single out men and say this is a territorial man and that a college man, and we will give rights to one and we won't to the other, it is a grand mistake and one that ought not to be perpetuated in this Council, and I, for one, do not agree with it at all. Dr. Sangster has intimated that the question of cost brought up last year was brought up for the purpose of defeating the motion, or rather defeating the idea, of increasing the committee. Now, if Dr. Sangster would go back a little further than he did to-night, he would find when the committee was considerably larger that the bill of expense was very considerable, and if he got into the transactions of that committee he would find that they took upon themselves a very large amount of work, that they shifted examinations from one place to another, and they interfered in many ways ; so that the Council, about the year 1879, or somewhere there—I do not remember the exact date—were obliged to curtail that committee and cut down the numbers, and give them instructions right in the Council that under the Statute they were not to meet unless it was absolutely necessary. And that is the reason why Dr. Sangster is able to trace along a few years without any special expense. We have kept a tight rein on that Executive Committee ever since, simply because we found it to be one of the most difficult committees to control in the entire Council. And it has become the custom to appoint three men, and the custom has been for a number of years to appoint the President, the Vice-President and one other man, giving the homœopaths one man, I think, on the committee. One object of the small committee was that if they did meet, the expense might be kept down. The Solicitor was consulted on the matter, and it was considered that it would be within the letter of the law, that the President and Vice-President might be elected to that committee, and if elected to that committee with one other man it would fill the letter of the law ; and that was all we wanted to accomplish, just to fill the letter, so that if an emergency cropped up we had the men ready to do whatever work was necessary. Now, I hold that that system is a reasonable and a good system ; it has worked well, as Dr. Sangster has shown you by the small amount of cost it has incurred ; and it has gone on satisfactorily in that way, and I see no good reason why we should depart from that and appoint a much larger committee ; neither do I see any good reason why you should introduce a source of discord by singling out men and making one side territorial men and always watching that they shall have a certain representation, and by singling out men from the other side. I hold that every man is here by statute and on the same basis, and all should be treated exactly in the same way so long as they are here. I do not know that it is necessary to make any further remarks upon this subject. I think the Council fully understand that I do not object to the personnel that has been nominated by Dr. Sangster, but I do object, and object very strongly, to the principle upon which they are nominated. I object to putting a large number on that committee, and I object to putting members on because they are territorial members—I object to singling them out on any such principle as that. A point was raised that for a good portion of the year that committee really were the Council, and that they (if I understand Dr. Sangster) kept information from members of the Council. I do not know whether I understand Dr. Sangster correctly, but I certainly understood him to say that they kept information from the Council. Now, if Dr. Sangster said that, I should like to know whether or not it is correct. I was on that Executive Committee, I think, a couple of years, and I am perfectly certain that during the time I was on there was no information kept from the members of the Council at all ; and I would like to know whether the Executive of this last year have hidden away in their pockets or some place else transactions that we ought to have known and that they have kept from us. I, for one, do not think there is any particular force in that argument, and I do not think there is any fact in it. I think there is no transaction, probably, they have had as to which any member of the Council wants to get information that that information would not be given. Under these circumstances I do not feel disposed to change the nomination that I have made, and I will stand by it. My nomination is that the President, Vice-President and one other member form the Executive Committee.

Dr. GEIKIE—I am not going to detain the Council more than a minute or two. I am fully in accord with what Dr. Williams has said, and I deprecate, and in the very strongest way, this splitting up of the Council or an attempt continually being made to put the Council into little classes of one kind and another. I am a representative of the College, it is true, but I have behind me not far from a thousand graduates, and if that is not almost more than a territorial representative's share I do not know what is. I have been long enough in the Council to remember the expensive plan and to know the cheaper plan and the better plan is that that has been recently adopted. I heartily approve of following out that plan by appointing a committee consisting of the three gentlemen named, the President, the Vice-President and Dr. Campbell, as has been suggested. The committee has been inexpensive, and properly inexpensive of late years ; and we will come down on the President and his colleagues very very heavily if, during the ensuing year, there should be any unnecessary departure from this exceedingly good usage. I have no sympathy with creating a large Executive Committee, for it was ruinous in the old House, and if you bring it back again we do not know what the result would be in the new House ; besides that, it is altogether unnecessary, I contend, and is sure to cause mischief by splitting us up into this section, that section and the other section, setting one part of the Council, as it were, at sword's point with another, or tending in that direction.

Dr. BARRICK—Mr. President, I am very sorry that my name should have been mentioned and mixed up in a discussion of this kind. I should like to have seen this matter settled as a matter of principle. As Dr. Williams has very clearly stated, he deprecates the singling out of territorial and other representatives, and Dr. Geikie also protests against it. But a few days ago we had Dr. Geikie protesting because he had been left off the Committee on Education ; and why ? Because he was an ordinary member of this House ? No, but because he was a representative of a school. (Hear, hear.) Although the theory may be given that the Council should not be divided into sections, yet the effect, according to Dr. Geikie's own statement and according to his own strong and vigorous protest, is that the practice and theory do not go together. We have by-laws. Are we to be guided by our by-laws, or are we to be guided by a custom ? If we are to be guided by custom, then, I say, wipe out the by-laws. If we are to be guided by by-laws, then, I say, wipe out the custom. It is as clearly stated as it can be stated that the Executive Committee shall consist of three members, and, as in all the other committees, the President and Vice-President are ex-officio members of that committee. Then the custom is that we appoint the number in each of the other committees, and the President and Vice-President are ex-officio members. Why then depart from that custom, if custom is such a good thing. with regard to Executive Committee ? Or, if the by-laws are to be followed, why then should we depart from the by-laws ? If we stick to the by-laws in all the other committees, why should we depart from the by-laws in this one particular thing ? If we are to have by-laws, let us carry them out. If our by-law is not right, then we had better make the by-law right, but as long as that by-law is there I shall contend that we must fulfil the letter of that by-law and treat that the same as the others. So much then for the custom, so much then for the by-laws. The next point is the question whether this committee are of any use at all ; what do this committee do ? The by-law says, "The Executive Committee shall take cognizance of and action upon all such matters as may be delegated to it by the Council, or such as may require immediate interference or attention between the adjournment of the Council and its next meeting." This Council meets just once a year, and there are large interests involved and a large amount of money to be expended during the year, and this Executive Committee have to supervise and control that. If it was not necessary to have so large a committee, then the time for considering that was when we were forming the by-law, and not at the present time, when we are in this state of transition with regard to this building, when we are looking around for chances perhaps to dispose of it ; and when we are in that condition with regard to legislation that this Executive Committee may be called together to take action, as they were this year, and they had to take action this year ; and this year the Executive Committee had to exercise their authority in certain cases to get bills withdrawn from the House ; they had to take the responsibility of allowing Dr. Young to register on certain conditions ; and there may be matters of greater importance than that to be decided. In the case of Dr. Young, had not the Executive Committee not decided that matter then and there that bill of Mr. German's would have been through, and would have brought up perhaps a good deal of unpleasant discussion. There are things constantly arising and calling for attention, and I point to that bill as one of them I know that had to be dealt with then and there. The Executive Committee were on hand to deal with it, and the three members had to assume that responsibility. I thought then, and I think now, that where so great a responsibility had to be assumed it was fortunate these three men were together ; I thought then it was a good thing that we had an Executive Committee, and it was a good thing the three of them could be present ; and I thought it would have been better, and would have made their position stronger and made their influence felt with the Government, if five of them had been there representing this Council as its Executive Committee instead of three members ; and therefore I contend, as a matter of safety, and as a matter of dividing the responsibility, that it is expedient and right we should have three members besides the ex-officio members. And it would then be right because it would be in accordance with the by-law and would tend towards maintaining the safety of the funds and better looking after the concerns of this Council during the interval. As a matter then of principle, I am sorry any names were connected with either of these resolutions because we should first have settled the question, "Shall we or shall we not respect our own by-laws?" If we cannot respect our own by-laws, how are we to expect 2,500 medical practitioners in this Province to respect our by-laws? These are a few of the many reasons that I can see why, and I feel strongly upon this point, there should be an Executive Committee appointed according to our by-laws, or else we should change the by-laws.

Moved by Dr. BROCK, seconded by Dr. LOGAN, in amendment to the amendment, That Drs. Campbell, Barrick and Williams be the Executive Committee for the year 1896-97.

The President read the amendment to the amendment.

Dr. MOORE—My object in moving this amendment to the amendment is to reconcile the difference that exists in the Council on this question. If this amendment to the amendment carries we can then obey our by-laws and have the President and Vice-President ex-officio members of this committee; and this will do away with the argument of Dr. Barrick, and I think settle the question satisfactorily to the Council. While I am on my feet in connection with this, I might ask that the Registrar be instructed to index the report of our proceedings for this year in order to make it useful to members of this Council, for without an index it is useless to us for purposes of reference.

Dr. MOORE—I only intend to say a few words, and my remarks are mostly drawn forth by what Dr. Barrick has said. He tells us that this committee have a large amount of work to do. Now, I had two years' experience upon this committee, and I never had anything to do; and I think, Mr. President, you have had one or two years' experience upon it and you had but very little to do. We have been crying for economy here for some time, and I do not know any gentleman that has cried more strongly upon the economical point than my friend Dr. Barrick; he wants everything cut down to about the smallest point possible, and I quite agree with him on that; and I want to say that on the very score of economy this committee was formed as it was and has been for several years back, I can't tell you just how many, but some ten or twelve years at all events, composed of the President, Vice-President and one other member of the Council. The opinion of Mr. Osler was taken upon this question, and he said it was quite competent for us to elect the President and Vice-President and one other member, and that then the committee would be complete and our by-laws would be complied with. Now, why we should to-day, when the funds of the Council are in such a low condition, add more members to this committee, is something I cannot quite understand. They have discharged their duties, which have not been very onerous in the past, to the satisfaction apparently of their fellow-members of the Council, and why these three gentlemen cannot do it next year seems to me very strange; and I shall vote for Dr. Williams' motion and vote for the good old custom, and the custom that does comply with our by-laws according to the information we got from our Solicitor.

Dr. SANGSTER—May I ask that the opinion of Mr. Osler be read to the Council?

The PRESIDENT—I do not think it was given in writing.

Dr SANGSTER—When was it given?

Dr. WILLIAMS—It was long ago; the opinion was given at the time the three men were put on the committee, instead of five.

Dr. SANGSTER—May I ask when the change from five was made?

Dr. WILLIAMS—I can't tell from memory; you can look it up from the minutes.

Dr. SANGSTER—I see the change was made from the by-law from three to five in 1886, but the by-law was not respected. I should imagine that Mr. Osler, if he was consulted at all, would have been consulted at that time and that he would have instructed the Council then to have changed the by-law. It never has been actually five.

Dr. WILLIAMS—It was actually five, and it was changed to the three; and Mr. Osler was consulted to see whether or not that would comply with the spirit of the by-law, and he informed us that we could elect the President and Vice-President and that would conform to the by-law. That was why it was done; it was done purely as a matter of economy.

Dr. SANGSTER—The Announcements that I have only run back to 1887-8, and the Executive Committee of that time is set down as three members. Perhaps the Registrar will tell us when it was an Executive Committee of five?

The REGISTRAR—I couldn't tell without the record.

Dr. BRAY—I cannot tell Dr. Sangster when the change was made, but I know the Executive Committee were not always confined to the five; I have been in the Council when we had ten on the Executive Committee. I was a member of the Council with Dr. Williams and others when we protested so strongly against it that we cut it down to three members—the President, Vice-President and one other gentleman; and the committee were instructed not to meet unless it was absolutely necessary. I was a member of that committee for two years and never was called on to meet my colleagues on the committee; and during those two years that committee never cost the Council one cent. It is only on extraordinary occasions the Executive Committee have to meet. While I was President of the Council I was on that committee, and we did a lot of business by communicating through the mail with one another. That is what is done in most cases. It was an extraordinary reason that brought the committee together this last year, and I think last year was the first year that the committee were ever called on to meet. But I have known that committee since I have been in the Council to cost nearly as much as the Council did, and the work was very imperfectly done, too ; and I remember very well when this question arose that Mr. Osler's opinion was got, and that his opinion was as has been stated here, though I cannot tell you at what date it was given ; and I know ever since he gave that opinion the committee has consisted of three members and no more.

Dr. MOORE—I see in 1881 we had six on the Executive Committee, and in 1882 it was cut down to three and has remained at that ever since.

Dr. BARRICK—In what year was the by-law introduced ?

Dr. SANGSTER—In 1886.

. Dr. MOORE—In 1878 we had thirteen on the Executive Committee. (Refers to book.)

Dr. ARMOUR—I just want to say a word or two. Dr. Moore has called attention to the fact that in 1881 there were six on the Executive Committee, and turning up the report of our financial year I find that in 1881 the Executive Committee cost the Council nothing, so that according to that the increase of a member or two will not matter much. There are now three motions before the chair which all appear to be, in a manner, substantive motions ; however, I just want to call the members' attention to the difference between the two last motions. Dr. Sangster has moved that Drs. Campbell, Barrick and McLaughlin be the Executive Committee for the year ; and Dr. Brock has moved, in amendment, changing that simply by the substitution of the name of Dr. Williams for Dr. McLaughlin. I have no objections to Dr. Williams being there, for he would make a very able representative on any committee of this Council, but I think it is only fair to ask, and it will be only fair in you to give us, that representation on the Executive Committee.

The PRESIDENT—Dr. Armour, you say, " Give us ; " who do you mean ?

Dr. ARMOUR—To give those representatives here who work with me and my friends Dr. Sangster, Dr. McLaughlin and others ; you may say "the members representing the Defence Association."

Dr. BRAY—There can be no such thing in this Council.

Dr. ARMOUR—Yes ; my friend Dr. Williams deprecated the idea of Dr. Sangster pointing out the sources from which the representation in this College comes, but before he got through he rather destroyed the effect the outrage that in a measure this seemed to cause to his sense of propriety——

The PRESIDENT—You must keep to the subject.

Dr. ARMOUR—I am speaking to the subject.

The PRESIDENT—Not now.

Dr. ARMOUR—When I get through my sentence you will see I am keeping to the subject. Before Dr. Williams got through he incidentally remarked it was the custom to place one homœopath on the committee ; surely that was acknowledging, as Dr. Geikie did the other day, that there were different sources of representation in this Council.

The President put the amendment to the amendment, and on a vote having been taken declared it lost.

The President put the amendment, and on a vote having been taken declared it lost.

The President put the original motion, and on a vote having been taken declared it carried.

Dr. Sangster asked for the yeas and nays.

The Registrar took the yeas and nays as follows :

Yeas—Drs. Bray, Britton, Brock, Campbell, Dickson, Emory, Fowler, Geikie, Graham, Henderson, Logan, Luton, Machell, Moore, Moorhouse, Rogers, Shaw, Thorburn, Williams. —19.

Nays—Drs. Armour, Barrick, Hanly, Henry, Sangster and Thornton—6.

Moved by Dr. MOORE, seconded by Dr. WILLIAMS, That the following gentlemen constitute the Legislation Committee for the ensuing year : Drs. Britton, Barrick, Emory, Sangster, Thorburn, Williams and Machell. Carried.

Moved by Dr. BROCK, seconded by Dr. BARRICK, That the Official Announcement shall be indexed. Carried.

Dr. Emory asked and obtained leave to present a special report of the Committee on Examinations.

Dr. EMORY presented and read report of the special committee appointed to consider the question of examinations.

To the President-and members of the Ontario Medical Council:

The special committee appointed to consider the question of examinations beg leave to report as follows :

1st. We recommend that By-law No. 70 be amended by striking out the word "seven" in Clause 4, and substituting therefor the word "five."

2nd. That the time allotted to each candidate with each Examiner be extended from ten to fifteen minutes.

3rd. That it be an instruction to the Examiners in Descriptive Anatomy and Medical and Surgical Anatomy that their papers for the written examination in said subjects shall each contain ten questions.

W. J. HUNTER EMORY, Chairman.

Adopted in Council.   A. F. ROGERS.

Moved by Dr. EMORY, seconded by Dr. MOORE, That the report be adopted.

The President read the motion.

Dr. WILLIAMS—I would just like to offer a word or two in explanation of that for fear some person else shall be got into the unpleasant feeling about the matter that I got into myself. You will observe there that the clinical examinations are apparently in the ordinary time of an oral examination, which is fifteen minutes ; and when we think about it, fifteen minutes at a clinical examination seems like nothing. That view produces an uncomfortable feeling ; you think you have the name of doing something when you really do nothing. But I met the Examiner this afternoon, and had a talk with him about it ; and according to what he tells me the practice is, the candidates have about an hour apiece in place of fifteen minutes. They are taken into a ward where there are about twenty beds, one ward provided for medical students and the other for the surgeon ; and there is an Assistant Examiner in the ward with the students. The students are taken into that ward in groups of about eight, and they are assigned to certain patients, and are allowed about an hour to examine their cases and make their preparations ; then the Examiner gets at them and he spends about fifteen minutes questioning them on the cases that they have had, which practically gives them in the neighborhood of an hour to work up their cases, and they can tell it all within fifteen minutes without any trouble ; so I think the examination in a clinical line is in that way perfectly satisfactory, while if it were just a fifteen minute examination it would be an absurdity.

The President put the motion, and on a vote having been taken declared it carried.

On motion of Dr. Campbell, seconded by Dr. Dickson, the Council adjourned at 9.30 p.m., to meet at ten o'clock to-morrow morning.

FIFTH DAY.

SATURDAY, June 13th, 1896.

The Council met at 10 a.m., according to motion for adjournment, the President in the chair.

The Registrar called the roll, and the following members were present :

Drs. Armour, Barrick, Bray, Brock, Campbell, Dickson, Emory, Fowler, Geikie, Graham, Hanly, Henderson, Henry, Logan, Luton, Machell, Moore, Moorhouse, McLaughlin, Reddick, Rogers, Rosebrugh, Sangster, Shaw, Thorburn, Thornton, Williams.

The minutes of the last maeting were read by the Registrar, and confirmed, and signed by the President.

NOTICES OF MOTION.

None.

READING OF COMMUNICATIONS, PETITIONS, ETC.

None.

MOTIONS OF WHICH NOTICE HAS BEEN GIVEN AT A PREVIOUS MEETING.

Dr. Machell asked and obtained leave to introduce a motion without notice.

Moved by Dr. MACHELL, seconded by Dr. SANGSTER, That in view of the use of the Ontario Medical Library to every member of the profession throughout the Province, the rental is hereby reduced to the nominal sum of $1.00 per annum.   Carried.

Moved by Dr. BRAY, seconded by Dr. MOORHOUSE, That the rules be suspended for the remaining portion of this session.   Carried.

Moved by Dr. SHAW, seconded by Dr. MOORE, That the Registrar be instructed to acknowledge the receipt of Dr. O'Reilly's letter inviting the members of the Council to attend the Toronto General Hospital, and expressing to Dr. O'Reilly the Council's appreciation of the invitation, and regret at not being able to accept the same for want of time. Carried.

Moved by Dr. EMORY, seconded by Dr. LUTON, That By-law No. — to amend By-law No. 70, in accordance with the resolution passed at last evening's session, be now read the first time. Carried.

The by-law received its first reading.

Moved by Dr. EMORY, seconded by Dr. MOORE, That the Council resolve into Committee of the Whole for the purpose of reading a second time By-law No. — to amend By-law No. 70. Carried.

Council in Committee of the Whole. Dr. Sangster in the chair.

The Chairman read the by-law.

Dr. MOORHOUSE—I would like to ask the mover of this resolution his reason for bringing in this alteration.

Dr. EMORY—I should just reply that the Council last night adopted the recommendation of the committee to make that change. I am merely introducing the by-law by order of the Council.

Moved by Dr. EMORY, That the by-law as read be adopted. Carried.

Moved by Dr. EMORY, That the committee rise and report. Carried.

The committee rose. The President in the chair.

Moved by Dr. EMORY, seconded by Dr. MOORE, That By-law No. — amending By-law No. 70 be read the third time, numbered, signed by the President, and sealed with the seal of the College of Physicians and Surgeons of Ontario. Carried.

BY-LAW No. 74 TO AMEND BY-LAW No. 70.

That Paragraph 2 of Section 4 is amended by erasing the word "seven" and substituting therefor the word "five."

J. H. SANGSTER,
Chairman Committee of Whole.

Adopted in Council. A. F. ROGERS, President.

Moved by Dr. WILLIAMS, seconded by Dr. MOORE, That the mover have leave to introduce a by-law for the purpose of settling the annual fee, and that it be now read the first time. Carried.

The by-law received its first reading.

Moved by Dr. WILLIAMS, seconded by Dr. MOORE, and resolved, That the Council go into Committee of the Whole for the purpose of reading the by-law a second time.

The President read the motion.

Dr. ARMOUR—I desire to speak to this motion. It will be remembered that last year I opposed the assessment of the fee, for the reason that I considered it unnecessary except for the carrying of this building, and at that time I did not think we should assess it for that purpose. We are, however, in a little different position this year; our finances are in a much improved condition, according to our estimates, which have not yet been presented, but which should have been presented before this by-law is introduced, because there is some recommendation in the financial report about this; that should have been done before the by-law was presented. However, the Finance Committee will pardon me for referring to the estimates here, so that this can be disposed of at the present time. This year, it would appear, we are in a much better position financially than we were last year; that, without the assessment of an annual fee, our estimates will show us that we have an expectation of a surplus of about $7,000.00. Now, with this prospect before us, I think it would be very unwise to again assess this annual fee. I will not detain you longer, but will content myself with thus briefly entering my protest against this assessment.

The President put the motion, and on a vote having been taken declared it carried.

Council in Committee of the Whole. Dr. Shaw in the chair.

The Chairman read the by-law.

Moved by Dr. WILLIAMS, That the by-law be taken up clause by clause. Carried.

Dr. CAMPBELL—Before this is proceeded with, I would like to ask if it would be possible to lay on the desks of the members any statement as to the number of delinquents and the payment of past assessments and the amount due, which might be of some assistance to the members.

The PRESIDENT—Dr. Pyne can have that statement placed on the members' desks at once.

The Registrar distributed copies of the statement referred to, showing the members in arrears.

Dr. CAMPBELL—My intention was to ask for a simple statement as to the amount paid in, how.many had paid, and how many had not paid ; so that the Council could judge of the necessity of adopting means of collecting that would equalize the payments so that all the people would be alike, and I think perhaps it might save trouble if we can get the statement showing how many there are who have not paid and how many have paid.

The REGISTRAR—Up to the 31st of December, 1895, 1,133 members paid their assessments ; this amounted to $6,800.00 odd.

Dr. REDDICK—What proportion of those men were very much in arrears ?

The REGISTRAR—Most of these were men recently in arrears, but some were a long time in arrears. One member was in to see me yesterday who owes $26.00, and he said he would send me a cheque this week.

Dr. MOORHOUSE—What was the largest sum paid by any one man ?

The REGISTRAR—$20.00 was the largest sum, excepting a member of the Council who paid $26.00.

The Chairman read Clause No. 1.

On motion of Dr. Williams, Clause No. 1 was adopted.

The Chairman read Clause No. 2.

On motion of Dr. Williams, the clause was adopted.

Dr ARMOUR—I think it is not right for the appointed members to vote on this ; when it comes from a committee appointed by the Council, I think that territorial members only should vote on this.

The CHAIRMAN—I think Dr: Armour is right, the vote should be only by the territorial members. I will put the vote again.

The Chairman again read Clause No. 2.

On motion of Dr. Williams, Clause No. 2 was adopted.

The Chairman read the preamble.

On motion of Dr. Williams the preamble was adopted as read.

Moved by Dr. WILLIAMS, seconded by Dr. HENRY, That the committee rise and report the by-law as read and passed in Committee of the Whole. Carried.

The committee rose. The President in the chair.

Moved by Dr. WILLIAMS, seconded by Dr. BRAY, and resolved, That the by-law be now read and finally passed, signed, sealed and numbered.

BY-LAW No. 75.

Whereas it is necessary and expedient that an annual fee be paid by each member of the College of Physicians and Surgeons of Ontario towards the general expenses of the College ;

And whereas by By-law No. 69 of the Council of the said College, it was enacted that Section 41a of the Ontario Medical Act be suspended until the 1st day of June, 1896, then to come into force in case a sufficient amount of dues is not paid to cover the bank liability ;

And whereas a sufficient amount of dues has not been paid, and it is expedient to remove all doubts as to the coming into force of the said section ;

Now therefore the College of Physicians and Surgeons of Ontario enacts as follows :

1. Each member of the College shall pay to the Registrar, towards the general expenses of the College for the current year, an annual fee of the amount of two dollars ($2,00), pursuant to the provisions of Section 27 of the Ontario Medical Act.

2. And it is hereby declared and enacted that Clause 41a of the Ontario Medical Act has been in force from the 1st of June, 1896, and is now in full force and effect.

Adopted in Committee of the Whole.

G. M. SHAW,
Chairman Committee of the Whole.

Adopted in Council. A. F. ROGERS.

The President read the motion.

Dr. McLAUGHLIN—I do not propose making any observations of any length, but I want the Council to thoroughly understand that a large section of the profession is opposed to this under the present state of affairs. I am opposed to it ; I do not think it should be passed. I think it is wrong in principle, and without any further remarks, because my opinions are known in the Council, and I do not wish to take up the time of the Council, I shall vote against it and ask for the yeas and nays.

Dr. SANGSTER—I am in somewhat a similar position. I am not going to make any lengthy remarks. There is no doubt that a large section of the profession is strongly, I might say violently, opposed the reinstation of the coercive clauses of the Act, and in many cases to the assessment itself. I believe that in certain places all the physicians in the town have passed resolutions stating that they would not pay one dollar of that tax while the money resulting was appropriated to purposes quite outside the Medical Act. This

Council show no disposition to economize, they still cling to Micawber Hall and seem disposed to continue to ; and it is into this corner lot most of this money goes ; and the profession are opposed to the tax. They have a strong conviction, and I have a strong conviction, that this Council are quite capable of spending whatever money may flow into their coffers ; but I have an equally strong conviction that if they made honest attempts to economize, if their economical ideas proceeded any farther than words, that that tax would not be necessary. I still regard the tax as unnecessary, and I still regard it as unconstitutional and vexatious. I am opposed to the tax, and I am speaking on behalf of that part of the profession which is opposed to it.

Dr. HENRY—I rise merely to repeat what I have repeated for some years. We cannot get on without the tax ; that is apparent to every person ; we must have money to carry on the work of the Council. But I am opposed to the mode of collecting it ; I am opposed to the coercive legislation. I think the profession have done very well this last year, and I believe if we were to allow that clause to remain in abeyance for another year the profession would respond, perhaps better than they did last year. I will vote against the reimposition of Section 41a, on the ground that I do not like the coercive character ; while I admit that the money is required and that every man should pay his fee, for I think it is unjust that I and a few others should pay, while others, again, go scotfree.

Dr. THORNTON—While I would like to direct my efforts to harmonize the conflicting elements of the profession and of this Council, I feel thoroughly satisfied that this by-law and its influences will tend directly in the opposite way, and therefore I feel bound to vote against it.

Dr. WILLIAMS—Mr. President, I think it is, perhaps, useless for us to discuss this matter at any very great length, and I think the gentlemen who have spoken have displayed a good deal of judgment in that particular, and I must commend them for not having gone into the matter more fully than they did, because the opinions of all the Council are well known. I think I may say, as well as every member of the Council may say, that we are opposed to paying that fee if it were not necessary. Do you think I would like to go into my pocket for two dollars and give it out if I could see an honest and good and feasible way of doing without it ? We only want to pay because we feel it is necessary to pay it. Then, why do we support the "coercive clauses," as they are called ? We do not support them because we love them. We do not love them a bit more than the rest of the profession do, not one of us ; but we support them because it is the only possible way that has been presented to us by which the whole profession may be placed on an equality, placed on the same common platform—that when one pays the others shall pay ; they all should pay alike, because they all derive like advantages. That is our view. We do not love the coercive clauses, neither do we love the assessment, but we look upon it as a necessity ; and the best and most feasible and fairest way it can possibly be carried out. I do not just care to follow Dr. Sangster in his intimation that the Council might be more economical and then this would not be necessary. I will not take the trouble to go over some votes of the Council since our present meeting, or we might point out that where the majority of the Council were inclined to an economical course the so-called economical men were inclined to draw us into a little more expense. I think the members of the Council are not looking for extravagance and waste, but sometimes we are compelled to do things from expediency which we believe to be the best under the circumstances—not perhaps that we love them, or not perhaps that they would be our opinion if we could fix things just as we liked ; but rather to get it in the best and most satisfactory way under the circumstances. I believe, in the administration of public business, that the man who can take hold of circumstances and fit his proceedings to those, is the successful man ; not the man who fixes up a theory in advance and opposes everything because it does not come just in harmony with his theory. As I said before, we do not love these things more than the rest, but we look upon this as the most practicable and most feasible and the best under the circumstances.

Dr. REDDICK—I, like the rest, do not like to take up unnecessarily any time of the Council. I will vote against this because I think it is wrong in principle and because a majority of the members of the constituency that sent me here told me to do so.

Dr. BRAY—My reasons for supporting this are strengthened by what Dr. Armour said prior to going into Committee of the Whole. He says our finances are in a very much better state now than they were this time last year, and I would ask him the reason of that. Is it not because of the passage of this by-law last year, with the coercive clause, if you term it so, being suspended ? Is that not the cause of our financial condition being better ? We heard the Registrar say there was something in the neighborhood of $7,000.00 paid in last year ; and I would like to ask you how much was paid in before the clause was suspended, three years ago ? There was not $300.00 paid in. Now, that being the case, is it fair to those gentlemen who paid the $7,000.00 that others who will not pay anything should receive the benefits ? I say no ; and for that, and if for no other reason, I would support this motion, and my constituents uphold me in it. My constituents say to me, " If you go down there and do not make every man pay, we think it is very unfair indeed to those who have paid, and we will not pay another dollar ; and, moreover, if there is any possibility of getting back what we have paid, we will endeavor to get it back unless other gentlemen in the profession are placed in the same position as we are." I have given you one reason, I could give you many others, why we should pass this motion, and I say the arguments in opposition to this motion only strengthen me in my support of it.

Dr. DICKSON—I propose to vote for the by-law. I would hesitate if I thought the number this list represents was the number opposed to pay the fee, but I take it if we subtracted from this list those who are dead and those who are absent from the Province and those who are refusing to pay because a certain proportion have failed to pay and are unwilling to pay, we will find the number of those opposed is very small indeed.

Dr. ARMOUR—Mr. President, I am rather surprised at the composure with which many members of this Council undertake to carry out the conditions contained in this by-law. This threat was made to the profession a year ago ; in fact, we can go away back to 1881 or 1882, when it was first introduced,—you all know with what result then, and you know with what result within the past year. Although it has been hanging over the heads of the profession for the last year, there is over half of the profession who have not paid their fees and who are not going to be forced in that way to pay them. The main contention that has been brought up here why this Section 41a should be applied at the present time, is that some have paid and others have not. I maintain that if this fee is an improper fee, as evidently the majority of the profession view it, the fact that a few members of the profession should have paid it is no reason why any other members should pay it. We must not assume, or we cannot reasonably assume, that those who have paid during the past year, or any considerable portion of them, approve of either the tax or the penal coercion. I know in my division quite a large number have paid, but they have paid it protestingly ; and they tell me that they paid it rather than have any legal or other troubles about it, on account of the small amount of the tax. They have paid it, but they object to the principle, they object to the tax ; and they object to a penal coercion being applied to the profession ; and if it comes to a test, they say they are willing to hold out to the last against this Council in that matter. I believe there are fully two-thirds of the profession who are opposed to this penal coercion, and if the Council insist on forcing it on them they will resist the Council to the last extremity.

Dr. SHAW—I will be guided very much in what I have to say by the example of those who have spoken, by being very brief. I have to say in the first place I would have to regard myself as an anti-coercionist on this by-law ; in the second place, I think it is my conviction, at any rate it is my constituents' conviction, that until the Council show some desire and make some effort, as a Council, to curtail the expenses which are connected with the proceedings throughout the year, they will not willingly pay the annual dues. The majority of them feel that they should pay annual dues, but until they are convinced that the business of the Council is carried on more economically, I think the majority of them would pay it very reluctantly.

Dr. DICKSON—Does Dr. Shaw think this Council have willingly increased the expenditure?

Dr. SHAW—Nobody does that.

Dr. DICKSON—I thought Dr. Shaw was speaking for his constituents, and it was his own opinion we were extravagant in the conduct of the affairs of this Council.

Dr. SHAW—I am very glad to reply to that ; my conviction, as expressed here a few days ago, was that we were spending more money than the finances of this Council would permit. I said it then, and I repeat it now, and I am prepared to repeat it here from day to day, not only for my constituents, but for myself.

Dr. CAMPBELL—I have nothing to say of the merits of the question one way or another, but owing to the unfortunate absence of Dr. Roome, the representative of the territorial division in which I live, I wish to place before the Council the sentiments of the physicians of the city of London, without comment. That body, at the commencement of this agitation, through a mistaken idea of the situation, as you all know strongly memorialized the Legislature against the actions of the Medical Council. The opinion of that body is now shown in the copy of a resolution passed at the regular meeting of the London Medical Association on February 10th, 1896. I may say that I am not a member of that Association ; it is composed of the general practitioners of the city.

Dr. ARMOUR—How many members were present at that meeting ?

Dr. CAMPBELL—I cannot tell you.

Dr. ARMOUR—It might lead to a false impression. There might have been only three or four present at that meeting, and if that was the case, it would have very little weight.

Dr. BRAY—I want to answer that question, because I know ; I was communicated with by the President and Secretary of that Association, and there were twenty-seven members present when that resolution was passed.

Dr. CAMPBELL—I do not know anything about that ; I know that resolution was passed unanimously by this Association and was published in the journal, and was never objected to.

Dr. BARRICK—The position I took last year in this matter, and which I take now, is strongly in accordance with what Dr. Armour has stated, in this respect, that the estimates of the year should be discussed by this Council before we incur any of the expenses for the present year. As we have been doing business, the Council are open to the charge of being extravagant. Now if the estimates had been before us, Dr. Shaw would have been in a position to point out to us, when we were discussing the estimates of the year, and to state in what particular item we were being extravagant, and it would have been better for him then to have pointed out in what way we could have avoided this extravagance. I am sure that every member of this Council will easily be led in a way that will lead to economy and efficiency in conducting the business of this Council, but there is just this, that Dr. Shaw has not an opportunity, the estimates have not been presented, and therefore in making a charge of that kind it is unfair to this Council and it is unfair to every medical man in this Province to charge this Council with being extravagant when he cannot point wherein we can lessen the expenses of the Council. I hope that at another session we will have in the early part the estimates brought forward. Dr. Armour has said that the Finance Committee this year are preparing estimates for the year, but how can the Finance Committee prepare the estimates when they do not know what we are to pay for printing and publishing this Announcement——

The PRESIDENT—You are getting away from the subject, Dr. Barrick ; you must keep to the subject.

Dr. BARRICK—How am I going to vote for that by-law unless it can be shown to me that we are using every other means of retrenchment? (Hear, hear.) I submit that the estimates should be given to us first. In the face of the statement of last year, I maintain that we cannot carry on the affairs of this Council without those estimates. We tried some years ago, as Dr. Bray has said, without that by-law, and we got about $300.00 in. Last year we tried, with the by-law with the penal clause suspended, and we collected $7,000.00 ; and our improved financial condition is now a result of the passage of that by-law last year. (Hear, hear.) As I understand this matter, although that by-law comes into force now, it cannot be acted on for another year. Am I correct in that?

Dr. BRAY—It is in force now.

Dr. BARRICK—I understand that it cannot be acted on until it has been in force another year.

Dr. BRITTON—That is correct.

Dr. BARRICK—That we cannot act on that for another year, so that we will have a very good sample this year of what we can do ; and if by another year we find that the responses have come in sufficiently, we can easily rescind that by-law next year, before it is actually put into force ; and then we will have before us what we got without the by-law, what we got with the by-law with the penal clause suspended, and we will have what we received with the penal clause in force, without having to bring an action. Then if we have the estimates brought in next year, there is no one in this Council who is more ready and conscientiously prepared than I am to stop the carrying into force of that section, just as long as it can be shown that it is not required and just as long as the estimates can convince me that we can carry on the affairs of this Council without forcing that clause. But it is perfectly clear from the Treasurer's report last year, that such a thing at present cannot be done, and therefore I must this year support that motion.

Dr. BROCK—My views upon this subject have been expressed at a previous meeting of the Council, and I find no reason to change my former opinion. I will not detain you longer, but will content myself with saying that the members who are now owing this Council, whom I have spoken to as delinquents, declare that they cannot view with composure the fact that we are not taking active steps to collect money from every person who is owing the Council, and their only reason for refusing payment is that we are not enforcing payment by every individual who owes us.

Dr. SANGSTER—It has been stated that if that by-law passes in its present form no action can be taken upon it, in regard to what the Council calls the delinquent debtors, until a year from next December or from the coming December. If I understand the Act aright, on the 31st of December the Registrar is required to notify those who have not paid, and forthwith, two months after that, we erase their names from the Register. I would like this to be clearly understood. A good deal of misapprehension prevails in the profession, and I am quite sure that if you can convince the electorate that you are standing practically on legal grounds in regard to your by-law, that you would have nearly every dollar of the past dues paid into the Council. The resolution asking for this the other day you thought wise to throw out, but I would like that every member of our College resident through the country should be in a position to clearly comprehend his exact position in regard to this Council. If he has to pay now and does not pay before the 31st of next December, will it be the duty of the Registrar, as I take it it will be, two months after that, to notify him that his name is erased from the Register, or will the suspension of action in that matter go on until a year from next December ? Perhaps Dr. Williams or some other gentlemen that are in the inner circle would just explain that.

The PRESIDENT—Your question is to me. I think the matter is probably a legal interpretation ; it is an interpretation of a section of the Act, and no doubt before any action is taken, the Solicitor, Mr. Osler, will be requested by the Registrar to tell him whether he shall act next November, or whether he shall act a year from next November.

Dr. SANGSTER—Then I submit that advice should be obtained now. I am quite certain you will have actions enough on your hands, but why multiply them by leaving anybody in doubt until action is taken ?

The PRESIDENT—Dr. Williams would probably be able to explain it from his standpoint, but I am quite satisfied, before any action is taken, the Solicitor's advice would be had.

Dr. SHAW—Perhaps I might be permitted to rise to a matter of privilege, although I have spoken already. Dr. Barrick, I think, was kind enough to say, if I understood him aright, that until I could point out that there was excessive expenditure in some way in connection with the Council and their proceedings, I should not charge the Council with spending more money than was necessary to carry on their proceedings. Is that right ?

Dr. BARRICK—That is correct.

Dr. SHAW—Mr. President, I think I pointed out three or four days ago very plainly that in my opinion the Council were paying out more money towards conducting the annual session of the Council than in my opinion the finances would permit. I thought I had pointed out then that if Dr. Barrick (and the rest of us) would accept $2.50 a day for five days, less than he now accepts for his sessional allowance, the Council would be saving in round figures one thousand dollars to the profession. I think I showed that very plainly, and I think Dr. Barrick will admit that my figures were correct ; but he rather chose to put the $12.50 in his pocket, which I think would have been a very small sum indeed for each member of the Council to have left in the hands of the Treasurer, and have thus saved the profession of the Province one thousand dollars. I think that is sufficient justification for the observation I have made.

Dr. WILLIAMS—I felt somewhat amused at Dr. Sangster speaking as though I was in the inner circle. I have not learned up to the present that there was any special inner circle in this Council. I thought that every man who came into the Council stood upon exactly the same platform and that they were in the inner circle——

Dr. ARMOUR—I rise to a point of order. Dr. Williams has already spoken to this motion.

The PRESIDENT—On the request of the chair, he is now speaking again.

Dr. ARMOUR—The Chair has answered the question.

The PRESIDENT—I have asked Dr. Williams to answer.

Dr. ARMOUR—He is not answering it.

The PRESIDENT—Dr. Williams is in order.

Dr. WILLIAMS—I am replying to a little pleasantry of Dr. Sangster's. I want to say that every man in this Council is in the same inner circle as I am, and I claim I am in order because I moved this resolution, and I have a right to reply later on ; but now I am not going to speak on the resolution, but simply to answer the question of Dr. Sangster, to the best of my ability. I will ask you, gentlemen, to turn up the Act, which you will find in the Register, on pages xxviii and xxix. (Reads Section 41a, Sub-section 1.) Then passing on to Sub-section 5, we find : " After twelve months' default in taking out such certificate, and if two months' notice of such default be given by registered letter, addressed to the registered address of such defaulter, the Registrar shall, if payment has not been made by the defaulter, erase the name of the medical practitioner so in default from the Register, and the provisions of this Act as to unregistered medical practitioners shall forthwith apply." We are dealing with the year 1896, and my explanation is that that fee is legally due on the 1st of January, 1896, and is supposed to be payable any time through the year, and members of this Council are allowed until the 31st of December of the year 1896 to pay that fee, and they are not considered in default until that 31st of December arrives. Then we start into 1897, and under Section 5 our members have a right to become one year in default, which takes us to the 31st of December, 1897, and then there must be two months' notice after that. So that they have two years and two months in which to get in their $2.00 payments. I submit that that is not a very coercive measure to any member of the profession.

Dr. SANGSTER—That is satisfactory. I merely wanted it correctly placed. As to the inner circle, I will still retain my convictions, and I feel very much that I am in the outer circle, whether Dr. Williams is in the inner circle or not.

The PRESIDENT—We are all in the one circle, for the benefit of the profession.

The President put the motion for the third reading, and on a vote having been taken declared it carried.

Dr. Sangster called for the yeas and nays.

Dr. WILLIAMS—I would specially like the yeas and nays.

The Registrar took the yeas and nays as follows :

Yeas—Drs. Barrick, Bray, Brock, Campbell, Dickson, Emory, Graham, Hanly, Henderson, Logan, Luton, Machell, Rogers, Williams—14.

Nays—Drs. Armour, Henry, McLaughlin, Reddick, Sangster, Shaw, Thornton—7.

Dr. WILLIAMS—I think in the record of that vote going into the Announcement attention should be called to the fact that the College representatives did not vote, otherwise the inference might be drawn by the profession that the vote was taken in a weak Council, that a part of the members were away, while really it is in a full Council, so far as this vote is concerned. I think this should in some way be made clear to the profession.

Dr. McLAUGHLIN—I think that is very important, and I think it might be added that the Government of our country has gone a little in the direction of incapacitating these men, and I hope they will completely incapacitate them in time.

Dr. GEIKIE—We have no votes on this question. Is it legal for us to offer our annual assessment ? I would not on any account do anything illegal in that way.

Moved by Dr. SANGSTER, seconded by Dr. McLAUGHLIN, That the opinion of the Solicitor be obtained promptly regarding the validity of the Council's action, founded on the substitution of resolutions in lieu of by-laws, covering the following particulars : 1st, the constitution of the Executive Committee ; 2nd, the payment of per diem allowances to any of the committees ; 3rd, the payment of any moneys to the Examiners ; 4th, the payment of any salary to the Official Prosecutor ; 5th, the fixing of the time of examinations ; and, 6th, the double examination at Kingston and Toronto.

The President read the motion.

Dr. WILLIAMS—I have no objection to that motion being carried, but I have some objection to its wording. I think it is unnecessary for Dr. Sangster to insinuate or state, as he does there, that the Council amend by-laws by resolutions. I submit that the Council have more sense than that, and that they have not done so. It may be, in places where it is a question of opinion as to whether it needs a by-law or a resolution. But the Council know perfectly well they cannot amend a by-law by a resolution. If Dr. Sangster is willing to eliminate that part of his resolution, I am satisfied the whole Council will assist him in getting the fullest explanation and information from the Solicitor ; but I think it is objectionable to put in something of that sort in the resolution, casting a serious reflection upon the Council's knowledge of how to transact public business.

Dr. SANGSTER—I think the usual practice when a resolution is introduced or a motion is introduced is that the mover should have the privilege of explaining his motion before any objection is taken to it, and I think my friend, Dr. Williams, would have been more in order and would have displayed more of his usual good taste if he had adopted that course now. I do not, have not, and had not the intention of casting a reflection on the Council. My resolution was somewhat hastily worded after I came into the room. I had not thought of moving it until I came in. If things were done irregularly in the past, I am quite prepared to absolve the Council for a large amount of responsibility in regard to that irregularity, for I believe the Council inherited these irregularities from their predecessors, and my anxiety is that we shall not go on in the same irregular manner ; and I think I would have been false in my duty to my fellow-members in this Council if I did not call attention to certain irregularities that existed in the past. When at the beginning of last session it was pointed out that the payment of $3.00 for hotel expenses was not covered by a by-law, but merely by resolution or a report of the committee, it was claimed by one of the members that that was tantamount or equivalent to the authority of a by-law. I differ from that very strongly ; I think there are legal rulings utterly opposed to it. I am not asking that they shall be gone into now ; but with regard to the relative value of by-laws and resolutions, I have a strong opinion in my own mind of the far greater force of the one than the other, and that opinion is borne out by a thing that occurred toward the last days of the closing session of the Dominion Parliament. It will be within the memory of most members of the Council that the Hon. Mr. Haggart had then to introduce an Act authorizing the Canadian Pacific Railway Company or its Executive to cover certain matters by resolution that in the charter were only covered by by-laws. I think that is a proof of the supremacy of the binding nature of a by-law and of the impossibility of covering by any resolution that which by the Act is only covered by a by-law. With regard to these matters, I think that the composition of your Executive Committee is covered by a by-law, and that by-law declares it shall be composed of three members ; that is, with the exclusion of those who are ex-officio members. It was said here last night that some time in the dim past an opinion was obtained from Mr. Osler covering this. If that opinion was obtained, it ought to be in existence, and if it is in existence and can be read to this Council, that first clause of my resolution will not, of course, be of any effect. The payment of per diem allowances is already provided for by by-law ; but there is no authority, I take it, in your by-laws to pay your Examiners one cent, and the Act distinctly says that the sum allowed to them shall be settled by a by-law. So, with regard to your Public Prosecutor. I will point that out if you will just give me a moment's time to find the by-law. I would have had these prepared if I had proposed before coming into the room to move this matter——

Dr. WILLIAMS— At page lxiv. you will find the by-law. It is By-law No. 70, Clause 4.

Dr. SANGSTER—That covers the matter of Examiners. But as I read your Medical Act, there is no provision in it for paying any member of your committees one dollar. There is no provision in the Act, as I take it, and I only ask the Council to make themselves sure on that point by a reference to their Solicitor. As I say, there is no authority given in the Act to pay any of the committees one dollar. I am quite sure that when this Act was projected its projectors had no thought of paying any of the committees anything. The idea was that the services of the committees would be given gratuitously, as it is now, as a rule, given on the majority of the committees. In Acts of Incorporation where it is designed a payment shall be made to committees, it is specifically there stated ; for instance, in the Municipal Act the wording is not merely as it is in this, that the Council shall have authority to pay their members any reasonable allowances for attendance at Council meetings, but in the Municipal Act it is provided that the Council shall have authority to pay their members reasonable allowances for attendance at Council and committee meetings. Those words "committee meetings," are left out of the Medical Act. It may be legal for you to pay members of committees without those words, but I think it is an important point to obtain your Solicitor's opinion on that matter. In one of the committees—the committee that proposed to discuss the per diem allowance to members—I called attention to that fact, and it was looked up, but it was thought of no importance. I think it is of importance. Then, with regard to the time of examinations, you have in your Act a provision that distinctly says you shall fix that only by by-law. I fail to find that by-law, or any reference to a by-law covering the determination of the time at which examinations shall be held. At page xxii. of the Register, the last two lines of Clause 28 are to the effect that such examinations are to be held at Toronto or Kingston, at such time and in such manner as the Council may by by-law direct. It covers both points ; it points to the fact that you can only cover that by by-law ; and the word "or" strictly precludes you from holding examinations "at Toronto and Kingston," as you do now. Last year that was distinctly adverted to, and I call your attention to it again. The first year examinations were held at Kingston alone, and the next year they were held at Toronto ; the next year they should have gone back to Kingston, but it was deemed inexpedient, and somewhat expensive, and the Act was changed in 1874 by the elimination of the word "and," not as was claimed last year by a mere clerical error, but by the direct intention of the Legislature, and those who had the Act in charge at that time. The Act was changed by the substitution of the word "or" for the word "and," and as it exists at present I claim that you have no power under that by-law to hold examinations at both Toronto and Kingston. The last two lines of Clause 28, to which I have referred, distinctly intimate that you fix the time of examinations by by-law and not by mere resolution. I may be wrong in these points, but I think I am not, and there are other points of a similar nature I could call attention to——

Dr. WILLIAMS—I call your attention to page xvi., Clause 3, and I ask Dr. Sangster, does that not cover the point of paying Examiners ?

Dr. SANGSTER—You have not fixed their fees by by-law.

Dr. WILLIAMS—We have.

Dr. SANGSTER—Last year ?

Dr. WILLIAMS—Yes, and before that.

The PRESIDENT—I would refer Dr. Sangster to page lxiv. of the Announcement.

Dr. SANGSTER—But that was last year. The attention of this Council had been called to that, and last year for the first time the payment to the Examiners was covered by by-law. When my attention was drawn to it, and I read it, I stated that that removed my contention with regard to the Examiners. But it does not touch my contention with respect to the other matters. You all seem to suspect when I rise to say something that I have the intention to lead the Council somewhere ; but I assure you my intention is to put the Council straight in the future. You do not seem to like the tonics we administer, but I hope the time will come when you will admit, if there was some strychnine in them, they were bracing and vivifying.

Dr. FOWLER—In regard to the statement of Dr. Sangster, as to the substitution of the word "or" for "and" in that Act, I wish to state simply that there was a distinct agreement made when this Act was drawn out, that the examinations should be held at Kingston as well as at Toronto. This was changed and the word "or" was inserted in some way without any authority, and without corresponding with the authorities at Kingston in any way whatever. I think it would be gross injustice to Kingston to withdraw the examinations from there.

Dr. SANGSTER—Just one word to correct a misapprehension. I have no desire to trench upon the point Dr. Fowler alludes to ; I have no intention of saying that no examinations should be held at Kingston as well as Toronto, but I merely point out the fact. You cannot convince the Legislature that there are any clerical errors—this is a great institution for clerical errors—in their Acts. At least, I imagine you cannot. And the word " or " is in that Act, and it is specific ; and I claim until that word " or " is removed or until your Solicitor expresses a legal opinion, that it is not of no material moment. This Council do not stand upon safe ground in continuing the examinations both at Kingston and at Toronto. This is my position.

Dr. CAMPBELL—I think there is no objection on the part of anyone to getting the opinion of the Solicitor on those points. The only objection I have is that which Dr. Williams has referred to, as to certain words in the preamble of the resolution ; and I move to amend by striking out the words " Founded on substitution of resolutions in lieu of by-laws."

Dr. MOORE—And there are some points we do not need the opinion of the Solicitor on.

Dr. SANGSTER—I have no desire to include words that seem offensive to the present Council or to the members of the old Council that are now here. I thought I had covered that by disclaiming such an intention ; when I was speaking, I stated they had no doubt inherited it from their predecessors, but, however, if it is a mere objection to a word, without amendment, I am willing that that word should be eliminated ; I am willing that, as Dr. Williams suggests, that word should be struck out.

The PRESIDENT—I have now struck out the words, " Founded on substitution of resolutions in lieu of by-laws."

The President then put the motion as altered, and on a vote having been taken declared it carried.

Moved by Dr. BROCK, seconded by Dr. CAMPBELL, That it be an instruction to the Finance Committee, before the meeting of the Council in 1897, to consider how best to curtail the expenses of this Council.

The President read the motion.

Dr. ARMOUR—That question came up last year, and it was the opinion of some of the older members that a standing committee could not meet to discharge any duties except when the Council were in session. If that is the case, this committee would not be able to hold a meeting and attend to this matter.

The PRESIDENT—I will add to the motion, " Without expense to the Council."

Dr. DICKSON—Does that refer to the committee next year ?

Dr. WILLIAMS—The Finance Committee this year can consider and report on that.

Dr. BARRICK—There is a by-law defining the duties of the Finance Committee. It says, " they shall prepare a detailed statement of the necessary estimates of money required by the Council for the year, and report the same for the consideration and action of the Council." If that statement is presented early in the session, that will answer the purpose, and the whole Council can then consider the best way to reduce the expenditure. We are now on the fifth day of our meeting, and that important matter, which in nearly all deliberative bodies is brought up at an early stage, has not yet been prepared. If we respect our by-laws, there is no need for a resolution of that kind.

The PRESIDENT put the motion as follows : " That it be an instruction to the Finance Committee, before the meeting of the Council in the year 1897, to consider how best to curtail the expenses of the Council, without expense to the Council." And on a vote having been taken declared it carried.

INQUIRIES.

None.

REPORTS OF STANDING AND SPECIAL COMMITTEES.

Dr. CAMPBELL—I am entrusted by the Chairman of the Registration Committee to submit a report of that committee.

Dr. CAMPBELL presented and read the Report of the Registration Committee. The report was received.

Dr. BARRICK presented and read the Report of the Committee on Printing. The report was received.

CONSIDERATION OF REPORTS.

Moved by Dr. CAMPBELL, seconded by Dr. SHAW, That the Council go into Committee of the Whole on the Report of the Committee on Registration. Carried.

Council in Committee of the Whole. Dr. Thornton in the chair.

Clauses 1 and 2 of the report were read, and on motion adopted.

The Chairman read Clause 3.

Dr. CAMPBELL—I will state our reasons in brief for that. The case of Lang is simply this ; he was a British licentiate, a registered practitioner. Unfortunately for himself, though he had completed his course while the old Act was in force, he did not register in

8

Great Britain until that old Act was repealed, and he could not register here. But he seems to be something of the same class as one who was proposed to be registered into the profession at the last session of the local Legislature, and as that will no doubt give him a chance to get into the Legislature, we thought it might be well to forestall him by giving him the same terms as the Council granted to the party named there, and permitting him to register on taking the Final examination and on payment of the fees. He graduated in 1887 and registered in 1888.

The PRESIDENT—The British Medical Amendment Act was passed in 1886.

Dr. CAMPBELL—Are you sure the Amendment Act was passed in 1886 ? I think it was in 1888.

The PRESIDENT—It was passed and came into force in 1886.

Dr. CAMPBELL—I would not be absolutely sure about that.

Dr. SANGSTER—I have the strongest possible objection to the expediency of the recommendation of the Registration Committee on that point. I think when the Legislature takes the Council by the throat, as it did last session, with regard to any favored individual, and it becomes a question whether we will permit a general law covering such points to be enacted or accept the special case which is being forced upon us, we have no alternative but to submit. But I think this Council will stultify itself by accepting cases of that kind. To do this practically cuts off the two years of study required by this Council ; and it does more than that. The Act states that a British practitioner shall acquire the rights that this man is seeking to acquire only after he has been five years domiciled in Great Britain. I think this would be a retrograde step for this Council to take, and an injustice to our universities, and I therefore oppose it.

Dr. ROGERS—On the occasion referred to—the case of Dr. Young, which case came up before the Legislature last year—the Executive Committee were reluctantly forced to consider the matter as a special case. In that case Dr. Young certainly had gained a certain amount of special influence, and, if you will notice, the report of the Executive Committee says there were special features and special reasons ; and we did this to prevent it becoming a precedent. We took the greatest care in the world to prevent it becoming a precedent ; for if it had become a precedent, the next applicant that came along could take advantage of it. We would be practically nullifying our rules for the benefit of this gentleman who says he passed in 1887. As the Act was passed in 1886, we in Canada have a right to ask that they should pass certain examinations, and I think this Council ought to go very slowly in allowing any man to escape the Primary examination, for that is what they are trying to escape. It is not only that he is going to escape the fifth year, but the Primary examination on Latin, and materia medica, and all those practical subjects will be passed by. They do not pass a Primary examination in Great Britain ; they pass there on a little surgery and a little midwifery, and are entitled then to become medical practitioners. I would not be afraid to say that any of our men of any qualifications at all could go over there and get through in two months.

Dr. WILLIAMS—You should explain that going from here, from a recognized school, and the Primary is accepted.

The PRESIDENT—Yes. I speak of any place, any colony, where they have a Primary, that Primary is accepted. But we want to know and to be sure that they know the Primary subjects. This gentleman would escape showing he knows the Primary subjects. I move, therefore, that that part of the report be struck out.

Dr. BRITTON—I was present on the occasion when the representatives of the Council before the committee of the Legislature agreed (agreed because they chose the least of two evils), to register one person whose name was given. The alternative was to have the bill known as the German Bill passed through the House, and of course that would then have included all cases. The committee of the House having agreed to withdraw that German Bill on condition that one particular individual should be registered in that way, is equivalent to saying that no such future legislation as that would be enacted, that it was not intended it should be applied to all persons. And we did not establish a precedent, and it was not so understood by the committee of the House, I think, nor was it understood by any member of this Council who was present on that occasion ; I do not think a solitary member understood it should be taken that that was a precedent or direction for us for all time to come, or most certainly we would have said, No, we will not register him ; go ahead with your German Bill, if this is to be taken as a precedent. I am perfectly certain if the Hon. Mr. Ross, the chairman of the committee, was here, he would say he did not intend to establish a precedent on which we were to act hereafter. Our action on that occasion was simply to get over a difficulty into which the Government were thrown in a certain way. It is not necessary for me to enter into particulars of that case, but I know very strong pressure was brought to bear ; and the Government do not control matters just as we do ; the Government are controlled to a certain extent by matters of policy ; therefore, it is not for us to question too much what the Government did on that occasion, but I think we here should establish no precedent of that kind. If we determine to establish such a precedent, let us go about it the right way and change the by-law relating to the matter and let it say that all British practitioners who choose to do so may come here and register by passing the Final examination. I was not present when this clause was read, but I believe it is a clause recommending that a certain person should be registered on the same conditions as the party to whom I formerly referred. I would certainly oppose that clause ; and I beg to remind you that the case of the gentleman registered in the way spoken of was not a matter of choice with us, but a matter of force, and I think we showed our good judgment in accepting the better alternative of the two.

Dr. SANGSTER—I think there is one other point that is settled, and I will just state it in half a dozen words. The Council are in the possession of the legal opinion from Mr. Osler, that we have no power to legislate for individuals, that our power is limited to legislating for classes.

Dr. HENRY—It appears that the Government are responsible for allowing Dr. Young to come in without complying with the regulations. I understand that the gentleman whom the committee recommend now to be registered is even better qualified than Dr. Young. Why did the Government interfere ? What pressure was brought on them ? It seems to me it was purely a political matter. Was it because Dr. Young happened to have a lot of friends and had important relatives in this city and elsewhere ? I think we ought to know this, because I consider it was a contemptible thing for the Government to do.

Dr. BRITTON—I do not think we have any right here to question the motives of the Government in the matter, nor have we any right to go into particulars of what pressure was brought to bear on the Government. We have simply to say here that the conclusion of the Government was that the German Bill should go through its second reading and be carried in the House, or else we should register that gentleman.

Dr. HENRY—Then it will have to go to the country and to the profession that a man who has prominent friends and who has influence, no matter what his qualifications are, must be admitted if the Government lifts its finger, but the poor man's son who has failed in a mark or two is to be refused.

The CHAIRMAN—I understand the committee have made a certain recommendation, and we must confine ourselves to that recommendation.

Dr. WILLIAMS—I am in favor of striking out that recommendation. I do not take the case that was dealt with last year as being one that was intended to establish a precedent for the Council. This is not an exceptional action for the Legislature ; it is notorious that when they want to make a man a lawyer without going through the regular course of study they can do so ; and they can make doctors too, I suppose, by Act of Parliament ; and I dare say if they tried, they could make even dentists and other things. But while it is notorious that they make lawyers (because they put one lawyer through without taking the regular course of study), it does not follow that Osgoode Hall must accept every other man on the same terms. In the case of the German Bill, they did not actually put through that bill, but they could have put it through. But because of that it does not pledge us to accept everybody on exactly the same terms, any more than Osgoode Hall would accept every applicant to enter their ranks as they did the lawyer who was put through by the Legislature. I am opposed to this clause of the report and I will support it being struck out.

Dr. MOORE—I think the members of this Council ought to be a little more careful about censuring the Government ; they should remember that the Government have power, as Dr. Williams has said, to make doctors. We have it on record where they have made a doctor, in the Rainy River District. I may be mistaken, but I think he was prosecuted. I will have to refer to our Registrar as to that.

The REGISTRAR—Yes, he was then a resident of the disputed territory.

Dr. MOORE—I think, after the treatment we have received at the hands of the Legislature, it is in bad taste for us to accuse them of doing anything wrong, or to impute evil motives, or to say they desire to do anything that is not in accord with the wishes of this Council.

Dr. CAMPBELL—Both individually and as a member of the committee, it is perfectly immaterial to me what action the Council take. The committee suggested that line of action simply as one the result of which might not injure the profession, and it might save us having a little more experimenting in the Legislature again.

The Chairman put the motion to strike out Clause 3 of the committee's report, and on a vote having been taken declared it carried.

Clauses 4 and 5 were read, and on motion adopted.

Moved by Dr. CAMPBELL, That the committee rise and report.

The committee rose, the President in the chair.

Moved by Dr. CAMPBELL, seconded by Dr. SHAW, That the report of the Committee of the Whole be adopted.

To the President and members of Council of College of Physicians and Surgeons of Ontario :

Your Registration Committee beg leave to report on the various matters submitted to them as follows :

1. Certain letters concerning Dr. E. A. B. Rose, we recommend to be referred to the Special Committee on Prosecutions.

2. Application of Dr. Gunn, of Montreal, in the matter of Dr. F. B. Elliott, we recommend be referred to Committee on Complaints.

3. Clause 3 erased. Dr. Laing to comply with regulations.

4. In examining the credentials of those qualified for registration during the year ending July 13th, 1896, as instructed by the Council, we find the number to be ninety-nine, of whom 88 are registered on the report of the Board of Examiners, and eleven on the report of the Committee on Complaints.

5. After consultation with the Registrar, we recommend that all orders for the printing of blank diplomas be signed by both President and Registrar, and that the lithograph plate of the diploma be kept by the Registrar in the vault.

J. W. ROSEBRUGH, Chairman.

Adopted as amended in Committee of Whole.

W. F. THORNTON, Chairman Committee of Whole.

Adopted as amended by striking out Clause 3.   A. F. ROGERS.

The President read the motion.

Dr. WILLIAMS—Before that is adopted, I wish to call attention to the fact that there is a provision made under the British Medical Act of 1886, by which colonies may take steps to secure reciprocal registration. Under that we have the power, as they have in Great Britain, where they have fixed the matter so that a person shall be ten years domiciled before he can get reciprocal registration. If we were to take steps on that here, we would have the same right to fix the time that they should be domiciled in England. I throw out this idea so that between now and the next meeting of the Council it may receive some consideration. If I am correct, and it would remedy the difficulty, I think we should move to get reciprocal registration, and fix the time that they should be domiciled in Great Britain before they can come here and claim registration, which time might be fixed at five or ten years.

The President put the motion, and on a vote having been taken declared it carried.

On motion by Dr. Sangster, seconded by Dr. Henderson, the Council adjourned to meet at 2 o'clock p.m.

AFTERNOON SESSION.

In accordance with motion to adjourn, the Council met at two o'clock. The President, in the chair, called the meeting to order.

The Registrar called the roll, and the following members were present : Drs. Armour, Barrick, Britton, Brock, Campbell, Emory, Fowler, Geikie, Graham, Hanly, Henderson, Logan, Luton, Rogers, Sangster, Thorburn, Thornton and Williams.

The Registrar read the minutes of the preceding meeting.

Dr. SANGSTER—Before the minutes are confirmed I wish to ask the Registrar which of the per diem allowances is erased ?

The REGISTRAR—The one that is erased is the per diem allowance to any of the committees ; the payment to the Examiners is in.

Dr. WILLIAMS—I think that was the one that was intended to be erased ; the wrong one appears to have been erased, and it ought to be corrected.

The minutes were then confirmed as amended, and were signed by the President.

NOTICES OF MOTION.

None.

READING OF COMMUNICATIONS, PETITIONS, ETC.

None.

MOTIONS.

None.

ENQUIRIES.

Dr. SANGSTER—I would enquire as to the probability of our getting through to-night. If we do not get through before a certain hour in the afternoon a large number of us will be kept here till Monday morning at any rate, and I myself would be kept here until Monday evening before I could take a train for home.

The PRESIDENT—I am unable to answer Dr. Sangster's question, because I do not know what business is to come before the Council.

Dr. SANGSTER—It is a matter of economy ; that is the point I wanted to make.

Dr. WILLIAMS—Is that economy in word or in fact ?

Dr. SANGSTER—Economy in fact. I do not think any attempts at economy in words are made from this side of the House—the opposition ; but that will be for the profession to judge. It might be a matter of serious consideration to the Council as to what is the most economical mode of proceeding. It is evident we are not going to get through till a very late hour, and it seems to me it is impossible to get through to-night at all because there are some two or three reports coming up that will entail long discussion, and that discussion you cannot stop.

Dr. WILLIAMS—There are only two or three reports.

Dr. EMORY—The Printing Committee report is very short.

Dr. BRITTON—The report of the Education Committee is complete and ready.

REPORTS OF SPECIAL AND STANDING COMMITTEES.

Dr. BRITTON presented and read the report of the Education Committee. The report was received.

Dr. HENDERSON presented and read the report of the Finance Committee. The report was received.

CONSIDERATION OF REPORTS.

Dr. Barrick read the report of the Printing Committee.

Dr. BARRICK—With regard to leaving this in abeyance, I have to say we found the tenders varied from $1.63 to $2.30 per page. The various firms tendering asked how many pages they would be required to print, but we could only give an approximate number ; and it was the opinion of the committee that if we had these typewritten copies of the transactions and the copy of the Announcement before us, we could go to two or three of the lower tenderers, that when they know definitely what work was required to be done, and how many pages there would be, we could then get a tender more favorable than any we have yet received. If the Council decide that there are to be no advertisements in the Announcement, then tenders will be given upon the same lines that they are now, but we find in the last Announcement there were fifteen pages of advertisements, and if the Council would allow us to seek advertisements we think we might get sufficient advertisements to pay for half if not the whole of the cost of the Announcement. In estimating the expense of publishing our Announcement for this year, we found that last year we had 271 pages of proceedings of this Council, and I think 64 pages of the Announcement, making in all 300 and some odd pages. Now, if you do not talk too long this year about 150 pages will be about the right thing to allow for the report of the proceedings of the Council, and that with the 64 pages will make a book of about 200 pages, and a book of 200 pages at the lowest estimate we have now would cost us $330.00. Then for the Announcement alone, taking 64 pages, the same as last year, at the lowest tender (thirty cents) would cost $19.20. Then I tried to find out how much per printed page our stenographic work is going to come to, so that we will know pretty nearly what our publication of the Announcement and of the proceedings is to cost us, and I found out last year we paid, as I have been informed by the Registrar, $256.00 for stenographic work in reporting and preparing for printing 271 pages ; that I found cost us then about 94 cents per page. According to that, then, the 150 pages which we have estimated will be in the stenographic report at 94 cents, would cost $141.00. In addition to the figures I have already given you we would have postage on 2,500 copies at six cents each, amounting to $150.00. The total of those figures amounts to $640.20. Now, it is just a question whether the game is worth the powder, not for this year, but for next. If we decide there are to be no advertisements in this Announcement, and if we are prepared to pay $640.00 a year for this work, well and good ; but if we are allowed to seek for advertisements it is probable we may be able to reduce that amount by perhaps $300.00 ; and if we can reduce the cost of sending this Announcement with a verbatim report to every medical practitioner at about $300.00 or $350.00, it seems to me the game would be worth the powder, but if it is to cost $640.00 it is just a question. I just mention that matter so that we can see exactly how we stand. In the report I mention nothing at all about the advertisements, and it is for you to decide whether that course will be adopted, and whether we shall take advantage of any advertisements so as to reduce the cost.

Moved by Dr. BARRICK, seconded by Dr. WILLIAMS, That the Council go into Committee of the Whole for consideration of the Printing Committee's report. Carried.

Council in Committee of the Whole.

Dr. Thorburn in the chair.

The Chairman read the first clause of the report.

Dr. WILLIAMS—I would like to ask if the committee have compared these prices with the prices we paid for the last two or three years, when I believe we had a contract for similar work.

Dr. BARRICK—I find the same defect here as I find right along. I have here a statement of the Treasurer which has been audited, and I have looked over it to find out what we paid for this journal last year. I expected to find it, but all I found in the Treasurer's report is that $150.00 was paid, and that that was for the balance of 1894-95. I failed to find in that report anything at all of what was paid for this journal last year, but I do find the stenographic report of the proceedings, special reports and typewriter copying, etc., came to $357.00 ; and I learned from the Registrar that $256.00 of that was paid the stenographer for preparing the work for this Announcement ; that item of $357.00 is the only item in the Treasurer's report bearing on this matter. I am perfectly aware that $350.00 was granted to this journal last year for doing this work, but I fail to find any record of it in the Treasurer's report.

Dr. WILLIAMS—Perhaps the Registrar can tell us what the contract was last year and the year before.

The REGISTRAR—Last year the contract was $360.00, and prior to that it was $600.00. The payment of the amount for last year does not appear in the Treasurer's report because the account is not all settled up ; only the stenographer's fees have been paid, and that the journal have to pay us back again.

Dr. BARRICK—That is the reason I made the point, because the tenderer got the advantage of the fifteen pages of advertisements in this Announcement ; and the position I took was, that if we got the advantage of the advertisements in this Announcement we would be able to reduce the $640.00 of which I have spoken to perhaps less than $360.00 of last year.

Dr. EMORY—I think I could further illustrate the question about which Dr. Williams is speaking. Last year we paid $360.00 for sending a free journal, the stenographer's report, and had our Announcement and our advertisements published in the journal. I have in my hand the bill for printing this journal, and I find the printing cost the journal people $616.68, and that they paid $210.00 postage to send this to the members of the College, and they paid to our stenographer $256.00, making in all $1,082.60 which our contract cost the journal publishing company, and for which we paid them $360.00. I mention this to show that the Printing Committee last year were very economical in their work. Further, I might say that this year we did not find anyone foolish enough to come forward with any such proposition to the Printing Committee——

Dr. WILLIAMS—I am very sorry.

Dr. EMORY—I am very sorry, too. We are of the opinion that when the typewritten matter is in our hands the Registrar can advertise for tenders, and we will get a much more favorable tender than any now in. There are only two tenders in now, the lowest of which is from the Dominion Medical Publishing Company, or the Nesbitt Company ; they offer to send their journal free to every member of the college for 25 cents a member, which will cost us about $400. I think there is very little necessity for taking up time in discussing this report ; it seems to me it is very simple, and that the business way to treat this subject is the way the committee suggest.

Dr. SANGSTER—I wish, before the matter is disposed of, to call your attention to the fact that it should be somebody's duty to see that the printed matter in the report of our proceedings is properly corrected and looked after. I think in that matter that I myself have something specially to complain of. I am greatly concerned that the grammar and punctuation of my little efforts, as printed in that report, are of a nature to disgust any ten-year-old public school-boy in the Province, because the official editor, or official somebody to whom that matter has been entrusted, has evidently peculiar notions of his own regarding grammar and punctuation, notions not in accordance with those of Lindley Murray and other grammarians ; and in that respect, except where a matter has been clearly——

Dr. WILLIAMS—Perhaps you were rattled, as the boys say, when you made your speech.

Dr. SANGSTER—I am not apt to become rattled. I was about to remark in that respect, with regard to the grammar and punctuation, except where the matter appears to have been clearly taken out of his hands, he has treated friend and foe with impartiality. I am not much concerned to note that, whether deliberately or otherwise, what I have stated is at times, apparently purposely, made incoherent and incomprehensible. I do not believe in these days that those whose good opinion I value much could be persuaded that I cannot, or that I do not, commonly express myself coherently and in fair English. While entering this protest, I beg to say that I do not think any of these inaccuracies are due to our official stenographer. I have the utmost pleasure in testifying that I think our stenographer is perfectly impartial, and I think if any changes or any inaccuracies have crept into the proceedings they have done so after the transcript of his notes left his hands. The whole probabilities point to the fact that his report is an exact replica of our debates, but I claim that either the stenographer's report should not merely in most cases, but in every instance, give the *ipsissima verba* of every debate in this Council, or that opportunities should be given to every member of this Council to correct his speeches before they appear in printed form. I do not think it should be open to any member of the Council to modify, to take from or add to, his speeches as they are when delivered ; but I think he should be permitted to see that they are properly punctuated, and that they are grammatical in their construction, so as to convey to the electorate an exact impression of what he intended to convey. I do not suppose that the medical profession care very much about our eloquence, or attempts at eloquence, in this Council, or that they would be greatly concerned if our report were reduced to a mere bald statement of the resolutions passed and the votes taken thereon. But I claim that if your Hansard is to carry any value with the profession it should be kept so exact as to give the words of our debate, or otherwise that every member should be permitted to correct his little efforts so as to put them in proper ship-shape.

Dr. BROCK—I have a motion that I think, if I could have brought it forward at the commencement, would have settled the question at once. I beg to move, seconded by Dr. ARMOUR, "That the offer by Dr. Barrick to get the Announcement at as low a rate as possible and canvass for advertisements at no extra cost to this Council be accepted." The words "no extra cost" put in, not implying that he is not to take a commission——

Dr. ARMOUR—Would you allow me to suggest that you should just move that that clause of the report be adopted.

Dr. WILLIAMS—Personally I take strong objections to our committee going to work to canvass for advertisements. I think that is no part of the business of this Council ; it is a commercial transaction that the Council may burn their fingers at ; and whether they burn their fingers or not it brings the Council into disrepute in getting into things outside of their legitimate business, and I object to it. I think if you put the advertisement proposition in another way and let some house prepare the Announcement for you, and if they want to get advertisements that should be their business. But I do not think this Council should hunt for advertisements to put in the publication of our proceedings at all.

Dr. McLAUGHLIN—I like to see my friends coming to the doctrine we have been speaking of on this side of the House ; that is, that the Council should not go outside of their legitimate work. I say this, if putting advertisements into that is going to reduce the cost of it, I think it would be well to allow the publisher to put the advertisements there ; but let these advertisements be subject to the sanction of the committee, because I do not want Dr. McCully's advertisement there, nor do I want any person advertising quack nostrums, nor anything that would be contrary to the feeling of the profession at large. I would not object to proper advertisements being put there, but I think that advertisements should be looked over either by the Registrar or by the committee before they are permitted to go in.

Dr. BROCK—I do not suppose for one instant that if any member of this Council took the duty upon himself of obtaining advertisements that he would put one objectionable advertisement into the Announcement.

Dr. McLAUGHLIN—You misunderstand me. It was Dr. Williams' suggestion that the publisher should put them in ; I say, if the publisher did, that the committee should see they were not of an objectionable character.

Dr. ROGERS—I personally do not see any reason why our Announcement should not have legitimate advertisements in it. I do not think that this Council stand in any more exalted light than a great university—McGill University, for instance. McGill University issues its announcement or calendar every year, and there are generally a few advertisements in it, at the back. It is the duty of the Registrar of the university, if he can get good advertisements that are paying advertisements and nice advertisements, to allow them to appear in the back of that announcement. I do not think, myself, that there can be any great reason why proper advertisements should not appear in the back of our Announcement ; and I personally would have the greatest confidence in Drs. Barrick and Emory, and would feel sure that if any advertisements were sent in to the office of the Registrar, if they secured them, they would not be objectionable. I do not say they should canvass for them, but they will get them in various ways ; and I have no doubt they will be selected properly. I have great confidence not only in Drs. Barrick and Emory, but equally great confidence in the Registrar, if it is left in his hands. I think the suggestion of the committee is a very valuable one and may enable us to save three or four hundred dollars, and I think we ought to adopt that suggestion.

Dr. BARRICK—All I want is to have this point settled : Are you going to allow advertisements, or are you not ? If you say "No," the matter ends. But if you are going to allow advertisements, in asking for tenders from the different persons we should know whether we can give them the privilege of using fourteen, or fifteen, or a certain number of pages for advertisements, to be approved of by a committee this Council may appoint. That is one way of doing that, and it is the best way.

Dr. WILLIAMS—I would not object to that at all.

Dr. CAMPBELL—While the debate has been proceeding I drew up this suggestion, " And that the privilege of inserting the advertisements, subject to the supervision of the Council, be made a condition of the tender."

Dr. SANGSTER—I think it is important to have the matter settled, as Dr. Barrick says. I believe the advertisements, if they are put in, will be a source of very material revenue. But I thoroughly agree with Dr. McLaughlin that this Council step out of place when they seek for advertisements. I see no objection to the introduction of the advertisements in the way mentioned, and I think it would be an inducement to those who tender to tender at a lower rate if they are permitted to insert advertisements. I do not know how much the income received from advertisements in the journal amounts to, but I believe it may be a very material matter. The value of any publication as an advertising medium depends largely upon the circulation and largely upon the character of the persons to whom the publication is sent ; and I can conceive that the Annual Announcement as an advertising medium may be a very important one. I know that in *Munsey's Magazine* each page of advertisements costs $500.00 for a single insertion. I do not suppose a page of our Announcement would amount to anything of that kind, but I can conceive it would be freely taken at a cost of $10.00 or perhaps $20.00 a page, and I think, therefore, it would go far towards determining what sum any house would be prepared to publish that Announcement for.

Dr. BROCK—Speaking to my resolution, I am personally aware that every page of your medical journal can be made worth from $50.00 to $150.00 for advertising——

Dr. SHAW—Do you mean each issue ?

Dr. BROCK—No, by the year ; yearly.

Dr. SANGSTER—When I say $500.00 for *Munsey's*, it is for each issue—each page of advertisements for each issue is worth $500.00.

Dr. CAMPBELL—I move to amend the clause by adding thereto, " And that the privilege of inserting advertisements, subject to the approval of the committee, not being on the first page of the cover, be made a condition of the tender."

Dr. BROCK—I have withdrawn my amendment, and I accept Dr. Campbell's.

Dr. EMORY—I conceive that making that a condition of the tender will limit our tenders along that line to the existing medical journals ; we will get no printing-house to enter into any such bond as that. But I believe that Mr. Wasson or some of the men in his employ would be very willing to undertake it and solicit advertisements ; and that would not be the Council doing it, but would be a private enterprise of his own, soliciting advertisements on commission. I think the printing-houses will do this work cheaper than the journals. I think both courses should be left open to the committee.

Dr. GEIKIE—You can leave it safely in the hands of the committee.

Dr. BARRICK—I think the number of advertisements should be limited.

Dr. CAMPBELL—No, leave it to the committee.

Dr. HENRY—Is there any provision for a free journal ?

The CHAIRMAN—No.

On motion, the clause was adopted as amended.

Dr. BRITTON—I would suggest just here, in order to meet the difficulty Dr. Sangster has spoken of, that the stenographer be instructed, in transcribing his notes, to make any changes in the typewritten copy that are necessary in order to render the wording of the Announcement grammatical without changing the sense.

Dr. MOORE—I think the full meaning should be given, but if there is a clerical error it should be quite competent for the stenographer to make such changes as may be necessary, and he should not be interfered with either.

Dr. McLAUGHLIN—It struck me it would be well, if it is practicable, that the stenographer should supervise the proofing of the sheets ; that is, that he should attend to the proof-reading, because no one knows better exactly what was said ; and I think if that were done we would get a much more accurate report of the proceedings of the Council.

The CHAIRMAN—That would mean an additional cost.

Dr. ARMOUR—I notice in the last copy of the proceedings the discussions are published and then the by-law or the report which the Council were dealing with is published away from them altogether. I think it would be well if in each instance the report was published and then the discussion on it should follow after, consecutively ; and so with the by-laws. The profession have complained to me a great deal that they could not understandingly read the report of the proceedings last year on that account.

The CHAIRMAN—I do not know that that is an objection, because you find in a great many journals, in the publication of the proceedings, that the by-laws or regulations and rules are in a separate part of the book entirely, and even the introduction of a new one, when it is passed, is placed along with the others and the discussions are in a separate place. I should think it is rather difficult to understand them when they are mixed up together.

Dr. Reddick—It is a very wise suggestion and a very useful suggestion. Half of the members do not, I presume, pretend to read this journal through ; and it is a difficult matter to turn up any particular report or any by-law just at once unless you know almost the whole book by heart. We have a by-law which makes it necessary to place every by-law in a book by itself, and also in the Announcement by themselves ; the suggestion that I wish to make particularly is that the by-laws for each year be placed all together, all consecutively, either in the back or front of our proceedings, and not mixed up here and there where it is a difficult thing to find them.

Dr. Dickson—The Announcement is to be indexed.

The Chairman put the motion to adopt the clause "We are of opinion, after due consideration, that when a typewritten copy of the matter referred to be printed and placed in our hands, we will be able to get the work done for less than the tenders now in our possession, and we recommend that the letting of the contract be left to Drs. Barrick and Emory, the members resident in the city." Carried.

Dr. Britton—Is that with the understanding that the stenographer may correct any grammatical errors without changing the substance ; that in having his notes transcribed he will be placed in the position to correct grammatical errors that may exist and to look after the punctuation ?

Dr. Sangster—That would inevitably involve some proof-reading, and it would be unjust to demand that from the stenographer unless his allowance is increased in proportion.

Dr. Britton—I wish to ask the stenographer whether it would cost any more if he were allowed discretion to correct grammatical errors.

The Stenographer stated that the correction of grammatical errors would not entail any extra expense, but he would not undertake to read the proof or correct the printer's punctuation.

Dr. Sangster—I am perfectly satisfied if the stenographer undertakes to see that the punctuation and gross grammatical errors are changed.

Moved by Dr. Henry, That it be requested of the Printing Committee to endeavor to make some satisfactory arrangements such as was done last year, so as to place in the hands of the members of the College of Physicians and Surgeons of Ontario a free journal.

Dr. Henry—I understand the *Dominion Medical Monthly and Ontario Medical Journal* offer to put in the hands of every medical man in Ontario a journal at twenty-five cents a year for each member. I understand the difference between the tenders received from this journal and the other journals amounts to quite a sum ; and if we accept the lower tender we could well afford to pay the twenty-five cents for the journal and place it in the hands of the medical profession. I do not think there ever was an act of the Council that gave such satisfaction as that free journal. It allayed a great deal of the bad feeling. I am satisfied if you allow this company that got up the journal to place advertisements such as we see in there—and I do not object to any of them, nor do I think that they can be objected to—they can well afford to furnish every man in the profession with a free journal and make money out of it ; and I think it would be very much better to have them do that than to have the Printing Committee soliciting advertisements. I would like to see this done and see a free journal sent to the members of the profession.

Dr. Britton—The other day we discussed this matter for two or three hours, and I took up some time in discussing it. I took up that time because I felt we had been very unwise from the start in sending a free journal to the profession, and I gave my reasons then and no doubt those reasons will appear in the Announcement ; the gentlemen present gave me good attention, and I have no doubt they will remember what I said on that occasion. There were others who spoke on the same line. I think it would be very unwise for us to allow this motion to pass, and I shall vote against it, but I shall spare the Council the infliction of any further remarks on the question ; I do not wish to repeat myself or to bring forward arguments which I did before, because I feel very well satisfied that notwithstanding my original resolution was lost, as well as the amendment and the amendment to the amendment, the Council will certainly vote against a free journal.

Dr. McLaughlin—We have expressed our opinion pretty freely and I do not intend to waste words on this. In my judgment we have no power to pass that resolution and carry it out ; we have no power, as far as I can see, under the Medical Act whereby we can take the funds of the Council and buy a journal and send it to the profession. We have just as much power to take the funds of the Council and buy a pair of boots and send them to the members of the profession in Ontario. I think this is beyond our jurisdiction altogether, and I think we had better drop it.

Dr. Henry—I object to dropping it. Heretofore the Council did not pay one cent for this journal, but it was sent gratuitously by the publishers of the journal. If you adopt the course we did in the past year they will send the medical journal to the profession free.

Dr. McLaughlin—I do not object to that, but I object to the payment of twenty-five cents for each member.

Dr. EMORY—I think we can answer Dr. Henry's question in one moment. We asked all the journals to state to the Printing Committee what they were willing to do in that line, and we have their answers before us. The *Dominion Medical Monthly* offered to send it to each member for twenty-five cents apiece, and the only other journal that offered it at all was the *Canadian Medical Review*, and they offered it at $1.00 a year to each member.

Dr. ROGERS—While we used to be able to get a journal, now it is impossible for the Printing Committee to make arrangements, and I have no doubt Dr. Henry is, and many of the other members are, sorry that we cannot have a journal going to the members this year. Next year perhaps some other journal will come forward and make an offer, but just now we cannot afford to spend $600.00.

Dr. HENRY—What is the reason we cannot get it still? If you would allow the publisher of this to put in the same advertisements I will guarantee you will get a free journal; I know the company will place in the hands of the profession a free journal. I am aware we cannot take the funds of the Council and send a free journal, but we have not done that, we have not been paying for it; it is the good will of the publishers that send it.

Dr. SANGSTER—It is within the power of every journal in the Province to send a free journal to every member of the profession in the Province if they like; but the question, as I understand, is whether the Council shall permit the journal to put advertisements at the back or front. We have no authority to prevent or restrict; each journal is at liberty to do as it likes in that respect. Dr. Henry seems to be under the impression that the Council can obtain it without making some payment to the journalists for the work done; I think that is a mistake. If he wants the name of the Council connected with the journal, so that the journal shall appear as the journal of this Council, or as an official medium between this Council and the electorate, then I have the strongest possible objections to anything of that kind.

Dr. HENRY—I do not wish that at all; all I say is that if we do not ask the publisher to eliminate such advertisements as Dr. Barrick and others advise, we can get a free journal sent to every medical man in the Province.

Dr. LUTON—As a member of the Printing Committee, I have listened to all the remarks that have been made. The Printing Committee afforded opportunities for everyone who desired to do our printing to put in tenders for that purpose; and the medical journal publishers had an invitation to send in what they would do it for. One journal publishing company offered to do all the general printing for so much per page, and to send a free journal for twenty-five cents per head. For the Council to pay twenty-five cents per head means between six and seven hundred dollars, and then over and above that there is over $200.00 of postage to be paid by somebody, which makes it quite a big sum; and the Printing Committee did not think that under the circumstances we would be wise, on financial grounds, to recommend that such a thing as that should be done.

The CHAIRMAN put Dr. Henry's motion as follows : " That it be requested of the Printing Committee to endeavor to make some satisfactory arrangement such as was done last year, so as to place in the hands of the members of the College of Physicians and Surgeons of Ontario a free journal," and on a vote having been taken declared the motion lost.

On motion, the committee rose, the President in the chair.

Moved by Dr. BARRICK, seconded by Dr. EMORY, That the report of the Committee of the Whole on the report of the Printing Committee be adopted. Carried.

PRINTING COMMITTEE REPORT.

To the President and members of the Medical Council :

Your Committee on Printing beg leave to report as follows :

1st. That tenders were solicited from ten firms, as follows : (A) Printing and binding of twenty-five hundred copies of Announcement and transactions, under one cover, at so much per page of printed matter. (B) Ten hundred copies of Announcement only at so much per page. (C) Sending free medical journal to each registered practitioner.

2nd. That we received seven tenders for printing and binding and two for free journal.

3rd. That the amounts of the tenders varied from in " A," $1.63 to $2.30 per page ; in " B," $1.65 to 30 cts. per page ; in " C," $1.00 to 25 cts. for every registered practitioner.

We are of opinion, after due consideration, that when a typewritten copy of matter required to be printed is placed in our hands, we will be able to get the work done for less than the lowest tender now in our possession, and recommend that the letting of the contract be left to Drs. Barrick and Emory, the members resident in the city.

All of which is respectfully submitted.

June 13th, 1896.   E. J. BARRICK, Chairman Printing Committee.

Amendment to Printing Committee report :

And that the privilege of inserting advertisements, subject to the approval of the committee, not being on first page of cover, be made a condition of the tender.

Adopted as amended. A. F. ROGERS.   JAMES THORBURN, Chairman.

Moved by Dr. BARRICK, seconded by Dr. McLAUGHLIN, that the report of the Committee of the Whole be adopted. Carried.

Dr. BRITTON presented the report of the Education Committee.

Moved by Dr. WILLIAMS, seconded by Dr. GEIKIE, That the reading of this report be dispensed with, and that the Council go into Committee of the Whole and the report be read clause by clause. Carried.

Council in Committee of the Whole.

Dr. Armour in the chair.

Dr. BRITTON read the first clause of the report, and said : I must explain this a little. The *Record* had the only authentic copy of all the names of those who had received these Buchanan diplomas which, according to his representation, were false and had been purchasable, and he offered to supply a full list of those names, wherever the holders of such diplomas might live. We, as a committee, concluded it would be unwise to incur all that expense, that we had nothing whatever to do with the Buchanan diplomatists, who might be in Mexico or anywhere else, other than with those in Canada ; and that is the reason why we instructed the Registrar to get a copy only of the list of the holders of those diplomas in Canada.

On motion Clause 1 of the report was adopted.

Dr. BRITTON read the second clause of the report and said : I omitted to state that the petitions from the faculties of each institution, and also petitions signed by students of each of those institutions were received, and these were considered also. For reasons which I will mention later on I could hardly consistently move the adoption of Clause 2 of the report, and I will therefore leave that motion to some other member of that committee.

Dr. CAMPBELL moved the adoption of Clause 2 of the report.

Dr. GEIKIE—That does not substitute the eight months' session for the six months' session, but it appears merely to make it optional. Our college was one of the consenting parties. If I understand it, this merely permits the eight months on the part of any college which chooses to enter upon it, and that was not our idea or the idea of any one of the colleges as far as I know ; it was to be compulsory upon all ; that is to say, if one adopts it the whole of us would have to, because otherwise it would be worth nothing ; it would not be adopted by anybody unless it were understood that the eight months' session was to take the place of the six months' session. As to taking away the fifth year the colleges simply agreed upon that because they considered that four terms of eight months, thirty-two months, gave eight months more study than we really require now, and we considered that that might be accepted, and we thought it ought to be accepted in lieu of the fifth year. That was our position. So that an optional eight months' session would be no boon to us, and I do not suppose any of the colleges would enter upon it under these circumstances ; I don't believe ours would.

Dr. ROGERS—Then why did you apply for it ?

Dr. GEIKIE—In order that the teaching might be better done. We agreed that the colleges should comply with it in a certain way, doing away with the summer session and the fifth year ; the four terms of eight months would give thirty-two months of medical teaching, and I am sure the students would be turned out better than they are now with the four terms of six months, giving them twenty-four months, and the fifth year, six months of which may be passed with a medical man, which as a general rule means six months loitered away.

Dr. ROGERS—Not necessarily. The trouble is you want to get rid of the fifth year. Why don't you come out and tell the Council ?

Dr. GEIKIE—I have told you the facts. I have secreted nothing.

Dr. SANGSTER—I would like to ask the chairman of the committee whether there is .any supplementary clause attached to the clause just read ?

Dr. BRITTON—No, there is not.

Dr. SANGSTER—That is the only place where that issue comes up in the report ?

Dr. BRITTON—The only place.

At the request of Dr. Williams, Dr. Britton again read Clause 2 of the report.

Dr. GEIKIE—I am sure we would not feel disposed to go into it if it was merely made an optional matter.

Dr. BRITTON—Mr. Chairman, there are several thoughts in connection with this that I would like to express. I will try and make it as brief as possible, and I will try and keep within my limit also, and perhaps a good deal within the limit. Last year the matter came up in the first place before this Council, and it was then decided by the Council that in as much as the representations came only from two teaching bodies—I am not positive but I think only two—that it would be better to defer the matter until there was opportunity for further conference between the teaching bodies of the Province. This year it came before us in the form of two petitions ; the first petition was from a conjoined meeting of the different faculties—the University of Toronto, Trinity Medical College, the Woman's

Medical College and the Western University. Queen's University, to some extent, did not take the same view as the others, and in the first instance I believe the Western University was not disposed to go into the scheme, but however it did later agree to do so. The petition has not been read in Council yet and I will read it in order that the Council may know what they have to deal with. [Reads petition.] I believe a copy of the circular referred to in this petition has been put in the hands of each member of this Council and therefore there is no need for me to read it, as I believe everybody here has it. In this connection I might read what is some explanation of this circular, and emphasizes the fact that the University of Toronto (and I think I might apply that to the other three institutions) is very anxious to maintain the standard, and they do not desire so much the doing away with the fifth year as they do desire an opportunity of lengthening the session so that they may do more efficient work, and so that the students will not be crowded too much with work, because we have increased the amount of work a student necessarily has before him before we give him his license.

Dr. GEIKIE—I was present at that meeting as one of the representatives, and the representative colleges were equally anxious about the fifth year, thinking with the eight months' course the fifth year would not be necessary because the extra two months would be a very good quid pro quo.

Dr. BRITTON—I think perhaps Dr. Geikie misunderstood my words. What I meant to emphasize was that the primary thing the University of Toronto desired is that it may have an opportunity to extend its sessions to eight months for the reasons I have given. The University of Toronto also thinks that that is quite an equivalent for the fifth year's work.

Dr. GEIKIE—Exactly ; that is it.

Dr. BRITTON—What we do desire is to have an eight months' session and if possible to do away with the fifth year's work. When Dr. Geikie spoke I was about to read a letter from the Dean of the Medical Faculty of the University of Toronto to me. So strong is the feeling in the University of Toronto regarding the necessity for extending the sessions that supposing it were to stand alone I feel very well satisfied (although there has been no definite step taken in that direction) that it would take the initiative even though it might possibly lose financially to some extent, and it might lose to a large extent ; but however that is, the conviction of the members of the Medical Faculty of the University of Toronto I think is unanimous. I have spoken to a good many, and it is represented to me as unanimous, and I have no doubt it is so. I also said we had a petition from the students. These petitions have been signed by the students from the different colleges, and I will simply read the heading of the petition ; it is virtually the same thing, but there is one statement to be made about the petition that is important. Perhaps I can give you the substance in shorter terms than those set forth in the petition, and therefore I will give you the substance. They asked for the changes to be made, such as are mentioned in the petition from the faculties ; and they also state that objection may be taken to making these changes on account of the fact that a great many teachers are studying medicine—call them occasional teachers. There are ninety-nine in all petitioning ; and they state that amongst that number there are twenty-eight teachers, and these teachers have signed themselves as such. Their plea is that it will not interfere at all with their work, because when they engage in teaching, as a stepping-stone towards medicine, the teaching is ordinarily done before the medicine is commenced ; and whether the interval in the summer be six months or only four—that is, whether we have a six or an eight months' session—it will make no difference to them because it is next to impossible for a teacher to secure a position for either four or six months in the summer, especially when you take from that time the two months of summer holidays. That is one important fact that I see in the petition from the students. The students' petition has been signed, as I said before, by ninety-nine. No one refused to sign, and it would have been signed, I suppose, by three times ninety-nine were it not that the petition was circulated, I believe, after the schools had ceased teaching, at any rate when a great many of the students were away ; I suppose that is the reason.

Dr. GEIKIE—Do I understand if this is carried by the Council it does not affect the schools at all because it is optional ?

Dr. BRITTON—There are a number of features I would like to go into, but I fear my time is up unless the Council will be indulgent with me. (Cries of "Go on, go on.")

The CHAIRMAN—You have four minutes yet.

Dr. BRITTON—I was one of those who originally voted for the five years' term, the resolution for which was carried on a close division, in fact on a tie as far as I can remember, the chairman of the Committee of the Whole or the President (I have forgotten which) giving the casting vote ; and I must say that the contention of the faculties is a correct one, that they were not consulted, so far as I know, before this was done. The fifth year was added on virtually without their knowledge of it. As to the respective advantages of having an eight months' session instead of a six months' session, or, on the other hand, of having a fifth year, so long as a student is here in the city of Toronto or elsewhere at a medical school pursuing his studies, and under the eye of the medical faculty, it is pretty difficult for him to shirk his work to a great extent, or at any rate he is more likely to do his work than were he left to himself to choose where he would pursue his studies ; that is, to choose whether or not he will put six months in some registered practitioner's office. I have known a good many medical students who were supposed to be in the doctor's office, and amongst those I could name a good many who have not been in the office more than two or three times in the six months ; and for that reason I think that a certificate from a physician that a student has been in his office for six months amounts to nothing, and it is no guarantee to us. The six months in the physician's office really amounts to six months' holiday. I grant you there are exceptions, that there are students who are anxious to acquire knowledge, and who will devote their time faithfully for the six months, and get all the advice and instruction they can from their tutor, but I think these are the exceptions. I have read the wording as to that six months, and I cannot determine whether it is obligatory or not as to spending six months in an hospital or some other institution in clinical work. However, at the very outset, according to my argument, the fifth year means only six months' actual work. Now, if we add on two months to each session, we add on eight months in all to the time that the student must work. He must work a session of eight months on one side or six months on the other, so far as the time of the work is concerned. If my resolution carries I think we have a guarantee that the student has to put in more actual time on his work than he would were the clause of the report to carry. Dr. Geikie has spoken of the unfairness that would arise were it left optional——

Dr. GEIKIE—I would rather say unsatisfactoriness ; I think that would apply better and make it more clear, instead of using the word "unfairness." I mean the colleges should work together in perfect harmony, and we would like to have it so that we would be all in the same line, because we ought not to be one taking one course and another taking another course.

Dr. BRITTON—Then I will use a milder term, and say it would be very unsatisfactory for one institution ; and I have already stated that I believe the University of Toronto, being permitted by that clause, will go ahead single-handed, if necessary, or if forced to ; and it will be unsatisfactory for that institution, it would be unsatisfactory for Trinity Medical College, and unsatisfactory for any other institution that adopted eight months' to feel that some other institution or institutions retained the six months' session. I declare, if I had to start to study medicine over again I would probably do just the same as the majority of other young men do ; that is, I would go where I would have to spend the least time ; I would be unwise enough to do that. That is the tendency of all young men ; they are anxious and ambitious ; every young man when he gets to be about seventeen is anxious for a moustache and to be twenty-one ; and then when he gets to be twenty-one he wants to hurry and get through medicine. I say it would be unsatisfactory if left permissible ; and I think it very important if you make the change I suggest.

Dr. WILLIAMS—I want to move an amendment to it, and if it is your pleasure it can be discussed at the same time. The amendment I propose is, "And we further recommend that the Announcement be amended on page x. to the following effect : After the session of 1896–97, two courses of not less than eight months each shall be required." That leaves the five years as it is, but lengthens out the session. We should word this so that it will make the session eight months long instead of six months, all through, where it is necessary to make a change.

Dr. FOWLER—I object to that. I rise for the purpose of protesting against the changes in the calendar in regard to doing away with the fifth year of work. I look upon that pretty much in the same light as if an attempt were to be made to do five years' work in four. I think that the work would be exceedingly crowded to have eight months' sessions, even if there were no fifth session at all. We find in regard to many students that they get worn out even at the end of the six months' session, and to continue their work for eight months would certainly, I think, do a great deal more harm than good. I feel, however, the great necessity that exists for the fifth year, and I cannot understand, when the Council have deliberately arranged for a fifth year of practical work, why that should now be interfered with in any sense whatever. (Hear, hear.) I conceive that the fifth year of practical work is of far more use than half a dozen eight months' sessions. We find under these sessions that students will be obliged to do more or less practical work, partly, perhaps, in the surgeons' offices and also in chemical and pathological laboratories and hospital work ; and to be sure that these studies shall be a benefit to the student, provision was made for an examination at the end of the fifth year ; the student then has to come back to the Medical Council to be examined to see how he has spent his time during the fifth year of medical study. I should, then, strongly protest against the extension of the eight months' session for various reasons. We find, for instance, independent of the fatigue that is brought about amongst students when working continuously during even six months, that they need some change, not only for the benefit of their health, but also often with a view of getting means to prepare them for the next session ; and I think it would be an exceedingly great hardship for many students who are working their own way towards a profession to be deprived of the opportunity of doing so by being compelled to work almost continuously all the year round at their medical studies. We have medical students who act as pursers on the boats in the summer, and many go into the woods for various kinds of work, and in other ways they earn money to put them through. This proposed change would be very well in the case of the rich young men, but we do. not wish to execute men who are struggling on to get an education for themselves, and this continuity of work undoubtedly would have that effect. For these and various other reasons I protest against any change being made in the curriculum which was so carefully considered and which included a fifth year of practical work.

Dr. SANGSTER—I am a little at sea as to the meaning of the last resolution proposed. May I have it read ?

The REGISTRAR read, " Moved by Dr. Williams, That the clause be amended by adding ' And we further recommend that the Announcement be amended on page x., after Clause 5, to the following effect : After the session of 1896–97, two courses of not less than eight months each shall be required.' "

Dr. SANGSTER—Is it Dr. Williams' intention that we should do away with the fifth year ?

Dr. WILLIAMS—No ; I simply want to put that in form that it shall be after 1897 an eight months' session instead of six months.

Dr. SANGSTER—I have no long speech to make upon that clause. This fifth year ques-tion was discussed in full four years ago, and a very great deal of eloquence was expended on the part of the Council (some of the members are here present) upon the great impor-tance of that fifth year of clinical study ; and a great deal of capital has been sought for, and perhaps won, on the part of the old Council for thus putting up the requirements of the curriculum. Now, to use a word of my friend, Dr. Geikie's, I wish to say just on behalf of the profession that any putting up of the length of session from six to eight months, on the part of the universities, or on the part of the Council, is quite satisfactory ; but any attempts to touch that fifth year of clinical work is unsatisfactory.

Dr. THORBURN—When this subject was brought up this last year I thought the Council were making a mistake in adding the fifth year to it. As a rule, the men who study medi-cine here are older than they are in Europe, but still there, instead of having their ordinary six months they are now having nine months, and they find it is much more to the advan-tage of the student than even adding the fifth year, which I believe they are to do after this. In six months it is very well known that they do not get more than five months' study ; whereas if they had an eight months' course they are kept at their work, like other students of other institutions, and they do not find it confusing or oppressive. There might be a six months' course for those who are too poor to pay for the whole nine months, but the oppor-tunity of making enough money in the two or three or four months left is very rare indeed, therefore I wish to record my vote in favor of the eight months' lectures and four years' course.

Dr. MOORHOUSE—I feel constrained to speak on this question. I have refrained from occupying the attention of the Council because I thought a great deal of time had been wasted needlessly, but in this, I think it is my duty to speak, as being a representative of one of the universities or teaching bodies concerned in this resolution now before you. I might say, when we first received information from the Toronto faculties that this matter was under consideration, we thought at that time that Kingston was heart and soul with the Toronto schools ; and I believe it was understood at that time by Toronto that Kingston was a unit with them. We for some time looked upon it with some degree of coldness, and thought it was an innovation, and like all other new movements it naturally strikes one with disfavor, and we naturally viewed it with disfavor ; but after having looked over the matter, and having become a little more familiarized with the idea, although, of course, at first there was scarcely anybody in our faculty that looked upon it with favor, we gradually dropped in in favor of the scheme, till at last there would not be more than two or three members of our faculty who would not be in favor of it ; and to make sure of the matter, a week or ten days before this meeting, I, being Dean of the faculty, called the faculty together to take their consensus of opinion ; and I found there was a large majority who would support the eight months' course. I think the Executive Committee did wisely in not forcing this eight months' session upon the schools in the session ensuing, in 1896–97 ; but Dr. Williams' amendment, I think, very well covers the ground, to make it compulsory on all the schools to teach an eight months' session during 1897-98 ; but 1896-97 should be left as it is unless the schools voluntarily undertake to so teach. This will prepare the way gradually, and work up the popular mind so that they can receive it when it does come and be prepared to act upon it. I have very great faith in Dr. Fowler's judgment as an old educationist ; I certainly believe he has had great experience, but I think he is looking upon this movement somewhat with a little misapprehension. First of all, allow me to say, in your Annual Announcement you make it obligatory upon all the medical schools and teaching bodies to teach a certain number of lectures in each session, one hundred in some subjects, seventy-five, fifty and twenty-five each for others. This eight months' session does not imply the number of lectures are to be increased ; we do not expect that, and we do not want it ; we want the same number of lectures we give inside of the five or six months extended over the longer period of eight months; and in this way the students will not be compelled to work so hard. Dr. Fowler complains and says the students are overworked, and I say they are overworked ; by the time they go through the various lectures and clinical subjects and dissections, the student that does his work faithfully is overworked. In this way they could have more time for a breathing spell ; for instance, take in the practice of medicine and surgery, where you give 100 numbers in about five months, which is about the time these lectures generally close up—about March—you have five lectures on the great subjects a week, chemistry and physiology, and by extending it over a longer interval of eight months you may only have three lectures ; and that will allow the subjects to work in, dovetail one on the other, so that a student can more carefully digest that which he has received and follow up the teaching by reading some of the more extended works and not be prescribed down to some of the briefer works or abridgements that students are compelled to use, and which, I am sorry to say, are too much used among students—little pocket books, little remembrancers and that sort of thing. Instead of using those they should read more widely and extensively. The members of this Council range from perhaps fifty years to twenty years' standing, some of them I know are of fifty years ; for instance our friend Dr. Fowler is now in his jubilee year (Applause). These men forget that the teaching now is so greatly changed to what it was at the time of their getting their education—Dr. Fowler does not forget because he is a teacher, but it is only those who are actively engaged as Dr. Fowler, Dr. Geikie and I, in teaching who know the great multiplicity of the subjects the student has to take up, subjects that were not taught when I was a student twenty-five years ago ; we have nearly doubled the amount of studies we had then. I think we cannot go astray if we vote for the apparently raising of the session from six to eight months during the session of 1897-8. With those few words of observation I would urge upon the Council to give it consideration and not to vote hastily against it, but to vote in favor of it. As to Dr. Fowler's other argument about a great many young men working for their livelihood when studying medicine, I think when the Council say a student shall put in that time in study they do not mean he is to put in half of that time to study and half the time to teaching school or splitting rails or collecting tickets on the boats. Personally I have very little faith in the fifth year's study, I do not give a snap for it, and I think four years with eight months' sessions is infinitely superior to four years of six months' sessions and a year for loafing idleness. You may have certificates from medical men that students have been engaged in actual work in their offices, but you all know how you sign such certificates, how your consciences hinted to you you were not doing right, but you did it because it was some personal friend ; and you all know that certificates are obtained in that way from the hospitals. We do not know whether those students have been actually hard working as they should have been ; a certificate from an hospital does not guarantee this any more than the certificates which many of us have so often given, without the requirements perhaps having been complied with. But in the case of a student following an eight months' tuition for four years, being constantly under the supervising eye of the teacher, he has his work progressively going on before him and he has the weekly examination which generally takes place in every class; and if our session were lengthened to an eight months' session instead of a six months' session we would give the teacher time for more genuine testing of the student's knowledge, and opportunities of setting him right on those subjects in which he is deficient, and explaining matters to him, and so on. I think we, as a Committee on Education, have not the power of recommending this to you, but we left it in an open way until it could be properly discussed before the Council, and then the Council could use their judgment on the matter.

Dr. FOWLER—I would ask Dr. Williams if he would change his motion to read "That it be referred to the medical colleges to consider the question whether it would be advisable over the fifth year to add the eight months' session." I think it would be an unwise thing to pass a rule that the eight months' session should be established at the present time.

Dr. WILLIAMS—I have just changed the wording of my resolution and it would be better to have the Registrar read it so that the Council will know the form it is in.

The REGISTRAR read the resolution as follows: That the following be added, "We further recommend that after the session of 1896-97 the winter course shall be eight months long instead of six months, and no summer session shall be required."

Dr. FOWLER—This should be considered by the various colleges.

Dr. WILLIAMS—That is a recommendation to the Council ; if the Council adopt that then it becomes compulsory.

Dr. Fowler—Then, I think it is a mistake.

Dr. Dickson—Is that the eight months in addition to the five years ?

Dr. Williams—Yes, leave the five years alone.

Dr. Dickson—I would say, if I am not mistaken, McGill College has adopted a nine months' session ; and if for no other reason I think we should, as far as possible, accommo. date the students coming here, and we know a great many are coming here for examination. I see by the proposed arrangement that the meeting of the Council will be delayed for two weeks, until the third week ; I think it would be desirable to make it longer. The third Tuesday will hardly be late enough for the colleges here.

Dr. Williams—We have a by-law to introduce on that.

Dr. Britton—I might say I conferred with teachers from the different bodies here in Toronto and they are quite satisfied it should be postponed to the third Tuesday of May. The representatives from the different teaching bodies were quite satisfied to have the examination postponed to the third Tuesday in May. That would be late enough.

Dr. Moorhouse—The examination is usually on the third Tuesday in March ; that is postponing it two months later.

Dr. Moore—I have no desire to say anything to pull down the standard of education, but I shall have to vote against Dr. Williams' resolution, because Dr. Williams is actually giving more than they are asking for, in one way, and not what they are asking for in another ; we are neither complying with the desires of the University of Toronto, nor Trinity Medical School, nor the Western University, nor with the desires of Queen's University. I think we had better go a little more slowly. If we go to work and put up the fence so high, put the barrier so high, we will have the Patrons around our ears again, just as sure as the world. If we go to work and make it five years' study and lengthen out the session from six months to eight months and put a stumbling block in the way of genius, in the way of the poor man's son, you will hear the poor farmer coming and saying the farmer's son cannot get a chance to get home and plant potatoes and hoe corn and help take off the crop ; and we will have trouble again. I think we had better make haste slowly and leave this off for a time. We have only entered nicely upon the five years' course, and if there was anything that has seemed ridiculous in this Council it is the fact that we have been tinkering with this curriculum every year—either went up or down or got sidetracked. I think it is time we called a halt and let the five years' course go on a while. Surely these great schools here are not afraid of a little university like Queen's, two hundred miles distant. And let me tell you, the people down there are poor ; and I do not think any member of this Council thinks less of a man when he enters upon the study of medicine and has got to stick his nose into an anatomy or some other medical work for some five years, because he goes and hoes corn or to be a purser on a steamboat or something of that kind. If he can earn an honest penny to pay an honest debt I think we will let him do it, as long as he passes his examinations. It has been stated a certificate from a doctor is not any good ; there are times I will grant it is no good, but I have known men to be certified as attending lectures when they were not there at all.

Dr. McLaughlin—That was down in your division.

Dr. Moore—No, I believe it occurred in other places, but we won't deny the fact it does occur even down there. I think it is a valuable thing for a student, if he is a good student and desires to advantage himself and desires to obtain the information that he can obtain in a doctor's office, to have that six months' experience in a doctor's office, especially if it is the office of a good man who does a good deal of work and is up with the times ; to my mind it is worth as much as six months in the hospital. I have had students in my office, and I am only a poor country practitioner, and those students learned a good deal there. I think we have hardly any hospitals in this Province or in Montreal who would certify a student stayed there six months when he was not there. We have had the five years' term only for a short time ; we have had the four courses of six months each and have found they worked pretty well ; and if we did anything right it was when we endeavored to make our work more practical——

Dr. Sangster—I do not think the resolution touches the five years' work.

Dr. Moore—This resolution points, I think, or the desire of the profession points out it should be reduced to four years. I have a right to discuss that. Dr. Britton has said, and properly said (he generally is pretty proper), that they would have thirty-two months of continuous study ; but let us take the five years with its six months' courses and that will give us twenty-four months, and adding to that ten weeks of a summer session, gives twenty-six and a half months ; and supposing the student does loaf six months and recruits his health by hoeing corn, by putting all this together you have got a little over thirty-two months ; and you have allowed him to go home and help his mammy and daddy by his work on the farm, or by standing behind the counter selling tea and coffee. Another thing I want to say is that I do not think that because two or three universities or schools decide upon a certain thing that another university should be just taken by the throat, so to speak, and chucked into the holé that the others have prepared, without being given an opportunity to kick a little ; and we propose to kick a little. If it suits these gentlemen to have an eight months' course let them have it, but give us another year or two to get ready, because we are slow down there——

Dr. MOORHOUSE—That is what we are doing.

Dr. MOORE—You are only giving us one session. I do not think I will take up the time of the Council more than a minute or two more ; I want simply to insist upon it that we move slowly. We need not go backwards. I refuse to go backwards ; I am not ashamed to go slowly and I do not want to go wrong, but I refuse to go back. I believe if you leave the thing as it is for a little time we will not be making any mistake, and if the report as it is now is adopted I think it will answer all the purposes necessary.

Dr. ROGERS—I just want to say one word in regard to this matter ; I want to ask the Council to consider very carefully what is before them. The report of the committee is before this Council ; they have asked to postpone a date at which the examinations of the Council will be held, and the date of the Council meeting. That has been the report of the Committee on Education after hours and hours of serious consideration ; and I think it was almost universally concluded that it would be best to postpone the date of the examinations and the Council meeting. Why ? Simply, so that those schools that wanted to have an eight months' session could have it, and so that those schools that did not want to have it should not be compelled to. Not hurriedly, but for hours has this been considered and talked over ; the report is now before us ; and on behalf of the Education Committee I ask this Council for their serious consideration. One or two members of the Education Committee got up and asked for a change. It does seem to me it is hardly fair to the Education Committee, after the serious consideration they have given this report, to alter it. I want to take up some of the points made by Dr. Britton and Dr. Geikie ; they say the six months' course is not long enough. But they do not have a six months' session ; they hardly ever have more than a four months' session—very little more ; there is hardly a school in this Province that gives more than a four months' session ; the students come about the 10th or 15th October and they stop work about the 1st March, and out of that time is taken two weeks for holidays.

Dr. MOORHOUSE—They do not stop till the middle of March.

Dr. ROGERS—I emphatically declare I know of dozens of students that stop their work on the 1st of March.

Dr. MOORHOUSE—That is the more argument for the eight months' session.

Dr. ROGERS—Why don't you say they shall complete the full six months' session ?

Dr. GEIKIE—So they do.

Dr. ROGERS—They do not do it. If we were to increase the session to an eight months' session the colleges cannot control their students ; they cannot get them to attend the full six months, and if they cannot control them in six months they cannot control them in eight months. What would be the consequence of this ? We would simply get about the same as we get now, except we only demand a certain number of lectures. But there is something else behind all this. I do say if the Council make an eight months' session you will find representations made to the Minister of Education at the next session, and you may expect to come down next session to fight a bill which will be put in to take off the fifth year. They will say, perhaps, as was said in regard to matriculation, the Council are going so fast we really must have a check put on them ; and Mr. Ross, in the quietest and kindest and pleasantest possible way, will agree to the request of our school friends, and the bill will be put in that any person who has attended lectures for four sessions of eight months each shall be allowed to come up for examination. The profession of medicine who pay the shot and pay the bills of this Council must be respected a little bit. The Legislature has put out its hands and taken hold of the matriculation and shown that we must go backwards, and I say I will never be a party to allow them to take off that fifth year or do anything that will make an excuse to the Legislature to take it off for us. I emphatically state that any fair student can get up the whole of his work in four sessions of six months each, and I do not take the word of men who say they cannot, when I know of institutions, even Queen's University, who turn out excellent students in four sessions of six months each. They come to us with a large deputation and say, we must have an eight months' session ; we cannot give enough knowledge in six months, it is impossible. We say, we will postpone the date of the examinations so as to let you have the session, so that you can make the session. What do they do ? I believe the only institution here which says it will try, and it is an institution I respect very highly, is Toronto University. Trinity says they won't do it. We give them a chance for an eight months' session, but the only one willing to take advantage of it is Toronto University.

Dr. GEIKIE—No, you are mistaken ; we said we might not like it unless all did it.

Dr. ROGERS—I understood Dr. Geikie to say what I have said.

Dr. GEIKIE—No.

9

Dr. ROGERS—What we say is, we only demand a six months' session, but we are raising our course so that any school that wishes an eight months' session may have it ; and when we have done that we have enabled our friends who represent the teaching bodies of this city to go to the Minister of Education and to say to him that we have so far raised up the requirements of the medical education that he will have to put his hand out and interfere with us. We will save ourselves trouble by leaving this alone, and I would strongly urge on Dr. Williams to leave the matter as it was left in the Committee on Education, to withdraw his motion and vote for the adoption of the report of the Education Committee. It will do no harm, if in a year from now we find all the schools are taking an eight months' session, to take it up, but in the meantime we should leave it alone and have no reference to it at all. Dr. Britton has said the six months in a doctor's office was no good. I do not say the student shall go into a doctor's office for six months. Dr. Moorhouse has said that the time spent by the student in the doctor's office was a time of loafing. I want to ask him if a student takes a year after he graduates in going to the hospitals in the Old Country, whether he is loafing ?

Dr. MOORHOUSE—No.

Dr. ROGERS—I would like to ask Dr. Moorhouse how many students he knows who loafed in the last year ?

Dr. MOORHOUSE—I don't know.

Dr. ROGERS—Then why does Dr. Moorhouse use those arguments ?

Dr. MOORHOUSE—I beg your pardon. I do know students who loaf if they have a chance.

Dr. ROGERS—We know of many students who, after they have got their practice of medicine up and their surgery, obstetrics and all their book work, go to New York, Boston, Philadelphia, and even to Europe, and take a year in the hospitals ; and the Council years ago said to the students, we will give you encouragement to go there, but if there is any poor fellow, such as those Dr. Moore has spoken of, who says " I can't afford to do so," and goes to the doctor's office for six months and does a fair amount of work, he can, if necessary, show an affidavit that he has studied there for six months. They must put in one year of clinical work after they have got through their book work. For these reasons I ask the Council to seriously consider what they are doing. We do not want to be caught in any little trap this time—at least I do not want to be—and I ask you to adopt this report as it is.

Dr. MOORE—There was a point I forgot to speak of. I want to point out to this Council this fact, that when we put on the eight months' course we keep the poor man's son two months longer away from home ; if we keep him two months longer away from home somebody has got to pay for it. Another thing is it is very hard to get board for much less than $5.00 a week, and that would make $40.00 we take out of the boy or out of his father by keeping him two months longer ; and in that way, if we put in four sessions, we wring $80.00 out of the poor man's pocket, and $20.00 would pay the fees to this Council.

Dr. MCLAUGHLIN—I can remember, as a student, and I presume the times have not changed much, we began at eight o'clock to listen to lectures, and listened for two or three hours ; then we ran away to the hospital and had some lectures, and kept it up till nine o'clock at night. I say that any student subjected to a treatment of that kind in getting his education must receive into his head information, if it is information at all, in such a way that he will be muddled up, and when the day is over it will be difficult for him to know what he has learned. I have another argument to present to you. I am not a stickler for lectures, I do not think that there is such a vast deal of good done by lectures; and my own personal experience is that when I was a student I obtained as much information and I crystallized it into form and order better from the standard books, by making notes and condensing them, than I did from lectures. The lectures were useful to me in leading my mind to be concentrated more upon points that I had overlooked. In that way I think the lecture was a good thing ; it guided me to those ideas and thoughts that in reading I had overlooked. I think the eight months' course is the sound course, because the lectures need not begin at eight o'clock, and there need not of necessity be so many lectures in a day ; we would have fewer lectures, more digestion, and what is more important still, far more clinical observation. We have in the city of Toronto, the city of Kingston and the city of London not the vast opportunity for clinical observation for students that they have in London (England), New York, Paris, Berlin and other places. Not having that opportunity, I say it is wise to extend the time, and the student will have in the eight months very much more opportunity for seeing the practical side of his profession than he would in the limited six months ; therefore, my contention is that if this Council desire to put their education upon a good and a sound basis, and to get abreast of the best teaching bodies of the world, we must get away from the six months' session and have the eight months' session. I approve of the fifth year provided it is well used, provided a student is able to go to some of the cities where there are more opportunities for clinical observation and clinical studies than a small place like Toronto can afford. I think it is time well spent. Whilst I maintain these views I also feel that the legislation in the Council has not partaken sufficiently of the character of the laws of the Medes and Persians. I do not say our laws should be unalterable, but at the same time I do not think that there should not be that continuous tinkering and alteration that have characterized the treatment of our curriculum for some time past. While I say that, I do not mean to advance the idea that I am not prepared to vote for this resolution if we are all clear it is the best thing for the students and for the medical education of this country. If that is so, then I think we ought to go forward to-day and adopt it, and I am disposed to think it will be adopted. There has been an *ad miseri cordium* argument adopted to-day about the poor student, that if this is adopted the poor students will suffer ; but I venture if this is not adopted the poor patients will suffer. We ought to consider in our legislation the people of this country, and put them and their interests paramount to the medical profession or the students or anything else. The question is, which will prepare the student for the best practitioner, the most useful man for the country ? I think the eight months in which the student digests more thoroughly everything he learns in his education will fit that man for a better practitioner than the student who only spends six months. It is true that in the last month (it was in my day and I presume it is still) that the boys run away, and begin to fag, and do not attend lectures ; they will probably do that in the seventh month under the new regime, if we adopt it, but still they will have seven months of solid study and direction by their teachers. I think it would be wise for us to adopt the eight months' session ; I feel disposed to accept that. Let us make it a fixed thing and not be altering our curriculum so often, and I think it will be a great benefit to the people, and not only to them but to the students who will become our future practitioners.

Dr. THORNTON—Whatever may be the necessity for change in the future, or however wise it may be to make changes in the future, at the present time I am going to follow the words of my opponents in the Council last year, "I think the time is not opportune." I do not pretend for a moment to be able to discuss this question from the university point of view, and I do not know that I am particularly qualified from the professional point of view, but I feel that I have a duty to discharge. There is nothing in connection with the work of this Council, since this question has been talked of, that I have devoted more attention to or made more enquiries about than this particular question. I do not pretend to say that it will not be wise for changes to be made in the future. I will not say that it is not wise to discuss this question as it has been discussed to-day. There may be a great deal of good come out of the discussion, and it may pave the way for a different state of things ; but on careful enquiry from men that are able to express opinions and who have a great deal of force with them, I have found that if we, at the present time, on the lines asked in that clause of the report, make those changes we will place an extra amount of work on our Registrar, and we will double the work of our Complaints Committee, and we will open up a mighty breach between the profession and the teaching bodies and pave the way for the Patrons or other organizations that may spring into existence to go to our legislative halls and not only ask to upset the changes we are making now but the whole Medical Act. I have found invariably with the leading members of the profession that there is, and particularly on the part of the public and those that are educating their sons in medicine, a deep rooted and a growing dislike to this continual tinkering with our curriculum, and to the continual making of changes ; and the feeling is such at the present time that if those changes are made it is going to tend to bring about the results which I have just enumerated, and for that reason I will vote for wiping out the clause and for leaving the matter just as it is.

Dr. CAMPBELL—I have helped all I could in the past to secure for the profession a high matriculation standard and a high standard of professional education, and I think we have succeeded in getting it, and we have a good standard. Our standard compares well with the standards of other countries in America and in Europe ; it is a good standard, and I think we should let well enough alone for a little while. (Hear, hear.) Complaint has been made repeatedly that we are continually changing. Possibly if we change now we may improve somewhat, but what is the necessity for making experiments and trying to improve when, under all the circumstances, we are doing remarkably well. Again, I say, let well enough alone. We do not want to give opportunity for people to effect changes in the Medical Act by getting the idea that we are endeavoring to make ourselves a too closely protected organization. I objected last year to raising the standard of matriculation on that account, and events proved that those of us who objected were correct ; we were going faster than the popular sentiment would endorse ; and now if we go faster in raising our professional educational standard than popular sentiment will endorse we will have our wings clipped again. Let us be careful and not give any opportunity to Patrons, School men, or anybody else, to go to the Legislature and endeavor to get our privileges reduced, and the standard we have adopted reduced. Let well enough alone. For that reason I am disposed to vote against any change whatever.

Dr. SANGSTER—I would not rise to say anything but for one remark of the last speaker. The changes made in the Legislature by the Ross Bill had no reference whatever to the elevation of the standard of matriculation accomplished here last year. That standard was not to go into force till 1897. The changes made in the Legislature at the request of somebody were made because the Education Committee too closely astringed their proceedings last year, so as to insist that no man should be permitted to claim registration as a matriculate unless he had passed what was announced, and had been announced for some years past, as the one sole and imperative requirement for matriculation. Nothing that was done in the House had the slightest reference or was founded in any way upon what was done or said last year in reference to the raising of the standard in 1897.

Dr. BRITTON—I beg leave to move in amendment to the amendment, That Clause 2 be struck out and the following inserted : " That four sessions of eight months each be demanded, and that the summer session and fifth year of clinical work be abolished." I have not a word to say in relation to that because whatever I have said referred to the facts contained in it.

Dr. WILLIAMS—I have refrained from making any remarks on this subject till the present. I think my object in introducing that resolution is partially attained already. I wanted by that resolution to elicit the feelings of the Council on this subject ; and I wanted at the same time to give the schools and the profession a warning that that step was going to be taken. Now, I have made the motion in such a way that after the next year it should be taken. I am not prepared to say whether that would be stepping a little too soon or not. That will be for the Council to say, but my own impression is that it is the right step to take, but whether or not we are taking that step too soon I am not prepared to say. It does not lengthen the time for a student ; the years would still be the five years ; it is just changing the work during the five years. We seem to occupy rather an awkward position ; we are told that we are in danger of getting into trouble with the Patrons on one hand, and if you look on the other side we are in danger of getting into trouble with the profession ; so that we stand in the middle, I won't say between the devil and the deep sea, because I would not know which to call the devil ; but still we are just in that position that we require to move with some considerable care. My own impression is that the schools need to take warning that this step is going to be taken ; and though my resolution may be voted down to-day, it, either by me or by somebody else, probably will be brought up at no distant day, and that step will have to be taken. Now, as I understand the amendment of Dr. Britton, it is to take the four eight months' sessions, but to abolish the fifth year.

Dr. BRITTON—And the summer session.

Dr. WILLIAMS—Now, that is a sort of half step. Mine you may call a full step, and his is the half step. And then, we come down to the recommendation of the report, and that is, to allow it to be optional with the schools, only to fix the period of holding the examinations at a time that if they felt they wanted to take that course they can then have their examinations. I think that is about the way the matter stands ; we have the three propositions, one that allows it to be optional with the schools as to what step they will take ; the other one takes the four eight months' sessions without the summer session and without the fifth year ; and the other one takes the four eight months' sessions with the fifth year and without the summer session ; and I think we are in a position to cast our votes on this without any trouble.

The Registrar read the amendment by Dr. Williams, and read Dr. Britton's amendment to the amendment.

The Chairman put the amendment to the amendment, and on a vote being taken declared it lost.

The Chairman read the amendment of Dr. Williams.

Dr. BRITTON—I would like to ask Dr. Williams through you, Mr. Chairman, for some information as to whether he means that to be added to the original clause or to be substituted for it.

Dr. WILLIAMS—It is worded : " And we further recommend ; " that is, in addition.

Dr. MOORE—You mean the four sessions of eight months and the five years ?

Dr. WILLIAMS—Yes.

The Chairman put the amendment, and on a vote having been taken declared it lost.

The Chairman then put Dr. Campbell's motion, That the second clause of the report be adopted. Carried.

Dr. Britton read the third clause of the report.

The PRESIDENT—Could not the Registrar give us that resolution now ? The resolution is that the therapeutics be placed with the practice of medicine instead of pathology.

Dr. BRITTON—It has come to my recollection that I did move that the subject of therapeutics, being an important one, a separate paper be given ; and it was subsequently decided by the Council that that paper should be given by the Examiner in medicine. The reason it has been referred here is because the Examiner who took both subjects, therapeutics and pathology, felt it was unwise for any one to attempt to take both, because in a certain sense they are so foreign and not closely allied. I do not think that it is necessary to take special action.

The Chairman put the motion to adopt the third clause of the report. Carried.

Dr. Britton read Clauses 4, 5, 6, 7, 8, 9, 10, 11, 12, 13, 14, 15, 16, 17 and 18 of the report, which, on motion, were adopted as read.

The Chairman read Clause 19 of the report.

Dr. Rogers—The Executive Committee recommended that Mr. Bremner be recommended to the Council favorably, and the facts are such that it seems to me really a great hardship.

Dr. Britton—I will read the original communication from Mr. C. W. Bremner, which is dated October 4th, 1895. The applicant had a personal interview with me last year. He is a brother of Dr. Bremner, who, until recently, was practising in Ontario, but who has gone to South America, where, I believe, he is establishing a private hospital ; and I am fully persuaded that it is the intention of the applicant to go down there as soon as he takes his degree in the Toronto University and secures his license from the College, if he can be allowed to secure it at the same time.

Dr. Sangster—Will you explain the object of the petition ?

Dr. Britton—The object of the petition is to be allowed to be registered as a student in the four-year course. He had all the qualifications, and far more than were necessary in 1892 ; in fact, he was qualified some years before and he knew that the four-year course was prescribed, and I presume he also knew—I would not say that—that the change was going to be made in 1892. I do not suppose he did know. But he did not know he would be allowed to register until he was actually engaged in the study of medicine.

Dr. Geikie—I move that his request be granted.

Dr. Thorburn—I second that.

Moved by Dr. Thorburn, seconded by Dr. Campbell, To strike out the word "not" in Clause 19 of the report. Carried.

Clause 19, on motion, was adopted as amended.

Dr. Britton read Clause 20 of the report, and stated that this might be condensed afterwards by the Registrar and the Executive Committee.

Dr. Britton moved the adoption of the clause. Carried.

Dr. Britton read Clause 21 of the report.

Dr. Geikie—I move that the report be amended by having embodied in it a recommendation that in the first line the word "fifty" shall be substituted for the word "sixty." I do that for the reason that, as you know, when a man passes, for instance, four Primary subjects, receiving 50 per cent. on each, he gets 200 marks, while another who gets 68, 65, 50 and 49, receives no credit at all. The second man makes a great many more marks, but he is not even allowed his subjects, because we have a double standard. This is a mistake. We should take the ordinary pass standard of 50 per cent. and 20 per cent. added if a person happens to be one mark short in any subject, and to give the man three branches, provided he comes up to our pass standard, is doing the Council no wrong. It is not hurting anything, and there is not a student in the country who does not desire that amendment made. I have one illustration where a man got 59, 59, 59 and 49 ; he should get credit for these four. I beg leave to move that that motion be adopted.

Dr. Sangster—If you proceed in that direction, there is only one finality you can come to, and that is, nothing. If you adopt 50 instead of 60, there is nothing to prevent another gentleman coming in and saying, " Here is a gentleman who got 49½, 49½ and 49½, and he got nothing." The next year you get it down further, and say, " Here is a gentleman who got 39½, and so on, and nothing was allowed." I say, when you fix a standard you have to keep to it, and not proceed by half marks. I think we prepared a large amount of trouble for the Registrar last night in permitting certain persons to register that had not been recommended for registration by the Examiners. As an old teacher and an old Examiner, I believe there is only one clear way for this Council to follow, and that is to fix a rule and never depart from it.

Dr. Geikie—In answer to you, I would like to say that I have not fixed upon a lower standard, but if a man makes 50 per cent. in three subjects he ought to be credited with them. This is your own standard, not a fresh standard.

Dr. Shaw—Clause 5, Section V., seems to cover the point raised by Dr. Geikie. I do sympathize to some extent with the position he takes, but I think this clause would enable the Council to relieve the hardship. It leaves the matter in the hands of the Council if there is a hardship ; and sometimes it does appear that there is a hardship. A candidate may take 70 per cent. in one subject, 65 in another, 59 in another, and fall under 50 in the fourth, and according to the technical interpretation of Sub-section 9, Section III., he would have to be declined. A case of that kind might seem a hardship, but

I think Clause 5, Section V., gives the Council the power of coming to their relief in cases of that character.

The Chairman put Dr. Geikie's amendment, which on a standing vote being taken was declared lost.

Dr. BRITTON moved the adoption of Clause 21 of the report. Carried.

Dr. Britton read Clauses 22, 23, 24 and 25 of the report, which on motion were adopted as read.

Dr. Britton read Clause 26 of the report.

Dr. THORBURN—I would like to make some remarks about that before it is put. I was at the last meeting of the Dominion Medical Association at Kingston, and this subject was discussed. It had been up on several former occasions, and we all felt it was most desirable that there should be uniform registration and the same curriculum, if possible. The different Provinces, except Ontario, were particularly anxious for it. They admitted, however, the difficulties in the way, but they asserted we were the stumbling block. It was shown to them that it was not so, that we had a provision in our Act that allowed us to confer equal powers on the different Provinces if they come up to our standard. You will observe there that it is not true that we could be registered in England if we were a uniformity. I am not prepared to say who it was, but somebody gave his word at that meeting that an application had been made by Quebec to that effect, and that the minister who submitted it from Canada said it was impossible to entertain it, that no single Province could get that provision ; but if we were a unit in the Dominion we would get it without any question. I moved yesterday, or the day before, that a committee be appointed to meet the different delegates from the different Provinces at Montreal in August next. I was then told it was in this report, and I withdrew it. I hope that you will consider that, and let the two men be considered as delegates upon this occasion. The meeting is on the 26th, 27th and 28th, and if there had been some correspondence before, they can get there in the morning and consider the matter, with no delay or expense. I suggested the names, which as President of the Association I had a right to do, of our friend Dr. Bray, who is familiar with our rights, and Dr. Pyne ; I would also suggest the name of Dr. Cameron, but I am sorry to say he is not here, and I would like if you could name some other gentleman. I find the Quebec fellows have a pretty large majority, and I would like to have our party strengthened.

The CHAIRMAN—Is it intended that the delegates that will be sent will be sent at the expense of the Council?

Dr. THORBURN—No, I think not ; they will be any members who are going there.

Dr. BRAY—This matter came up before this Council some three or four years ago, and there was a delegation appointed from the Council with the understanding that they should not receive anything ; I was one of the parties appointed. We talked a lot, but nothing came of it. Dr. Thorburn mistakes, I think, about all the Provinces, except Ontario, being willing and anxious to go in. Certainly the old Maritime Provinces and Quebec are very anxious to reciprocate with Ontario, but we are told that the delegates from British Columbia and Manitoba did not want anything of the kind ; it was not to their advantage ; that while it was to our advantage here, we were graduating any number of students and hadn't room for them, and they would flock up there, they were not graduating any more than they wanted up there, and they would not be coming here ; and while that lasted they would not consent. Those were the reasons that they gave, and they would not enter into it at all. I think it would be a very grand thing if we could have this. I have advocated for ten years or more to have reciprocity between the Provinces. They have different courses ; British Columbia three years, others four, and we require five. If you can assimilate the standard of matriculation and medical education, I think any other difficulty can be got over. But that is one great difficulty ; another difficulty is the clause in our own Act, referring to any Province that has an examining body independent of the schools. I think perhaps there should be some give and take on the part of all these Provinces ; and I think if there was a delegation sent from this Council it would show we had a desire to do what we could in the matter. I would be very glad to have a delegation sent from here if it is understood it will be no expense to this Council. We chose members likely to attend the Dominion Medical Association, which was held in Ottawa at that time, and it is to be held in Montreal this time. I do not know how many they ask for, but would it not be just as well for this Council to give any gentleman, who intends going, authority, and ask him to attend as a delegate of this Council?

Dr. BRITTON moved the adoption of Clause 26, and also moved that the following be added to it : "That any members of this Council who will visit the meeting of the Canadian Medical Association at Montreal in August next, be requested to act in concert as a committee to meet the committees from the other Provinces, and to report to the Council at the next session, without expense to the Council."

Dr. WILLIAMS—Before that clause is passed, I want to make a remark about it. I do not agree in one respect with Dr. Bray at all ; he seems to think the great stumbling block is in our Act. It seems to me that it is not there but in the fact that the other Provinces have no control of their examinations ; they simply accept graduates from the different schools and register them, on condition that they pass their matriculation. Now, I think that is the foundation difficulty of the whole trouble. So far as the matriculation is concerned, I think that trouble could be assimilated without any great difficulty—I think likely at a conference. And if they keep themselves to the matriculation it should be very easily adjusted, and that might be of some advantage to the students or to the persons wishing to register in the different Provinces. There is the medical curriculum, and I think there will be some little difficulty in getting them all to agree upon that, but ultimately those two points will be conceded. The third point, which is the fundamental point of the whole, getting examinations held independently of the teaching bodies, the same as we have here ; that is a point they are not likely to agree upon for some considerable time, and I think that is the foundation to the whole thing. We could certainly not recommend this Province to go into a reciprocal condition with any of the other Provinces if they accept students from the schools that might be scattered about the country without any knowledge at all as to how their standard may be.

Dr. THORBURN—The object of the committee is to consider that.

The Chairman put the motion for the adoption of Clause 26 of the report, and on a vote having been taken declared it carried.

Dr. Britton read Clause 27 of the report, which on motion was adopted as read.

Dr. Britton read Clause 28 of the report.

Dr. BRITTON—I might explain to some members of the committee that this matter came up after the adjournment of the committee last night, when it was too late to ask the committee to remain any longer, consequently the Secretary and myself went over that again this morning. It is not a very important matter, at any rate. However, we considered some of the text books were getting a little antiquated, and we thought it better to have them replaced. I have introduced this without consulting all the members of the committee ; I have consulted some of them.

Dr. BRITTON moved the adoption of Clause 28.

Dr. GEIKIE—Should it not be stated that the books are not placed in the order of merit ? That is important. For instance, in physiology, Kirke is placed before Foster, and Foster is much the more encyclopædic.

Dr. BRITTON—I think it would be for a teacher to advise his pupils.

Dr. GEIKIE—The Council are supreme, and the teacher recommends the book agreed on by the College.

Dr. BROCK—We have now a course of ten lectures on mental diseases, and I would ask that a text book by a very well known medical man of this city, and one who has all respect, should be placed on the list ; the book I refer to is "Mental Diseases," by Dr. Daniel Clark ; it is a new work.

Dr. SHAW—Is it any good ?

Dr. MOORHOUSE—I do not think I would put that on without having it supervised.

Dr. WILLIAMS—I have been spoken to about it, and it has been recommended very highly to me. It is said to be a very clever little work ; whether it is or not I do not know. I have not seen it. With reference to the Medical Council putting down a list of text books, it would be just as well if the entire list was struck out, and let the teachers indicate to the scholars what books they choose.

Dr. MOORE—Dr. Clark is undoubtedly a very clever man, but he holds many radical views.

Dr. BRAY—In reply to what Dr. Williams has said, if they are all wiped out, I have just learned from a gentleman who knows, that if we name our text books they get them in with a great deal less duty to pay, and I think for that reason we should name them.

Dr. DICKSON—If this Council name the text books they should have a conference of the teaching bodies of the Province, and let them come to an understanding of the books to be chosen. I think it would be better to do so than for this Council at a short session, or in committee, to determine the list. There should be a conference.

Dr. BRITTON—Before the Secretary and myself decided to make any change in the list to be submitted to the Council for approval, we had a consultation with some of the medical faculty of the University of Toronto, and on composing the list as it appears in their annual announcement we came to the conclusion to suggest these changes which I speak of now.

Dr. GEIKIE—You mean the text books ?

Dr. BRITTON—Yes.

Dr. MACHELL—I move that the American Text Book of Obstetrics be added to that ; it is the most recent, and, I believe, the most complete, and the best work for the students to read.

Dr. BRITTON moved that Clause 28, as amended, be adopted. Carried.

Dr. BRITTON moved that the committee rise and report. Carried.
The committee rose. The President in the chair.

To the President and members of the Medical Council of the College of Physicians and Surgeons of Ontario :

GENTLEMEN,—Your Education Committee were convened on the 9th inst., when Dr. Britton was elected Chairman and Dr. Moorhouse as Secretary. A sub-committee to aid the Chairman, consisting of Drs. Williams and Moorhouse, were appointed.

1. F. K. Reybold, of Philadelphia *Record*, sent a communication *re* Buchanan diplomas. Your committee recommend that the Registrar reply, asking for a copy of all the names of those holding such diplomas in Canada.

2. A deputation consisting of representatives from the University of Toronto, Trinity Medical College and the Woman's Medical College was received in reference to prescribing sessions of eight months each instead of six as at present existing ; also as to the desirability of eliminating the summer session and the fifth year of clinical work. After due consideration your committee concluded that in order to encourage and strengthen the hands of any teaching bodies in their efforts to secure a higher standard of professional training who may choose to adopt the eight months' session, it will be wise for this Council to fix the time of the Spring examination for the third Tuesday in May. In order to give sufficient time for the Examiners to report, it is also recommended that the by-law be so amended that the Council shall meet on the third Tuesday of June. We also recommend that students presenting tickets of eight months' sessions be exempted from attendance on the summer session.

3. On the 11th inst. the committee met and considered the report of the Board of Examiners. It was decided to ask the Registrar to look up a former resolution to the effect that a separate paper be set in therapeutics by the Examiner in Medicine, as it appears anomalous that the same Examiner should take both therapeutics and pathology.

4. Mr. Geo. A. Fish made application to be allowed his Primary examination, provided he has the license of the Royal College of Physicians and Surgeons of Great Britain. We recommend that he be referred to Sub-section 12, Section II. of Announcement of 1895-96.

5. It is recommended that W. F. Mayberry be allowed to take his Intermediate and Final examinations at the end of the fourth year, seeing that he took the B.A. Science course.

6. It is recommended that the petition of J. T. Clarke, of Foxboro, Ont., be not granted.

7. It is also recommended that the petition of G. Welsh, Dutton, Ont., be not granted.

8. Your committee recommend that the petition of Wellington Stephens, Trafalgar, Ont., be not granted.

9. C. W. McLeay, B.A., London, Ont., petitioned to be put on the four year course. Your committee recommend that his petition be granted, and that he be referred to Sub-section 2 of Section II., Annual Announcement.

10. Geo. S. Cameron, Oil City, Ont. It is recommended that he be granted his standing in the Primary examination upon completing his matriculation.

11. J. H. Fleming, St. George, Ont., petition not granted.

12. A. E. Burrows, Kingston, Ont., petition not allowed.

13. John McCormack, Glenlea, Man., petition granted.

14. Omer Rochon, of Clarence Creek, Ont., petition granted.

15. P. Ross. We recommend that he be required to complete his matriculation.

16. W. J. Fletcher, Chatham, Ont., request to be granted.

17. W. A. Kelly, Chatham, Ont., request to be granted.

18. Thomas M. Harrowell, Regina, N.W.T., request not granted.

19. W. C. Bremner, Toronto, Ont., petition allowed.

20. As your committee inferred from the character of the circular *re* Matriculation in Medicine recently issued by the Education Department that the Government had misunderstood some of the conditions of the agreement between the Special Committee appointed by the Legislature and the Legislation Committee and Executive of this Council, a sub-committee consisting of Drs. Sangster and Britton were appointed to wait on the Minister of Education. This was done, and with the result that the Hon. Mr. Ross cordially consented that such changes be made in the Departmental regulations as would harmonize with our convictions as to the exact nature of the original compact, and consequently expressed his willingness that we should arrange matriculation on that definite line.

Accordingly we recommend that the conditions for registration of matriculates be as follows :

(1) Any person who presents to the Registrar of the Medical Council a certificate that he has passed the examination conducted by the Education Department on the course pre-

scribed for matriculation in arts, including chemistry and physics, shall be entitled on payment of the lawful fees on that behalf to registration as a medical student within the meaning of Section 2 of the Ontario Medical Act.

(2) Any person who before this date has not passed the examination in all the subjects prescribed for matriculation as aforesaid, shall be entitled to registration as a medical student on submitting to the Registrar a certificate that he has completed such examination by passing in the remaining subjects of such matriculation, including chemistry and physics.

(3) Any student in medicine who submits to the Registrar certified tickets that he has attended not less than two courses of lectures at any chartered medical school or college in Canada, shall be entitled on payment of the lawful fees in that behalf, to take the Primary examination, provided that the standing obtained at such examination may not be allowed until such student presents to the Registrar the matriculation certificate.

(4) A certificate from the Registrar of any chartered university conducting a full arts course in Canada, that the holder thereof matriculated prior to his enrolment in such university and passed the examination in arts prescribed for students at the end of the first year, shall entitle such student to registration.

(5) Any person who on or before the 1st day of November, 1895, had passed the examination of any university in Canada, for matriculation in arts, or the matriculation examination conducted by the Education Department entitling to registration in arts with any university in Canada, or an examination entitling to registration with the Medical Council subsequent to July 1st, 1888, shall be entitled to registration on submitting to the Registrar a certificate to that effect signed by the proper officer in that behalf.

Synopsis.—From 1st July, 1888, to 1st November, 1892, second-class non-professional certificate with Latin. Since 1st November, 1892, the junior matriculation certificate with physics and chemistry, as prescribed and conducted by the Education Department of Ontario.

We understand that on the date of the conference above referred to, the Executive passed a resolution instructing the Registrar to accept applicants on the terms enunciated, and we fully approve of its action.

21. Dr. Geikie's resolutions were duly considered, and it is recommended that Sub-section 9 of Section III. remain unchanged, and that no reduction be made in the minimum percentage for pass in chemistry.

22. A communication was received from Dr. W. L. Yeomans *re* the five years' course ; petition not granted.

23. Also one from A. Grasett Smith, not allowed.

24. Benton C. Hazelwood asks to be registered as a matriculate. Request granted.

25. Petition of O. A. Marshall. Must conform to the regulation.

26. Your committee have carefully examined the report of the Committee of the Canadian Medical Association concerning inter-provincial registration.

(1) We concur in the regret expressed in the first clause of the report, and think all reasonable effort should be made to remove the disability expressed in the following words of the communication : " A graduate in medicine entitled to practise in one Province is not free to exercise his functions in all the Provinces of this large but sparsely settled Dominion."

The second clause reads as follows : " That this condition of things prevents the names of medical practitioners in this Dominion being placed on the British Register, becoming thereby British practitioners, which the Council of Medical Education of Great Britain has more than once signified its willingness to grant."

Your committee are not aware of the correctness of this contention, and are firmly pursuaded that as far as Ontario is concerned it is not correct. Provision is made in the British Medical Act, Clause 17, Sub-section 1, indicating the steps necessary by a colony to secure reciprocal registration, which seems to be imperative before the names of Canadian practitioners can appear on the British Register, which steps this Province has not taken.

The third clause is as follows : " That with this end in view it is therefore most desirable that there should be a uniform standard of matriculation, a uniform standard of medical education, and a uniform method of examination for the whole Dominion."

We quite concur in this, and think that the method of examination is the underlying difficulty in the matter.

We could not recommend that under existing circumstances we should have reciprocity with all the Provinces, for there are those over whose medical examinations there is no Council supervision. The examinations conducted by schools may not necessarily be above suspicion.

We are of the opinion that as to uniformity of matriculation and uniformity in medical studies there would be little difficulty in arriving at satisfactory arrangements, and we further believe that were these steps secured they would be of some advantage to those engaged in the study of medicine.

The fourth clause suggests the sending of one or more delegates to a Dominion Committee for the purpose of adjusting a suitable curriculum and carrying out the suggestions contained in the communication, and that such committee be requested to forward their finding to each of the provincial Councils and to the Secretary of the Dominion Association before its next annual meeting.

Your committee would recommend that two members be appointed for this purpose to meet delegates from other Provinces at such time and place as can be satisfactorily arranged. Any members of committees to be delegates without expense to this Council. Carried.

27. We recommend that the personnel of the Board of Examiners be as follows :

Dr. F. LeM. Grasett, Toronto ....   *Anatomy, Descriptive.*

Dr. Mundell, Kingston ....   *Theory and Practice of Medicine.*

Dr. H. Howitt, Guelph ....   { *Midwifery, Operative and other than Operative, and Puerperal and Infantile Diseases.*

Dr. A. S. Fraser, Sarnia ....   *Physiology and Histology.*

Dr. A. B. Welford, Woodstock ....   *Surgery, Operative and other than Operative.*

Dr. H. Williams, London ....   *Medical and Surgical Anatomy.*

Dr. G. Acheson, Galt ....   *Chemistry, Theoretical and Practical, and Toxicology.*

Dr. H. B. Small, Ottawa..........   *Materia Medica and Pharmacy.*

Dr. C. V. Emory, Hamilton ......   *Medical Jurisprudence and Sanitary Science.*

Dr. C. O'Reilly, Toronto..........   *Assistant Examiner to the Examiner on Surgery.*

Dr. Third, Kingston ....   *1st Assistant Examiner to the Examiner on Medicine.*

Dr. W. P. Caven, Toronto........   { *2nd Assistant to the Examiner on Medicine, Pathology and Therapeutics.*

Dr. D. J. Sinclair, Woodstock ....   *Homœopathic Examiner.*

28. We recommend the following list of text books :

I. General Text Books.

Anatomy—Gray, Quain, Cunningham's Practical Anatomy.

Physiology—Foster, Kirke, Yeo.

Chemistry—Roscoe, Attfield, Remsen and Jones, Richter, Simons.

Materia Medica—Ringer, Mitchell Bruce, Hare's Therapeutics, British Pharmacopœia.

Surgery—Erichsen, Treves, Walsham, Mansell Moulin.

Medicine—Hilton Fagge, Strumpell, Osler.

Clinical Medicine—Gibson and Russell, Vierordt.

Midwifery and Gynæcology—Lusk, Playfair, Thomas Mundé, Hart and Barber, and American Text Book of Obstetrics.

Medical Jurisprudence and Toxicology—Taylor, Reese.

Pathology—Ziegler, Green, Woodhead, Coates.

Sanitary Science—Wilson, Louis C. Parke.

Diseases of Children—Eustace Smith, Ashby and Wright, Goodhart.

II. Homœopathic Text Books.

Materia Medica—Hahnemann, Hering.

Medicine and Therapeutics—Goodno, Arndt, Raue Pathology and Diagnostics, Lilienthal.

Surgery—Fisher, Helmuth.

Midwifery—Guernsey, Ludlam.

All of which is respecfully submitted.

W. BRITTON, Chairman.

Carried. Adopted as amended.

J. P. ARMOUR,
Chairman Committee of Whole.

A. F. ROGERS, President.

Moved by Dr. BRITTON, seconded by Dr. MOORHOUSE, That the report of the Committee of the Whole be adopted. Carried.

Moved by Dr. WILLIAMS, seconded by Dr. BRITTON, That the Registrar be and is hereby instructed to make all necessary clerical alterations in the Announcement to adapt it to the year 1896-97, and such other alterations as have been authorized by the Council. I may say that this is a resolution we have usually passed in committee ; this year it was forgotten

Dr. McLAUGHLIN—I would like to inquire what is meant by "clerical errors."

Dr. WILLIAMS—Did I put it "errors" ?

The PRESIDENT—No, alterations.

Dr. WILLIAMS—For instance, this Announcement would be dated one year ; we want to have changed all things that become necessary to change by a change of the year. Sometimes we made it our business to go through and change these figures, but latterly we have instructed the Registrar to do it.

Dr. GEIKIE presented the report of the delegate to the British Medical Association, which met in London, England, in August of last year.

The report was received.

To the College of Physicians and Surgeons of Ontario :

The undersigned begs to report having conveyed, as directed to do by letter from the Registrar of the College, given by order of the Council last session, the hearty good wishes and greetings of this Council to the British Medical Association, which met in London, England, in August of last year.

I met that great body assembled under the chairmanship of the late lamented Sir Russell Reynolds, and as heartily as I was able conveyed our greetings to our British brethren. The message thus conveyed was well received and cordially reciprocated by the chairman on behalf of the British Medical Association.

All of which is respectully submitted. W. B. GEIKIE.

Toronto, June 13th, 1896.

Adopted. A. F. ROGERS, President.

Moved by Dr. WILLIAMS, seconded by Dr. MOORE, That Dr. Geikie's report be adopted. Carried.

Moved by Dr. WILLIAMS, seconded by Dr. SHAW, and resolved, That the mover have leave to introduce a by-law to amend By-law No. 39, and that it now be read a first time.

The President read the motion.

Dr. WILLIAMS—This is a by-law rendered necessary because of the adoption of the Education Committee's report.

The President put the motion, and on a vote having been taken declared it carried.

The by-law was read a first time.

Dr. WILLIAMS moved, seconded by Dr. HENRY, and resolved, That the Council do now go into Committee of the Whole to read a second time the by-law to amend By-law No. 39. Carried.

Council in Committee of the Whole. Dr. Logan in the chair.

The Chairman read the by-law.

Dr. WILLIAMS—The report read, I think, "the third Tuesday in June." I had written a by-law for the first Tuesday in July. I think it is necessary to count up whether or not we will have sufficient time to go into the Examiners' reports and have the matter ready for the Council before the first week in July. Dr. Pyne gave me the time that was consumed usually, and as near as I could make out it would require from four to six weeks, and I thought the first Tuesday in July would be as early as we could count upon. If you are all satisfied with that I will let it stand ; if you think an earlier day would do we will put it back a week.

Dr. BRAY—The first Tuesday of July might be the first of July, which would be a very awkward day.

Dr. WILLIAMS—It has been suggested that persons like to get away the first week in July. If Dr. Pyne will tell us he thinks there is sufficient time to get the work done, I have no objection to the fourth Tuesday in June.

Dr. WILLIAMS moved the adoption of the by-law. Carried.

Dr. WILLIAMS moved, seconded by Dr. BRITTON, That the committee do now rise and report the by-law passed in Committee of the Whole.

The committee rose. The President in the chair.

Dr. WILLIAMS moved, seconded by Dr. MOORE, and resolved, That the by-law be now read a third time and finally passed, signed, sealed and numbered. Carried.

By-law No. 76.

Whereas the Council of the College of Physicians and Surgeons of Ontario has power to make rules and regulations or pass by-laws governing the Council in its proceedings and times of meeting ; and whereas it is expedient that By-law No. 39 be amended,

Therefore be it enacted, and it is hereby enacted, that the first clause be amended by striking out the words "second Tuesday in June" and substituting the words "first Tuesday in July."

GEO. LOGAN, Chairman Committee of the Whole.

Adopted.   A. F. ROGERS, President.

FINANCE COMMITTEE'S REPORT.

Dr. HENDERSON presented the Finance Committee's report.

The report was received.

Dr. ARMOUR moved, seconded by Dr. DICKSON, That the Council go into Committee of the Whole to consider the Finance Committee's report.   Carried.

Council in Committee of the Whole.   Dr. Bray in the chair.

Dr. Henderson read Clause 1 of the report.

Dr. ARMOUR—I want to draw the attention of the Council to one item in connection with this section, a very small matter ; that is, the payment to the *Ontario Medical Journal*. We agreed to pay that journal $300.00 for a certain service.   That service was very indifferently performed.   However, I will not refer to that ; but it has been usual that what was paid to them was placed in a separate item in the financial statement, but that has not been done this year.   It is mixed up with what was paid to the stenographer and what was paid to the *Journal*.   There was an item of $347.19 paid to the stenographer for proceedings and other special reports ; when we come to investigate it, we find $256.00 of this was paid on account of the *Ontario Medical Journal*.   In addition to that, the *Ontario Medical Journal* received $150.00.   In all, last year the *Ontario Medical Journal* received $406 00, when the stipulated contract was for $360.00.   We looked into this matter to ascertain how they had got more than their contract, and we find, by going away back to 1893, the first year the *Journal* had the contract with the Council, they were paid $500.00 that year, and, so far as we could learn, the intention of the Council was that they were fully paid up for that year.   The contract at that time was that they were to be paid $50.00 a month for each issue of the *Journal*. After they got the contract in the first place the *Journal* began in August, and they issued ten issues of the *Journal* in that year, and consequently they received $500.00 only.   In 1894 they received $600.00, according to the contract ; in 1895 they received $600.00 ; and in 1896, instead of $360.00, they received $406.00.   Now I find that the Journal Company are asking for the payment of $54.00 additional to make up the $600.00 for 1893.   Perhaps the older members of the Council will know whether that is correct, but I could not find or get any reason to believe that it was not the intention of the Council in 1893, when we paid the Journal Company $500.00, that we paid them all they were entitled to at that time.   That is all I have to say regarding that matter.

Dr. Henderson read Clauses 1, 2, 3 and 4 of the report, which on motion were adopted.

Dr. Henderson read Clause 5 of the report.

Dr. ARMOUR—We passed a by-law last year which stipulated the amount which was to be paid and the Auditor did the work knowing that.   Of course, it is left at our discretion whether we pay him more or not.   We have provided to pay him more for the future.   He did the work knowing the consideration was fixed.   I think we should not set aside a by-law by a report of this kind.

The CHAIRMAN—I do not think you are setting aside a by-law by paying him more.   It is a very common thing to give a man a bonus.

Dr. THORBURN—What is given to the Auditor is generally at the end of the year ; it is settled by the parties.   He may understand it is so and so, but each and every year you have got to name the sum.

Dr. BROCK—We named the sum of $20.00 last year.

Dr. McLAUGHLIN—It is a very strange principle you are establishing.   You pass a by-law for what purpose?   To bring, in a special way, before a body that it will be clearly understood what the grant is and the amount to be given.   Surely you do not over-ride that by resolution ; if you do you open the door that may lead to serious mischief hereafter. I would provide a special by-law or give him $60.00 for the ensuing year, rather than alter that.   I do not think you have any right to do it.

Dr. BARRICK—It seems to me that this is, a very exceptional case.   It is the first year we have ever had an Auditor appointed by this Council

The CHAIRMAN—No, not the first year.

Dr. BARRICK—Has there ever been an Auditor appointed by by-law before?   I think you will find that I am correct, that last year was the first time that this Council ever appointed an Auditor by by-law. As one of those who supported the appointment of that Auditor I was not aware, and very few of the members of this Council were aware, what duties that Auditor would have to perform, whether they were more or whether they were less, whether they were worth $20.00, $30.00 or $40.00 ; and the Auditor in accepting that position, not knowing what the work to be done was, was just as much in the dark in deciding whether he should accept that amount as we were in offering it. And therefore I think it is quite proper for us now, when you understand what the work has been, and Dr. Pyne has stated that there was a good deal of work to be done, and the Auditor now knows what the work is and feels he was underpaid, that the figures we have adopted here in this exceptional case should pass without any discussion.

Dr. ARMOUR—I move that that clause of the report be struck out.

Dr. McLAUGHLIN—I second that motion, because while I have no objection that in some way or other the Auditor should get the full amount of his remuneration, I would like it to be done in a way that we would not establish a precedent that might be worked for some bad purpose. I think if we have laws that demand that money should be granted by by-law we should stick to it and not be over-riding by-laws by simple resolutions.

The Chairman put Dr. Armour's motion that the clause be struck out.

Dr. DICKSON—Will you support a motion to grant the additional sum ?

Dr. McLAUGHLIN—I am willing to support a lawful motion. I am willing to change the other to $60.00 so that he shall get a proper remuneration, but I do not believe in breaking a by-law in a mode of this kind.

The CHAIRMAN—You think the $40.00 is right, but you object to the way in which it is given.

Dr. BROCK—We settled by by-law that Dr. Carlyle was to receive $20.00 last year. We have settled by by-law that he is to receive $40.00 this year. That settles the question. He received $20.00 for last year, he will receive $40.00 for this year.

Dr. ARMOUR—But this report will permit him to receive $40.00 for last year.

Dr. BROCK—I can hardly understand a report coming in this way that is a by-law last year. It leaves him so that he may demand more and the Council may be compelled to give it to him.

Dr. ARMOUR—That clause in the report refers to Dr. Carlyle's communication, and it gives it to him for last year.

Dr. BROCK—I understood when you put this item here that the Auditor should receive for the next year $40.00. When I came to the Council I found Dr. Barrick had already prepared a by-law to that effect, naming the very sum which you wish to put in, and I considered the $40.00 was for this year.

The CHAIRMAN—Let us change the report to $20.00 and have it understood that Dr. McLaughlin or somebody else shall move that on account of the Auditor's services being greater than we supposed they would be, we grant him a bonus of $20.00.

Dr. ARMOUR—We do not need to strike out the figure only ; strike out the whole clause.

Dr. McLAUGHLIN—I think it is a pity that Dr. Carlyle, having accepted the by-law, did not submit to the remuneration offered. If I had been in that position I would not come to the Council and ask for more money. If he would just allow that matter to drop and get us out of the difficulty into which we will get——

Dr. Henderson reads clause.

Dr. DICKSON—That reads as if for this year's remuneration ; that is what I understood in the committee.

Dr. HENDERSON—It is for the past year. It does not say so in the report.

Dr. McLAUGHLIN—I move that that be struck out; it is not very clear what is meant, but the intention is very clear he is to get $40.00 instead of $20.00.

Dr. BARRICK—Is the result of that that Dr. Carlyle gets nothing at all ?

The CHAIRMAN—No, there is a by-law fixing his remuneration at $20.00 and he gets that.

Dr. BROCK—We have inserted in our estimates for this year, "Auditor $40.00." We have settled by by-law his payment for last year ; that is settled.

The CHAIRMAN put the motion made by Dr. Armour, seconded by Dr. McLaughlin, That the clause of the report be struck out, which on a vote being taken was declared carried.

Dr. Henderson read Paragraphs 7 and 8 of the report, which on motion were adopted as read.

The CHAIRMAN—That is all the Discipline Committee have cost the Council this past year.

Dr. Henderson read Paragraph 9 of the report, which on motion was adopted as read.

Dr. Henderson read Clause 10 of the report.

Dr. HENDERSON—One of those letters has already been read and it is on a par with all the others, so that I do not think it would be necessary to read them.

Dr. Armour—I want to ask through the Chairman a question of Dr. Henderson, the Chairman of the Finance Committee, whether there are any other communications bearing on this subject received by the Registrar or by the College.

Dr. Henderson—Not that I am aware of.

Dr. Thornton—I understand these are in connection with the assessment tax.

The Chairman—I do not know ; I believe they are.

Dr. Thornton—Are those the only communications received by the Registrar in connection with the tax, or are they a selection out of the ones he did receive ?

The Registrar—Members sending their fee often write a letter with it.

Dr. Thornton—Do the writers of those letters send their fee with them ?

The Registrar—No, some did not.

Dr. Thornton—Why are those letters taken and perhaps some others excluded ?

. The Registrar—Because they requested them to be brought before the Council. I do not put a man's letters before the Council, enclosing fees, unless he asks me.

On motion Clause 10 was adopted.

Dr. Henderson read Clauses 11, 12, 13, 14, 15, 16 and 17 of the report, which on motion were adopted as read.

Dr. Henderson read Clause 18 of the report and said : Dr. Aikins has done his work very well and the work has increased materially. We think his salary ought to be increased and I move the adoption of Clause 18 of this report.

Clause 18 of the report was adopted as read.

Dr. Henderson read Clauses 19 and 20, which on motion were adopted as read.

Dr. Henderson read Clause 21.

Dr. Thornton—There was never a committee appointed to dispose of it.

Dr. Armour—You had better say the proper committee, that will make it right.

On motion Clause 21 of the report was adopted.

Dr. Henderson read Clause 22 of the report, which on motion was adopted as read.

Dr. Henry—I may say I think he is well entitled to it. I know he was up in my section of the country once or twice ; and one fellow he did good work with and brought him to time. The Kickapoo Indians heard that the magistrate wouldn't take security and the fellow skipped. I know from my experience Mr. Wasson has done a great deal of good.

On motion Clause 23 of the report was carried.

Dr. Henderson moved the adoption of the financial statement. Carried.

Dr. Henderson moved the adoption of the reports of the Auditor, also approximate statement of receipts and expenditure.

Dr. Barrick asked to have the estimates read.

Dr. Henderson—This is simply an approximation.

Dr. Henderson read estimates.

Dr. Henderson moved the adoption of the report as amended in Committee of the Whole. Carried.

FINANCE COMMITTEE REPORT.

To the President and members of the Ontario Medical Council :

Gentlemen,—Your Committee on Finance beg to submit the following report :

The Treasurer's statement with accompanying report of Auditor, according to instructions from this Council, were placed before you on the first day of the session, thereby giving an opportunity to every member to know our present financial standing.

We have carefully examined the Registrar's books, and all accounts and papers referred to us, and have compared them with the financial statement of the Treasurer, and have pleasure in stating that after due consideration of the same we find them to be correct, both officers having discharged their duties in their usual efficient manner.

The petitions and accounts referred to us have also been duly considered, and we recommend as follows :

The account of our Solicitor, B. B. Osler, for services rendered to date, certified by Registrar as correct, of $190.05, to be paid.

Also that of Rolph, Smith & Co., for diplomas and cases, $103.40.

Dr. F. Fowler's account, for acting as Deputy Registrar at Kingston, $40.00, the Auditor considering his remuneration inadequate to the labor required of him. We advise $40.00.

The Harper account Queen vs. J. E. Fox, payment to Harper, $12.50, and Crown Attorney Farewell, $24.50, be paid.

The Discipline Committee meeting of present session, $37.50.

Re insurance on elevator. We accepted that of the Ontario Accident Company, their tender being the lowest.

The letters received *re* assessment dues from Drs. M. H. Aikins, Mencke, Lang, Jackson, Preston, Bibbie, Clemeshaw, Jackes, Matheson, Peters, Bell, Bingham, Arnott and the Lóndon Medical Association, we recommend to be read for your deliberation.

In the case of Ezra Briggs, no action to be taken.

In the case of Dr. E. B. O'Reilly, objecting to being assessed while absent from the Province for a period of eight years, as he was disfranchised from voting by the Council, we agree to accept his payment of fees from 1892 to date.

Colfax's request granted on account of illness during examination.

To save extra labor for Registrar and Treasurer, we suggest that all members of Council may pay assessment dues direct to Registrar before receiving their sessional allowance.

We recommend that the temporary loans from the bank be arranged, if possible, at a less rate of interest, and as two loans amounting to $4,400.00 are now due, that immediate provision be made for the same, and for the necessary bank accommodation to defray expenses of present meeting of Council, by the officers appointed for that purpose.

In supplying certificates under the Act the members of College must pay all arrears before receiving such certificate.

We also advise that it be left to the discretion of the Registrar whether the Official Announcement be supplied to others than members of the Council.

On account of increased labor and extra time devoted in the interests of the Council, we recommend that the salary of the Treasurer be $500.00 per annum.

We believe that the necessities of the Council demand the annual fee of $2.00 to be collected, and recommend that steps be taken to that end.

In regard to Council building, we advise that the Property Committee be authorized to arrange for its disposal, or act as they deem best in the interests of your body.

In reference to Prosecutor, we recommend the re-engagement of Mr. Wasson, at a salary of $600.00 per annum, but before proceeding in doubtful cases, he must receive the approval of the committee appointed for that purpose, and in view of his loss the past year in connection with prosecutions amounting to nearly $400.00, we recommend that he be paid $200.00 to partially compensate him for his loss.

We append financial statement :

Assets.

Building and site	$100,000	00
Assessment dues uncollected	11,000	00
" " for 1896	˙5,000	00
Council chamber and office furniture	3,000	00
Cash in bank	45	00
Total	$119,045	00

Liabilities.

Mortgage on building	$60,000	00
Notes in bank now due	4,400	00
Estimated cost of present session	3,500	00
Accounts ordered to be paid	435	45
Total	$68,335	45
Balance in favor of Council	$50,709	55

Appended hereto are the reports of Auditor, also an approximate estimate of receipts and expenditure.

All of which is respectfully submitted.

G. HENDERSON, Chairman of Committee.

V. L. BRAY, Chairman Committee of Whole.

Adopted as amended. A. F. ROGERS.

To the members of the Council of the College of Physicians and Surgeons of Ontario :

GENTLEMEN,—I beg to submit herewith my report for the Council year 1895–1896, just past :

Receipts.

Balance on hand, June 12th, 1895, at credit of College account, in Imperial Bank of Canada...........................		$1,015 62
One registration fee, referred to in last year's statement......		20 00
Assessment dues—collected from members of the Council	$235 00	
Assessment dues—collected by the Registrar.......	3,378 00	
Assessment dues—collected by bank..............	3,470 00	
	$7,083 00	7,083 00
Deduct amount collected by the Treasurer from Council members	235 00	
	$6,848 00	

This sum represents the actual amount of assessment dues collected during the year.

Office rents, new building.................................		3,215 86
Registration fees...		1,631 00
Fines of persons practising illegally.......................		793 02
Fees for professional examinations, Fall............$1,410 00		
" " " Spring 8,505 00		
		9,915 00
Temporary loans, Imperial Bank		61,503 90
Total receipts..........................		$85,177 40

Disbursements.

Council meeting, June, 1895—		
Members' allowance $4,189 49		
Stenographic report of proceedings, special re-.ports typewritten, copying, etc., etc........	337 43	
		$4,526 92
Salaries—		
Registrar $1,800 00		
Treasurer	400 00	
Official Prosecutor.................... $35 54		
550 00		
	585 54	
		2,785 54
Official Prosecutor, T. Wasson—		
Amount of fines collected from illegal practitioners		793 02
Prosecutions—Legal, stenographic and other expenses		1,067 80
Discipline Committee for 1894–1895.......................		308 65
Printing diplomas, examination papers, etc., etc.............		279 65
Ontario Medical Journal Publishing Company, balance of contract for 1894–1895................................		150 00
Executive Committee....................................		78 08
Legislation Committee....................................		124 48
Disbursements *re* Legislation		56 63
Holding Professional Examinations—		
General expenses $197 25		
Examiners' fees, etc, Fall.................. 579 45		
" " Spring 1,543 04		
		2,319 74

Assessment dues collected from Council members, paid over to
the Registrar...................................... $235 00
Fees returned to students............................... 140 00
Audit of Treasurer's books and vouchers for 1894–1895...... 25 00
Registrar's office supplies (including postage on circulars to
members of the College, etc., $383.50) 517 75
Treasurer's office expenses, etc., for Council years 1894–1895
and 1895–1896.................................... 30 00
Interest on mortgages to Canada Life Assurance Company.... 3,000 00

Temporary loans repaid—

Discounts $64,093 95
Interest................................. 606 05
———— 64,700 00
Interest on overdrafts 24 35
Bank charges, re collection of assessment dues, costs, commis-
sions, etc.. 111 26

New Building Maintenance—

Caretaker $510 00
Elevatorman and fireman..................... 315 00
Gas....................................... 238 89
Water 483 20
Carpenter's repairs......................... 210 43
Plumbing repairs 152 47
Painting, glazing, paperhanging, etc........... 91 97
Elevator repairs 103 73
Electric and pneumatic bell service repairs...... 43 90
Miscellaneous repairs....................... 60 28
Building supplies and repairs................. 256 00
Commission on rent collections 150 82
Telephone for year.......................... 45 00
Insurance on boiler 20 00
Heating 510 46
Taxes.................................... 665 81
———— 3,857 96
Balance on deposit in Imperial Bank...................... 45 57
————
$85,177 40

Balance as per statement $45 57
Balance as per Bank pass-book $114 62
Cheques outstanding 69 05
———— $45 57

All of which is respectfully submitted.

W. T. Aikins, Treasurer.
Toronto, June 3rd, 1896.

I have audited the books of the College of Physicians and Surgeons of Ontario for the year ending May 31st, 1896 ; I have also compared the receipts and vouchers with the income and expenditure. I have found all correct and satisfactory. The above statement corresponds with the books.

J. Carlyle, Auditor.

Estimates for 1896-97.

Receipts.

Assessment dues, say.................................... $15,000 00
Rents of building, say................................... 4,200 00
Registration fees, say 2,000 00
Examinations, say 9,000 00
————
$30,200 00

Expenditure.

Fees owing to members of Discipline Committee ..	$37	00
Present meeting, say	3,000	00
Salaries	2,800	00
Discipline Committee—prosecutions, printing, etc.,	500	00
Legislation	500	00
Examinations	2,400	00
Fees returned to students, say	200	00
Auditor	40	00
Registrar's office supplies	500	00
Treasurer's office supplies	15	00
Interest on Mortgage	3,000	00
Room rent free.		
New building maintenance—		
Caretaker	510	00
Elevatorman and fireman	315	00
Gas	238	89
Water	483	20
Carpenter's repairs	210	43
Plumbing repairs	152	47
Painting, glazing, paperhanging, etc.	91	97
Elevator repairs	103	73
Electric and pneumatic bell service repairs....	43	90
Miscellaneous repairs	60	28
Building supplies and repairs	256	00
Commission on rent collections	150	82
Telephone for the year	45	00
Insurance on boiler	20	00
Heating	510	46
Taxes	665	81
	$3,857	96
	$16,347	96
Say, unforeseen contingencies	1,000	00
	$17,347	96

Copy of a resolution passed at a regular meeting of the London Medical Association, February 10th, 1896.

Moved by Dr. Ferguson, seconded by Dr. Arnott, and resolved, That the London Medical Association recognizes the services rendered to the medical profession by the Council of the College of Physicians and Surgeons of Ontario, in maintaining an efficient standard of medical education for students, providing for the registration of licentiates, guarding the rights of registered practitioners, prosecuting unlicensed practitioners, and erasing the names of practitioners guilty of infamous or disgraceful conduct in a professional respect.

This Association accordingly holds it to be the duty of every member of the College of Physicians of Ontario promptly and loyally to pay the annual assessment fee levied in accordance with the provisions of the Ontario Medical Act, for the maintenance of the general expenses of the College ; and it is further claimed that members of the College taking exception to any of the administrative acts of the Council should seek reforms by way of the medical electorate rather than by attempting to withhold the payment of assessments authorized by the statute and indispensable to the very existence of a Council.

Yet this Association begs to protest against By-Law No. 69, passed by the Council on the 28th of June, 1895, which suspends the penal clause of Section 41a of the amended Medical Act for Ontario until June 1st, 1896, then to come into force only "in case a sufficient amount of dues is not paid in to cover the bank liability." This Association submits that said qualification is grossly unjust to members of the profession who have paid or may pay their assessment prior to June 1st, 1896, and affords a loop-hole to delinquents who are disposed to shirk payment of their fees. The Association recommends the Ontario Medical Council either to rescind said clause of the by-law, or, otherwise, to furnish every member on payment of his fee a guarantee that no other member shall be permitted to escape payment of his legal indebtedness to the Council.

And resolved further, that a copy of these resolutions be forwarded to the Registrar and to the medical journals of the Province.

To the President and members of the Medical Council of the College of Physicians and Surgeons of Ontario :

GENTLEMEN,—I beg leave to submit for your consideration my annual report commencing June 1st, 1895, and ending May 31st, 1896, giving a detailed statement of fines imposed, amount collected, and expenses incurred in carrying out the provisions of the Ontario Medical Act.

Previous to June, 1895, the Council paid all expenses and received all fines from prosecutions, paying me a salary of $400.00 a year. In nearly all cases the amount of convictions was equal to the amount of expenses, but the trouble was to collect the fines, as a number went to jail, others skipped out, and some appealed, which made the amount paid out by the Council largely in excess of receipts.

At the meeting of the Council in June, 1895, at the suggestion of the Council, I signed an agreement to pay all expenses in prosecutions and to receive all fines, making my salary $600.00 a year. I have endeavored to the best of my ability to carry out my contract, and at the end of the year find myself several hundred dollars out of pocket.

I may state that a good deal of that is owing to complaints from medical men all over the Province, who after receiving a notice from the Registrar to pay the dues, in a great many cases the answer was that there was a quack in their district and they desired to be protected from such. I took three men with me and made an investigation of nearly all the places reported. I found a great many of them were over a year ago, the parties having gone away, and some that under our Act we could not convict. I had to pay all the expenses incurred. Since then I have had to be very careful what cases I undertook to prosecute so that I could get a conviction to try and cover expenses. Even in some cases where conviction has been had we never got the fines, as some of the defendants go to jail, others skip out. It is a well-known fact that the magistrate invariably, if he knows the prosecutor is interested in the fines, will dismiss the case, and in nearly every case the defendant will employ counsel to defend him.

In the case of Prof. Crane, of Buffalo, who was arrested and tried at Dunville, the expenses amounted to over $150.00, and the result a conviction and a fine of $25.00, and defendant went to jail for one month.

Also in the case of Professor Gustin, of Orangeville, who was allowed out on his own bail by the magistrate and skipped.

In the case of Black, of Toronto, who went to attend a patient in Orangeville, accompanied by a doctor from Toronto, who made the examinations, and Black then prescribed the herbs. Evidence was taken in this by a stenographer, and solicitors on both sides, and the case was dismissed and the expenses were heavy. Some parts of the accounts I am still disputing.

In the case of Druggist Wright, of Toronto Junction. This case was remanded several times, and a petition and letters were sent to the President, asking him to stay proceedings, counsel and witnesses had to attend at each day's trial, which was very costly, and he was only fined $25.00 and costs.

There have been a number of appeals, the Council paying the cost of the same.

Dr. N. Washington's appeal dismissed with costs, Washington having gone to reside in Milwaukee, U.S.A. A second charge was laid against him in Crysler. I served him with a summons in Toronto, but he did not appear, so I went to Crysler and got the trial proceeded with in his absence. He was fined $50.00 and costs. The fine is not yet paid, he having gone to the States ; a warrant is issued for his arrest.

In the case of W. F. Coulson, representing the M. V. Lubon Medicine Co. Two years ago I prosecuted him, he was convicted and fined ; he appealed the case and had the conviction quashed. This year I worked up a stronger case, had him convicted and fined $75.00 and costs, and he again appealed, but the conviction was sustained with costs against him.

The Loftus Medicine Co. conviction was quashed without costs.

In the McCarthy appeal case the conviction was sustained with costs against him. Since then I have had him prosecuted and fined $75.00 and costs. He has again appealed to the Sessions in Brantford.

At the Council meeting in June, 1895, several medical practitioners were reported for unprofessional conduct. During the year I have been getting up evidence, which I have submitted to the Discipline Committee.

In regard to prosecutions, I might suggest that a Committee on Medical Infractions, the same as the Discipline Committee, could be appointed by the Council, so that all matters could be submitted to them instead of consulting the Solicitor when appeals and other matters are brought to my notice.

Trusting the above report will meet with your approval, and while I am in the service of the Council I shall endeavor to carry out your views and the spirit of the Medical Act.

Since the last meeting of the Council I have been appointed by the Federal Government a Constable in the Dominion Police Force (without salary), having authority in all parts of the Dominion.

All of which is respectfully submitted.

THOMAS WASSON,

Detective C. P. and S. O.

PROSECUTIONS.

Number of Cases Investigated, Prosecuted, Etc.

Name and Address.	Amount of Fine.	Amount Paid.
R. S. T. Gilmour, Wiarton........	$25 00	$25 00
James Beaton, Kincardine	25 00	25 00
Dr. G. E Fell, Ridgeway.........	35 00	35 00
J. S. Powley, Toronto............	25 00	25 00
William Gilbert, Huntsville.......	27 00	27 00
J. W. Black, Toronto.............	25 00	25 00
A. P. Sterrit, Toronto...........	35 00	35 00
Ruth Beasley, Toronto...........	25 00	25 00
Dr. N. Washington, Crysler......	50 00	50 00
W. R. McNab, Tara..............	25 00	25 00
T. A. Pine, Northbrook..........	25 00	25 00
F. H. McCarthy, Ottawa..........	40 00	40 00
Dr. A. Oumet, Ottawa...........	25 00	25 00
Mrs. R. Thompson, Ottawa.......	25 00	25 00
Mrs. R. Lange, Ottawa...........	25 00	25 00
T. A. Pine, Flinton.............	25 00	25 00
A. Robertson, Maberley..........	25 00	25 00
A. Finley, Mountain Grove........	25 00	5 00
Professor Glen, Wasego..........	25 00	Not paid
T. H. Blow, Wiarton............	25 00	25 00
Professor Millar. Walkerton.......	25 00	25 00
Dr. N. Washington, Crysler.......	50 00	Not paid
R. S. Sneadley, Toronto..........	25 00	25 00
H. R. Buckley, Toronto..........	25 00	25 00
Mrs. A. McKelvie, Ottawa....	25 00	Not paid
Professor Crane, Dunville........	25 00	Not paid
M. A. Graham, Toronto..........	25 00	Not paid
T. Pine, Northbrook.............	25 00	25 00
W. F. Coulson, Toronto..........	75 00	75 00
D. McCarthy, Paris..............	76 02	76 02
Loftus Med. Co., Stratford........	50 00	Not paid
Chas. Wright, Tor. Junction.	25 00	25 00
D. McCarthy, Paris..............	75 00	Not paid
Professor Gardeau, Thessalon......	25 00	Not paid

Total.. $1,113 02

Kickapoo Indians, Stevensville, case dismissed ; J. McKelvey, St. Catharines, no case ; Henry Musson, Allenburgh, no case ; Sent man to Cornwall to prosecute Washington, found he had skipped ; A. McLeod, Owen Sound, no case ; A. N. Cadieux, Toronto, case dismissed ; Mrs. Beauvine, Crysler, no case ; Mary A. Lebreik, Toronto, no case ; Mrs. A. McKelvie, Ottawa, gone to jail ; S. Townsend, Ottawa, withdrawn ; Prof. Gustin, Orange-ville, skipped, warrant for his arrest ; J. Bealing, North Bend, withdrawn ; Mrs. John Kane, Ottawa, no case ; Mrs. E. Thompson, Ottawa, no case ; Mrs. Ann Kelly. Ottawa, no case ; Mrs. W. Ackland, Ottawa, no case ; Mrs. Sharron, Clarkstown, no case ; Mrs. Beeton, Baytown, no case ; Dr. Jebb, Orangeville, left the day I arrived there ; Mrs. Mitchell, Delaware, no case ; J. W. Black, Orangeville, case dismissed ; Dr. High, Doon, information laid, he did not appear, warrant issued for his arrest ; Matilda Spring, Dorchester, no case ; Mr. Doreland, Hawkesbury, left the place, no case ; Joseph Zehr, Topping, could not be found, was travelling with his father ; Professor Shrieves, Moravian-town, no case ; J. H. Chatton, Fenelon Falls, no case ; Opticians, Ottawa, does not come under the Medical Act ; Mrs. J. E. Fox, Whitby, agent for Viavi, case dismissed ; Philo Crane, Dunville, went to jail ; Kickapoo Indians, Tilbury, the information laid, the professor skipped, there is a warrant out for his arrest ; James Upham, Gardo, case dis-missed ; Professor Gardeau, Georgina, fined $25.00 but skipped ; Kickapoo Indians, Chelsea, case dismissed with costs ; Professor Bell, Evanstown, no case ; Professor Chamberlain,

Toronto, evidence not sufficient, case withdrawn ; M. A. Graham, Toronto, fined, allowed time and skipped ; Mrs. Killakie, Toronto, no case. Dr. E. A. A. B. Rose, Portland, has been practising since being erased by the Council. I had to stop him and he promised to leave Ontario. I have interviewed a number of jewellers who advertise as opticians, and upon advice I find the Medical Act will not convict them. They are taught by a medical gentleman in Toronto. I went to Huntsville after Prof. Gustin, but I found that he had gone to Michigan ; I had a warrant for his arrest.

Prosecutions.—Twenty-five convictions paid, 8 convictions not paid, 23 investigations, no cases ; 6 cases dismissed, 2 gone to jail, 2 withdrawn, 4 skipped out, 5 appeals.

Receipts.

Thirty-four convictions amounting to.....................		$1,113 02
Total amount paid by Registrar to Prosecutor	$793 02	
Fines as unpaid, some having skipped, gone to jail, etc	320 00	
Total..................................		$1,113 02

Expenditure.

Amount of cash paid by Prosecutor................	$901 25	
Accounts received by Prosecutor but not yet paid....	277 00	
Total.................................		$1,178 25
Total amount of expenditure paid by Prosecutor in excess of fines received..		$385 23

THOMAS WASSON,
Detective C. P. and S. O.

DISCIPLINE COMMITTEE.

Expenditure.

Dr. E. A. A. B. Rose, Portland—Expenses of investigation in Brockville in May, 1895, which should have been in last year's accounts	$126 08
Amount for the several investigations since June, 1895, to June, 1896, inclusive	120 37
Total	$246 45

Toronto, June 1st, 1896.

The committee rose. The President in the chair.

Moved by Dr. HENDERSON, seconded by Dr. ARMOUR, That the report of the committee be adopted. Carried.

Dr. BARRICK—I have a motion. In order to enable the Printing Committee to carry out the instructions of the Council to have the Announcement and proceedings of the Council placed in the hands of all registered practitioners in this Province in August of this year, That it be an instruction to the Registrar and Stenographer to prepare and place in the hands of the sub-committee the matter required to be inserted therein at as early a date as possible. This Council have instructed our committee to have the Announcement printed and put into the hands of the registered practitioners in August. In order to enable us to do that we must have instructions to the Registrar and Stenographer to let us have the matter so that we can get tenders on it at as early a date as possible. Carried.

Moved by Dr. MACHELL, seconded by Dr. WILLIAMS, That the President now leave the chair and the Vice-President, Dr. Thorburn, take the chair. Carried.

The President left the chair.

The Vice-President, Dr. Thorburn, in the chair.

Dr. MACHELL—Mr. Vice-President, I beg to move that the thanks of the Council should be tendered to Dr. Rogers, our President, for the able, impartial and dignified manner in which he has presided over all the deliberations of the meetings of this Council now about to be ended.

Dr. WILLIAMS—Mr. Vice-President, I have very great pleasure in supporting that motion that has been read and I do so with a good deal of earnestness, because I believe the statements therein made are not simply formal but are correct in this case. The gentleman who presided over this meeting has done so in a very satisfactory manner, according to my mind. I believe the word "impartial" there is properly and justly used. I think he has presided in a very satisfactory manner to the Council. Under these circumstances, I have a very great deal of pleasure in seconding that motion.

Dr. McLAUGHLIN—I can join heartily in the expressions of good-will that we all must cherish towards Dr. Rogers. I take his rulings as being extremely fair. I think he has strained points very often in order not to be harsh ; and he has given us all, I think, abundant opportunity to express our opinions, and so far as I am concerned and have been able to observe, Dr. Rogers has been very fair and very just in his rulings.

Dr. LUTON—I am and have been very much pleased with the conduct of Dr. Rogers as President. I think he has made it as pleasant for us all as he possibly could. He has succeeded admirably in his efforts to preserve harmony and order.

The Vice-President put the motion.

Dr. THORBURN—This is a resolution seconded by Dr. Williams, and I cannot express too heartily my own personal feelings in this matter. At one time I must admit we thought he had a good deal to say, when he first came here, but he has come down to be one of the sober, solid judges.

Dr. MOORE—He is married.

Dr. THORBURN—And I respect him. Is it your pleasure that this vote of thanks be passed ?

The motion was carried amid very loud applause.

The Vice-President, Dr. Thorburn, tendered the vote of thanks to the President, Dr. Rogers.

The President in the chair.

The PRESIDENT—Vice-President of the Council, Gentlemen of the Council, Drs. Machell and Williams, I appreciate very much indeed this vote of thanks and I appreciate very heartily the kind, and nice things which have fallen from the lips of Drs. Williams, McLaughlin and Luton. I entered the chair with a certain amount of misgiving, as I had never filled an office of this kind in this Council before or in any body of that character. I have been President of Medical Associations, but this I realized was of a different nature. However, I determined to be absolutely fair, so far as my lights went in the first place ; secondly, to do the best I could to forward the business of the Council and to make every member of it feel satisfied as far as possible. Whether I succeeded or not it is for you to say. At any rate, I have done my best to serve the interests of the members here at this meeting, and as I have done now it will be my pleasure to do whatever I can between now and the meeting of the Council to forward the best interests of our College. I appreciate very heartily the assistance I have received from all our members and I thank you for this pleasant expression of good-will towards me. (Applause.)

Moved by Dr. SHAW, seconded by Dr. WILLIAMS, That the minutes of the last meeting be now read. Carried.

The Registrar read the minutes of this meeting of the Council.

Dr. SANGSTER—Before the business is finished I want to make one remark. I do not know whether I am in order or not, but if I am not I presume you will stop me as you are still President. I was not in the room when the motion was made to tender the vote of thanks to the President. As I implied in my first remarks at the beginning of the session, I was not very sanguine of receiving fair play in the Council during your presidency. I wish simply to state my great gratification and to say that I feel grateful to you personally as well as in my position as a member of this Council, for your dignified, impartial and kind manner in the chair, and I would like this to be, if it can be, inserted in the proceedings as well as any other remarks that may have been made in this connection.

The PRESIDENT—I very much appreciate the remarks that have fallen from Dr. Sangster. I certainly intended to be impartial and to be thoroughly fair, whatever else I was, or whatever my faults might be. I am only human, and I might err, but as to being impartial I would be that and if I have received the good-will of all the members I am very glad indeed ; and I am very glad to have these remarks made by Dr. Sangster, and I appreciate them very heartily.

The President declared the minutes confirmed as read.

Dr. WILLIAMS moved, seconded by Dr. MOORE, That the Council do now adjourn. Carried.

A. Y. SCOTT, M.D.   D. MacMILLAN.

MESSRS.
SCOTT & MacMILLAN

Wish to announce to the Medical Profession of Canada that they have begun the manufacture of

PHARMACEUTICAL
SPECIALTIES . . . . .

Their Laboratory has been fitted up with the most improved machinery, and is under competent and experienced supervision. This firm will be pleased to send to any medical man samples of their specialties, if notified by post-card. Physicians can depend absolutely upon all preparations turned out by SCOTT & MacMILLAN being up to full strength.

Their Specialties Comprise . . . . .

VITALLIC SYRUP
of the Hypophosphites.
FLUID CASCARA AROMATIC
10-30 min.
ESSENCE PEPSIN.
ELIXIR LACTATED PEPSIN.
SYRUP ACID HYDRIODIC.

CALISAYA CORDIAL.
APODYNA.
SYRUP TRIFOLIUM COMP.
SYRUP WHITE PINE COMP.
BEEF, IRON AND WINE.
SYRUP FERRI IODIDE.
ELIXIR CORDIAL, ETC., ETC.

Please specify on all prescriptions S. & M.   Telephone Communication.

RECOLLECT THE ADDRESS—

14 and 16 MINCING LANE, TORONTO

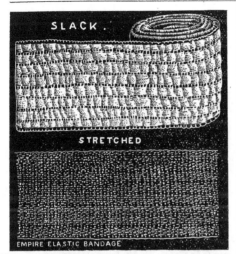

BABIES

Reared on **Robinson's Patent Barley,** when eight months old, should be fed upon **Robinson's Patent Croats,** with an occasional return to the Patent Barley.

※ ※ ※

Gruel should be made from the Patent Croats and with milk ; it then forms a perfect diet, with heat - producers, muscle, bone, and flesh - formers nicely balanced.

※ ※ ※

Manufactured (since 1823) only by

Keen, Robinson & Co., Ltd.

= = = LONDON = = =

Purveyors to H. M. the Queen.

Sold by Grocers and Druggists in 1-lb. and ½-lb. Tins.

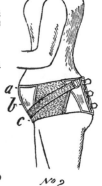
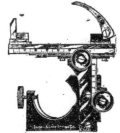

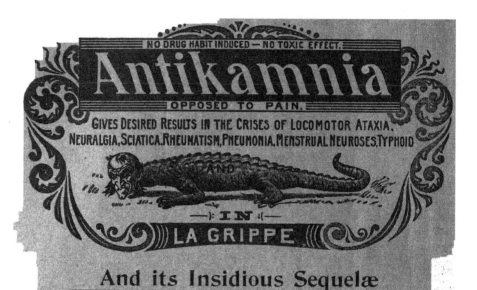
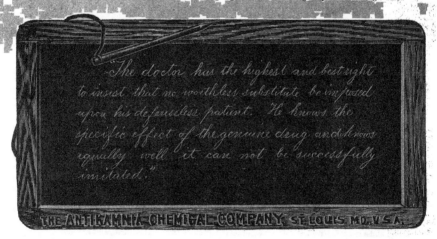